P9-DFN-914

THE GEOGRAPHY OF CHINA

SACRED AND HISTORIC PLACES

UNDERSTANDING CHINA

THE GEOGRAPHY OF CHINA

SACRED AND HISTORIC PLACES

EDITED BY KENNETH PLETCHER, SENIOR EDITOR, GEOGRAPHY AND HISTORY

Britannica®
Educational Publishing

IN ASSOCIATION WITH

ROSEN
EDUCATIONAL SERVICES

LONGWOOD PUBLIC LIBRARY

Published in 2011 by Britannica Educational Publishing
(a trademark of Encyclopædia Britannica, Inc.)
in association with Rosen Educational Services, LLC
29 East 21st Street, New York, NY 10010.

Copyright © 2011 Encyclopædia Britannica, Inc. Britannica, Encyclopædia Britannica,
and the Thistle logo are registered trademarks of Encyclopædia Britannica, Inc. All
rights reserved.

Rosen Educational Services materials copyright © 2011 Rosen Educational Services, LLC.
All rights reserved.

Distributed exclusively by Rosen Educational Services.
For a listing of additional Britannica Educational Publishing titles, call toll free (800) 237-9932.

First Edition

Britannica Educational Publishing
Michael I. Levy: Executive Editor
J.E. Luebering: Senior Manager
Marilyn L. Barton: Senior Coordinator, Production Control
Steven Bosco: Director, Editorial Technologies
Lisa S. Braucher: Senior Producer and Data Editor
Yvette Charboneau: Senior Copy Editor
Kathy Nakamura: Manager, Media Acquisition
Kenneth Pletcher: Senior Editor, Geography and History

Rosen Educational Services
Alexandra Hanson-Harding: Editor
Nelson Sá: Art Director
Cindy Reiman: Photography Manager
Matthew Cauli: Designer, Cover Design
Introduction by Carolyn Jackson

Library of Congress Cataloging-in-Publication Data

The geography of China: sacred and historic places / edited by Kenneth Pletcher.—1st ed.
    p. cm.—(Understanding China)
"In association with Britannica Educational Publishing, Rosen Educational Services."
Includes bibliographical references and index.
ISBN 978-1-61530-134-8 (library binding)
1. China—Geography. 2. Historic sites—China. 3. Sacred space—China. 4. China—History,
Local. I. Pletcher, Kenneth.
DS706.7.G46 2011
915.1—dc22

                                                                    2010002170

Manufactured in the United States of America

Cover: The main tourist street in Yangshuo with the famous karsts (steep hills) of
Guangxi province in the background. *Ed Freeman/Photodisc/Getty Images*; p. 18:
Fisherman with cormorant on bamboo raft on the Li River in Guilin, Guangxi province,
China. *Dennis Cox/Time & Life Pictures/Getty Images;* back cover: Summer Palace in
Beijing. © *www.istockphoto.com/Nikada.*

Page 18: Fisherman with cormorant on bamboo raft on the Li River in Guilin, Guangxi
Province, China. *Dennis Cox/Time & Life Pictures/Getty Images.*

CONTENTS

48

52

135

145

152

161

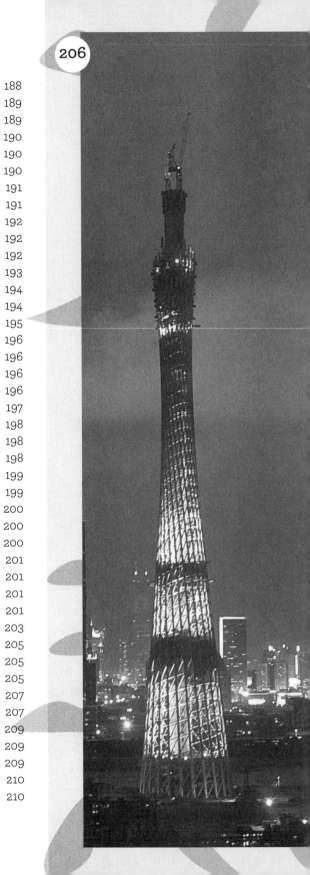

225

CHAPTER 11: SELECTED AUTONOMOUS REGIONS

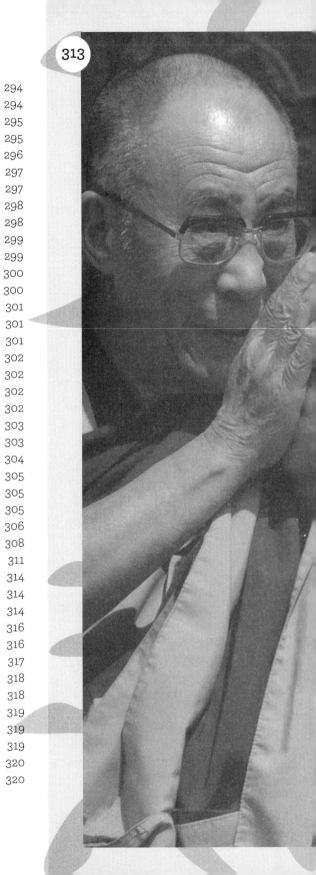

353

355

INTRODUCTION

The Three Gorges Dam, the world's largest when completed in 2006, is built across the Yangtze River in the heart of China. The project has been heavily criticized—to build the dam, more than 1.2 million people were moved from nearly 500 cities, towns, and villages, and 1,200 historical and archaeological sites were flooded. But proponents say it will help control deadly floods, create a deep-water reservoir, and allow for easier navigation for oceangoing freighters. Its 26 turbines will also create a massive amount of hydroelectric energy that will bring electricity to millions of people. Throughout its long history, the needs of China's people have spurred it to under-take giant projects that shape their land. That is a necessity, because although it is only slightly larger in area than the United States, China has today roughly 1 billion more people. In fact, about one in five people in the world is Chinese.

In this book, readers will learn how the contours, fertility, and weather patterns of China's land have shaped its people. They will also learn how China's population—the largest in the world—has put special pressure on the land. Peoples' needs for water, food, fuel, and space have caused them to change and mold the landscape over time. Readers will also get an overview of China, from its land-scapes to its cityscapes. This book explores many of the places that give China its character, from the Great Wall to vast mountain ranges to great cities and ancient provinces.

Eons before humans arrived, the Indian subcontinent was separate from the Asian mainland. Some 50 million years ago, India began crashing into Asia. The pressure created when the subcontinent was forced under the Asian landmass created the Himalayas, a vast mountain chain that has continued to slowly grow taller. The pressure also pushed up a wide region of land to the north of the mountains, so that today China is like a table tilting from west to east. This western part, the Plateau of Tibet (or Qiangtang), is known as the "roof of the world." The world's highest peak, Mount Everest, is in the Himalayas on China's border with Nepal. Just north of the Tibetan Plateau is the Turfan Depression, China's lowest spot, 508 feet (155 metres) below sea level. Also in western China, north of Tibet, lie the Kunlun Mountains. But the country generally slopes eastward until it reaches the Pacific Ocean. China's more than 50,000 rivers flow, with a few exceptions, from west to east.

The Huang He, or Yellow River, is the most northern of China's three main rivers. It rises on the Plateau of Tibet and drains into the Bo Hai (Gulf of Chihli), part of the Yellow Sea. The mighty river, which gets its name because it is so filled with silt that it appears to be yellow-brown in colour, enriches the land with the soil it deposits, making it fertile for farming. It also has been called "China's Sorrow" because the shifting river often overflows its banks and floods the North

China Plain. The Huang He has changed course many times. In the past 4,000 years for instance, the river has entered the Yellow Sea at points that vary as much as 500 miles (800 km).

The Yangtze is the longest of China's rivers, flowing from the Plateau of Tibet to the East China Sea north of Shanghai. It divides northern and southern China. The longest river in Asia, it is the third longest river in the world—3,915 miles (6,300 km). It is also has the greatest depth of any river in the world—in some spots it is as much as 500 to 600 feet (150 to 180 m) deep. Over history, the Yangtze has been responsible for many devastating floods along its fertile, highly populated banks.

The Xi is the most southern of China's great river systems; it flows from the Yunnan-Guizhou Plateau past picturesque mountains and into the Pearl River Delta, where it meets with two other rivers and flows into the South China Sea at Guangzhou. The Xi, whose flow is second only to the Yangtze, is 80 feet (25 m) higher in summer than winter because it is swelled by monsoon rains. Important cities line its banks as well.

Rainfall and temperatures in China vary greatly, and so do its soils. In general, the northern, wheat-growing, part of the country is cool and dry, and its soils tend to be alkaline. One important kind of soil in northern China is loess, which is very fertile but erodes away easily. In China, much of this loose, silty material is borne away by the Huang He. Some of the earliest evidence of human civilization in China has been found in the Loess Plateau.

In the south, the hot, humid weather is suitable for growing rice. Despite the acidity of the soil, skilled farmers have learned how to cultivate the land intensively enough to grow two or even three crops per year.

Urban grown accelerated in the mid-1980s as China entered the global economy. Today, some two in five Chinese live in cities. More than 70 cities have more than a million people, and several dozen top a half-million.

Rural life began to change in the late 1970s as China's industrial economy grew. When many farmers moved to cities to look for jobs, the government helped create light manufacturing jobs in thousands of villages to help raise the standard of living.

To fuel these jobs, China uses some of its vast hydrocarbon resources, such as coal, which is China's main fuel and which is found in every province. The country has oil reserves, as well as natural gas. Rivers remain important sources of hydroelectric power.

There are many world-famous tourist attractions in China. Among them is the world's longest human-made waterway, the Grand Canal (Da Yunhe). Begun in the 4th century BCE and expanded over the centuries, the canal is 1,085 miles (1,747 km) long and links Hangzhou (in the south) with Beijing (in the north). It is still being used to transport goods.

China has always been vulnerable to invasion from the north. From the Xiongnu to the Mongols, nomadic peoples have always been tempted by China's rich civilization. To protect its territory, the Chinese started building the Great Wall in the 7th century BCE. Over the course of many centuries and dynasties, one emperor after another expanded the wall until it spanned some 5,500 miles (8,850 km) from east to west across northern China and southern Mongolia. It was named a UNESCO World Heritage site in 1987. Tourists can see portions of the wall as it stretches over hills and visit beacon towers where soldiers once sent military signals to each other with smoke, fire, banners, and sound.

Visitors also can visit the ancient Qin Tomb near the modern city of Xi'an. There the first sovereign emperor of the Qin dynasty (Shihuangdi) built a funeral compound with some 8,000 life-size terracotta (baked clay) figures of soldiers and horses that were discovered, buried, in 1974, more than 2100 years after his death.

China has places of great natural beauty as well. The Huang Mountains in southern Anhui province have more than 400 scenic spots and hot springs. Crescent-shaped Lake Tai, between Zhejiang and Jiangsu provinces, has been settled since the first century BCE. Mount Wutai in the province of Shanxi is a cluster of five flat-top peaks and one of the great holy places of Buddhism.

The importance of serene beauty becomes apparent when travelers experience China's fast-growing cities. The skyline of Beijing, the nation's capital, is punctuated by modern skyscrapers, including many high-rise apartment buildings that house a growing number of the more than 15.8 million residents in the capital region.

Except for brief periods, Beijing has been China's capital for eight centuries. In the summer of 2008, millions of tourists visited Beijing for the Olympic Games. Development for the games greatly changed Beijing for its residents as well. On the one hand, the already blistering pace of change was sped up—the subway system was extended, new sports facilities were built, and so was housing. On the other, many hutongs—alleyways with quaint, traditional homes, were destroyed.

There is much to see in Beijing, such as the Forbidden City, a series of palaces within palaces built for China's emperors and first occupied in 1420. At the Museum of Chinese History, visitors can see evidence of human habitation of the area around Beijing dating to about 770,000 years ago—the age of the earliest bones of Peking man discovered near the city.

Among the cities of southeastern China that this book explores is Shanghai. With more than 18 million people in its metropolitan area, Shanghai is China's largest city. Located on the coast of the East China Sea, it is one of the world's largest ports. Its industries produce everything from steel to consumer electronics, which creates heavy pollution.

Shanghai is a hub of scientific and technological research, with the nation's most highly skilled workforce.

Next, readers will explore southern and western China. One of the greatest cities of southwest-central China, Chongqing is located where the Yantgze and Jialing rivers meet, 1,400 miles (2,250 km) from the sea. Settled more than 3,000 years ago, it was the capital of Nationalist China during World War II. Chongqing is so foggy from fall to spring that it is called the "fog capital" of China. Unfortunately, the thick fog not only makes it difficult for planes to land, but it also traps acid rain and soot. In the far west, Ürümqi is the capital of the Uygur Autonomous Region of Xinjiang. Most Uighurs are Muslim. Kazakh, Dungan, and Manchu peoples also live in Xinjiang, but the majority are Han Chinese, many of whom have come there since the 1990s.

Hong Kong, once British-ruled, and Macau, long under Portuguese rule, were returned to China at the end of the 20th century. Both are now designated special administrative regions under Beijing's control, though each has some economic and administrative autonomy. Hong Kong Island is volcanic in origin and sits in Victoria Harbor of the South China Sea. Hong Kong is densely packed with people speaking Cantonese, Mandarin and English. Macao is located on a peninsula in the South China Sea about 25 miles (40 km) from Hong Kong. Like Hong Kong, it is an important trading centre.

China also has five autonomous regions; two—Tibet and Xinjiang—are discussed here. They are neighbours and the largest and most remote of China's subdivisions. Tibet was brought into the People's Republic of China beginning in 1950, and this has remained a highly controversial issue. Lhasa, considered holy by Tibetan Buddhists, is its capital. The thousand-room Potala Palace in Lhasa was once the seat of the Tibetan government and the main residence of the Dalai Lama (religious leader; the current Dalai Lama went into exile in 1959). It was spared during the Cultural Revolution when many of China's historical and sacred objects were destroyed. A first palace was built there in the 7th century, but the current one, begun in 1645, was built there under the fifth Dalai Lama.

China has 22 provinces. Three—Shandong, Guangdong, and Sichuan—are explored here. Shandong, located on China's northeast coast, is the country's third most populous province. Its capital and chief cultural centre is Jinan. Among its many agricultural products are peanuts, which are pressed into oil, and also cotton, tobacco, hemp, and fruit. The province is also known for its silk production, and it is rich in coal and oil. It came under the influence of the Germans, British, and Japanese in the late 19th and early 20th centuries. Shandong is famous for being the home of China's greatest philosopher, Confucius, who was born in 551 BCE in Qufu in the southwestern part of the province. Visitors can still see his tomb, a tree he is said to have planted, and a well that he drank from.

Guangdong is the southernmost mainland province in China. This heavily populated province with its long coastline, had early exposure to Western influence.

The city of Guangzhou, some 90 miles (145 km) inland from the South China Sea near the head of the Pearl River, is the capital of Guangdong. Gangzhou was the first Chinese port visited by European traders, who called it Canton. Guangzhou, now with more than eight million residents, is one of the wealthiest and most Westernized cities in China. By the late 17th century the overpopulated Guangdong region had become a source of emigration, and in the mid-19th century these migrants began to pour into Southeast Asia and North America. Less than one fifth of land is cultivated, but some of the crops that are grown here include rice, rubber, palm oil, hemp, coffee, black pepper, sweet potatoes, tea, and some 300 kinds of fruit, including citrus, litchi, and pineapples. Cantonese cuisine features tasty dishes such as dim sum, noodles, seafood, and fresh vegetables.

Sichuan, the second largest province in China, is also famous for its food—though it is more hot and spicy than Cantonese and features flavourful ingredients such as chili peppers, garlic, and peanuts. Sichuan is located in central China, at the upper reaches of the Yangtze River, and most of its people are farmers. Mountains protect Sichuan from cold, so the growing season is very long. In the east, it has been called the "land of one million steps," because so much of the farmland consists of terraced hillsides—long narrow strips of land on steep slopes. Its capital city is Chengdu, and not far away are nature reserves, where rare giant pandas can be seen—it is a UNESCO world heritage site. In 2008, a large-scale earthquake killed tens of thousands of people in the province.

In this book you will learn more about these and many other distinctive features of China that help to make up this diverse and spectacular land.

Pearl River waterfront, Guangzhou (Canton), China. G. Richardson/Robert Harding World Imagery/Getty Images

CHAPTER 1

GEOGRAPHIC OVERVIEW

Within China's boundaries exists a highly diverse and complex country. Its topography encompasses the highest and one of the lowest places on Earth, and its relief varies from nearly impenetrable mountainous terrain to vast coastal lowlands.

RELIEF

Broadly speaking, the relief of China is high in the west and low in the east; consequently, the direction of flow of the major rivers is generally eastward. The surface may be divided into three steps, or levels. The first level is represented by the Plateau of Tibet, which is located in both the Tibet Autonomous Region and the province of Qinghai and which, with an average elevation of well over 13,000 feet (4,000 m) above sea level, is the loftiest highland area in the world. The western part of this region, the Qiangtang, has an average height of 16,500 feet (5,000 m) and is known as the "roof of the world."

The second step lies to the north of the Kunlun and Qilian mountains and (farther south) to the east of the Qionglai and Daliang ranges. There the mountains descend sharply to heights of between 6,000 and 3,000 feet (1,800 and 900 m), after which basins intermingle with plateaus. This step includes the Mongolian Plateau, the Tarim Basin, the Loess

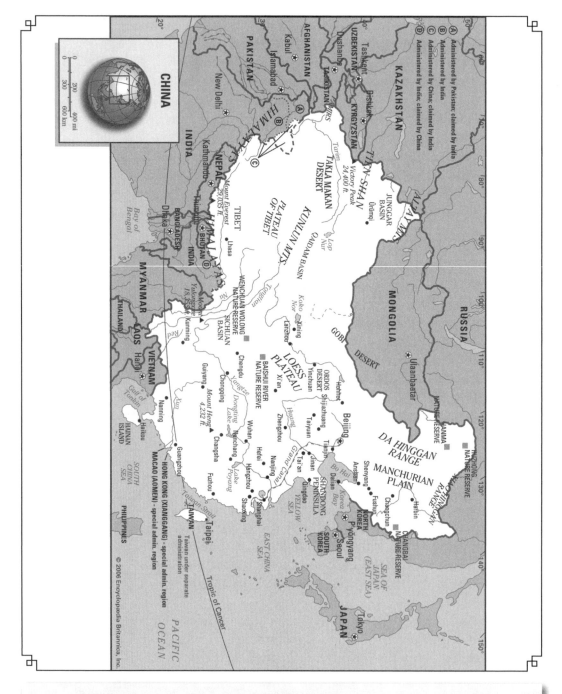

This map shows China and its special administrative regions.

Plateau (loess is a yellow-gray dust deposited by the wind), the Sichuan Basin, and the Yunnan-Guizhou (Yungui) Plateau.

The third step extends from the east of the Dalou, Taihang, and Wu mountain ranges and from the eastern perimeter of the Yunnan-Guizhou Plateau to the China Sea. Almost all of this area is made up of hills and plains lying below 1,500 feet (450 m).

The most remarkable feature of China's relief is the vast extent of its mountain chains; the mountains, indeed, have exerted a tremendous influence on the country's political, economic, and cultural development. By rough estimate, about one-third of the total area of China consists of mountains. China has some of the world's tallest mountains and the world's highest and largest plateau, in addition to possessing extensive coastal plains. The five major landforms—mountain, plateau, hill, plain, and basin—are all well represented. China's complex natural environment and rich natural resources are closely connected with the varied nature of its relief.

The topography of China is marked by many splendours. Mount Everest (Qomolangma Feng), situated on the border between Tibet and Nepal, is the highest peak in the world, at an elevation of 29,035 feet (8,850 m). By contrast, the lowest part of the Turfan Depression in the Uygur Autonomous Region of Xinjiang—Lake Ayding—is 508 feet (155 m) below sea level. The coast of China contrasts greatly between South and North. To the south of the bay of Hangzhou, the coast is rocky and indented with many harbours and offshore islands. To the north, except along the Shandong and Liaodong peninsulas, the coast is sandy and flat.

China is prone to intense seismic activity throughout much of the country. The main source of this geologic instability is the result of the constant northward movement of the Indian tectonic plate beneath southern Asia, which has thrust up the towering mountains and high plateaus of the Chinese southwest. Throughout its history China has experienced hundreds of massive earthquakes that collectively have killed millions of people. Two in the 20th century alone—in eastern Gansu province (1920) and in the city of Tangshan, eastern Hebei province (1976)—caused some 250,000 deaths each, and a quake in east-central Sichuan province in 2008 killed tens of thousands and devastated a wide area.

China's physical relief has dictated its development in many respects. The civilization of Han Chinese originated in the southern part of the Loess Plateau, and from there it extended outward until it encountered the combined barriers of relief and climate. The long, protruding strip of land, commonly known as the Gansu, or Hexi, Corridor, illustrates this fact. South of the corridor is the Plateau of Tibet, which was too high and too cold for the Chinese to gain a foothold. North of the corridor is the Gobi Desert, which also formed a barrier. Consequently, Chinese civilization was forced to spread along the corridor, where melting snow and ice in the Qilian Mountains provided water for oasis farming. The westward extremities of the corridor became the meeting place of the ancient East and West.

Thus, for a long time the ancient political centre of China was located along the lower reaches of the Huang He (Yellow River). Because of topographical barriers, however, it was difficult for the central government to gain complete control over the entire country, except when an unusually strong dynasty was in power. In many instances the Sichuan Basin—an isolated region in southwestern China, about twice the size of Scotland, that is well protected by high mountains and self-sufficient in agricultural products—became an independent kingdom. A comparable situation often arose in the Tarim Basin in the northwest. Linked to the rest of China only by the Gansu Corridor, this basin is even remoter than the Sichuan, and, when the central government was unable to exert its influence, oasis states were established; only the three strong dynasties—the Han (206 BCE–220 CE), the Tang (618–907 CE), and the Qing, or Manchu (1644–1911/12)—were capable of controlling the region.

Apart from the three elevation zones already mentioned, it is possible—on the basis of geologic structure, climatic conditions, and differences in geomorphologic development—to divide China into three major topographic regions: the eastern, southwestern, and northwestern zones.

THE EASTERN REGION

The eastern zone is shaped by the rivers, which have eroded landforms in some parts and have deposited alluvial plains in others; its climate is monsoonal (characterized by seasonal rain-bearing winds). Topographically the most complex of the three regions, it can be subdivided into ten second-order geographic divisions.

THE NORTHEAST PLAIN

The Northeast Plain (also known as the Manchurian Plain and the Sung-liao Plain) is located in China's Northeast, the region formerly known as Manchuria. It is bordered to the west and north by the Da Hinggan (Greater Khingan) Range and to the east by the Xiao Hinggan (Lesser Khingan) Range. An undulating plain split into northern and southern halves by a low divide rising from 500 to 850 feet (150 to 260 m), it is drained in its northern part by the Sungari River and tributaries and in its southern part by the Liao River. Most of the area has an erosional rather than a depositional surface, but it is covered with a deep soil. The plain has an area of about 135,000 square miles (350,000 square kilometres). Its basic landscapes are forest-steppe, steppe, meadow-steppe, and cultivated land; its soils are rich and black, and it is

occasional open valleys, they reach elevations mostly between 1,500 and 3,000 feet (450 and 900 m). In some parts the scenery is characterized by rugged peaks and precipitous cliffs. The highest peak is the volcanic cone of Mount Baitou (9,003 feet [2,744 m]), which has a beautiful crater lake at its snow-covered summit. As one of the major forest areas of China, the region is the source of many valuable furs and famous medicinal herbs. Cultivation is generally limited to the valley floors.

Da Hinggan (Greater Khingan) Range, southeast of Hailar, Inner Mongolia Autonomous Region, China. Richard Harrington/Miller Services Ltd.

a famous agricultural region. The river valleys are wide and flat with a series of terraces formed by deposits of silt. During the flood season the rivers inundate extensive areas.

THE CHANGBAI MOUNTAINS

To the southeast of the Northeast Plain is a series of ranges comprising the Changbai, Zhangguangcai, and Wanda mountains, which in Chinese are collectively known as the Changbai Shan, or "Forever White Mountains." Broken by

THE NORTH CHINA PLAIN

Comparable in size to the Northeast Plain, most of the North China Plain lies at elevations below 160 feet (50 m), and the relief is monotonously flat. It was formed by enormous sedimentary deposits brought down by the Huang He and Huai River from the Loess Plateau; the Quaternary deposits alone (i.e., those from the past 2.6 million years) reach thicknesses of 2,500 to 3,000 feet (760 to 900 m). The river channels, which are higher than the surrounding locality, form local water divides, and the areas between the channels are depressions in which lakes and swamps are found. In particularly low and flat areas, the underground water table often fluctuates from 5 to 6.5 feet (1.5 to 2 m), forming meadow swamps and, in some places, resulting in saline soils. A densely populated area that has long been under settlement, the North China Plain has the highest proportion of land under cultivation of any region in China.

THE LOESS PLATEAU

The Loess Plateau is a vast 154,000 square miles (400,000 square km) and forms a unique region of hills clad in loess (dry, powdery, wind-blown soil) and barren mountains between the North China Plain and the deserts of the west. In the north the Great Wall of China forms the boundary, while the southern limit is the Qin Mountains in Shaanxi province. The average surface elevation is

The Yan River at Yan'an, Shaanxi province, China, in the eastern portion of the Loess Plateau. A.Topping—Rapho/ Photo Researchers

roughly 4,000 feet (1,200 m), but individual ranges of bedrock are higher, reaching 9,825 feet (2,995 m) in the Liupan Mountains. Most of the plateau is covered with loess to thicknesses of 165 to 260 feet (50 to 80 m). In northern Shaanxi and eastern Gansu provinces, the loess may reach much greater thicknesses. The loess is particularly susceptible to erosion by water, and ravines and gorges crisscross the plateau. It has been estimated that ravines cover approximately half the entire region, with erosion reaching depths of 300 to 650 feet (90 to 200 m).

THE SHANDONG HILLS

The Shandong Hills are basically composed of extremely ancient crystalline shales and granites of early Precambrian age (i.e., older than about 2.5 billion years) and of somewhat younger sedimentary rocks dating to about 540–420 million years ago. Faults have played a major role in creating the present relief, and, as a result, many hills are horsts (blocks of Earth's crust uplifted along faults), while the valleys have been formed by grabens (blocks of Earth's crust that have been thrust down along faults). The Jiaolai Plain divides this region into two parts. The eastern part is lower, lying at elevations averaging below 1,500 feet (450 m), with only certain peaks and ridges rising to 2,500 feet and (rarely) to 3,000 feet (900 m); the highest point, Mount Lao, reaches 3,714 feet (1,132 m). The western part is slightly higher, rising to 5,000 feet (1,524 m) at Mount Tai, one of China's most sacred mountains. The Shandong Hills meet the sea along a rocky and indented shoreline.

THE QIN MOUNTAINS

The Qin (conventional Tsinling) Mountains in Shaanxi province are the greatest chain of mountains east of the Plateau of Tibet. The mountain chain consists of a high and rugged barrier extending from Gansu to Henan; geographers use a line between the chain and the Huai River to divide China proper into two parts—North and South. The elevation of the mountains varies from 3,000 to 10,000 feet (900 to 3,000 m). The western part is higher, with the highest peak, Mount Taibai, rising to 12,359 feet (3,767 m). The Qin Mountains consist of a series of parallel ridges, all running roughly west-east, separated by a maze of ramifying valleys whose canyon walls often rise sheer to a height of 1,000 feet (300 m) above the valley streams.

THE SICHUAN BASIN

The Sichuan Basin is one of the most attractive geographical regions of China. It is surrounded by mountains, which are higher in the west and north. Protected against the penetration of cold northern winds, the basin is much warmer in the winter than are the more southerly plains of southeast China. Except for the Chengdu Plain, the region is hilly. The relief of the basin's eastern half consists of numerous folds, forming a series of ridges and valleys that trend northeast to southwest. The lack of arable land has obliged farmers to cultivate the slopes of the hills, on which they have built terraces that frequently cover the slopes from top to bottom. The terracing has slowed down the process of erosion and has made it possible to cultivate additional areas by using the steeper slopes—some of which have grades up to 45° or more.

THE SOUTHEASTERN MOUNTAINS

Southeastern China is bordered by a rocky shoreline backed by picturesque mountains. In general, there is a distinct structural and topographic trend from northeast to southwest. The higher peaks may reach elevations of some 5,000 to 6,500 feet (1,500 to 2,000 m). The rivers are short and fast-flowing and have cut steep-sided valleys. The chief areas of settlement are on narrow strips of coastal plain where rice is produced. Along the coast there are numerous islands, where the fishing industry is well developed.

PLAINS OF THE MIDDLE AND LOWER YANGTZE

East of Yichang, in Hubei province, a series of plains of uneven width are found along the Yangtze River (Chang Jiang).

The plains are particularly wide in the delta area and in places where the Yangtze receives its major tributaries—including large areas of lowlands around Dongting, Poyang, Tai, and Hongze lakes, which are all hydrologically linked with the Yangtze. The region is an alluvial plain, the accumulation of sediment laid down by the rivers throughout long ages. There are a few isolated hills, but in general the land is level, lying mostly below 160 feet (50 m). Rivers, canals, and lakes form a dense network of waterways. The surface of the plain has been converted into a system of flat terraces, which descend in steps along the slopes of the valleys.

THE NAN MOUNTAINS

The Nan Mountains (Nan Ling) are composed of many ranges of mountains running from northeast to southwest. These ranges form the watershed between the Yangtze to the north and the Pearl (Zhu) River to the south. The main peaks along the watershed are above 5,000 feet (1,500 m), and some are more than 6,500 feet (2,000 m). But a large part of the land to the south of the Nan Mountains is also hilly; flatland does not exceed 10 percent of the total area. The Pearl River Delta is the only extensive plain in this region and is also the richest part of South China. The coastline is rugged and irregular, and there are many promontories and protected bays, including those of Hong Kong and Macau. The principal river is the Xi River, which rises in the highlands of eastern Yunnan and southern Guizhou.

THE SOUTHWESTERN REGION

The southwest is a cold, lofty, and mountainous region containing intermontane plateaus and inland lakes. It can be subdivided into two second-order geographic divisions.

THE YUNNAN-GUIZHOU PLATEAU

The Yunnan-Guizhou Plateau region comprises the northern part of Yunnan and the western part of Guizhou; its edge is highly dissected. Yunnan is more distinctly a plateau and contains larger areas of rolling uplands than Guizhou, but both parts are distinguished by canyonlike valleys and precipitous mountains. The highest elevations lie in the west, where Mount Diancang (also called Cang Shan) rises to 13,524 feet (4,122 m). In the valleys of the major rivers, elevations drop to about 1,300 to 1,600 feet (400 to 490 m). Particularly sharp differences in elevation and the greatest ruggedness of relief occur in the western part of the region, in the gorges of the large rivers. In the eastern part, karst processes (creating sinks, ravines, and underground streams in the limestone landscape) have developed very strongly. Scattered throughout the highlands are small lake basins, separated by mountains.

THE PLATEAU OF TIBET

The great upland massif called the Plateau of Tibet occupies about one-fourth of the country's area. A large

Stupa (Buddhist commemorative monument) on the bank of the Yarlung Zangbo (Brahmaputra) River, southern Tibet Autonomous Region, China. © Naomi Duguid/Asia Access

part of the plateau lies at elevations above 13,000 to 16,500 feet (4,000 to 5,000 m). The border ranges of the plateau (the Kunlun Mountains and the Himalayas) are even higher, with individual peaks rising to heights of 23,000 to 26,000 feet (7,000 to 8,000 m) and higher. As a rule, the interior (i.e., Tibet-side) slopes of these border mountains are gentle, while the exterior slopes are precipitous. The plateau's eastern and southern periphery is the source of many of the world's great rivers, including the Yangtze, Huang He, Mekong, Salween, Indus, and Brahmaputra. Only in the low valleys, chiefly along the Brahmaputra valley, are there centres of human settlement.

The Qaidam (Tsaidam) Basin, occupying the northwestern portion of the Plateau of Tibet, is the largest, as well as the lowest, depression in the plateau. The broad northwestern part of the basin lies at elevations between approximately 8,800 and 10,000 feet (2,700 and 3,000 m), and the narrow southeastern part is slightly lower. Gravel, sandy and clay deserts, semideserts, and salt wastes predominate within the basin.

THE NORTHWESTERN REGION

The northwest is arid and eroded by the wind and forms an inland drainage basin. It can be subdivided into three second-order geographic divisions.

THE TARIM BASIN

North of the Plateau of Tibet and at the much lower elevation of about 3,000 feet (900 m) lies the Tarim Basin. It is hemmed in by great mountain ranges: the Tien Shan (Tian Shan; "Celestial Mountains") on the north, the Pamirs on the west, and the Kunlun Mountains on the south. Glacier-fed streams descend from these heights only to lose themselves in the loose sands and gravels of the Takla Makan Desert, which occupies the centre of the basin. The Takla Makan is one of the most barren of the world's deserts; only a few of the largest rivers—such as the Tarim and Hotan (Khotan)—cross the desert, but even their flow is not constant, and they have water throughout their entire courses only during the flood period. The area of the basin is about 215,000 square miles (557,000 square km), and its elevations range from 2,500 to 4,600 feet (750 to 1,400 m) above sea level. Its surface slants to the southeast, where Lop Nur (a salt-encrusted lake bed) is situated.

THE JUNGGAR BASIN

North of the Tarim Basin is another large depression, the Junggar (Dzungarian) Basin. It is enclosed by the Tien Shan on the south, while to the northeast it is cut off from Mongolia by the Altai Mountains. The surface of the basin is flat, with a gentle slope to the southwest. The larger portion of the land lies at elevations between about 1,000 and 1,500 feet (300 and 450 m), and in the lowest part the elevation drops to just below 650 feet (200 m). In general the main part of the basin is covered by a broad desert with barchans (crescent-shaped sand dunes that move); only in certain parts are dunes retained by vegetation.

THE TIEN SHAN

The Chinese (eastern) part of the Tien Shan consists of a complex system of ranges and depressions divided into two major groups of ranges: the northern and the southern. The groups are separated by a strip of intermontane depressions that itself is broken up by the interior ranges. Ancient metamorphic rock constitutes the larger portion of the ranges in the interior zone; Paleozoic (i.e., about 250 to 540 million years old) sedimentary and igneous sedimentary beds form its northern and southern chains, while Mesozoic (about 65 to 250 million years old) sandstones and conglomerates fill the intermontane depressions in the interior zone and constitute the foothill

Tian Lake in the Bogda Mountains in the eastern Tien Shan, Uygur Autonomous Region of Xinjiang, China. K. Scholz— Shostal Assoc.

than 20 miles (32 km). Large rivers with heavy flows, such as the Ili (Yili) River and its tributaries, begin their courses there, and the predominantly alpine meadow steppe is one of the best grazing lands of China.

DRAINAGE

China has more than 50,000 rivers with individual drainage areas exceeding 40 square miles (100 square km). Of the total annual runoff, about 95 percent drains directly into the sea (more than 80 percent into the Pacific Ocean, 12 percent into the Indian Ocean, and less than 1 percent into the Arctic Ocean) and 5 percent disappears inland.

ridges. The height of the main Chinese chains of the Tien Shan is between 13,000 and 15,000 feet (4,000 and 4,600 m), with individual peaks exceeding 16,000 feet (4,900 m); the interior chains reach 14,500 feet (4,400 m). In the western part, where precipitation is adequate, large glaciers are formed, reaching a length of more

The three principal rivers of China, all of which flow generally from west to east, draining into the China Sea, are the Huang He, the Yangtze, and the Xi. The Huang He, which rises in the Kunlun Mountains, is the northernmost of the three; it drains into the Bo Hai (Gulf of Chihli), north of the Shandong Peninsula. The

Yangtze, the longest river in the country, rises in the Tibetan Highlands and flows across central China, draining into the East China Sea north of Shanghai. The Xi River, the southernmost of the three, rises in the Yunnan-Guizhou Plateau and empties into the South China Sea via the Pearl River Delta at Guangzhou (Canton).

The distribution of surface water in China is extremely uneven. Only a small part of the country has sufficient quantities year-round. Much of the country has abundant runoff but only during the rainy summer, when enormous surpluses of water are received. From the southeast to the northwest, the surface water decreases as the relief becomes more mountainous. A vast area of the northwest lacks water throughout the year. North China (north of the Qin Mountains–Huai River line), with its flat relief and long history of agriculture, contains almost two-thirds of China's cultivated land; paradoxically, because of scanty and erratic precipitation, the average annual runoff in the North accounts for only about one-sixth of the total for the country as a whole.

The mountains of the southeast and the mountainous Hainan Island have the most abundant surface water. Over the year they receive more than 60 inches (152 cm) of precipitation (in some places even more than 80 inches [203 cm]), of which almost two-thirds constitutes the runoff, so that a dense drainage network has developed. The amount of runoff is highest in the southeast, exceeding 40 inches (101 cm). It gradually diminishes toward the west and north, so that in the true deserts of the northwest it is usually less than 0.4 of an inch (1 cm). The arid climate of the northwest is reflected in the landscape of the dry steppes, which is characterized by richer grasses in the east, while in the west the landscape gradually changes to bare deserts.

In the lower reaches of the Yangtze, the Pearl River Delta, and the Chengdu Plain, a dense network of waterways has been developed. In the North China Plain and the Northeast Plain, most of the rivers have a linear flow, and tributaries are few and unconnected. In the inland drainage area there are very few rivers because of scanty precipitation. Extensive areas such as the Tarim Basin and northeastern Gansu province are often completely devoid of runoff. In those regions the rivers depend on melted snow and ice; in consequence, they are mostly small and are found only in mountains and mountain foothills. As they drain increasingly farther away from the mountains, most of them eventually disappear in the desert, while some form inland lakes. Because the northern part of the Plateau of Tibet is a cold desert, the rate of evaporation is slow, so that a denser network of rivers has developed; most of these, however, run into glaciated depressions, forming numerous lakes.

SOILS

China, with its vast and diverse climatic conditions, has a wide variety of soils.

Indeed, all the soil types of the Eurasian continent, except the soils of the tundra and the highly leached podzolic-gley soils of the northern taiga (boreal forest), are found in China. As a result of the climatic differences between the drier and cooler North and the wetter and hotter South, soils may be grouped into two classifications. Generally speaking, the soils north of the Qin Mountains–Huai River line are pedocals (calcareous) and are neutral to alkaline in reaction; those south of this line are pedalfers (leached noncalcareous soils), which are neutral to acid.

Apart from the great plateaus and high mountains to the southwest, marked soil zones are formed in China according to differences in climate, vegetation, and distance from the sea. The east and southeast coastal region is covered by the forest zone associated with a humid and semihumid climate, while the north and northwest inland regions belong mostly to the steppe zone, as well as to the semidesert and desert zone associated with a semiarid and arid climate. Between these two broad soil zones lies a transitional zone—the forest-steppe zone, where forest soils merge gradually with steppe soils.

Between the pedocals of the North and the pedalfers of the South lie the neutral soils. The floodplain of the Yangtze below the Three Gorges (the point where the river cuts through the Wu Mountains to empty onto the Hubei Plain) is overlain with a thick cover of noncalcareous alluvium. These soils, sometimes classified as paddy (rice-growing) soils, for the most part are exceedingly fertile and of good texture. The paddy soil is a unique type of cultivated soil, formed over a long period of time under the specific conditions of intensive rice cultivation.

Along the coast of North China are belts of saline and alkaline soil. They are associated with a combination of poor drainage and aridity, where precipitation is insufficient either to dissolve or to carry away the salts in solution.

The adverse effects of nature on the soil have been further intensified by centuries of concentrated cultivation, which has resulted in an almost universal deficiency of nitrogen and organic matter. The shortage of organic matter is primarily because farmers habitually remove crop stalks and leaves for livestock feed and fuel. The animal and human waste used for fertilizer contains too small an amount of organic matter to compensate for the loss of nutrients in the soil. The soils are also often deficient in phosphorus and potassium, but these deficiencies are neither so widespread nor so severe as that of nitrogen.

At one time, half of the territory of present-day China may have been covered by forests, but now less than one-tenth of the country is forested. Extensive forests in central and southern China were cleared for farmlands, resulting in the inevitable erosion of soils from the hillsides and their deposition in the valleys. Farmers have constructed level terraces, supported by walls, in order to hold back water for rice fields, thus effectively controlling erosion. Wherever elaborate terraces have been built, soil erosion is virtually absent, and stepped terraces have become one of the characteristic features of the rural landscape.

Excessive grazing and other practices that destroy the grass cover have also produced soil loss. When its valuable crumb structure is broken down and its porosity is lost, the topsoil is easily washed away through erosion in the rainy season; the wind produces the same effect in dry regions. The Loess Plateau, constantly buffeted by rain and wind, is especially vulnerable to soil erosion, which results in a distinctive landscape. Deep, steep-sided gullies cut the plateau into fantastic relief. The damage done by heavy rain in summer includes not only topsoil loss but also frequent flooding by silt-laden rivers.

CLIMATE

China's climatic diversity mirrors that of its topography, ranging from extremely dry, desertlike conditions in the northwest to a tropical monsoon climate in the southeast. In addition, it has the greatest contrast in temperature between its northern and southern borders of any country in the world.

THE AIR MASSES

The vast and topographically varied landmass of China lies in Asia, the world's largest continent, and faces the Pacific, the world's largest ocean, along an extensive shoreline. The country's climate is thus heavily influenced by the seasonal movement of large air masses between the Pacific and the Chinese mainland. The polar continental air mass, originating to the north in Siberia, dominates a large part of China during the winter; likewise, the tropical Pacific air mass exerts its influence during the summer. The sharply varied climatic conditions prevailing in summer and in winter are a direct result of the interaction of these two air masses, which are entirely different in nature.

The Siberian air mass, which is quite stable, is extremely cold and dry and often has marked layers of temperature inversion. After crossing the Mongolian Plateau, the air mass spreads southward and begins to invade North China, where it undergoes a series of rapid changes; its temperature rises slightly, and its stability decreases. During the day, the air there may be quite warm, but at night or in shaded places the cold is often unbearable. In general, the diurnal (daily) range of temperature is more than 18 °F (10 °C); in extreme cases it may exceed 45 °F (25 °C). Because North China is affected by this air mass most of the time, it is dry, with clear weather and an abundance of sunshine during the winter months.

The prevailing winter wind blows from November through March, but it changes direction as it moves to the south. In northern and northeastern China its direction is from the northwest, in eastern China it comes from the north, and on the southeastern coasts it is from the northeast. The height of the winter wind belt usually does not exceed 13,000 feet (4,000 m). As it moves to the south, the height decreases; in Nanjing it is about 6,500 feet (2,000 m), and in South China it is less than 5,000 feet (1,500 m). The Qin Mountains become an effective barrier to the advance of the cold waves to the south, particularly in the western section, where the average elevation of the mountains is mainly between 6,500 and 9,000 feet (2,000 and 2,700 m).

In China the tropical Pacific air mass is the chief source of summer rainfall. When it predominates, it may cover the eastern half of China and penetrate deep into the border areas of the Mongolian Plateau and onto the eastern edge of the Plateau of Tibet. In summer the Siberian air mass retreats to the western end of Mongolia, although it occasionally penetrates southward and sometimes may reach the Huai River valley, which constitutes a summertime battleground between the tropical Pacific and Siberian air masses.

The movement of the two air masses is of immense significance to the climate of central and North China. In summer, when the tropical air mass predominates, the frontal zone between the two shifts northward; as a result, North China receives heavier rainfall. When the

southeastern monsoon slackens, however, the frontal zone moves southward, and central China receives more rainfall, which can cause flooding. The activity of the tropical Pacific air mass in winter is confined to the southeast coastal areas; during that season, therefore, it frequently drizzles in the hilly areas south of the Nan Mountains, and morning fog is common.

Besides these two air masses, three other air masses also influence China's climate: the equatorial continental air mass (a highly unstable southwest monsoon), the polar maritime air mass, and the equatorial maritime air mass. Furthermore, because China is so vast and has such complex topography, the interaction between the air masses and relief produces a wide range of climatic conditions.

TEMPERATURE

Temperatures generally decrease from south to north. The mean annual temperature is above 68 °F (20 °C) in the Pearl River valley. It decreases to between 59 and 68 °F (15 and 20 °C) in the middle and lower reaches of the Yangtze, to about 50 °F (10 °C) in North China and the southern part of Xinjiang, and to 41 °F (5 °C) in the southern area of the Northeast, the northern part of Xinjiang, and places near the Great Wall. It drops below 32 °F (0 °C; i.e., freezing) in the northern part of Heilongjiang. The annual range of temperature between the extreme south and north is about 86 °F (48 °C). With few exceptions, January is the coldest month and July is the hottest.

South of the Qin Mountains–Huai River line, the mean January temperature increases progressively, rising from freezing to 72 °F (22 °C) on the southern coast of Hainan Island. Snow rarely falls, and the rivers do not freeze. North of this line, the temperature drops from freezing to -18 °F (-28 °C) in the northern part of Heilongjiang.

In April the mean temperature is above freezing for the whole of China, with the exception of extreme northern Heilongjiang. During that time the mean temperature for the Northeast Plain is between 36 and 46 °F (2 and 8 °C), and for the extensive plain between Beijing and Shanghai it is between 54 and 59 °F (12 and 15 °C). South of the Nan Mountains the mean temperature is considerably higher than 68 °F (20 °C). Along the coast of southern Guangdong, willows start to bud in late January, but in Beijing the budding of willows comes as late as early April.

In summer the temperature range between North and South China is quite small. In July the difference in temperature between Guangzhou and Beijing is only about 5 °F (3 °C), and the isotherms in July are roughly parallel to the coastline. In July the isotherm of 82 °F (28 °C) marks an extensive area. The hottest places in China are found along the valleys of the middle and lower Yangtze. The

mean July temperature of Nanchang and Changsha is well above 84 °F (29 °C), and in many years it exceeds 86 °F (30 °C).

In North China, autumn is generally cooler than spring. The mean October temperature in Beijing is about 55 °F (13 °C), and in April it is about 57 °F (14 °C). In South China, the reverse is true. The mean October temperature in Guangzhou is 75 °F (24 °C), but in April it is only about 70 °F (21 °C).

The middle and lower reaches of the Huang He are where China's civilization and agriculture first developed. There the seasonal rhythm is well marked, and the duration of each season is evenly spaced. In other parts of China, however, the duration as well as the starting and closing dates of each season vary among different regions. Summer is nonexistent in northern Heilongjiang, while there is no winter in southern Guangdong. At Kunming, in the Yunnan uplands, the climate is mild throughout the year, with only brief summer and winter periods.

In general, south of the Qin Mountains–Huai River line the mean daily temperature seldom falls below freezing, so that farming can be practiced year-round. In the Yangtze valley, two crops are usually grown annually, but north of the Great Wall only one crop per year is possible.

PRECIPITATION

Precipitation in China generally follows the same pattern as temperatures, decreasing from the southeast to the northwest. The annual total of certain areas along the southeastern coast amounts to more than 80 inches (203 cm). The Yangtze valley receives about 40 to 45 inches (101 to 114 cm). Farther north, in the Huai River valley, the annual rainfall decreases to some 35 inches (90 cm). In the lower reaches of the Huang He, only 20 to 25 inches (50 to 63.5 cm) falls annually. The Northeast generally receives more precipitation than the North China Plain, with upwards of 40 or more inches falling in the Changbai Mountains.

The southeast monsoon loses much of its moisture by the time it reaches the northern part of the Loess Plateau, where the annual precipitation is reduced to between 12 and 20 inches (30.5 to 50 cm). Northwest of a line linking the Da Hinggan (Greater Khingan), Yin, Lang, Qilian, and Altun ranges, the annual precipitation is less than 10 inches (25 cm). Because these regions are far from the sea, high mountains prevent the southern monsoon from reaching them, and only grasslands are found there. In western Inner Mongolia, the Gansu Corridor, and the Tarim Basin, the annual precipitation drops to 4 inches (10 cm) or less. These are areas of true desert, where sometimes not a single drop of moisture is received for several years.

The Junggar Basin and the Ili River valley of northern Xinjiang are open to the influences of the westerlies, and precipitation is heavier there. Precipitation

on the Plateau of Tibet, following the national pattern, decreases from southeast to northwest. More than 40 inches falls annually in the valleys in the southeastern part of the plateau, and the eastern edge receives 20 inches. However, in the enclosed Qaidam Basin in the north, the yearly total is only 4 to 10 inches.

The high variability of precipitation is another characteristic of China's climate. Usually, variability increases as annual amounts decrease, a circumstance that is closely connected with the country's high frequency of drought and flood. Spring rain is of immense significance to Chinese farmers, but spring is also the season with the highest variability. In South China the variability exceeds 40 percent, along the Yangtze it is about 45 percent, and in North China it is more than 50 percent. The variability of a vast area in North China exceeds 70 percent in some places; east of Beijing, for example, the rainfall variability in spring may even exceed 80 percent, as it also does in the central parts of the Yunnan-Guizhou Plateau.

Rain falls mostly in the summer months, when plants need water the most. This is an important asset for farmers, but summer rainfall is usually too intense. In July, when the frontal zone shifts northward, cyclones (circulation of winds around centres of low atmospheric pressure) are much more active in North China than in South China, and North China begins to receive heavier rainfall. More than half the area of the North China Plain records 0.8 inch (20 mm) of rainfall daily, and in some places it may reach as much as 1 inch (25 mm) or more daily. During that time, areas south of the Yangtze are covered by the tropical Pacific air mass, so that the weather becomes comparatively stable, the amount of rainfall usually decreases, and the average rainfall intensity is less than that of June. The intensity of August rainfall is in general less than that of July.

In the southeastern coastal regions, around Fuzhou and Shantou, the maximum daily rainfall may even approach 12 inches (300 mm). Such accumulations are directly related to the high frequency of typhoons (tropical cyclones) striking that part of the coast, usually during the period from May to November; July, August, and September are the three months when typhoons are the most frequent.

In May, typhoons usually strike the coast south of Shantou. Later in June they shift northward, arriving between Shantou and Wenzhou, and after July they invade areas north of Wenzhou. August has the highest frequency of typhoon invasions, when more than one-third of the typhoons reaching China arrive. After September the frequency of typhoons decreases, and the pattern again shifts southward. In October, typhoons usually land south of Wenzhou; the late typhoons arriving in November and December strike south of Shantou.

PLANT AND ANIMAL LIFE

The diversity of both China's relief and its climate has resulted in one of the world's widest arrays of ecological niches, and these niches have been filled by a vast number of plant and animal species. Indeed, practically all types of Northern Hemisphere plants, except those of the polar tundra, are found in China, and, despite the continuous inroads of humans over the millennia, China is still home to some of the world's most exotic animals.

FLORA

China's great topological and climatic diversity has produced a vast array of natural vegetation types. The country's total number of seed-plant species is approximately 30,000, representing some 2,700 genera; more than 200 of these genera are endemic to China. There are about 2,500 species of forest trees, including some 95 percent of the known broad-leaved types. Many of these trees are of economic importance, such as tung trees, camphor trees, varnish trees (*Rhus verniciflua*), star anise (which yields an oil used as a flavouring additive), and glossy privet (*Ligustrum lucidum*).

Contributing to the variety and inter-mixture of tropical and temperate plants in China are such factors as the lack of insurmountable topographic barriers, such as large stretches of desert, between the tropical, temperate, and subalpine zones; wind systems that alternate in

Bamboo grove in the garden surrounding the cottage of Tang dynasty poet Du Fu, in Chengdu, Sichuan province, China. © Joan Lebold Cohen—Photo Researchers

winter and summer; and the frequent occurrence of cyclones. If, for example, the vegetation of Heilongjiang province in the North and of Guangdong province in the South are compared, it is hardly possible to find a single common plant species, with the exception of certain weeds. In the taiga (boreal forest) zone of China's northern border region or in the high mountains, on the other hand, there are many plant species that are also found in the lands within the Arctic Circle, while in the Chinese tropics there are species that also grow south of the Equator. However, from the ecological point of view, the tropical forests of South China generally do not differ greatly from those of Indonesia and other Southeast Asian countries, and the desert and steppe vegetation of northwestern China is closely akin to that found in Mongolia or Kazakhstan. Furthermore, the Chinese taiga terrain of the frontier area adjoining Russia is essentially the same as that of Siberia.

A traveler in China may encounter practically all types of natural vegetation indigenous to the Northern Hemisphere, the exception being species of the polar tundra. There are mangrove swamps along the shores of the South China Sea; rainforests on Hainan Island and in southern Yunnan; and deserts, steppes, meadows, and savannas elsewhere, as well as regions where tropical and temperate coniferous and evergreen and deciduous broad-leaved plants prevail.

China may be divided—roughly along a diagonal from the southwest to the northeast—into two sharply different vegetation zones: the dry northwest and the humid southeast. The tropical area, adjoining the humid southeast, is geographically related more to Southeast Asia. In the northwest, where desertlike conditions prevail, are vast areas of sparse drought-resistant vegetation; within these areas, in the low-lying land and depressions, are patches of salt-tolerant plants, notably in the Junggar, Qaidam, and Gobi regions. Skirting the southern edge of the Gobi is a wide belt of grassland.

Animal Life

The profusion of vegetation types and a variety of relief have allowed a great diversity of animal life to develop and have permitted animals to survive there that elsewhere are extinct. Notable among such survivals are the great paddlefish of the Yangtze, the species of small alligator in eastern and central China, and the giant salamander (related to the Japanese giant salamander and the American hellbender) in western China. The diversity of animal life is perhaps greatest in the ranges and valleys of Tibet and Sichuan, the latter province being renowned as the home of the giant panda. The takin (a type of goat antelope), numerous species of pheasants, and a variety of laughing thrushes are found in all Chinese mountain ranges. China seems to be one of the chief centres of dispersal of the carp family and also of old-world catfishes.

The regional affinities of Chinese animal life are complex. Resemblances in the Northeast are to the fauna of the Siberian forests. Animals from Central Asia inhabit suitable steppe areas in northern China. The life of the great mountain ranges is Palearctic (relating to a biogeographic region that includes Europe, Asia north of the Himalayas, northern Arabia, and Africa north of the Sahara) but with distinctively Chinese species or genera. To the southeast the lowlands and mountains alike permit direct access to the eastern region. This part of China presents a complete transition from temperate-zone Palearctic life to the wealth of tropical forms distinctive of southeastern Asia. Tropical types of reptiles, amphibians, birds, and mammals predominate in the southernmost Chinese provinces.

CHAPTER 2

HUMAN INTERACTIONS WITH CHINA'S ENVIRONMENT

Despite China's diverse geographic features and biodiversity, the single most identifiable characteristic to many outside its borders is the size of its population. Some one-fifth of humanity is of Chinese nationality. The great majority of the population is Chinese (Han), and thus China is often characterized as an ethnically homogeneous country, but few countries have as wide a variety of indigenous peoples as does China. Even among the Han there are cultural and linguistic differences between regions; it is possible that the only linguistic commonality between two individuals from different parts of China may be the written Chinese language.

SETTLEMENT PATTERNS

Although China's population is enormous, the population density of the country is not uniformly high; vast areas of China are either uninhabited or sparsely populated. In general, population density increases from west to east and is especially heavily concentrated in the corridor between Beijing and Shanghai.

RURAL AREAS

An overwhelming majority of rural settlements in China consist of sizable compact (nucleated) villages, except in mountainous and hilly terrain where such compaction is not possible. The formation of such rural settlements is related to the increasing population and to a long historical background as well as to water supply (the practice of drilling deep wells, for instance) and to defense (especially, in former days, against attack by bandits). Many of the large villages have no urban atmosphere at all, even with populations of several thousand. Frequent markets may be held between such settlements to enable the peasants to barter their agricultural produce.

On the North China Plain, villages are fairly evenly distributed and are connected with one another by footpaths and cart tracks. Houses are built close together and are mostly made of sun-dried brick or pounded earth. Many of the market towns or even large villages are surrounded by walls. The number and length of the streets depend on the town's size and the nature of the terrain; some streets are merely narrow lanes.

Rural landscapes of central and southern China are dominated by rice fields. The Yangtze River delta has almost every type of human settlement, from the single farmstead to the fairly large market town. Villages to the south and east of Lake Tai in Jiangsu province are generally located 1 to 2 miles (1.6 to 3 km) apart, and since the 1980s many of these have been developed into small towns. Villages in central China, particularly on the lower Yangtze, are larger than those of North China; many have a few shops that serve not only the villagers but also the dispersed residents nearby. In the centre of dozens of such villages is a market town, which collects rural produce and distributes manufactured goods. Communication among the villages is mainly by boat, along the dense net of waterways. The most elegant structures in the landscape are the numerous stone bridges that span streams and canals. In the Chengdu Plain of the Sichuan Basin, a large part of the population lives in isolated farmsteads or scattered hamlets, surrounded by thickets of bamboo and broad-leaved trees.

Cave dwellings are another distinctive feature of the Chinese rural landscape. They are common on the Loess Plateau and particularly in northern Shaanxi, western Shanxi, and southeastern Gansu, where the loess cover is thick and timber is scarce. A cave dwelling has the advantage of being naturally insulated, making it cooler in summer and warmer in winter.

The economic reforms initiated in China from the late 1970s had a profound impact on rural settlement. Improvements in agricultural productivity created a vast pool of surplus labour. Many of these rural workers went to the cities in search of factory jobs, but a large number stayed behind, where they engaged in a growing system of rural industrial production termed "township enterprise." Usually engaged in light manufacturing for both domestic and export markets, these enterprises helped transform thousands of villages into partially urbanized towns and raised the standard of living for

A cavehouse in Shanxi province, China, close to the Huang He (Yellow River). China Photos/ Getty Images

millions of peasants. The new towns thus served as a link between the city and the countryside and became a significant factor in the rapidly growing rural economy.

URBAN AREAS

Urbanization and industrialization often have been closely related in China. The first major urbanization push began in the mid-1950s, as the government of the newly established People's Republic intensified its efforts to convert the country into an industrial power. Urban growth accelerated even more rapidly from the mid-1980s, with China's serious entry onto the global economic stage.

Thus, the rapid development of modern manufacturing industries and of communications in China produced a dramatic change in the urban landscape. Many new towns and cities have been built around manufacturing and mining centres. In the remoter areas of China, the first appearance of railways and highways contributed to the rapid growth of some entirely new towns, such as Shihezi in northern Xinjiang and Shiquanhe in western Tibet. Among larger cities, Ürümqi (Urumchi; capital of Xinjiang), Lanzhou (capital of Gansu), and Baotou (in Inner

Hailar, a railway city in Inner Mongolia Autonomous Region, China. Richard Harrington—Miller Services Ltd.

Mongolia) are examples where expansion has been extremely rapid. Lanzhou lies midway between southeastern and northwestern China. Baotou—formerly a bleak frontier town of traders, artisans, and immigrant farmers—has become one of the country's largest steel centres.

More than two-fifths of China's population is urban, up from less than one-fourth in 1975. While the urban-rural proportion is relatively low compared with more highly industrialized countries, it represents an enormous number of people—comparable to the total population of North America. More than six dozen cities have populations of more

than 1,000,000, and the populations of several other dozen are between 500,000 and 1,000,000. The distribution of China's large cities mirrors the national population distribution, with heavy concentrations in the eastern coastal provinces, lesser but still significant numbers in the central provinces, and considerably fewer in western regions.

CHINA'S LAND USE AND ITS ECONOMY

Despite China's size, the wealth of its resources, and the fact that about one-fifth of the world's population lives within its borders, its role in the world economy was relatively small until late in the 20th century. However, since the late 1970s China has dramatically increased its interaction with the international economy and has become a dominant figure in world trade. Both China's foreign trade and its gross national product (GNP) have experienced sustained and rapid growth, especially since foreign-owned firms began using China as an export platform for goods manufactured there.

The Chinese economy thus has been in a state of transition since the late 1970s as the country has moved away from a Soviet-type economic system. Agriculture has been decollectivized, the nonagricultural private sector has grown rapidly, and government priorities have shifted toward light and high-technology, rather than heavy, industries. Nevertheless, key bottlenecks have continued to constrain growth. Available energy has not been sufficient to run all of the country's installed industrial capacity, the transport system has remained inadequate to move sufficient quantities of such critical commodities as coal, and the communications system has not been able to meet the needs of a centrally planned economy of China's size and complexity.

China is the world's largest producer of rice and is among the principal sources of wheat, corn (maize), tobacco, soybeans, peanuts (groundnuts), and cotton. The country is one of the world's largest producers of a number of industrial and mineral products—including cotton cloth, tungsten, and antimony—and is an important producer of cotton yarn, coal, crude oil, and a number of other products. Its mineral resources are probably among the richest in the world but are only partially developed. China has acquired some highly sophisticated production facilities through foreign investment and joint ventures with foreign partners. The technological level and quality standards of many of its industries have improved rapidly and dramatically.

AGRICULTURE, FORESTRY, AND FISHING

Agriculture, forestry, and fishing collectively represent an important, though decreasing, proportion of China's overall economy. The once-dominant agricultural sector was surpassed decades ago by manufacturing and, more recently, by the service sector. Nonetheless, farming and related pursuits have continued to represent the single-largest proportion of the labour force, about two-fifths of the total.

FARMING AND LIVESTOCK

As a result of topographic and climatic features, the area suitable for cultivation is small: only about 10 percent of China's total land area. Of this, slightly more than half is unirrigated, and the remainder is divided roughly equally between paddy fields and irrigated areas. Good progress has been made in improving water conservancy. In addition, the quality of the soil in cultivated regions varies around the country, and environmental problems such as floods, drought, and erosion pose serious threats in many areas. Nevertheless, about two-thirds of the population lives in the countryside, and until the 1980s a large proportion of them made their living directly from farming. Since then many have been encouraged to leave the fields and pursue other activities, such as handicrafts, commerce, factory work, and transport; and by the mid-1980s farming had dropped to less than half of the value of rural output.

RICE

Rice is an edible starchy cereal grain and the plant by which it is produced. Roughly one-half of the world population, including virtually all of East and Southeast Asia, is wholly dependent upon rice as a staple food; 95 percent of the world's rice crop is eaten by humans.

The cultivated rice plant, Oryza sativa, is an annual grass of the Gramineae family. It grows to about 4 feet (1.2 m) in height. The leaves are long and flattened, and its panicle, or inflorescence, is made up of spikelets bearing flowers that produce the fruit, or grain.

Many cultures have evidence of early rice cultivation, including China, India, and the civilizations of Southeast Asia. However, the earliest archaeological evidence comes from central and eastern China and dates to 7000–5000 BCE. With the exception of the type called upland rice, the plant is grown on submerged land in the coastal plains, tidal deltas, and river basins of tropical, semitropical, and temperate regions. The seeds are sown in prepared beds, and when the seedlings are 25 to 50 days old, they are transplanted to a field, or paddy, that has been enclosed by levees and submerged under 2 to 4 inches (5 to 10 cm) of water, remaining submerged during the growing season.

The harvested rice kernel, known as paddy, or rough, rice, is enclosed by the hull, or husk. Milling usually removes both the hull and bran layers of the kernel, and a coating of glucose and talc is sometimes applied to give the kernel a glossy finish. Rice that is processed to remove only the husks, called brown rice, contains about 8 percent protein and small amounts of fats and is a source of thiamine, niacin, riboflavin, iron, and calcium. Rice that is milled to remove the bran as well is called white rice and is greatly diminished in nutrients. When white rice forms a major portion of the diet, there is a risk of beriberi, a disease resulting from a deficiency of thiamine and minerals. Parboiled white rice is processed before milling to retain most of the nutrients, and enriched rice has iron and B vitamins added to it. Rice is cooked by boiling. It is eaten alone and in a great variety of soups, side dishes, and main dishes in Oriental, Middle Eastern, and many other cuisines.

The by-products of milling, including bran and rice polish (finely powdered bran and starch resulting from polishing), are used as livestock feed. Oil is processed from the bran for both food and industrial uses. Broken rice is used in brewing, distilling, and in the manufacture of starch

Rice cultivation is extremely labour-intensive. This farmer in the eastern Zhuang Autonomous Region of Guangxi, China, is hand-planting rice seedlings. Shutterstock.com

and rice flour. Hulls are used for fuel, packing material, industrial grinding, fertilizer manufacture, and in the manufacture of an industrial chemical called furfural. The straw is used for feed, livestock bedding, roof thatching, mats, garments, packing material, and broomstraws.

In the 1960s, the so-called Green Revolution, an international scientific effort to diminish the threat of world hunger, produced improved strains of numerous food crops, including that known as miracle rice. Bred for disease resistance and increased productivity, this variety is characterized by a short, sturdy stalk that minimizes loss from drooping. Poor soil conditions and other factors, however, inhibited its anticipated widespread success.

The principal rice-producing countries are China, India, Japan, Bangladesh, Indonesia, Thailand, and Burma. Other important producers are Vietnam, Brazil, South Korea, the Philippines, and the United States.

Although the use of farm machinery has been increasing, for the most part the Chinese peasant depends on simple, nonmechanized farming implements.

Western China, comprising Tibet, Xinjiang, and Qinghai, has little agricultural significance except for areas of oasis farming and cattle raising. Rice, China's most important crop, is dominant in the southern provinces, many of which yield two harvests per year. In North China, wheat is of the greatest importance, while in the central provinces, wheat and rice vie with each other for the top place. Millet and kaoliang (a variety of grain sorghum) are grown mainly in the Northeast and some central provinces, which—together with some northern areas—also produce considerable quantities of barley. Most of the soybean crop is derived from the North and the Northeast, and corn (maize) is grown in central China and the North. Tea comes mainly from the hilly areas of the southeast. Cotton is grown extensively in the central provinces, but it is also found to a lesser extent in the southeast and in the North. Tobacco comes from central China and parts of the South. Other important crops are potatoes, sugar beets, and oilseeds.

Animal husbandry constitutes the second most important component of agricultural production. China is the world's leading producer of pigs, chickens, and eggs, and it also has sizable herds of sheep and cattle. Since the mid-1970s, greater emphasis has been placed on increasing the livestock output.

FORESTRY AND FISHING

Wholesale destruction of China's accessible forests over a long period of time gave way to an energetic reforestation program that has proved to be inadequate; forest resources are still fairly meagre. The principal forests are found in the Qin (Tsinling) Mountains and the central mountain ranges and in the uplands of Sichuan and Yunnan. Because they are inaccessible, the Qin forests are not worked extensively, and much of the country's timber comes from Heilongjiang, Jilin, Sichuan, and Yunnan.

China has a long tradition of ocean and freshwater fishing and of aquaculture, and it is the world's leading producer in both categories. The bulk of the catch comes from Pacific fisheries, with nearly all of the remainder from inland freshwater sources. Pond raising has always been important and has been increasingly emphasized to supplement coastal and inland fisheries threatened by overfishing and to provide valuable export commodities such as prawns. Aquaculture surpassed capture, in terms of overall tonnage, in the early 1990s.

RESOURCES AND POWER

China is well endowed with mineral resources, and more than three dozen minerals have proven economically important reserves. The country has rich overall energy potential, but most of it remains to be developed. In addition, the geographical distribution of energy places most of these resources far from their major industrial users. Basically, the Northeast is rich in coal and petroleum, the central part of North China has abundant coal, and the southwest has great hydroelectric potential. However, the industrialized regions around Guangzhou (Canton) and the lower Yangtze region around Shanghai have too little energy, while there is little industry located near major energy resource areas other than in the southern part of the Northeast. Thus, although energy production has expanded rapidly, it has continued to fall short of demand, and China has been purchasing increasing quantities of foreign petroleum and natural gas.

MINERALS

China's most important mineral resources are hydrocarbons, of which coal is the most abundant. Although deposits are widely scattered (some coal is found in every province), most of the total is located in the northern part of the country. The province of Shanxi is thought to contain about half of the total; other important coal-bearing provinces include Heilongjiang, Liaoning, Jilin, Hebei, and Shandong. Apart from these northern provinces, significant quantities of coal are present in Sichuan, and there are some deposits of importance in Guangdong, Guangxi, Yunnan, and Guizhou. A large part of the country's reserves consists of good bituminous coal, but there are also large deposits of

lignite. Anthracite is present in several places (especially Liaoning, Guizhou, and Henan), but overall it is not significant.

At the government's instigation, hundreds of small, locally managed mines have been developed throughout China in order to ensure a more even distribution of coal supplies and to reduce the strain on the country's inadequate transportation network. These operations produce about two-fifths of the country's coal, although their output typically is expensive and used largely for local consumption.

China's onshore petroleum resources are located mainly in the Northeast—notably at the Daqing oil field—and in the northwestern provinces of Xinjiang (particularly in the Tarim Basin), Gansu, and Qinghai; there are also reserves in Sichuan, Shandong, and Henan provinces. Shale oil is found in a number of places, especially at Fushun in Liaoning, where the deposits overlie the coal reserves, as well as in Guangdong. Light oil of high quality has been found in the Pearl River estuary of the South China Sea, the Qaidam Basin in Qinghai, and the Tarim Basin in Xinjiang. China contracted with Western oil companies to jointly explore and develop oil deposits in the China Sea, Yellow Sea, Gulf of Tonkin, and Bo Hai. The country consumes the bulk of its oil output and imports but does export some crude oil and oil products.

The true extent of China's natural gas reserves is unknown. It has proven reserves of some 42 trillion cubic feet (1.2

trillion cubic m), but estimates have ranged as high as 187 trillion cubic feet (5.3 trillion cubic metres). Exploration for natural gas, long at only modest levels, has been increasing. Sichuan province accounts for almost half of the known reserves and production. Most of the rest of China's natural gas is associated gas produced in the Northeast's major oil fields, especially Daqing. Other gas deposits have been found in Inner Mongolia, the Qaidam Basin, Shaanxi, Hebei, Jiangsu, Shanghai, Zhejiang, and off the southwest shore of Hainan Island.

Iron ore reserves are also extensive and are found in most provinces, with Hainan, Gansu, Guizhou, southern Sichuan, and Guangdong having the richest deposits. The largest mined reserves are located north of the Yangtze River and supply neighbouring iron and steel enterprises. With the exception of nickel, chromium, and cobalt, China is well supplied with ferroalloys and manganese. Reserves of tungsten are also known to be fairly large. Copper resources are moderate, and high-quality ore is present only in a few deposits. Discoveries have been reported from the Hui Autonomous Region of Ningxia. Lead and zinc are available, and bauxite resources are thought to be plentiful. China's antimony reserves are the largest in the world. Tin resources are plentiful, and there are fairly rich deposits of gold. There are important deposits of phosphate rock in a number of areas. Pyrites occur in several places, the most important of which are found in Liaoning, Hebei, Shandong, and Shanxi. China also has large resources of fluorite (fluorspar), gypsum, asbestos, and cement.

In addition, China produces a fairly wide range of nonmetallic minerals. One of the most important of these is salt, which is derived from coastal evaporation sites in Jiangsu, Hebei, Shandong, and Liaoning, as well as from extensive salt fields in Sichuan, Ningxia, and the Qaidam Basin.

HYDROELECTRIC POTENTIAL

China's extensive river network and mountainous terrain provide ample potential for the production of hydroelectric power. Most of the total hydroelectric capacity is in the southwest—notably in Sichuan, Yunnan, Tibet, and Hubei—where coal supplies are poor but demand for energy is rapidly growing. The potential in the Northeast is fairly small; however, it was there that the first hydroelectric stations were built (by the Japanese). As a result of considerable seasonal fluctuations in rainfall, the flow of rivers tends to drop during the winter, forcing many power stations to operate at less than normal capacity, while in the summer, on the other hand, floods often interfere with production. The massive Three Gorges project on the Yangtze River east of Chongqing, involving the construction of a dam and reservoir, has been producing hydroelectric power since 2003.

TRANSPORTATION

Great emphasis has been placed on developing the country's transportation infrastructure because it is so closely related to developing the national economy, consolidating the national defense system, and strengthening national unification. Nevertheless, China's domestic transportation system continues to constitute a major constraint on economic growth and the efficient movement of goods and people. Railroads, some still employing steam locomotives, provide the major means for freight haulage, but their capacity cannot meet demand for the shipment of coal and other goods. In addition, roads and waterways are providing an increasing proportion of China's overall transportation.

Initially, as China's railways and highways were mostly concentrated in the coastal regions, access to the interior was difficult. This situation has been improved considerably, as railways and highways have been built in the remote border areas of the northwest and southwest. All parts of China, except certain remote areas of Tibet, are accessible by rail, road, water, or air.

RAILWAYS

Railway construction began in China in 1876. Because railways can conveniently carry a large volume of goods over long distances, they are of especial importance in China's transportation system.

All trunk railways in China are under the administration of the Ministry of Railways. The central government operates a major rail network in the Northeast built on a base constructed by the Russians and Japanese during the decades before the establishment of the People's Republic of China in 1949 and an additional large system inside (that is, to the south or east of) the Great Wall. The framework for the railways inside the wall consists of several north-south and east-west lines.

Apart from those operated by the central government, there is also a network of small, state-owned local railways that link mines, factories, farms, and forested areas. The construction of these smaller railways is encouraged by the central government, and technical assistance is provided by the state railway system when it is thought that the smaller railways can stimulate regional economic development.

Coal has long been the principal railway cargo. The rather uneven distribution of coalfields in China makes it necessary to transport coal over long distances, especially between the North and South. The increase in the production of petroleum and natural gas has made necessary the construction of both pipelines and additional railways.

Since the late 1950s there has been a change in railway-construction policy. Prior to that time, most attention was paid to the needs of the eastern half of China, where most of the coal network is found; but since then, more emphasis has been given to extending the rail system into the western provinces and improving the original railway system, including such measures as building bridges, laying double tracks, and using continuous welded rail. In addition, certain important rail links have been electrified.

Since 1960 hundreds of thousands of workers have been mobilized to construct major lines in the northwest and southwest. In the 1970s new lines were extended into previously unopened parts of the country. In the 1980s new regions in the northwest were linked to the national market and opened up for development. The best example was the line built from Lanzhou in Gansu province westward into the oil fields of the Qaidam Basin. These projects, which were coordinated on a national level, contrast to the pattern prevailing before World War II, when foreign-financed railroads were built in different places without any attempt to coordinate or standardize the transportation and communications systems.

Even greater effort has been made since 1990 to speed up new railway construction and improve the existing network. A major new line runs southward from Beijing to Kowloon (Hong Kong) via Fuyang and Nanchang and eases strain on the other north-south trunk lines. The main east-west trunk line from Lianyungang on the east coast to Lanzhou now extends northwestward through Ürümqi (Urumchi) to the Xinjiang-Kazakhstan border, linking China to Central Asia and Russia. A third line, constructed southeastward from Kunming in Yunnan to the port of Beihai in Guangxi, greatly improves southwestern China's access to the sea, as does a new line that connects Lhasa in Tibet with Qinghai province. In addition, upgrades to track and equipment have facilitated high-speed passenger rail service between Beijing and Shanghai, Guangzhou, and Harbin.

ROAD NETWORKS

The first modern highway in China was built in 1913 in Hunan province. The highways of China may be divided into three categories: state, provincial, or regional highways of political, economic, or military importance; local highways of secondary importance, operated by counties or communes; and special-purpose highways, mostly managed by factories, mines, state farms, forestry units, or the military forces.

The most striking achievement in highway construction has been the road system built on the cold and high Qinghai-Tibetan plateau. Workers, after overcoming various physical obstacles, within a few years built three of the highest and longest highways in the world, thus markedly changing the transportation pattern in the western border regions of China and strengthening the national defense system. Of the three highways, one runs westward across Sichuan into

Tibet; another extends southwestward from Qinghai to Tibet; and the third runs southward from Xinjiang to Tibet.

Another early objective was to build a rural road network in order to open up commercial routes to the villages and to facilitate the transportation of locally produced goods. The wide dispersion and seasonal and variable nature of agricultural production, as well as the large numbers of relatively small shipments involved, explain why trucks are preferred for shipping. Similarly, trucks best bring consumer goods, fertilizers, and farm machinery and equipment to rural areas.

From the 1980s and especially since 1990, the emphasis has shifted to creating a nationwide network of major highways. Thousands of miles of multilane express highways have been constructed in and around the largest cities, and older two-lane roads have been widened to accommodate multiple lanes of traffic. Overall road mileage has roughly doubled since the early 1980s. Nonetheless, motor vehicle use has expanded much more rapidly than road construction, particularly in the major cities. In addition, a large proportion of China's road network is either unpaved or badly in need of reconstruction.

Large-scale highway construction spurred China to develop its motor vehicle industry. The first vehicle manufacturing plant dates to the mid-1950s, and by 1970 localized production was widespread in the country. The basis of the early industry was generally simple, usually an extension of repair shops in which vehicles of various types were produced to serve the needs of the locality. Vehicles produced by large state automotive factories generally were distributed only to state enterprises and military units. By the 1980s many vehicles, especially automobiles, were imported. Domestic automobile manufacture grew rapidly after 1990 as individual car ownership became increasingly possible, and it emerged as one of China's major industries. Several foreign companies have established joint ventures with Chinese firms.

WATERWAYS

Since ancient times, inland water transportation has played a major role in moving goods and commodities from production sources to consumption destinations. Railways and roads, though increasingly important to modern China's transportation network, cannot entirely supplant waterways. The high cost of construction prevents railways from being built extensively, and rail transportation conditions are often congested. Freight volume carried by highways is limited, and highways are not suitable for moving bulk goods. China's water transportation potential is great, but it is still far from being fully developed. Nonetheless, China has more than 75,000 miles (some 125,000 km) of navigable inland waterways, the most

Cargo barges on the Grand Canal at Suzhou, Jiangsu province, China. © Susan Pierres/Peter Arnold, Inc.

extensive system of any country in the world. The distribution of waterways is chiefly within central and South China, except for a few navigable streams in the Northeast.

One of the first goals of the communist government after it took power in 1949 was to establish a national network of waterways. It also initiated a program to build and refurbish port facilities and to dredge river channels. By 1961 some 15 principal waterways had been opened to navigation, focused on the Yangtze, Pearl (Zhu), Huai, and Han rivers, the Huang He (Yellow River), and the Grand Canal. Water transportation development has subsequently received considerable emphasis. Dredging and other improvements to inland waterways have been important to economic reconstruction, while capital and maintenance costs for water transportation have been much lower than those for railway transportation.

The Yangtze, the most important artery in China's waterway network, is also one of the most economically significant rivers in the world. Together with its tributaries, it accounts for almost half of the country's waterway mileage, while the volume of the freight it carries represents about one-third of the total volume carried by river transportation. Work undertaken in the mid-1950s to improve the middle course of the Yangtze allowed it to become navigable throughout the year from its mouth to Yibin in Sichuan. When the Yangtze is high in summer, it is navigable from its mouth to as far as

Chongqing for ships of up to 5,000 tons. Many cable-hauling stations had been established at rapids on the upper course of the Yangtze and of its major tributaries, such as the Wu River. Boats sailing against the current are hauled over the rapids with strong steel cables attached to fixed winches, thus augmenting their loading capacity, increasing speed, and saving time. Such improvements have permitted regular passenger and cargo services to be operated on the Yangtze.

The Xi River is second in importance only to the Yangtze, being the major water transport artery of South China. Ships of 1,000 tons can sail up the Xi to Wuzhou, while smaller craft can sail up its middle and upper courses as well as up the Bei and Dong rivers and the tributaries of all these streams. The Yangtze and the Xi are not icebound in winter. The Sungari (Songhua) River, flowing across the Manchurian Plain, is navigable for half of its course; it is icebound from November through March and crowded with traffic the other months of the year. The Amur (Heilong), Sungari, and Ussuri (Wusuli) rivers with their tributaries form a network of waterways totaling about 12,500 miles (20,100 km) in length. In the past the Huang He was little navigated, especially on its middle and lower courses, but mechanized junks now operate along the middle course in Henan.

The Grand Canal, the only major Chinese waterway running from north to south, passes through the basins of the Hai, Huang, Huai, Yangtze, and Qiantang rivers in its 1,100-mile (1,800-km) course from Beijing to Hangzhou. One of the greatest engineering projects in China, equal in fame to the Great Wall, it is the world's longest artificial waterway; some of its sections follow the natural course of a river, while other parts are hand-dug. Work on the canal began as early as the 4th century BCE and was completed by the end of the 13th century CE. It forms a north-south communications and transportation link between the most densely populated areas in China. From the latter part of the 19th century, however, because of political corruption, mismanagement, and flooding from the Huang He, the canal gradually became silted up, and the higher section in Shandong became blocked. Since 1958, efforts have been made to reopen the Grand Canal to navigation, this time also by larger modern craft. The canal is important in the north-south transportation of bulk cargoes, thus facilitating the nationwide distribution of coal and foodstuffs.

PORT FACILITIES AND SHIPPING

China's 8,700-mile-long (14,000 km) coastline is indented by approximately 100 large and small bays as well as some twenty deepwater harbours, most of which are ice-free throughout the year. Coastal shipping is divided into two principal navigation zones, the northern and southern marine districts. The northern district extends north from Xiamen (Amoy) to the North Korean border, with Shanghai as its administrative centre. The southern district extends south from

Amoy to the Vietnamese border, with Guangzhou as the administrative centre. Most of the oceangoing routes begin from the ports of Dalian, Qinghuangdao, Tanggu, Qingdao (Tsingtao), Shanghai, Huangpu, Zhanjiang, or Hong Kong. Shanghai, the leading port of China from the early 19th century, was eclipsed by Hong Kong when the latter was reincorporated into the country in 1997.

In 1961 China established a state-run marine shipping company and subsequently signed shipping agreements with many countries, laying the foundation for developing the country's ocean transport. That organization developed into the present-day China Ocean Shipping (Group) Company (COSCO), one of the world's largest shipping corporations. The Chinese government also invested heavily in water transportation infrastructure, constructing new ports and rebuilding and enlarging older facilities. A major effort has also been made to increase mechanization and containerization at major international ports. In addition, China has become one of the world's premier shipbuilding countries, satisfying domestic demand and exporting ships and oil-drilling platforms worldwide.

AVIATION

Air travel is particularly suited to China, with its vast territory and varied terrain. Chinese civil aviation has two major categories: air transportation, which mainly handles passengers, cargoes, and mail, traveling on both scheduled and non-scheduled routes; and special-purpose aviation, which mainly serves industrial and agricultural production, national defense, and scientific and technological research. The aims of civil aviation in China have been primarily to extend air routes; to strengthen the link between Beijing and other important cities, as well as remote border and interior areas; to develop special-purpose flights serving the needs of agriculture, forestry, and geologic prospecting; and to increase the number of large transport airplanes.

In the 1950s international aviation depended mainly on Soviet support, and all principal international air routes originally passed through Moscow using Soviet planes. As Sino-Soviet relations deteriorated in the late 1950s, China began to open direct air routes to other places as well. Thus, in addition to the original routes between China and the Soviet Union, North Korea, Mongolia, Vietnam, and Burma (now Myanmar), air routes were opened to several of China's neighbouring countries, the United States, western Asia, Europe, and Africa. After 1980 the number of air routes grew markedly; the addition of Hong Kong's international air traffic in 1997 constituted another significant increase.

Chinese civil air efforts were carried out solely by the state-run General Administration of Civil Aviation of China (CAAC) from 1949 until the mid-1980s. In an effort to improve efficiency and service, regional airlines were then introduced in competition with the airlines operated by the CAAC. In the early 21st century the CAAC's airline-operating responsibilities were being shifted to semiprivate companies.

Airport construction has increased greatly since Beijing's first modern civilian airport was built in 1958; that facility was replaced in 1980 by Capital Airport. Major projects since 1990 include new facilities at Macau (1995), Hong Kong (1998), Shanghai (2000), and Guangzhou (2004). The Chinese Air Force controls a large number of airfields; retired Air Force personnel have been the major source of civilian pilots. Airplanes, including various types of military aircraft, have long been made in China. Civil airliners for long-distance flights, however, are still mostly purchased abroad.

CHAPTER 3

MAJOR CHINESE PHYSICAL FEATURES

A s China's landmass is nearly as large as the whole of Europe, its geographic diversity is perhaps not surprising. However, not only is China home to many different kinds of geographic features, it contains some of the most famous and fascinating, including two of Asia's longest rivers, some of the continent's loftiest mountains, and one of its largest and driest deserts.

YANGTZE RIVER

The Yangtze River is the longest river in both China and Asia, and it is the third longest river in the world, with a length of 3,915 miles (6,300 km). Its basin, extending for some 2,000 miles (3,200 km) from west to east and for more than 600 miles (1,000 km) from north to south, drains an area of 698,265 square miles (1,808,500 square km). From its source on the Plateau of Tibet to its mouth on the East China Sea, the river traverses or serves as the border between ten provinces or regions. More than three-fourths of the river's course runs through mountains. The Yangtze has eight principal tributaries. On its left bank, from source to mouth, these are the Yalong, Min, Jialing, and Han rivers; those on the right bank include the Wu, Yuan, Xiang, and Gan rivers.

The name Yangtze—derived from the name of the ancient fiefdom of Yang—has been applied to the river mainly by those in the West. Chang Jiang ("Long River") is the name

used in China, although it also is called Da Jiang ("Great River") or, simply, Jiang ("[The] River"). The Yangtze is the most important river of China. It is the country's principal waterway, and its basin is China's great granary and contains nearly one-third of the national population.

The Upper Course

The upper course of the Yangtze flows across the Plateau of Tibet and descends through deep valleys in the mountains east of the plateau, emerging onto the Yunnan-Guizhou (Yungui) Plateau. Summers there are warm, and the winters are cold. The source of the Yangtze is the Ulan Moron (Wulanmulun) River, which originates in glacial meltwaters on the slopes of the Tanggula Mountains in southern Qinghai province on the border with the Tibet Autonomous Region. From the confluence of this stream with several others, the river flows generally easterly through a shallow, spacious valley, the bottom of which is studded with lakes and small reservoirs. This part of its

China's longest river, the Yangtze, separates the provinces of Sichuan (top) and Yunnan in southwest China. Frederic J. Brown/AFP/Getty Images

course lies in the higher regions of the Tibetan highlands.

The river's character changes sharply upon reaching the eastern limits of the highlands. There the river—which in this stretch is called the Jinsha—descends from a high elevation, winding its way south of the high Bayan Har Mountains and forming a narrow valley up to 2 miles (3 km) in depth. Individual mountain peaks exceed elevations of 16,000 feet (4,900 m) above sea level and are crowned with glaciers and perpetual snow. The steep, rocky slopes are cut with gorges and deep valleys. For several hundred miles the Yangtze flows in a southeasterly direction, before turning south to flow downward in rushing rapids. For a considerable distance the river flows through passes that are so steep that no room is left even for a narrow path. Villages, which are scarce in this area, are located high above the river. In this region the Yangtze runs close and parallel to both the Mekong and Salween rivers; all three rivers are within 15 to 30 miles (25 to 50 km) of one another and continue to flow in mutual proximity for a distance of more than 250 miles (400 km).

North of latitude 26° N these great rivers diverge, and the Yangtze turns east to pass through a winding valley with steep slopes. The river receives the waters of many tributaries, among which the Yalong River is the largest and contributes the most water. The Yangtze then widens to between 1,000 and 1,300 feet (300 and 400 m), reaching depths often exceeding 30 feet (9 m). In narrower gorges the water width decreases by almost half, but the depth increases sharply.

Near the end of the upstream part of its course, the Yangtze descends to an elevation of 1,000 feet above sea level. Thus, over the first 1,600 miles (2,600 km) of its length, the river has fallen more than 17,000 feet (5,200 m), or an average of more than 10 feet per mile (2 m per km) of its course. In the mountains, however, there is a substantial stretch where the fall of the river is considerably greater.

The Middle Course

The middle course of the Yangtze stretches for about 630 miles (1,010 km) between the cities of Yibin in Sichuan province and Yichang in Hubei province. The climate is characterized by hot summers and relatively mild winters, as the high mountains to the west protect the region from the cold north and west winds. Annual precipitation measures between 40 and 60 inches (101 to 152 cm), a large part of it occurring in summer; the growing season lasts for more than six months. In most of this segment, the river crosses hilly Sichuan province, where the lower mountains and plateaus connect the highlands of southwestern China with the Qin (Tsinling) Mountains lying between the Yangtze and Huang He (Yellow River) basins. Located in this

Xiling Gorge, in the Three Gorges section of the Yangtze River (Chang Jiang), as it appeared before completion of the Three Gorges Dam, Hubei province, China. © Wolfgang Kaehler

area is Chongqing, a major industrial centre and river port. The river's width there is from about 1,000 to 1,600 feet (300 to 500 m), and the depth in places exceeds 30 feet. The current is swift; the banks often are high and steep. The river falls some 820 feet (250 m) in Sichuan, more than a foot per mile (0.2 m per km) of flow.

As the Yangtze flows through eastern Sichuan and into western Hubei, it traverses the famous Three Gorges region for a distance of 125 miles (200 km) before debouching onto the plains to the east. The gorges have steep, sheer slopes composed mainly of thick limestone rocks. Prior to the completion of the Three Gorges Dam in 2006, the slopes rose some 1,300 to 2,000 feet (400 to 600 m) above the river, although with the creation of the reservoir behind the dam their height has been diminished fairly significantly. Nonetheless, they still present the appearance of fantastic towers, pillars, or spears. Qutang, the first gorge—about 5 miles (8 km) long—is the shortest;

prior to its inundation, the river there was considered the most dangerous for navigation, being extremely narrow with many rapids and eddies. Wu, the second gorge, stretches for about 30 miles (50 km); it is a narrow, steep corridor with almost vertical walls of heights up to 1,600 or even 2,000 feet (487 to 609 m) above the river. The last gorge, Xilang, is located upstream of Yichang and extends for a distance of 21 miles (34 km); limestone cliffs rise directly out of the water in some places, although with the rise of the reservoir to much lower heights than before. The gorges are rocky, and the walls are speckled with cracks, niches, and indentations. Even before the river was inundated, its depth in the gorges was considerable, increasing to between 500 and 600 feet (150 and 180 m) and giving the Yangtze the greatest depths of any river in the world.

THE LOWER COURSE

The lower part of the Yangtze basin is centred on the extensive lowland plains of east-central China. The region experiences a temperate climate with warm springs, hot summers, cool autumns, and relatively cold winters for the latitude. Monsoons (seasonally changing winds) dominate the weather of the region, and in the summer and autumn typhoons occur periodically. As the Yangtze exits from the Three Gorges Dam, near Yichang, it enters a complex system of lakes, marshes, and multiple river channels developed on the plains of Hunan and Hubei provinces. This vast region, lying at elevations below 165 feet (50 m), has served as a natural flood-regulation basin in recent geologic history. Three main tributaries (the Yuan, Xiang, and Han rivers) and many smaller ones join the Yangtze in this region, which also is where the current slows as the river reaches the plain. Water levels fluctuate considerably between the flood and low-flow seasons. In addition, the presence of a number of large lakes, including Dongting Lake and Lakes Hong and Liangzi, also causes considerable fluctuations in water volume. The total area of the lakes, at average water levels, is some 6,600 square miles (17,100 square km). The lakes are of national economic significance, mainly as fisheries.

At the edge of the Lake Liangzi plain, the Yangtze widens markedly, the course of its stream wandering in the form of a large loop. The width of the river is up to 2,600 feet (800 m), the depth is more than 100 feet (30 m), and the water current flows at a rate of about 3.5 feet (1 m) per second. The banks are built up for protection from floods. In the southern part of the plain lies Dongting Lake, which once was the largest freshwater lake in China but now has been reduced in area by silting and land reclamation; it shares four tributaries and two canals with the Yangtze, whose flow it serves to regulate. The surrounding area, agricultural and studded with lakes, is China's most important rice-producing region.

At the centre of the lakes region is the large metropolis of Wuhan. Situated on the Yangtze near the mouth of the Han River, it was formed in 1950 by the merger of the cities of Hanyang and Hankou on the left bank and Wuchang on the right bank and has become one of China's most important metallurgical-industry centres and river ports. Farther east, the Yangtze flows into a narrowing, picturesque valley and then passes onto the plain of Jiangxi province, which contains Lake Poyang, China's largest natural freshwater lake. The lake, with an average area of about 1,385 square miles (3,585 square km), receives the Kan River tributary and, in turn, is linked to the Yangtze by a wide tributary. The river then turns to the northeast, passes through a widening valley, and flows out onto the southern North China Plain. The width of the river increases at this point to between 3,000 and 6,000 feet (900 and 1,800 m), and the depth in places approaches 100 feet (30 m). In this region there are a number of large cities, including Anqing, Wuhu, and Nanjing. The Grand Canal (Da Yunhe), with a length of nearly 1,100 miles (1,800 km), is one of the longest canals in the world; it crosses the Yangtze in the vicinity of the city of Zhenjiang.

Dongting Lake

Dongting Lake (Chinese: Dongting Hu) is a large lake in northern Hunan province, south-central China. It lies in a basin to the south of the Yangtze River and is connected to the Yangtze by four channels. Typically, some two-fifths of the river's waters flow into the lake, the amount increasing during flood periods. The lake is also fed from the south by almost the entire drainage of Hunan province, with the Xiang River flowing in from the south and the Zi, Yuan, and Li rivers from the southwest and west. The waters of the entire lake system discharge into the Yangtze at Yueyang.

The lake's size varies greatly from season to season. Its normal size is about 95 miles (150 km) from east to west and 60 miles (95 km) from north to south, while its area is 1,089 square miles (2,820 square km). In flood periods, its water level may rise by as much as 50 feet (15 m), and the inundated area may increase by as much as 7,700 square miles (20,000 square km). It is now the second largest freshwater lake in China.

The lake, like Lake Poyang farther east, acts as a huge retention reservoir for the Yangtze. In the flood season (June to October) the waters of the Yangtze flood into the lake. During that time not only the Yueyang outlet but also two of the inflow channels (the Taiping and Ouchi streams) are navigable by large craft, which can also pass up the southern rivers. From October to April, however, more water is discharged from the lake than enters it, the water level falls, and much of the lake's area becomes dry land.

Large-scale construction projects have been undertaken to supplement the role played by Dongting Lake in regulating flooding on the Yangtze. In the northwest angle between the lake and the Yangtze, a huge artificial retention basin (built 1954–56) has floodgates through which the Yangtze can be diverted in time of need. The basin is kept empty and its floor under cultivation, except during the flood season. Called Lake Datong, it is regulated by a great barrage (dam) across the Taiping Stream entrance to Dongting Lake. Between the 1930s and the 1950s, much of the land along the lake banks and inside the dikes surrounding Dongting Lake was reclaimed, a process hastened by the gradual silting up of the lake from the huge amounts of sediment deposited by its inflowing rivers, especially the Yangtze. As a result, the area of the lake was reported to be 400 square miles (1,000 square km) smaller in the 1970s than it was in 1937. At one time, as a result of such reclamation, the lake was almost divided in two and was no longer able adequately to fulfill its regulatory function, causing flooding on the lower courses of the rivers flowing into the lake. In the 1950s, however, such reclamation was prohibited, and efforts were begun to reconnect the different sections of the lake system. In response to the serious flood disaster of 1998, the central and local governments launched several projects aimed at soil and water conservation, extending the limits of the lake, and reinforcement of the banks around the lake. In addition, the large Three Gorges Dam project, upstream from the lake, is intended to regulate the flow of the Yangtze and to limit flooding.

Dongting Lake provides a common nexus for the rivers of Hunan and a link between northern Hunan and the Yangtze. The cities around the lake's margin are the chief agricultural collection and distribution centres for the surrounding fertile plain. The lake is also a fishing ground, particularly noted for its carp during the winter months. The Zhangling Oil Refinery, built in 1971, is located on the edge of Dongting Lake and provides fuel oil for the province.

THE YANGTZE DELTA

The Yangtze delta, which begins beyond Zhenjiang, consists of a large number of branches, tributaries, lakes, ancient riverbeds, and marshes that are connected with the main channel. During major floods the delta area is completely submerged. Lake Tai, with an area of about 930 square miles (2,410 square km), is notable as the largest of the many lakes in the delta. The width of the Yangtze in the delta, as far as the city of Jiangyin, ranges from less than 1 mile to almost 2 miles (1.6 to 3.2 km); farther downstream the channel gradually widens and becomes a large estuary, the width of which exceeds 50 miles (80 km) near the mouth of the river. Major cities in the delta include Wuxi, Suzhou, and, at the river's mouth, Shanghai.

Before emptying into the sea, the Yangtze divides into two arms that drain independently into the East China Sea. The left branch has a width of about 3 to 6 miles (5 to 10 km), the right branch of

6 to 15 miles (10 to 25 km). Between the branches is situated Chongming Island, which was formed over the centuries by the deposit of alluvium at the mouth of the Yangtze. The depth of the river in places approaches 100 to 130 feet (30 to 40 m) but decreases to only several feet near the sea at the mouth of the river because of the presence of sandbars.

The section of the river from the mouth to 250 miles (400 km) upstream is subject to the influence of tides. The maximum range of the tides near the mouth is 13 to 15 feet (4 to 5 m). The Yangtze delta is rich in mud and silt and is dominated by fluvial and tidal processes.

The present-day bed of the Yangtze in this area is somewhat above the elevation of the plain. Thus, to protect the surrounding region from floodwaters, the banks of the main and other rivers are built up; the total length of banks on the Yangtze on which levees have been constructed is about 1,700 miles (2,740 km). Dams also have been built for flood protection on the shores of several lakes; the Qingjiang Reservoir, built for this purpose near Dongting Lake, has a design capacity of 194 million cubic feet (5.5 million cubic m). The delta is protected from the sea by two gigantic parallel banks that are faced with stone in most parts.

HISTORY

The Yangtze River basin is one of the longest-inhabited regions in China. Although much of China's political history has centred around North China and the Huang He basin, the Yangtze region always was of great economic importance to successive dynasties for its agricultural potential. The Grand Canal was built in order to transport grain from the Yangtze basin to the great northern capital cities; it is possible that the southernmost portion of the canal was in use as early as the 4th century BCE, and much of it was constructed in the 7th century CE.

Over the course of time the Yangtze has served as both a political and a cultural boundary. The river now demarcates the provinces constituting South China. The Yangtze also was the focus of many of the imperialist incursions into China in the 19th century and the first half of the 20th, with Shanghai at the river's mouth becoming the main foreign commercial base. Since 1950 the river and its basin have been the focus of much of China's economic modernization.

HUANG HE

The Huang He ("Yellow River") is the principal river of northern China. Often called the cradle of Chinese civilization, it is the country's second longest river, with a length of 3,395 miles (5,464 km), and its drainage basin is the third largest in China—an area of some 290,000 square miles (750,000 square km). The river rises in Qinghai province on the Plateau of Tibet and crosses six other provinces and two autonomous regions in its course to the Bo Hai (Gulf of Chihli), an embayment of the Yellow Sea. In its lower

Junks on the silt-laden Huang He near Zhengzhou, Henan province, China. Tim Megarry/Robert Harding Picture Library

reaches it is a shifting, turbulent, silt-laden stream that often overflows its banks and sends floodwaters across the North China Plain. For this reason, it has been given such names as "China's Sorrow" and "The Ungovernable." The word *huang* ("yellow") is a reference to the fine loess sediments that the river carries to the sea. The Huang He basin has an enormous population—exceeded by only a small number of countries—and the river and its tributaries flow past some of China's oldest cities, including Lanzhou, Baotou, Xi'an (Sian), Taiyuan, Luoyang, Zhengzhou, Kaifeng, and Jinan.

PHYSICAL FEATURES

The Huang He is divided into three distinct parts: the upper course through mountains, the middle course across a plateau, and the lower course across a low plain.

THE UPPER COURSE

The Huang He originates at an elevation above 15,000 feet (4,600 m) in the Bayan Har Mountains, in the eastern Plateau of Tibet. In its upper reaches, the river crosses two large bodies of water: Lakes Ngoring and Gyaring. These shallow lakes, each covering an area of about 400 square miles (1,000 square km), are rich in fish and freeze over in winter. The Huang He in this region flows generally from west to east. The broad highlands of the upper course rise 1,000–1,700 feet (300–500 m) above the river and its tributaries. The highlands consist of crystalline rocks that are sometimes visible as eroded outcroppings on the surface. The river enters a region of deep gorges, winding its way first southeast, then northwest around the A'nyêmaqên (Amne Machin) Mountains, where its fall exceeds 10 feet per mile (2 m per km), and then east again between the Xiqing and Laji mountains. Past the gorges, near the city of Lanzhou, it leaves the Plateau of Tibet. This marks the end of the upper Huang He, which is some 725 miles (1,165 km) from its source. The upper course drains a basin covering about 48,000 square miles (124,000 square km), consisting chiefly of inaccessible, highly mountainous, and sparsely populated terrain with a cold climate.

THE MIDDLE COURSE

The middle course of the Huang He, extending more than 1,800 miles (2,900 km), consists of a great loop and drains an area of about 23,000 square miles (60,000 square km). The river at first flows northeast for about 550 miles (880 km) through the sandy soils of northern Ningxia and of the western Ordos Desert; it has many rapids there, and in a number of places it narrows. The river then turns eastward and flows for another 500 miles (800 km) through alluvial plains in Inner Mongolia, in places branching into numerous distributary channels. In this stretch its fall is less than half a foot per mile (9 cm per km), and many of the channels have been developed over the millennia for irrigated agriculture. The Huang He then turns sharply to the south and flows for about 445 miles (715 km), forming the border between Shaanxi and Shanxi provinces. The river's width usually does not exceed 150–200 feet (45–60 m) in this section, as it cuts through narrow gorges with steep slopes several hundred feet (above 100 m) in height. The river then gradually widens, notably after receiving the waters of its two longest tributaries: first the Fen River of Shanxi province and then the Wei River of Shaanxi. At the confluence with the Wei, the river turns sharply to the east for

another 300 miles (480 km) as it flows through inaccessible gorges between the Zhongtiao and eastern Qin (Tsinling) mountains. The average fall in this stretch is slightly more than one foot per mile (20 cm per km) and becomes increasingly rapid in the last 100 miles (160 km) before the river reaches the North China Plain at the city of Zhengzhou.

Most of the middle course is cut through the Loess Plateau, which extends eastward from the Plateau of Tibet to the North China Plain at elevations ranging between 3,000 and 7,000 feet (900 and 2,100 m). The plateau contains terraced slopes as well as alluvial plains and a scattering of peaks sometimes rising more than 1,500 feet (450 m) above the plateau. Across this plateau, the river has cut at least six terraces, rising to more than 1,600 feet (500 m) above the present river level. The terraces, formed over the past 2.5 million years, provide an important record of landscape evolution and ancient environmental change in the region. The underlying rock systems are covered with thick layers of loose soils, consisting mainly of wind-deposited sand and loess. The loess strata reach thicknesses of 160–200 feet (48–60 m) and in some places as much as 500 feet (150 m). Through these loose deposits, the river has cut deep valleys, carrying away with it huge quantities of surface material, making this one of the most highly eroded landscapes in the world. The easily eroded loess soil accounts for the instability of the riverbed both in the middle basin, where the erosion is considerable, and on the plain, where deposition builds up the channel bed.

THE LOWER COURSE

Downstream from Zhengzhou, the Huang He broadens out to flow through Henan and Shandong provinces across the North China Plain. The plain is a great, nearly featureless alluvial fan broken only by the low hills of central Shandong; it was formed over some 25 million years as the Huang He and other rivers deposited enormous quantities of silt, sand, and gravel into the shallow sea that once covered the region. The plain has been densely inhabited for millennia and long has been one of China's principal agricultural regions. The river has changed its course across the plain several times, and the region's inhabitants have built extensive systems of levees and irrigation works in an attempt to control the river's flow. The area illustrates perhaps better than any other place on Earth how human activity has combined with natural forces to shape the landscape.

The lower Huang He is about 435 miles (700 km) long with an average fall of about 3 inches per mile (5 cm per km). Along the river are found occasional areas of sand dunes 15 to 30 feet (5 to 9 m) high. In general, however, the plain is an area of great floods because the riverbed, built up gradually by sediment deposits, lies above the surrounding land in many places. In the section north of the city of Kaifeng, the low-water level is some 15 feet (5 m) above the surrounding countryside, the mid-water level is between 19 and 23 feet (6 and 7 m), and the high-water level is sometimes as much as 30 to 35 feet (9 to 11 m) above that of the land. From Kaifeng to the Grand Canal (Da Yunhe), the levees are lower than farther upstream, rarely exceeding 3 to 6 feet (1 to 2 m) in height. Marshes are common. Below the Grand Canal, the height of the levees increases to between 13 and 16 feet (4 and 5 m) and in some places to 25 feet (8 m).

The delta of the Huang He begins approximately 50 miles (80 km) from its mouth and spreads out over an area of about 2,100 square miles (5,400 square km). The delta land is marshy, composed of mud and silt, and is covered with reeds. A sandbar at the river's mouth impedes navigation at low tide by boats drawing more than 4 feet (1.2 m) of water; at high tide the depth on the bar is 8 or 9 feet (2.4 or 2.7 m).

Until the late 20th century, the Huang He delta was one of the most actively growing deltas in the world, as the North China Plain continued to extend farther into the Bo Hai (the remnant of the ancient sea now covered by the plain). In the century from 1870 to 1970, the delta grew an average of more than 12 miles (19 km). Some outlying parts expanded even more rapidly: one area grew 6 miles (10 km) during the period 1949 through 1951, and another grew more than 15 miles (24 km) from 1949 to 1952. However, beginning in the 1950s, dam construction upstream—notably the Sanmen Gorge installation in Henan province—began to reduce the silt load that the river could carry to its mouth, and by the 1990s the delta was actually eroding.

HYDROLOGY

The lower Huang He has changed course radically throughout its geologic history. The river's decreased gradient and velocity on the plain cause its suspended load of silt to settle. As the riverbed builds up, the stream shifts course to occupy a lower level. In the past four millennia, the river has entered the Yellow Sea at points as much as 500 miles (800 km) apart. From the 3rd millenium BCE to 602 BCE, when it occupied its northernmost course, it flowed near the present-day city of Tianjin and entered the nearby Bo Hai. From 602 BCE to 70 CE, both the river and its mouth shifted to a point on the Yellow Sea south of the Shandong Peninsula. From 70 to 1048, the Huang He again shifted to the north, taking up a course near its present bed.

From 1048 to 1194, changes in the course of the river occurred farther inland, where the river enters the North China Plain. In 1194, the river occupied a course running to the southern edge of the delta. In that year, after protecting dikes had been ruptured, a second arm of the Huang He began flowing south of the Shandong Peninsula. From 1289 to 1324, the river took over the bed of the Guo River and a large part of the Huai River, entering the Yellow Sea well to the south of Shandong. It was stable for more than

500 years until the 1850s, when it again shifted to the north of the Shandong Peninsula, finally settling into its present course.

As the Chinese developed agriculture on the plain, they became more adept at building levees to stabilize the channel and thereby protect the inhabitants against the floods brought by shifts in the channel. Tens of thousands of miles of levees have been constructed through the centuries. The overall effect of these has been to delay flooding, but, because the riverbed has been elevated and confined artificially, levee breaching and channel shifts have become more dramatic and destructive than they otherwise would have been. The few hydraulic engineers who succeeded in decreasing rather than increasing the flood hazard have gained legendary status in Chinese history.

Breaks in the levees have been more frequent than course changes throughout history. Between 960 and 1048, there were thirty-eight major breaks, and twenty-nine more were recorded from 1048 to 1194. In later years such breaches were less frequent as a result of systematic improvements to the levee system. The slackening of these efforts during the Taiping Rebellion (1850–64) led to the major change in the course of the river that occurred from 1852 to 1854. In 1887 the Huang He burst the levees near the city of Kaifeng and began to flow into the Huai River, but engineering efforts succeeded in returning it to its former course in 1889. The flood of 1887 covered thousands of square miles, completely burying many villages under silt. In 1889 another flood destroyed 1,500 villages. The next major flood, in 1921, wiped out hundreds of populated places, mainly near the river's mouth. In the flood of 1933, more than 3,000 populated places were submerged and 18,000 people killed. Other floods occurred in 1938—when the levees were purposely broken near Zhengzhou to delay the advance of Japanese troops—and in 1949.

The Huang He carries an average annual volume of about 13.4 cubic miles (56 cubic km) of water down to the sea, a rate of about 62,500 cubic feet (1,770 cubic m) per second. The rate can be as much as 78,000 cubic feet (2,200 cubic m) per second in high-volume years and as little as 22,000–28,000 cubic feet (600–800 cubic m) per second in low-volume years. There also is considerable seasonal variation in its volume. The river has a low discharge rate—eight other Chinese rivers exceed that of the Huang He—because its basin encompasses large areas of arid or semiarid land, where considerable quantities of water evaporate or are diverted for irrigation. More than half of the basin's annual precipitation falls during the rainy season (July to October). The average annual precipitation for the entire basin is about 18.5 inches (47 cm), but its distribution is highly uneven. In some years the bulk of the river's volume comes from its tributaries. In the upstream areas, the main source is snowfall in the mountains, with the high-water level occurring in the spring. The highest water levels in the middle and lower parts of the river occur in July and August. Seasonal maximum flows can be considerable: 188,900 to 216,200 cubic feet (5,350 to 6,120 cubic m) per second near Lanzhou, 350,000 cubic feet (10,000 cubic m) near Longmen, and 1,270,000 cubic feet (36,000 cubic m; recorded in 1943) in the lower parts of the river.

The Huang He carries the highest concentration of sediment load of any river in the world, amounting to about 57 pounds of silt per cubic yard (34 kg per cubic metre) of water, as compared with 2 pounds (1 kg) for the Nile River, 9 pounds (5 kg) for the Amu Darya (the ancient Oxus River), and 22 pounds (13 kg) for the Colorado River. Floodwaters may contain up to 1,200 pounds of silt per cubic yard (710 kg per cubic metre) of water (70 percent by volume). The river, unimpeded, carried down to the sea about 1.52 billion tons of silt per year, a large part of it loess, which was loose and easily washed away. Other factors contributing to the high volume of silt included the steepness of the slopes, the rapidity of the current, and a lack of forested areas to check erosion. The reservoirs created by dams have allowed increasing quantities of silt to settle out.

The Huang He freezes over in parts of its middle section for several months each winter. On the North China Plain near Kaifeng, there are fifteen to twenty icebound days per year, but farther downstream there are none at all. Ice jams are broken up with the help of aerial bombardment or sometimes by artillery shelling.

ECONOMIC DEVELOPMENT

Water resources in the Huang He basin have been managed by irrigation and flood-control works of significant size since the 3rd century BCE. Modern hydraulic engineering techniques have been applied since the 1920s, while basin-wide multipurpose development efforts have been under way since the mid-1950s. The major accomplishments of that program have included giant hydroelectric dams at the Liujia Gorge and other gorges near Lanzhou and major irrigation projects—some with smaller hydroelectric stations—at several locations farther downstream. On the plain, levees have been strengthened and the flood-control system rationalized and integrated with reservoirs and with the Grand Canal (which crosses the Huang He in western Shandong province). Erosion-control measures on the Loess Plateau have reduced the silt load carried downstream. The key project has been the huge dam at the Sanmen Gorge upstream of Luoyang and the reservoir impounded behind it. The project has augmented flood control on the plain and has also provided water for irrigation and hydroelectric power generation, although silt deposition in the reservoir has reduced its functional capabilities.

As modern economic development has increased throughout the basin, however, pollution from industrial sources and agricultural runoff has also increased. In addition, the greater demand for limited water resources has caused shortages, which have been severe at times.

STUDY AND EXPLORATION

The Huang He and its floods have been central to the legend, folklore, and written history of Chinese civilization for more than three thousand years. Regular records of major floods and of changes in the river's course have been kept since the 6th century BCE, and water levels have been studied since 1736. The first European to explore the upper reaches of the Huang He was a Russian traveler, Nikolay Mikhaylovich Przhevalsky, in 1879 and 1884. Systematic study of the river basin was first undertaken in the 1950s by Chinese and Soviet scientists. Since the 1970s, this work has been carried on by Chinese scientists in cooperation with specialists from numerous other countries.

XI RIVER SYSTEM

The Xi River (Chinese: Xi Jiang or "West River") is the name applied to a system of rivers that combine to form the longest river of southern China. Together with its upper-course streams, the Xi River flows generally eastward for 1,216 miles (1,957 km) from the highlands of Yunnan province to the South China Sea and drains—along with the Bei, Dong, and Pearl (Zhu) rivers—a basin with an area of 173,000 square miles (448,000 square km). The Xi is shorter than the other important Chinese rivers—the Yangtze River (Chang Jiang) and the Huang He (Yellow River)—but it delivers an enormous quantity of water, and its volume of flow is second only to that of the Yangtze. The name Xi River is more narrowly applied only to its lower course.

LAND

The Xi itself drains an area of about 127,000 square miles (329,000 square km) of southern China and northern Vietnam. More than half of the river's basin is mountainous and lies between 1,650 and 9,900 feet (500 and 3,000 m) above sea level; more than two-fifths of the rest of the basin is occupied by hills between 330 and 1,650 feet (100 and 500 m) high. The lowlands of the river's delta account for only a tiny fraction of the total drainage area. Most of the mountains and hills in the basin are composed of limestone, and the river has cut a cavernous valley through them. The riverbed is broken by rapids and gorges, and its walls are often high and steep. The landscape is categorized as karst, in which the limestone rocks are honeycombed with tunnels, openings, and deep sinkholes caused by water action; the result is that much of the drainage runs underground.

The Xi's main headstream is generally considered to be the Nanpan River, which rises in the Yunnan-Guizhou Plateau at an elevation of about 6,900 feet (2,100 m). The Nanpan drops about 5,900 feet (1,800 m) in the first 530 miles (850 km) of its course and flows in a southeasterly direction through Yunnan province. It then forms part of the border between Guizhou province and the Zhuang Autonomous Region of Guangxi for a distance of about 535 miles (860 km).

Southeast of the town of Ceheng, the river receives the Beipan River and is then known as the Hongshui River. This section of the river flows about 400 miles (640 km) through a narrow valley with high, mountainous banks that tower about 850 feet (260 m) above the riverbed. The bed—between 165 and 1,000 feet (50 and 300 m) wide—is broken by rocky rapids that are less than 3 feet (1 m) deep and difficult to navigate. For the first 75 miles (120 km) of its course, the Hongshui continues to form part of the Guizhou-Guangxi border, flowing in an easterly direction until just before it reaches the town of Tian'e, where it makes a great bend to the south and flows through Guangxi. At Gongchuan, it turns northward and then resumes its easterly direction.

At Shilong, the river receives the Liu River—its major left- (north-) bank tributary—and is then called the Qian River. This section of the river is the shortest, no more than 75 miles (120 km) long, and the river drops about 50 feet (15 m) in this distance. The channel grows dramatically, occasionally achieving depths of 280 feet (85 m). For almost half its length, the Qian flows through the narrow, rock-strewn Dateng Gorge between the cities of Wuxuan and Guiping.

At the end of this section, the river receives its major right- (south-) bank tributary—the Yu River—and is then called the Xun River. The Yu River rises in southeastern Yunnan province and flows about 400 miles (750 km) eastward in Guangxi to the point at Guiping where it joins the Xian to form the Xun River. The Xun flows for about 120 miles (190 km) in an easterly direction, dropping a further 55 feet (17 m) and receiving the Beilu River on the right bank at Tengxian and the Gui River on the left bank at Wuzhou (Cangwu) on the border with Guangdong province.

Below Wuzhou, where it enters Guangdong, the river becomes known as the Xi. Its valley consists of a series of winding gorges and wide hollows. The Sanrong and Lingyang gorges narrow to widths of 230 to 260 feet (70 to 80 m) and are about 250 feet (75 m) deep. Throughout its 130-mile (210-km) length, the Xi drops only about 30 feet (10 m), flowing to the east until it joins the Bei River at Sanshui. It then turns south through the vast Pearl River Delta before emptying into the South China Sea west of Macau.

The Pearl River Delta is formed by three main rivers—the Xi, the Bei, and the Dong. At Sanshui, the Xi and Bei are linked by a short channel but then divide. The larger branch, the Xi, bends to the south and forms the western border of the delta, while a lesser branch, the Foshan, flows eastward into the delta itself. The Dong flows from the east and enters the delta's main channel, the Pearl River, just below Guangzhou (Canton). The Pearl River itself begins just below Guangzhou; Hong Kong is to the east and Macau to the west of the entrance to the Pearl River estuary, which is about 18 miles (29 km) wide.

Covering an area of about 1,500 square miles (3,900 square km) in southeastern Guangdong province, the delta is a complex network of river branches and channels divided by islands of alluvial soil and by hills that were once coastal islands. The fertile islands are only slightly above sea level and are protected from the sea by a system of flood dikes.

The Xi River's rate of flow more than doubles in the summer season. Most of the increased flow results from the summer monsoon rains, when torrential floods may occur and frequently cause catastrophic damage. The river is at its lowest during the dry winter period. Fluctuations in the water level during the year may vary by as much as 80 feet (25 m) at Wuzhou; in the lower course and the delta, variations in the level are smaller. Especially dangerous are the delta floods that result from a combination of flooding rivers and high tides.

PEOPLE AND ECONOMY

Throughout the mountainous part of its course, the Xi River has little relationship to the peoples who live in its vicinity. Most settlement occurs on small plots of land between mountains. The villages are isolated, compact agricultural units. River towns become more frequent in the hilly part of the Guangxi region, where the river is an artery of commerce; towns include Gongchuan, Qianjiang, Laibin, Guiping, Tengxian, and Wuzhou.

The Pearl River Delta is one of the most densely populated areas of China. The entire region is intensively cultivated. Rice is the most important crop, but wheat, corn (maize), sorghum, beans, and potatoes are also grown in the cooler, drier climate of the west. An intricate irrigation system includes more than 1,200 miles (1,900 km) of flood dikes. The delta's many channels are vital to Guangzhou's international commerce, as well as to trade with the interior.

Forests cover much of the mountainous region of the Xi River basin, especially in the north and west, the stretch along the border of Guizhou province being the most heavily forested. The more important tree species economically are pine, fir, camphor, tung, and bamboo. In the eastern part of the basin—notably in the low places of the maritime zone and in the valleys—the land is mostly cleared for cultivating crops, including rice, peanuts (groundnuts), sugarcane, hemp, tobacco, and fruit. The river contains an abundance of freshwater fish, and the waters of the Pearl River Delta are in some cases enclosed with bamboo fences and used for fish farming.

The Xi River is the great commercial waterway of South China, linking Hong Kong, Guangzhou, Macau, and other delta centres with Wuzhou and the interior. During flood time, the river is navigable for vessels drawing 16 feet (5 m) as far upstream as Wuzhou. The Xi basin contains more than 9,000 miles (14,500 km) of water routes, of which more than 6,800 miles (11,000 km) are in use. Steamships can sail along more than one-third of the total length of the waterways, while junks and small craft ply all the navigable waters. The water routes do not form an integrated system, however. Guangzhou, the largest city in the basin, does not have direct access to either the Xi or the Bei. The channels that connect the city to the water routes of the basin are winding and mud-filled and are navigable only by shallow-draft boats. Because most of the river branches of the delta are shallow, oceangoing vessels cannot reach Guangzhou but must dock at Huangpu (Whampoa), 10 miles (16 km) downstream. Navigation is hampered by low water on many tributaries and by rapids on some sections of the river system. In several places, as on the Yu River, river craft are pulled over the rapids with hand-worked windlasses. During low-water periods, transportation ceases on some rivers, including the Dong and the Bei.

KUNLUN MOUNTAINS

The Kunlun Mountains (Chinese: Kunlun Shan) comprise a major mountain system of southern Central Asia. The Kunluns extend west to east some 1,250 miles (2,000 km), from the Pamirs in Tajikistan in the west to the Kunlun Pass and the adjacent ranges of central Qinghai province in the east—Burhan Budai, Bayan Har, and A'nyêmaqên (Amne Machin). The width of the Kunluns varies considerably but rarely exceeds 125 miles (200 km). In the western margins, they form an Inner Asian rampart between the Plateau of Tibet and the Tarim (Talimu) Basin in western China. A northern fork of the Altun (Altyn Tagh) Mountains continues this alignment.

The western Kunlun Mountains, near Mazar, southwestern Uygur Autonomous Region of Xinjiang, China. © Jeffrey Alford/Asia Access

Physical Features

The southern face of the Kunlun Mountains rises no more than 5,000 feet (1,500 m) above the Plateau of Tibet, which itself averages some 15,000 feet (4,600 m) in elevation. From the perspective of the oases at the southern edge of the Takla Makan Desert to the north of the mountains, however, the Kunluns form a massive rampart blocking access to the icy barren expanses of the westernmost reaches of the Tibet Autonomous Region of China.

Physiography

Throughout much of their alignment, the Kunlun Mountains comprise two or three parallel ridges rather than a single crest. This is especially true in the western reaches. At the Sarykol Range where the Kunluns forge out from the Pamirs, a spur to the east called the Muztagata Range actually has some of the highest summits—Mount Kongur at 25,325 feet

(7,719 m), as well as Mount Muztagata at 24,757 feet (7,546 m). A major bifurcation occurs just south of the oasis town of Qiemo (Cherchen); there, the Altun Mountains branch in a northeasterly direction from the Arkatag Mountains at Mount Muztag (Muztagh), which at 25,338 feet (7,723 m) is the highest point in the Kunluns. To the east, the northern rim of the Kunluns then becomes the southern margin of the vast, high Qaidam (Tsaidam) Basin. High valleys with occasional saline lakes intersperse the medial Kunlun ridges.

The highest crest of the main range of the western Kunlun Mountains is Mount Keriya, at an elevation of 23,359 feet (7,120 m). Several peaks exceeding 20,000 feet (6,000 m) punctuate the skyline in the central to eastern reaches, including Mount Muztag and Bukadaban Peak (22,507 feet [6,860 m]). The surrounding plain lies above 16,000 feet (4,900 m); hence, these mountains do not have the prominence of other high mountains in Asia. Soil zonation is simple in structure, with steppe soils and desert soils predominating, both including those of the alpine group. Organic content is low, and bogs, moors, and saline depressions are common at the lower altitudes. Eolian erosion results in scattered large sand dunes.

GEOLOGY

The principal folded structures and granitic rocks of the Kunlun Mountains date to about 250 million years ago, a time during which there was much mountain building in the Eastern Hemisphere. The inner depressions of the Kunluns, however, are relatively recent structures in their entirety, being formed by deposits that are no more than 26 million years old; only the largest of them, the Qaidam Basin, contains a thick sedimentary cover of which Jurassic deposits (i.e., those roughly 150–200 million years old) represent the oldest strata. The Kunlun Mountains also represent a region of geologically recent movements of Earth's crust, and a considerable amount of seismic (earthquake) activity still occurs, particularly associated with the Altun strike-slip fault system.

DRAINAGE AND GLACIATION

The Kunlun Mountains form a part of that region in Central Asia in which there is only internal drainage, associated mainly with the Tarim and Qaidam basins to the north and the basins of the Plateau of Tibet to the south. Only the most easterly spurs of the mountain system, where the source of the Huang He (Yellow River) is located, have drainage systems that empty into the ocean.

There are two river networks in the Kunluns: the large streams that rise in the Karakoram Range to the southwest and in northern Tibet, cutting through the entire chain of Kunlun ranges by way of gorges, and the small streams that drain the slopes of the peripheral ranges.

The major rivers form lengthy, zigzag valleys; several supply irrigation water to the oases on the northern rim of the Kunlun Mountains.

Although they receive some rainwater, the Kunlun rivers are fed mainly by snows and glaciers. The volume of flow thus varies with the seasons; 60 to 80 percent of it occurs in the summer months, when intensive thawing of snow and ice in the mountains is combined with maximum precipitation. High evaporation of snow and glacial meltwater has resulted in the formation of extensive salt pans.

In spite of the great elevation, there is little glaciation in the Kunluns because of the extreme dryness of the climate; snow cover persists only along the deep crevices of the highest peaks. The main centres of glaciation occur at elevations of about 23,000 feet (7,000 m). All the glaciers are notable for their unusual steepness and for their paucity of meltwater.

CLIMATE

The Kunlun Mountains are almost totally isolated from the climatic influence of the

Satellite image of a large dust storm in the Takla Makan Desert, northwestern China. MODIS Rapid Response Team/NASA/GFSC

Indian and Pacific Ocean monsoons. Instead, they are under the constant influence of the continental air mass, which causes great annual and diurnal temperature fluctuations. Maximum aridity occurs in the middle segment of the mountain system; to the west and east, however, the climate is somewhat moderated.

In the most arid part of the Kunlun Mountains, precipitation is less than 2 inches (50 mm) annually in the foothills and about 4 to 5 inches (100 to 150 mm) in the high elevations; near the Pamirs and the Tibetan mountains, the amount of annual precipitation increases to about 18 inches (460 mm). In the lower tier of mountains (those bordering the northern plains), the average temperature is 77 to 82 °F (25 to 28 °C) in July and not lower than 16 °F (- 9 °C) in January; in the upper tier of mountains and on the border of Tibet, however, the average temperature in July is less than 50 °F (10 °C) and often falls to - 31 °F (- 35 °C) or lower in winter.

The extremely sharp daily fluctuations of temperature in the high-elevation zone create conditions of intense weathering from heat and frost, producing enormous quantities of loose material in those areas. Also characteristic of the Kunlun Mountains are their high winds, the strongest of which occur in autumn; the winds of the Qaidam Basin are particularly noteworthy.

PLANT AND ANIMAL LIFE

The desert or, at best, steppe conditions prevailing throughout the Kunlun Mountains inhibit development of vegetation. Much of the terrain consists of rock deserts. Occasional stagnant water pools provide browsing and water for several wild ungulates, such as the Tibetan gazelle and Tibetan goat antelope (chiru), along with large herds of wild asses (kiang) and clusters of wild yaks. In the more humid western mountains, argali sheep (*Ovis ammon*) graze on the high grasslands. On the upper crags, blue sheep (*Pseudois nayaur*), Ladakh urials, and ibex range sporadically throughout the western reaches. Willow thickets near watercourses frequently contain brown bears, and wolves are endemic; the snow leopard is rare. Many migratory waterfowl visit the lakes during seasonal migration.

PEOPLE AND ECONOMY

Despite the extreme climatic and topographic conditions, the Kunlun Mountains and adjacent areas support permanent and migratory populations. On the northern slopes are found Uighurs, up from the oases, and occasional Mongols. South to the northern areas of Tibet, Tibetan pastoral nomads have commandeered large expanses of formerly abandoned steppe grazing lands. Mountain Tajik and Kyrgyz remnants occupy the few settlements in the deep valleys of the western mountains adjacent to the Karakoram and Pamir ranges. Chinese (Han) are ubiquitous, with concentrations along the extensive and well-maintained network of gravel roads that has been constructed since 1949's establishment of the People's Republic.

Irrigation in a few areas sustains limited crop farming; otherwise, pastoralism constitutes the economic base, with a focus on yak and yak crossbreeds, sheep, goats, and occasionally cattle. High-yielding strains of wheat, barley, peas, potatoes, and rapeseed occupy the greater part of Tibet's arable land. The grass crop is low in volume but high in nutrients and protein.

The hard-surfaced trans-Tibetan road from Dunhuang to Lhasa serves the settlements in Qinghai. Golmud, itself a modern city rising from the windblown flats of the Qaidam Basin, is a railway terminus. Several other major roads from the Tarim Basin oases penetrate the Kunlun massif. Trucks supply vegetables, building materials, motor fuel, and sundry goods to the farthest settlements and deliver raw materials such as petroleum, soda ash, and coal from extraction sites to nearby towns.

STUDY AND EXPLORATION

The northern rim of the Kunlun Mountains, skirting the Tarim Basin, served for centuries as the southerly branch of the Silk Road that, until the 16th

Herding goats along the ancient Silk Road, northern Takla Makan Desert, China. Bob Thomason/Tony Stone Worldwide

century, connected China with Central and Southwest Asia. Wool and salt were the main products brought down from the heights of the Kunluns to the oases on the edge of the Takla Makan Desert. Small regional Buddhist monasteries retained Tibetans as serfs, but repeated Muslim incursions from the north kept the Kunluns in a state of flux.

British attempts to tap the trading potential of Chinese Turkistan spurred adventurers to probe the western end of the Kunluns, but it was not until the end of the 19th century that explorers such as the Swede Sven Anders Hedin mustered enough resources to plot the western Kunlun Mountains. Several travelers used the east-west route in Tsinghai, through the eastern extensions of the Kunluns and Golmud as an alternative route to the Gansu Corridor. With the founding of the People's Republic of China, these peripheral territories came under central control, and Chinese scientific expeditions explored throughout the area. Major Chinese scientific accomplishments have defined the geology, glaciation, soils, and vegetation of the Kunlun Mountains. Another study, entailing international cooperation, has focused on the physiological and ecological adaptability of the various Kunlun ethnic groups to the high marginal environment adjoining the range's southern rim.

Beginning in the 1980s, numerous geological expeditions have been undertaken by Sino-French and Sino-American teams to examine the evolution of the Kunlun Mountains and in particular the nature of tectonic movements along the Altun fault system.

TAKLA MAKAN DESERT

The Takla Makan Desert (Chinese: Taklimakan Shamo) is the great desert of Central Asia and one of the largest sandy deserts in the world. It occupies the central part of the Tarim Basin in the Uygur Autonomous Region of Xinjiang, northwestern China. The Takla Makan's area extends about 600 miles (960 km) from west to east, and it has a maximum width of some 260 miles (420 km) and a total area of approximately 123,550 square miles (320,000 square km). The desert reaches elevations of 3,900 to 4,900 feet (1,200 to 1,500 m) above sea level in the west and south and from 2,600 to 3,300 feet (800 to 1,000 m) in the east and north.

PHYSICAL FEATURES

The Takla Makan is flanked by high mountain ranges: the Tien Shan to the north, the Kunlun Mountains to the south, and the Pamirs to the west. There is a gradual transition to the Lop Nur basin in the east; in the south and west, between the sandy desert and the mountains, lies a band of sloping desert lowland composed of pebble-detritus deposits.

PHYSIOGRAPHY

Several small mountain ranges and chains, composed of sandstones and clays of Cenozoic age (i.e., formed within about the past 65 million years), rise in the western part of the Takla Makan. The arc-shaped Mazartag Mountains, located between the Hotan and Yarkand (Ye'erqiang) river valleys, arch toward the southwest. Some 90 miles (145 km) long and 2 to 3 miles (3 to 5 km) wide, and with a maximum height of 5,363 feet (1,635 m), they rise an average of only 1,000 to 1,150 feet (300 to 350 m) above the surface of the sandy plain. Nearby is another insular range, surrounded on all sides by massifs of moving sands; Rosstagh Mountain, also known as Tokhtakaz Mountain, reaches an elevation of 5,117 feet (1,560 m), and the range rises from 600 to 800 feet (180 to 240 m) above the plain. Both ranges are covered by a shallow mantle of eluvium and rock debris that support only sparse, desert-type vegetation. In the north, the sands of the Takla Makan form a clear boundary with the vegetated Tarim River valley.

The general slope of the plain is from south to north, and the rivers running off from the Kunlun Mountains flow in that direction. The Hotan and Keriya river valleys have survived up to the present day, but most of the shallower rivers have been lost in the sands, after which their empty valleys were filled by windborne sand.

The surface of the Takla Makan is composed of friable alluvial deposits several hundred feet thick. This alluvial stratum has been affected by the wind, and its wind-borne sand cover is as much as 1,000 feet (300 m) thick. The relief consists of a variety of eolian (wind-formed) topographic features and variously shaped sand dunes. These eolian sand dunes were formed through the weathering of the alluvial and colluvial deposits of the Tarim Basin and of the foothill plains of the Kunluns and eastern Tien Shan. The size of the larger sand-dune chains is considerable: they range from 100 to 500 feet (30 to 150 m) in height and 800 to 1,650 feet (240 to 500 m) in width, with a distance between the chains of 0.5 to 3 miles (1 to 5 km). The highest eolian topographic forms are the pyramidal dunes, rising 650 to 1,000 feet (200 to 300 m). In the eastern and central parts of the desert, networks of hollow dunes and large, complex sand-dune chains predominate. They also are common in the western portion of the desert (east of the Hotan River valley), where transverse and longitudinal (with respect to the wind) topographic forms coexist. On the edge of the desert, semipermanent, clustered sand dunes with tamarisk and nitre bushes—as well as clayey regions with disconnected sand dunes—predominate. Such a diversity in eolian features is a result of the complex wind conditions of the basin.

CLIMATE

The Takla Makan's climate is moderately warm and markedly continental, with a maximum annual temperature range of 70 °F (39 °C). Precipitation is extremely low, ranging from 1.5 inches (38 mm) per year in the west to 0.4 inch (10 mm) annually in the east. The air temperature in the summer is high, rising to as much as 100 °F (38 °C) on the eastern edge of the desert. In July the average air temperature is 77 °F (25 °C) in the eastern regions. Winters are cold: in January the average air temperature is 14 to 16 °F (-10 to -9 °C), and the lowest temperature reached in winter generally falls below -4 °F (-20 °C).

Northerly and northwesterly winds prevail in the summer in the western region. These two air currents, on meeting near the desert's centre at the northern extreme of the Keriya River, create a complex circulation system that is clearly reflected in the topography of the sand dunes. In the spring, when the surface sand becomes warm, ascending currents develop, and northeasterly winds become particularly strong. During that period, hurricane-force dust storms, filling the atmosphere with dust to altitudes up to about 13,000 feet (4,000 m), often occur. Winds from other directions also raise clouds of dust into the air, covering the Takla Makan with a shroud for almost the entire year.

DRAINAGE

Since the Tarim Basin is an internal-drainage basin, the entire runoff from the surrounding mountains collects in the depression itself, feeding the rivers and the groundwater strata. In all probability, the groundwater table under the Takla Makan's sands flows from the west to the arid basin of Lop Nur in the east. The importance of precipitation in moistening the sands and feeding the groundwaters is slight, however, because of its small quantity and high rate of evaporation. The rivers draining the Kunlun Mountains penetrate about 60 to 120 miles (100 to 200 km) into the desert, gradually drying up in the sands. Only the Hotan River crosses the centre of the desert and, in summer, occasionally carries its waters to the Tarim River.

PLANT AND ANIMAL LIFE

Vegetation is extremely sparse in the Takla Makan; almost the entire region is devoid of plant cover. In depressions among the sand dunes, where the groundwater lies no deeper than 10 to 15 feet (3 to 5 m) from the surface, thin thickets of tamarisk, nitre bushes, and reeds may be found. The thick strata of moving sands, however, prevent the wider spread of this vegetation. The vegetation is richer along the edges of the desert—the area where the sand dunes meet the river valleys and deltas and where the groundwaters lie comparatively close to the surface. There, in addition to the plants mentioned above, a number of species characteristic of river valleys are found: Turanga poplar, oleaster, camel thorn, members of the Zygophyllaceae (caltrop) family, and saltworts. Sand dunes in hummocks frequently form around the scrub.

The animal life of the Takla Makan is also extremely sparse. Only in peripheral regions of the desert, in ancient and modern river valleys and deltas where water and vegetation appear, is the fauna more diverse. Herds of gazelles are found in open spaces, and there are wild boars in river-valley thickets. Wolves and foxes are among the carnivores. Until the beginning of the 20th century, tigers could still be found, but they have since been exterminated. Rare animals include the Siberian deer, which inhabits the Tarim River valley, and the wild camel, which at the end of the 19th century roamed over much of the Takla Makan as far as the Hotan River but now appears only occasionally in the eastern desert region.

There are a large number of rabbits, gerbils, field mice, and jerboas in the sand dunes; among insectivores, the long-eared hedgehog and bats are common. Small, tufted larks and the Tarim jay are the most common birds.

PEOPLE AND ECONOMY

There is no fixed population in the Takla Makan. Hunters make periodic visits, but the area territory is not used by stock breeders because of the virtual absence of vegetation.

Since 1950, the Chinese government has encouraged the emigration of sedentary agriculturalists into the marginal lands on the edges of the Takla Makan. The yields from these low-capacity lands, however, drop after a few years, and the agriculturalists have had to move on. Because the fertility of the soil is so low to begin with, the fallow fields have tended

to become desert rather than to revert to grassland. In addition, the more recent market-oriented rural reforms have encouraged a rapid expansion of herd sizes, which in turn have led to overgrazing and further intensified the desertification process.

In the 1950s, oil was discovered near Korla, at the northern edge of the Takla Makan. Even greater deposits were discovered beginning in the 1980s along the southern rim and in the central portion. The exploitation of these sites has been undertaken despite the extremely difficult working conditions encountered in the desert. Transportation across the shifting sands has remained hazardous, though roads exist surrounding the edge of the desert, and new ones have been built across the centre of the desert from Korla to Yutian in the south, near the Kunluns.

Tensions between Han (Chinese) authorities and the dozen or so Hui (Muslim) minority peoples native to the Takla Makan have existed for centuries. Chinese migration into the region, coupled with Islamic fundamentalist agitation elsewhere in Asia and minority unrest across the border in the Central Asian republics, has fostered more open hostility by local peoples against the Chinese.

STUDY AND EXPLORATION

The fabled Silk Road caravan route connecting China with Central Asia and Europe skirted the northern and western fringes of the Takla Makan. Buddhism reached East Asia in the first centuries

CE over this great trans-Asian road, and most of China's foreign trade and other outside contacts came by this way as well. By the 15th and 16th centuries, however, sea routes to East Asia had replaced the old overland routes. For several centuries, the desert and its oasis towns became a mysterious backwater for Europeans. The towering mountain ranges surrounding the Takla Makan on three sides and the daunting Gobi on the remaining side severely restricted access to a region that was already extremely hazardous to traverse.

Thus, successful scientific exploration of the desert itself did not begin until the late 19th century. The first European to make a notable study of the region was Swedish explorer Sven Anders Hedin, who returned from his first trek (1893–98) with artifacts of a completely forgotten Buddhist civilization that had flourished there for much of the 1st millennium CE. Hedin's discoveries and maps stimulated and aided many others, including Germany's Albert von Le Coq, American Langdon Warner, and the greatest of the archaeological explorers of the Takla Makan, Sir Aurel Stein. On his first expedition, which set out in 1900, Stein excavated several towns buried in the sands and retrieved a large amount of monumental Buddhist art. This expedition set off an international race to rob the Takla Makan of its ancient treasures, which ceased only in the mid-1920s when the Chinese forbade further exploration. Most of the subsequent study of the region was undertaken by researchers from China and the Soviet Union (until 1992), although some Europeans and Americans also have visited the area.

CHAPTER 4

SPOTLIGHT ON CHINA'S WORLD HERITAGE SITES AND OTHER NOTABLE LOCATIONS

China's natural and cultural landscape is remarkable for its diversity. In addition to some of the world's most spectacular scenic areas, the country contains many of the world's oldest and most recognizable cultural treasures. The United Nations Educational, Scientific and Cultural Organization (UNESCO) includes a significant number of Chinese sites on its World Heritage list. Most prominent among these cultural and natural features is the renowned Great Wall, one of the best-known man-made objects on Earth.

GREAT WALL OF CHINA

The Great Wall of China (Chinese: Wanli Changcheng or "10,000-Li Long Wall") is an extensive bulwark erected in ancient China. One of the largest building-construction projects ever undertaken, the Great Wall actually consists of numerous walls—many of them parallel to each other—built over some two millennia across northern China and southern Mongolia. The most extensive and best-preserved version of the wall dates from the Ming dynasty (1368–1644) and runs for some 5,500 miles (8,850 km) east to west from Mount Hu

Tourists on a section of the Great Wall of China near Beijing. © Marius Hetrea

near Dandong, southeastern Liaoning province, to Jiayu Pass west of Jiuquan, northwestern Gansu province. This wall often traces the crestlines of hills and mountains as it snakes across the Chinese countryside, and about one-fourth of its length consists solely of natural barriers such as rivers and mountain ridges. Nearly all of the rest (about 70 percent of the total length) is actual constructed wall, with the small remaining stretches constituting ditches or moats. Although lengthy sections of the wall are now in ruins or have disappeared completely, it

is still one of the more remarkable structures on Earth. The Great Wall was designated a UNESCO World Heritage site in 1987.

Large parts of the fortification system date from the 7th through the 4th century BCE. In the 3rd century BCE, Shihuangdi (Qin Shihuang), the first emperor of a united China (under the Qin dynasty), connected a number of existing defensive walls into a single system. Traditionally, the eastern terminus of the wall was considered to be Shanhai Pass in eastern Hebei province along the coast of the

Bo Hai (Gulf of Chihli), and the wall's length—without its branches and other secondary sections—was thought to extend for some 4,160 miles (6,700 km). However, government-sponsored investigations that began in the 1990s revealed sections of wall in Liaoning, and aerial and satellite surveillance eventually proved that this wall stretched continuously through much of the province. The greater total length of the Ming wall was announced in 2009.

HISTORY OF CONSTRUCTION

The Great Wall developed from the disparate border fortifications and castles of individual Chinese states and kingdoms. For several centuries, these powers were probably as concerned with protection from their near neighbours as they were with the threat of barbarian invasions or raids.

EARLY BUILDING

About the 7th century BCE, the state of Chu started to construct a permanent defensive system. Known as the "Square Wall," this fortification was situated in the northern part of the kingdom's capital province. From the 6th to the 4th century, other states followed Chu's example. In the southern part of the Qi state, an extensive perimeter wall was gradually created using existing river dikes, newly constructed bulwarks, and areas of impassable mountain terrain. The Qi wall was made mainly of earth and stone and

terminated at the shores of the Yellow Sea. In the Zhongshan state, a wall system was built to thwart invasion from the states of Zhao and Qin in the southwest. There were two defensive lines in the Wei state: the Hexi ("West of the [Yellow] River") and Henan ("South of the River") walls. The Hexi Wall was a fortification against the Qin state and western nomads. Built during the reign of King Hui (370–335 BCE), it was expanded from the dikes on the Luo River on the western border. It started in the south near Xiangyuan Cave, east of Mount Hua, and ended at Guyang in what is now the Inner Mongolia Autonomous Region. Henan Wall, built to protect Daliang (the capital, now Kaifeng), was repaired and extended in King Hui's later years. The Zheng state also built a wall system, which was rebuilt by the Han state after it conquered Zheng. The state of Zhao completed a southern wall and a northern wall; the southern wall was built mainly as a defense against the Wei state.

After administrative reorganization was carried out by Shang Yang (died 338 BCE), the Qin state grew politically and militarily to become the strongest among the seven states, but it was frequently raided by the Donghu and Loufan, two nomadic peoples from the north. Therefore, the Qin erected a wall that started from Lintiao, went north along the Liupan Mountains, and ended at the Huang He (Yellow River).

In the Yan state, two separate defensive lines were prepared—the Northern Wall and the Yishui Wall—in an effort to defend the kingdom from attacks by northern groups such as the Donghu, Linhu, and Loufan, as well as by the Qi state in the south. The Yishui Wall was expanded from the dike of the Yi River as a defense line against Qi and Zhao, its two main rival states. It began southwest of Yi City, the capital, and ended south of Wen'an. In 290 BCE, the Yan state built the Northern Wall along the Yan Mountains, starting from the northeast in the area of Zhangjiakou in Hebei, passing over the Liao River, and extending to the ancient city of Xiangping (modern Liaoyang). This was the last segment of the Great Wall to be erected during the Zhanguo (Warring States) period.

In 221 BCE, Shihuangdi—the first Qin emperor—completed his annexation of Qi and thus unified China. He ordered removal of the fortifications set up between the previous states because they served only as obstacles to internal movements and administration. In addition, he sent General Meng Tian to garrison the northern border against incursions of the nomadic Xiongnu and to link the existing wall segments in Qin, Yan, and Zhao into the so-called "10,000-Li Long Wall" (2 *li* equal approximately 0.6 mile [1 km]). This period of construction began about 214 BCE and lasted a decade. Hundreds of thousands of soldiers and conscripted workers laboured on the project. With the fall of the Qin dynasty after Shihuangdi's death, however, the wall was left largely ungarrisoned and fell into disrepair.

THE HAN THROUGH YUAN DYNASTIES

During the reign of the Han emperor Wudi (141–87 BCE), the wall was strengthened as part of an overall campaign against the Xiongnu. From that period, the Great Wall also contributed to the exploitation of farmland in northern and western China and to the growth of the trade route that came to be known as the Silk Road. In 121 BCE a 20-year project of construction was started on the Hexi Wall (generally known as the Side Wall) between Yongdeng (now in Gansu) in the east and Lake Lop Nur (now in Xinjiang) in the west. According to *Juyan Hanjian* ("Juyan Correspondence of the Han"), the strongpoints set up along the wall included "a beacon every 5 *li*, a tower every 10 *li*, a fort every 30 *li*, and a castle every 100 *li*."

The main work on the wall during the Dong (Eastern) Han period (25–220 CE) took place during the reign of Liu Xiu (Guangwudi), who in 38 ordered the repair of four parallel lines of the Great Wall in the area south of the Hexi Wall. The Great Wall served not only for defense but also to centralize control of trade and travel.

During the Bei (Northern) Wei dynasty (386–534/535 CE), the Great Wall was repaired and extended as a defense against attacks from the Juan-juan and Khitan tribes in the north. According to *Wei shu: Mingyuandi Ji* ("History of Wei: Chronicle of Emperor Mingyuan"), in 417, the eighth year of the reign of Mingyuandi (409–423), a part of the Great Wall was built south of Changchuan, from Chicheng (now in Hebei) to Wuyuan (now in Inner Mongolia) in the west, extending more than 620 miles (1,000 km). During the reign of Taiwudi (423–452), a lower and thinner wall of rammed earth was built around the capital as a complement to the Great Wall. Starting from Guangling in the east, it extended to the eastern side of the Huang He, forming a circle around Datong. In 549 after the Dong Wei kingdom moved its capital east to Ye, it also built a segment of the Great Wall in the area of contemporary Shanxi province.

In order to strengthen its northern frontier and prevent invasion from the west by the Bei Zhou, the Bei Qi kingdom (550–577) launched several big construction projects that were nearly as extensive in scope as the building projects of the Qin dynasty. In 552 a segment was built on the northwestern border, and only three years later the emperor ordered the recruitment of 1.8 million workers to repair and extend other sections. The construction took place between the south entrance of Juyong Pass (near modern Beijing) and Datong (in Shanxi). In 556 a new fortification was set up in the east and extended to the Yellow Sea. The following year a second wall was built inside the Great Wall within modern Shanxi, beginning in the vicinity of Laoying east of Pianguan, extending to the east beyond Yanmen Pass and Pingxing Pass, and ending in the area around Xiaguan in Shanxi. In 563 the

emperor Wuchengdi of the Bei Qi had a segment repaired along the Taihang Mountains. That is the part of the Great Wall found today in the area around Longguan, Guangchang, and Fuping (in Shanxi and Hebei). In 565 the inner wall built in 557 was repaired, and a new wall was added that started in the vicinity of Xiaguan, extended to the Juyong Pass in the east, and then joined to the outer wall. The segments repaired and added during the Bei Qi period totaled some 900 miles (1,500 km), and towns and barracks were established at periodic intervals to garrison the new sections. In 579, in order to prevent invasions of the Bei Zhou kingdom by the Tujue (a group of eastern Turks) and the Khitan, the emperor Jing started a massive rebuilding program on areas of the wall located in the former Bei Qi kingdom, starting at Yanmen in the west and ending at Jieshi in the east.

During the Sui dynasty (581–618), the Great Wall was repaired and improved seven times in an effort to defend the country against attacks from the Tujue. After the Tang dynasty (618–907) replaced the Sui, the country grew much stronger militarily, defeating the Tujue in the north and expanding beyond the original frontier. Thus, the Great Wall gradually lost its significance as a fortification, and there was little reason for repairs or additions. During the Song dynasty (960–1279), however, the Liao and Jin peoples in the north were a constant threat. The Song rulers were forced to withdraw to the south of the lines of the Great Wall built by the Qin, Han, and Northern dynasties. Many areas on both sides of the wall were subsequently taken over by the Liao (907–1125) and Jin dynasties (1115–1234). When the Song rulers had to retreat even farther—to the south of the Yangtze River (Chang Jiang)—repairs to the wall or extensions of it were no longer feasible. Limited repairs were carried out once (1056) during Liao times, but only in the area between the Yazi and Huntong rivers.

In 1115, after the Jin dynasty was established, work was performed on two defensive lines at Mingchang. The old wall there—previously called the Wushu Wall, or Jinyuan Fort—ran westward from a point north of Wulanhada, then wound through the Hailatu Mountains, turning to the north and then to the west again, finally ending at the Nuanshui River. The second of the lines was the new Mingchang Wall, also called the Inner Jin Wall or the Jin Trench, which was constructed south of the old wall. It started in the west from a bend in the Huang He and ended at the Sungari (Songhua) River.

During the Yuan (Mongol) dynasty (1206–1368), the Mongols controlled all of China, as well as other parts of Asia and sections of Europe. As a defensive structure, the Great Wall was of little significance to them; however, some forts and key areas were repaired and garrisoned in order to control commerce and to limit the threat of rebellions from the Chinese (Han) and other nationalities.

The Ming Dynasty to the Present

Rulers during the Ming dynasty (1368–1644) ceaselessly maintained and strengthened the Great Wall to prevent another Mongolian invasion. The majority of the work took place along the old walls built by the Bei Qi and Bei Wei.

Most of the Great Wall that stands today is the result of work done during the reign of the Hongzhi emperor (1487–1505). Starting west of Juyong Pass, this part of the wall was split into south and north lines, respectively named the Inner and Outer walls. Along the wall were many strategic "passes" (i.e., fortresses) and gates. Among them were Juyong, Daoma, and Zijing passes, the three closest to the Ming capital Beijing. Together they were referred to as the Three Inner Passes. Farther west were Yanmen, Ningwu, and Piantou passes, known as the Three Outer Passes. Both the Inner and Outer passes were of key importance in protecting the capital and were usually heavily garrisoned.

After the Qing (Manchu) dynasty (1644–1911/12) replaced the Ming, there was a change in ruling strategy called *huairou* ("mollification"), wherein the Qing tried to pacify the leaders and peoples of Mongolia, Tibet, and other nationalities by not interfering with local social, cultural, or religious life. Because of the success of that strategy, the Great Wall was repaired less frequently, and it gradually fell into ruin.

DESIGN OF THE FORTIFICATIONS

The Great Wall had three major components: passes, signal towers (beacons), and walls.

PASSES

Passes were major strongholds along the wall, usually located at such key positions as intersections with trade routes. The ramparts of many passes were faced with huge bricks and stones, with dirt and crushed stones as filler. The bastions measured some 30 feet (10 m) high and 13 to 16 feet (4 to 5 m) wide at the top. Within each pass were access ramps for horses and ladders for soldiers. The outside parapet was crenellated, and the inside parapet, or *yuqiang* (*nüqiang*), was a low wall about 3 feet (1 m) high that prevented people and horses from falling off the top. In addition to serving as an access point for merchants and other civilians, the gate within the pass was used as an exit for the garrison to counterattack raiders or to send out patrols. Under the gate arch, there was typically a huge double door of wood. Bolts and locker rings were set in the inner panel of each door. On top of each gate was a gate tower that served as a watchtower and command post. Usually it stood one to three stories (levels) high and was constructed either of wood or of bricks and wood. Built outside the gate, where an enemy was most likely to attack, was a *wengcheng*, a semicircular or polygonal parapet that shielded the gate from direct assault. Extending beyond the most strategic *wengcheng*s was an additional line of protection, the *luocheng*, which was often topped by a tower used to watch those beyond the wall and to direct troop movements in battles waged there. Around the gate entrance, there was often a moat that was formed in the process of digging earth to build the fortifications.

SIGNAL TOWERS

Signal towers were also called beacons, beacon terraces, smoke mounds, mounds, or kiosks. They were used to send military communications: beacons (fires or lanterns) during the night or smoke signals in the daytime; other methods such as raising banners, beating clappers, or firing guns were also used. Signal towers, often built on hilltops for maximum visibility, were self-contained high platforms or towers. The lower levels contained rooms for soldiers, as well as stables, sheepfolds, and storage areas.

WALLS

The wall itself was the key part of the defensive system. It usually stood 21.3 feet (6.5 m) wide at the base and 19 feet (5.8 m) at the top, with an average height of 23 to 26 feet (7 to 8 m), or a bit lower on steep hills. The structure of the wall varied from place to place, depending on the availability of building materials. Walls were made of tamped earth sandwiched between wooden boards, adobe bricks, a brick and stone mixture, rocks, or pilings and planks. Some sections made use of existing river dikes; others used rugged mountain terrain such as cliffs and gorges to take the place of man-made structures.

In the western deserts, the walls were often simple structures of rammed earth and adobe; many eastern ramparts, such as those near Badaling, were faced with stone and included a number of secondary structures and devices. On the inner side of such walls, placed at small intervals, were arched doors called *juan*, which were made of bricks or stones. Inside each *juan* were stone or brick steps leading to the top of the battlement. On the top, on the side facing outward, stood 7-foot-high (2 m) crenels called *duokou*. On the upper part of the *duokou* were large openings used to watch and shoot at attackers, and on the lower part were small openings, or loopholes, through which defenders could also shoot. At intervals of about 650 to 1,000 feet (200 to 300 m), there was a crenellated platform rising slightly above the top of the wall and protruding from the side that faced attackers. During battle, the platform provided a commanding view and made it possible to shoot attackers from the side as they attempted to scale the wall with ladders. On several platforms were simply structured huts called *pufang*, which provided shelter for the guards during storms. Some platforms, as with signal towers, had two or three stories and could be used to store weapons and ammunition. Those at Badaling commonly had two stories, with accommodations for more than 10 soldiers on the lower level. There were also drainage ditches on the walls to shield them from damage by excessive rainwater.

MILITARY ADMINISTRATION

Each major stronghold along the wall was hierarchically linked to a network of military and administrative commands. During the rule of Shihuangdi, twelve prefectures were established along the wall, and in the Ming period the whole fortification was divided into nine defense areas, or zones. A post chief (*zongbingguan*) was assigned to each zone. Together they were known as the Nine Border Garrisons.

TRADITION AND CONSERVATION

The Great Wall has long been incorporated into Chinese mythology and popular symbolism, and in the 20th century it came to be regarded as a national symbol. Above the East Gate (Dongmen) at Shanhai Pass is an inscription attributed to the medieval historian Xiao Xian, which is translated as "First Pass Under Heaven," referring to the traditional division between Chinese civilization and the barbarian lands to the north.

Despite the wall's cultural significance, roadways have been cut through it at several points, and vast sections have suffered centuries of neglect. In the 1970s a segment near Simatai (68 miles [110 km] northeast of Beijing) was dismantled for building materials, but it was subsequently rebuilt. Other areas have also been restored, including just northwest of Jiayu Pass at the western limit of the wall; at Huangya Pass, some 105 miles (170 km) north of Tianjin; and at Mutianyu, about 55 miles (90 km) northeast of Beijing. The best-known section, at Badaling (43 miles [70 km] northwest of Beijing), was rebuilt in the late 1950s; it now attracts thousands of national and foreign tourists every day. Portions of the wall around Shanhai Pass and at Mount Hu, the eastern terminus, also had been rebuilt by 2000.

OTHER CULTURAL SITES

Although the Great Wall of China is perhaps its best-known cultural landmark, other great national treasures provide glimpses into China's past—including the majestic Forbidden City, the immense Grand Canal, the heavenly Potala Palace, the archaeologically significant Longmen and Mogao caves, and the early human remains found at Zhoukoudian. Tributes to Confucius (temple complex of Qufu), the Buddha (Yungang caves), and past emperors (Qin tomb) mirror values of previous generations.

FORBIDDEN CITY

The Forbidden City (Chinese: Zijincheng) encompasses the imperial palace complex at the heart of Beijing. Commissioned in 1406 by the Yongle emperor of the Ming dynasty, it was first officially occupied by the court in 1420. It was so named because access to the area was barred to most of the subjects of the realm. Government functionaries and even the imperial family were permitted only limited access; the emperor alone could enter any section at will. The 178-acre (72-hectare) compound was designated a UNESCO World Heritage site in 1987 in recognition of its importance as the centre of Chinese power for five centuries, as well as for its unparalleled architecture and its current role as the Palace Museum of dynastic art and history.

The architecture of the walled complex adheres rigidly to the traditional Chinese geomantic practice of feng shui. The orientation of the Forbidden City, and for that matter all of Beijing, follows a north-south line. Within the compound, all the most important buildings, especially those along the main axis, face south to honour the Sun. The buildings and the ceremonial spaces between them are arranged to convey an impression of great imperial power while reinforcing the insignificance of the individual. This architectural conceit is borne out to the smallest of details—the relative importance of a building can be judged not only from its height or width but also by the style of its roof and the number of figurines perched on the roof's ridges.

Among the more notable landmarks are the Wu (Meridian) Gate, the Hall of Supreme Harmony (Taihedian), and the Imperial Garden (Yuhuayuan). The Wu Gate is the imposing formal southern entrance to the Forbidden City. Its auxiliary wings, which flank the entryway, are outstretched like the forepaws of a guardian lion or sphinx. The gate is also one of the tallest buildings of the complex, standing 125 feet (38 m) high at its roof ridge. One of its primary functions was to serve as a backdrop for imperial appearances and proclamations. Beyond the Wu Gate lies a large courtyard, 460 feet (140 m) deep and 690 feet (210 m) wide, through which the Golden River (Golden Water River) runs in a bow-shaped arc. The river is crossed by five parallel white marble bridges, which lead to the Gate of Supreme Harmony (Taihemen).

North of the Gate of Supreme Harmony lies the Outer Court, heart of the Forbidden City, where the three main administration halls stand atop a three-tiered marble terrace overlooking an immense plaza. The area encompasses some 7 acres (3 hectares)—enough space to admit tens of thousands of subjects to pay homage to the emperor. Towering above the space stands the Hall of Supreme Harmony, in which the throne of the emperor stands. This hall, measuring 210 by 122 feet (64 by 37 m), is the largest single building in the compound, as well as one of the tallest (being approximately the same height as the Wu Gate). It was the centre of the imperial court. To the north, on the same triple terrace, stand the Hall of Central (or Complete) Harmony (Zhonghedian) and the Hall of Preserving Harmony (Baohedian), also loci of government functions.

Farther north lies the Inner Court, which contains the three halls that composed the imperial living quarters. Adjacent to these palaces, at the northernmost limit of the Forbidden City, is the 3-acre (1.2-hectare) Imperial Garden, the organic design of which seems to depart from the rigid symmetry of the rest of the compound. The garden was designed as a place of relaxation for the emperor, with a fanciful arrangement of trees, fish ponds, flower beds, and sculpture. In its centre stands the Hall of Imperial Peace (Qin'andian), a Daoist temple where the emperor would retreat for contemplation.

The Forbidden City ceased to be the seat of Qing (Manchu) imperial government with the Chinese Revolution of 1911–12. Some of the ancient buildings (which had been repaired and rebuilt since the 15th century) were lost to the ravages of the revolution and during the war with Japan (1937–45); however, the site was maintained as a whole. Puyi, the last Qing emperor, was permitted to live there after his abdication, but he secretly left the palace (and Beijing) in 1924. In the late 20th century, several of the palace buildings were restored.

The film *The Last Emperor* (1987), which portrays the life of Puyi, was filmed in part within the Forbidden City.

GRAND CANAL

The Grand Canal (Chinese: Da Yunhe, also called Jing-Hang Yunhe; "Beijing-Hangzhou Canal") is a vast series of waterways in eastern and northern China that link Hangzhou in Zhejiang province with Beijing. Some 1,085 miles (1,747 km) in length, it is the world's longest man-made waterway, though, strictly speaking, not all of it is a canal. It was built to enable successive Chinese regimes to transport surplus grain from the agriculturally rich Yangtze (Chang) and Huai river valleys to feed the capital cities and large standing armies in northern China.

The oldest part of the canal lies between the Yangtze and the city of Huaiyin (formerly called Qingjiang) in Jiangsu province, which was originally on the Huang He (Yellow River) when that river followed a course much farther to the south. This section, traditionally known as the Shanyang Canal, in recent centuries has been called the Southern Grand Canal (Nan Yunhe). This ancient waterway was first constructed as early as the 4th century BCE, was rebuilt in 607 CE, and has been used ever since.

China's first great canal system, which created a northeast-southwest link from the Huang He (when the Huang had a northern course) to the Huai River, was built beginning in 605 during the Sui dynasty (581–618). Known as the New Bian Canal, it remained the chief waterway throughout the Tang period (618–907) and the Northern Song period (960–1125/26).

The need for a major transportation link again arose during the Yuan (Mongol) dynasty (1279–1368), because its capital at Dadu (Beijing) required a grain-supply system. In 1282–83, the decision was made to build a new canal from the Huang He—which since 1195 had changed its course southward and taken over the former mouth of the Huai below Huaiyin—to the Daqing River in northern Shandong province, which was dredged to give an outlet to the sea. The mouth of the Daqing, however, silted up almost immediately. An alternative canal, cut across the neck of the Shandong Peninsula from the harbour of Qingdao (Tsingtao) to Yixian, also proved impracticable and was abandoned. Eventually another stretch of canal, the Huitong Canal, was built to join Dong'e Zhen on the Huang He with the Wei River at Linqing. In this way, the modern Grand Canal came into being. During the Yuan period, however, canal transportation was expensive and inefficient, and most grain went by sea.

At the beginning of the Ming dynasty (1368–1644), the capital was at Nanjing. After Beijing again became the seat of government in 1403, the whole canal—including the section from Linqing on the Wei to its junction with the Huang He, which was dredged and repaired—remained in operation until the 19th century. It comprised six main sections: (1) a short canal from the outskirts of Beijing to Tongzhou, (2) a canalized river joining the Hai River to Tianjin and then joining the Wei River as far as Linqing, (3) a section in Shandong rising over comparatively high ground from Linqing to its highest point near Jining and then falling again to a point near Xuzhou, a difficult stretch using a series of dams, sluices, and locks supplied with water from a number of small rivers flowing off the Mount Tai massif and from the string of lakes southeast of Jining, (4) a stretch from Xuzhou that followed the southern course of the Huang He as far as Huaiyin, (5) a section from Huaiyin following the ancient Shanyang Canal south to Zhenjiang on the Yangtze, and (6) a section south of the Yangtze where the canal, there called the Jiangnan Yunhe, ran southeast and then southwest for some 200 miles (320 km) via Suzhou to Hangzhou.

In the 19th century, a series of disastrous floods broke the dikes of the Huang He (which began to shift to its present northern course), caused great problems in the section of the canal between Xuzhou and Huaiyin, and cut across the canal between Linqing and Jining. After the Taiping Rebellion (1850–64) and the Nian Rebellion (1853–68), the use of the canal as the major supply line to Beijing was abandoned, and the canal gradually fell into disrepair in its northern sections. After 1934 the Chinese government carried out extensive works on the canal between Huaiyin and the Yangtze; ship locks were constructed to allow medium-sized steamers to use this section, which was dredged and largely rebuilt.

New work was begun in 1958 to restore the whole system as a trunk waterway able to carry ships of up to 600 tons. Between 1958 and 1964, it was straightened, widened, and dredged; one new section 40 miles (64 km) long was constructed, and modern locks were added. The canal can now accommodate medium-sized barge traffic throughout its length. The main traffic, however, is concentrated in the southern half. The canal is also used to divert water from the Yangtze to northern Jiangsu province for irrigation, making possible double cropping of rice.

LONGMEN CAVES

The Longmen caves are a series of cave temples carved into the rock of a high river bank south of the city of Luoyang, in

Empress as Donor with Attendants, *limestone relief with traces of colour, from Binyang cave, Longmen, Henan province, China, c. 522, Bei (Northern) Wei dynasty; in the Nelson Atkins Museum of Art, Kansas City, Missouri.* Courtesy of the Nelson-Atkins Museum of Art, Kansas City, Missouri (Nelson Fund)

Henan province, east-central China. The cave complex, designated a UNESCO World Heritage site in 2000, is one of China's most popular tourist destinations.

The temples were begun late in the Bei (Northern) Wei dynasty (386–534/535), in the Six Dynasties period. Following the transfer of the Bei Wei capital from Pingcheng (present-day Datong, Shanxi province) south to Luoyang in 495, a new series of cave temples was begun there. These were based on the precedent of an ambitious series of caves built in the preceding decades at Yungang.

The Bei Wei caves at Longmen (including the well-known Guyang and Binyang caves) are intimate in scale and display complex iconography that is elegantly crafted into hard stone. The Buddha images—clothed in the costume of the Chinese scholar, with a sinuous cascade of drapery falling over a flattened figure—provide an example of what is known as the Longmen style, in contrast to the blockier Yungang style. Construction at the site continued sporadically throughout the 6th century and culminated in the Tang dynasty (618–907) with the construction of a cave shrine, known as Fengxian Si. This truly monumental temple was carved out over the three-year period between 672 and 675. The square plan measures about 100 feet (30 m) on each side, and a colossal seated Buddha figure upon the back wall, flanked by attendant figures, is more than 56 feet (17 m) high.

MOGAO CAVES NEAR DUNHUANG

The Mogao Caves—also called the Caves of the Thousand Buddhas (Chinese: Qianfo Dong)—constitute an extensive cave complex near the city of Dunhuang in western Gansu province, northwestern China. Dunhuang is situated in an oasis in the Gansu-Xinjiang desert region at the far western limit of traditional Chinese settlement along the Silk Road across Central Asia, and it was the first trading town reached by foreign merchants entering Chinese-administered territory from the west. The renowned Mogao Caves were designated a UNESCO World Heritage site in 1987.

Dunhuang was a great centre of Buddhism from 366 CE to the fall of the Xi (Western) Xia dynasty in the early 13th century. It was one of the chief places of entry for Buddhist monks and missionaries from the kingdoms of Central Asia, and in 366 these Buddhists founded the first of what are now known as the Mogao Caves. From that period onward, the town was a major Buddhist centre and place of pilgrimage. There were a number of monastic communities that played a predominant role in local society and to which successive governors were generous patrons.

In one of the cave temples, a rich collection of about 60,000 paper manuscripts, printed documents, and fragments dating from the 5th to the 11th century was walled up about 1015. When discovered in 1900, this collection was found to include not only Buddhist but also Daoist, Zoroastrian, and Nestorian scriptures, as

Deer Jataka fresco painting, 8th century, in cave 257, Mogao Caves, Dunhuang, Gansu province, China. Holle Bildarchiv, Baden-Baden

Lhasa, southern Tibet Autonomous Region, southwestern China. It is situated atop Mar-po-ri (Red Mountain), 425 feet (130 m) above the Lhasa River valley, and rises up dramatically from its rocky base. Completed in 1648, Potrang Karpo (White Palace) once served as the seat of the Tibetan government and the main residence of the Dalai Lama; from the mid-18th century, it was used as a winter palace. Completed in 1694, Potrang Marpo (Red Palace) houses several chapels, sacred statues, and the tombs of eight Dalai Lamas; it remains a major pilgrimage site for Tibetan Buddhists.

King Srong-brtsan-sgam-po commissioned the building of a palace in Lhasa in the 7th century. Significantly smaller and less elaborate than its 5-square-mile (13-square-km) successor, it was named the Potala ("Pure Land" or "High Heavenly Realm") for reasons that are not historically documented, although Mount Potala in India seems the likely source. Tibetan Buddhists acknowledge the Dalai Lama as the incarnation of Avalokiteshvara (Guanyin), a bodhisattva whose home was on Mount Potala.

Srong-brtsan-sgam-po's palace was later destroyed, and in 1645 the fifth Dalai Lama ordered the construction of a new castle that could accommodate his role as both a religious and a government leader. Lhasa was again chosen as the location because of its importance as a pilgrimage site and its proximity to the three main Buddhist monasteries of Sera, 'Bras-spungs (Drepung), and Dga'-Idan (Ganden). The new Potala was built on

well as vast numbers of secular texts. Although most of the manuscripts and documents were sold to foreigners, the caves still contain murals and painted statuary. Many of the nearly 500 caves in the Mogao complex were opened to the public after 1949.

POTALA PALACE

The Potala Palace is an immense religious and administrative complex in

Mar-po-ri for the security provided by an elevated position; until its use declined in the mid-18th century, the Potala was a major Tibetan military fortress.

Of more than 1,000 rooms in the Potala, the ones considered most holy are the Chogyal Drubphuk and the Phakpa Lhakhang, remnants from the original palace of Srong-brtsan-sgam-po; the latter houses the sacred Arya Lokeshvara (Avalokiteshvara) statue. More than 200,000 statues and 10,000 altars are located within the sacred complex. Its value was recognized by China's Cultural Relics Commission, and the palace was spared during the Cultural Revolution. The Potala was designated a UNESCO World Heritage site in 1994. Two other locations—Tsuglagkhang, or Gtsug-lag-khang (Jokhang) Temple, one of the holiest places in Tibetan Buddhism, and the Norbuglingka (Nor-bu-gling-ka; Jewel Palace), the former summer residence of the Dalai Lama—were added to the World Heritage site in 2000 and 2001, respectively.

Potala Palace complex, Lhasa, Tibet Autonomous Region, China. Adam Crowley/Getty Images

QIN TOMB

The great Qin tomb complex is a major Chinese archaeological site near the ancient capital city of Chang'an, Shaanxi province, in north-central China, now near the modern city of Xi'an. It is the burial place of the first sovereign emperor, Shihuangdi of the Qin dynasty (221–207 BCE), who unified the empire, began construction of the Great Wall of China, and prepared for death by constructing a 20-square-mile (50-square-km) funerary compound. The treasures of the Qin tomb began to come to light only some 2,100 years after the emperor's death.

In March 1974, a work brigade of farmers drilling a well discovered a subterranean chamber that archaeologists later found contained an army of some 8,000 life-size terra-cotta soldiers (assembled from separately fired sections but given individually detailed faces) and horses, along with richly adorned chariots of wood (now disintegrated) and of bronze; iron farm implements; bronze and leather bridles; objects of silk, linen, jade, and bone; and such weapons as bows and arrows, spears, and swords, cast from an unusual thirteen-element alloy, which are still shiny and sharp today. The clay figures, once brightly painted with mineral colours, were grouped into a specific military formation—a configuration of vanguard bowmen and crossbowmen, outer files of archers, groups of infantrymen and charioteers, and an armoured rear guard—that followed the military prescriptions of the time. Three nearby chambers were also discovered in the 1970s—one holding more than 1,300 ceramic figures representing a smaller, complementary force of foot soldiers, chariots, and cavalry; one with sixty-eight members of what probably represents an elite command unit; and one that is empty. Buried above and around many of the broken figures are the remnants of timber roofing, which may have collapsed because of a fire shortly after the emperor's death. These four so-called Xi'an digs are covered with protective roofing and, even as the archaeologists' work proceeds, serve as the unique in-site Museum of Qin Figures. A new exhibit hall was opened above one of the pits in 1994.

The buried army faces east, poised for battle, about three-quarters of a mile from the outer wall of the tomb proper, guarding it from Shihuangdi's chief former adversaries, who had come from that direction. In pits nearby have been found the remains of seven humans (possibly the emperor's children), a subterranean stable filled with horse skeletons, an assemblage of half-size bronze chariots, seventy individual burial sites, a zoo for exotic animals, and other artifacts.

The tomb itself, which may have been looted shortly after its completion, remains unexcavated. It lies within an inner wall and beneath a four-sided pyramid mound that was originally landscaped to appear as a low, wooded mountain. The interior is reputedly a vast underground palace that took about 700,000 conscripted workmen more than 36 years to complete. The historian Sima Qian (c. 145–c. 87 BCE) wrote:

> The labourers dug through three subterranean streams, which they sealed off with bronze to construct the burial chamber. They built models of palaces, pavilions, and offices and filled the tomb with fine vessels, precious stones, and rarities. Artisans were ordered to install mechanically triggered crossbows set to shoot any intruder. With quicksilver the various waterways of the empire, the Yangtze and Yellow rivers, and even the great ocean itself were created and made to flow and circulate mechanically. With shining pearls the heavenly constellations were depicted above, and with figures of birds in gold and silver and of pine trees carved of jade the earth was laid out below. Lamps were fueled with whale oil so that they might burn for the longest possible time.

The compound was declared a UNESCO World Heritage site in 1987. Archaeological excavations on the site continued into the 21st century, and archaeologists anticipated that it would take years to unearth the entire tomb complex.

The region surrounding the Qin tomb holds the mausoleums of several other ancient Chinese rulers, including those of Taizong, second emperor (626–649 CE) of the Tang dynasty, and the Han emperor Wudi (141–87 BCE).

THE CONFUCIAN TEMPLE COMPLEX OF QUFU

The city of Qufu in west-central Shandong province, eastern China, lies 70 miles (110 km) south of Jinan. In ancient times, Qufu was the capital of the small independent state of Lu, which flourished from the 6th to the 4th century BCE. Qufu is best known as the birthplace and place of residence of Confucius (Kongfuzi, or Kongzi), the ancient sage who founded Confucianism. Confucius was born in Qufu in 551 BCE, and in the later part of his life, he forsook his previous wanderings and returned to live at his birthplace, writing, editing, and teaching numerous disciples there until his death in 479 BCE.

The Great Temple of Confucius in the town was built in 1724. Inside the large ceremonial hall of the temple is a large statue of Confucius, surrounded by statues of his disciples. The temple itself stands within a larger oblong walled enclosure that covers about 49 acres (20 hectares) and around which the town of Qufu expanded. Inside the enclosure is an extensive complex of Confucian temples, shrines, monuments, and pavilions. The enclosure contains a house that stands on the site of the one Confucius lived in, an ancient tree said to have been planted by the sage, and a well from which he drank.

Inside the town of Qufu, but lying outside the temple enclosure, is an elaborate complex of buildings that was the residence of Confucius's descendants, the Kong family. Through the centuries, the Kongs were the guardians of the temple complex and the administrators of the town of Qufu; the 76th lineal descendant of Confucius lived in the town before World War II. Lying outside the north gate of the temple enclosure is the family cemetery of the Kongs, which contains the tomb of Confucius.

Qufu has long been a major site for pilgrims and tourists who come to visit the temples, the tomb, and the other surviving memorials to China's greatest sage. The entire complex, both inside and outside the temple enclosure, was designated a UNESCO World Heritage site in 1994.

YUNGANG CAVES

The Yungang caves form a series of magnificent Chinese Buddhist cave temples, created in the 5th century CE during the Six Dynasties period (220–598 CE). They are located about 10 miles (16 km) west of the city of Datong, near the northern border of Shanxi province (and the Great Wall) in northern China. The cave complex, a popular tourist destination, was designated a UNESCO World Heritage site in 2001.

The caves are among the earliest remaining examples of the first major flowering of Buddhist art in China. About twenty major cave temples and many smaller niches and caves were formed by excavating a low ridge of soft sandstone stretching more than half a mile (about 1 km) from east to west. Some of the caves served merely as cell-like enclosures for colossal figures of the Buddha (up to about 55 feet [17 m] tall), while others contained chapels.

The earliest five temples were instituted by the head of the Buddhist church, a monk named Tanyao, about 460 CE; their construction was among the first acts of propitiation sponsored by the foreign Tuoba, or Bei (Northern) Wei, rulers (386–534/535) as a result of their persecution of Buddhism during the period between 446 and 452. The colossal Buddha images in each cave were equated with the first five emperors of the Bei Wei, thus emphasizing the political and economic role that the court imposed upon Buddhism.

The remaining temples were mainly constructed in subsequent decades until 494, when the Bei Wei court was moved to the city of Luoyang (Henan province) and a new series of cave temples was instituted at the site of Longmen.

The predominant sculptural style of the innumerable images (primarily of the Buddha, with ancillary figures) is a synthesis of various foreign influences—including Persian, Byzantine, and Greek—but ultimately derived from the Buddhist art of India. Late in the period of major work at the site, a new "Chinese style" appeared, based on indigenous styles and forms; Yungang, however, is considered to embody the first style, while the later caves at Longmen embody the "Chinese style."

ZHOUKOUDIAN

One of the world's most renowned archaeological sites is located near the village of Zhoukoudian, Beijing municipality, northern China, 26 miles (42 km) southwest of the central city. The site, including some four residential areas, has yielded the largest known collection of fossils of the extinct hominin *Homo erectus*—altogether some 40 incomplete skeletons, which are commonly known as the Peking man fossils. Remains of anatomically modern humans (*H. sapiens*) have also been excavated there. The discoveries at Zhoukoudian have proved vital to advancing the study of human evolution.

The hominin remains were found within a series of scree- and loess-filled clefts (inaccurately referred to as "caves") in a limestone cliff. In 1921 the Swedish geologist and fossil hunter J. Gunnar Andersson became intrigued by tales of "dragon bones" that local people found in the clefts and used for medicinal purposes. Andersson explored the clefts and discovered some quartz pieces that could have been used as early cutting tools. This discovery lent credence to his theory that the bones were actually human fossils. In 1927 the Canadian anthropologist Davidson Black retrieved a hominin molar from the site. On the basis of that finding, he identified a previously unknown hominin group, which he named *Sinanthropus pekinensis* (i.e., Peking man). Large-scale excavations began in 1929.

In the years that followed, archaeologists uncovered complete skulls, mandibles, teeth, leg bones, and other fossils from males and females of various ages. The specimens were eventually classified as *H. erectus*. Many of the fossil-bearing layers have been dated, and the results suggest that the site was first occupied more than 770,000 years ago and then used intermittently by *H. erectus* until perhaps 230,000 years ago. If these dates are correct, Zhoukoudian documents the relatively late survival of this species.

Further discoveries at the site demonstrated that Peking man was fairly technologically sophisticated. Stone scrapers and choppers as well as several hand axes indicated that Peking man devised various tools for different tasks. Excavators also claimed to have uncovered ash deposits consisting of charred animal bones and stones indicating that Peking man had learned to use fire for lighting, cooking, and heating. This discovery resulted in a drastic revision of the date for the earliest human mastery of fire. A reanalysis of the site in 1998, however, revealed no evidence for hearths, ash, or charcoal and indicated that some of the "ash" layers were in fact water-laid sediments washed into the sites from the surrounding hillsides. The bones and stones were charred not by human activity but by lightning-induced fire.

During World War II the more notable fossils were lost during an attempt to smuggle them out of China for safekeeping; they have never been recovered.

Following the war, excavations resumed, and many more fragments of *H. erectus* were unearthed; however, some areas remain unexcavated. In 1987 Zhoukoudian was placed on the list of UNESCO World Heritage sites. In 1995 concern over the deterioration of the clefts, parts of which were in danger of collapsing, led to the establishment of a joint UNESCO-China project aimed at preserving the site and encouraging investigations there.

NATURAL SITES

China is renowned for its many places of great natural beauty. Often these sites are associated with ancient religious practices and are places of pilgrimage or of retreat. The Huang, Lu, and Wuyi mountain systems; Lake Tai; and the Tai and Wutai peaks are among the top tourist destinations in the country.

HUANG MOUNTAINS

The Huang Mountains (Chinese: Huang Shan) constitute a complex mountain system in southern Anhui province, China. Some 160 miles (250 km) in length, the range has a generally southwest-to-northeast axis, extending from the area east of Lake Poyang to the eastern point of the province near Guangde. Its general elevation is about 3,300 feet (1,000 m), but individual peaks exceed that; Mount Guangming is 6,040 feet (1,840 m) high. A secondary range, somewhat lower in elevation, known as the Jiuhua Mountains, runs parallel to the main range to the north along the southern bank of the Yangtze River.

The range takes its name from its most famous peak, Mount Huang ("Yellow Mountain"), which is renowned for its magnificent scenery. Known in ancient times as Mount Yi, Mount Huang received its present name in 747 CE. It was the retreat of the Chan (Zen) Buddhist master Zhiman, who founded a temple that later became famous as the Xiangfu Monastery. From that time onward, it became a popular place for sightseeing, with its great stands of pines, its mountain streams and waterfalls, and its many strangely shaped rocks, caves, grottoes, and hot springs.

Mount Huang was designated a UNESCO World Heritage site in 1990. It rises in a scenic area that encompasses some 60 square miles (155 square km), protected by an outlying conservation area of an additional 55 square miles (140 square km). Its landform is unique, as one peak rises after another among unpredictable mists and clouds, making it an ever-changing scene of magnificent natural beauty. There are more than 400 scenic spots with strange-shaped pines, fantastic-looking rocks, a sea of clouds, and hot springs, which are among the most popular attractions of the Mount Huang area.

The Huang Mountains form the watershed between the Yangtze and Xin'an rivers, the latter a tributary of the Fuchun River. The principal route crosses the range to the west of the peak of Mount Huang itself, running from Taiping in the north to Shexian in the south.

Much of the area remains heavily forested with fir and pine, and lumbering is an important local industry, as is the production of tung oil, lacquer, and similar products. The major product of the area is, however, tea.

LU MOUNTAINS

The Lu Mountains (Chinese: Lu Shan) constitute a famous mountain area in northern Jiangxi province, southeastern China. Situated to the south of Jiujiang and west of Xingzi, it looks north over the Yangtze River (Chang Jiang) valley and east over Lake Poyang. It forms the eastern extremity of the Mufu Mountains. Its highest peak, Dahanyang, is about 4,836 feet (1,474 m) above sea level. The Lu Mountains were venerated as a holy area from ancient times, when they were called the Kuang Mountains. In early times, they were the home of many prominent Buddhists and the intellectual centre of Daoism from the 6th to the 8th century. The Lu Mountains also have associations with many famous poets and literary figures, who referred to them as Kuanglu. Before World War II, the mountains still had some 300 temples and Daoist shrines and were a popular summer resort for Western residents of Shanghai and the coastal cities; the area has continued to thrive as a resort. The mountains and surrounding region also have been the subject of geological studies of glaciers of the Quaternary Period (i.e., about the past 2.6 million years).

The Lu massif forms a horst-style fault block that integrates mountains, rivers, and lakes into one unit. It combines a celebrated mountain with beautiful scenery and is renowned worldwide for its grandeur, unusual shape, and elegance. Designated a UNESCO World Heritage site in 1996, the Lu Mountains scenic area encompasses some 117 square miles (302 square km) and is protected by an outlying zone of 193 square miles (500 square km).

LAKE TAI

Lake Tai (Chinese: Tai Hu) is a large body of water between Zhejiang and Jiangsu provinces, eastern China. Roughly crescent-shaped, it is about 45 miles (70 km) from north to south and 37 miles (59 km) from east to west; its total surface area is about 935 square miles (2,425 square km). The lake lies in a flat plain and is connected with a maze of waterways that feed it from the west and discharge its waters eastward into the East China Sea, via the Wusong, Liu, Huangpu, and other rivers. In addition to these natural waterways, there is an intricate pattern of canals and irrigation channels associated with the lake. Only on the northeast side is the lake bounded by uplands—a ridge of hills that also outcrop in the lake as islands, many of which, because of silting, have been joined to the shoreline.

The surrounding area has been settled since the 1st century BCE, but the irrigation system mostly dates from the 7th

A path in the Lu Mountains, Jiangxi province, China. Heather Angel

century CE and later. Reclamation and drainage improvements were conducted intensively between the 10th and 13th centuries; large-scale flood control measures were undertaken in the 11th and again in the 15th century. Similar improvements have been carried out in more recent times: drainage canals and dikes have been built, and an ever more complex irrigation pattern has emerged. In the 1930s the Chinese Nationalist government established a water conservancy authority for the lake that the Chinese communist government replaced after 1949 with a water conservancy assembly that also became responsible for the surrounding area.

Some of the islands in the eastern part of the lake are traditionally famous Daoist and Buddhist religious sites, and several thousand people live on them, raising fruit and fishing in the lake. Lake Tai has historically been considered a place of great natural beauty, and the area, particularly in the east near Suzhou and in the north around Wuxi (both in Jiangsu), attracts many tourists.

By the early 21st century, however, the improper disposal of chemicals and sewage had caused a toxic algae to form on the lake's surface, thereby threatening the quality of drinking water for people living nearby. In 2007 the Chinese government began a large-scale cleanup project. Many local factories were closed and water treatment regulations made more strict as part of a five-year plan to improve water quality.

Mount Tai

Mount Tai (Chinese: Tai Shan) is a mountain mass with several peaks along a southwest-northeast axis to the north of the city of Tai'an in Shandong province, eastern China. Comprising several peaks along a southwest-northeast axis, the massif consists of a much-shattered fault block, mostly composed of archaic crystalline shales and granites and some ancient limestones. The highest point, Tianzhu Peak, reaches a height of 5,000 feet (1,524 m). Mount Tai was originally known as Daizong or Daishan. Since Qin times (221–207 BCE) it has also been known as Dongyue ("Eastern Mountain"), one of the five holy mountains of China, and has usually ranked as the first among them. The other four are: Mount Heng in Hunan province (south), Mount Hua in Shaanxi province (west), Mount Heng in Shanxi province (north), and Mount Song in Henan province (central).

Historically important in the cult of official state rituals, Mount Tai was the site of two of the most spectacular of all the ceremonies of the traditional Chinese empire. One of them, called *feng*, was held on top of Mount Tai and consisted of offerings to heaven; the other, called *chan*, was held on a lower hill and made offerings to earth. These ceremonies are often referred to together as *fengchan* (worship of heaven and earth) and were believed to ensure a dynasty's fortunes. They were carried out at rare intervals— during the Xi (Western) Han dynasty (206 BCE–25 CE) in 110, 106, 102, and 98

BCE; during the Dong (Eastern) Han dynasty (25–220 CE) in 56 CE; and by emperors of the Tang dynasty (618–907) in 666 and again in 725.

Mount Tai was not only the site of imposing state ceremonies. It was also home to powerful spirits for whom rituals were performed in spring for a good harvest and in autumn to give thanks for a harvest completed. Since Mount Tai was the chief ceremonial centre for eastern China, rites were also performed to seek protection from floods and earthquakes.

Mount Tai became associated with a wide range of beliefs that were derived from folk religion and connected with Daoism, a philosophy integral to Chinese life and thought for more than 2,000 years. It was considered to be the centre of the yang (male) principle, the source of life, and from the Dong Han period onward, it was believed that the spirits of Mount Tai determined all human destiny and that after death the souls of people returned to Mount Tai for judgment. The name of the most important spirit, originally Taishan Fujun ("Lord of Mount Tai"), was, with the emergence of organized Daoism, changed to Taiyue Dadi ("Grand Emperor of Mount Tai"). In Ming times (1368–1644) the centre of the popular cult was transferred from the spirit himself to his daughter, Taishan Niangniang ("The Lady of Mount Tai")—also called Bixia Yunjun ("Goddess of the Colourful Clouds")—whose cult had begun to grow from about 1000 and who became a northern Daoist equivalent to the Buddhist Guanyin (Kuan-yin) or to Avalokitesvara (bodhisattva of mercy), whose cult was powerful in central and southern China.

The slopes of Mount Tai have long been covered with temples and shrines dedicated to the complex pantheon of associated spirits. In the past, vast numbers of pilgrims visited it annually, and a great festival was held in the third month of the Chinese year. Mount Tai has a long history of grandeur, and, in addition to religious structures, it has many towers, pavilions, and other cultural relics. Designated a UNESCO World Heritage site in 1987, it is an important part of Chinese history and culture.

MOUNT WUTAI

Mount Wutai (Chinese: Wutai Shan) is a mountain in northeastern Shanxi province, northern China. It is actually a cluster of flat-topped peaks, from which it takes its name, *wutai* meaning "five terraces"; the highest peak is 10,033 feet (3,058 m) above sea level. It is also the name of a mountain chain, a massif with a southwest-northeast axis that is separated from the Heng Mountains to the northwest by the valley of the Hutuo River; the Hutuo curves eastward around the chain's southern flank to flow into the Huangbizhuang Reservoir and then the North China Plain in Hebei province, where it joins the Hai River system.

Mount Wutai is particularly famous as one of the great holy places of Buddhism.

Great numbers of temples, including some of the oldest wooden buildings surviving in China, are scattered over the mountain. The largest temples—such as Xiantong, Tayuan, and Pusading—are grouped around the town of Taihuai Zhen.

Prior to its association with Buddhism, Mount Wutai appears to have been designated a holy mountain of Daoism during the later Han dynasty (25–220 CE). It came into prominence in the 5th century during the Bei (Northern) Wei dynasty (386–534/535), when, as Qingliang Mountain, it became identified as the dwelling place of Manjusri (Chinese: Wenshushili) bodhisattva (a being who voluntarily postpones Buddhahood in order to work for worldly welfare and understanding). The cult of Manjusri intensified during the Tang dynasty (618–907). In early Tang times, Mount Wutai was closely associated with the patriarchs of the Huayan (Kegon) school of Buddhism, becoming the principal centre of their teaching. During that period it attracted scholars and pilgrims not only from all parts of China but also from Japan, who continued to visit and study there until the 12th century.

Many of the other monasteries in the region were attached to Chan (Zen) Buddhism, which during the 9th century enjoyed the patronage of the provincial governors of the neighbouring areas of Hebei. This arrangement protected Mount Wutai from the worst ravages of the great religious persecution that occurred from 843 to 845. Under Mongol rule in the late 13th century, Tibetan Buddhism was first introduced to Mount Wutai. During the Qing dynasty (1644–1911/12), the Tibetan Buddhist religion was an important element in relations between the Chinese court and its Mongol and Tibetan vassals, and the state gave lavish support to monasteries inhabited by lamas (monks); Mount Wutai was one of the principal monastic centres.

Few of the present buildings are from earlier periods, but the main hall of Foguang Temple, dating from 857, is one of the oldest surviving wooden buildings in China. In addition, the main hall of Nanchan Temple, originally dating to at least 782, was reconstructed in 1974–75. In 2009 Mount Wutai was designated a UNESCO World Heritage site.

WUYI MOUNTAINS

The Wuyi Mountains (Chinese: Wuyi Shan) is a mountain range on the border between Fujian and Jiangxi provinces, southeastern China. Originally used in reference to a cluster of peaks in northwestern Fujian, the name is now applied generally to the range along a southwest-northeast axis forming the northern and central parts of the Fujian-Jiangxi border. The individual peaks of the Wuyi range reach about 6,000 feet (1,800 m) above sea level. Situated in an area with many caves and spectacular scenery, the Wuyi Mountains have long been associated with cults of Daoism, a philosophy that has influenced all aspects of Chinese culture for more than 2,000 years. Ziyang Shuyuan, a well-known academy established in 1183 by the famous Neo-Confucian philosopher Zhu Xi (1130–1200), flourished there in the 18th and 19th centuries; its ruins have been partially rebuilt.

The range is crossed by a number of passes, two of which are traversed by railroads. One railroad line, completed in 1957, runs from Yingtan (in Jiangxi) through Tieniu Pass to Xiamen (Amoy) in Fujian; a branch line, completed in 1959, connects Waiyang to Fuzhou (both in Fujian). A second main line, completed in 1997, runs from Hengfeng (in Jiangxi) through Fenshui Pass to Nanping (in Fujian). To the northeast of the range are the somewhat higher and even more rugged Xianxia Mountains, which extend into Zhejiang province.

Heavily forested and sparsely populated, the Wuyi Mountains are famous for their timber and bamboo and have long been renowned for their fine tea. From the 13th to the 17th century, the government maintained special offices in the area to control tea production.

The Wuyi Mountains area has some of the most beautiful natural scenery in China, and the region is a popular tourist attraction. A protected area of about 38 square miles (100 square km) was designated a UNESCO World Heritage site in 1999.

CHAPTER 5

BEIJING

The great city of Beijing (conventional Peking) is a province-level municipality and the capital of the People's Republic of China. Few cities in the world have served for so long as the political headquarters and cultural centre of an area as immense as China. The city has been an integral part of China's history over the past eight centuries, and nearly every major building of any age in Beijing has at least some national historical significance. The importance of Beijing thus makes it impossible to understand China without a knowledge of this city.

More than 2,000 years ago, a site north of present-day Beijing was already an important military and trading centre for the northeastern frontier of China. In 1267, during the Yuan (Mongol) dynasty (1206–1368), a new city built northeast of the old—called Dadu—became the administrative capital of China. During the first five decades of the subsequent Ming dynasty (1368–1644), Nanjing (Nanking) was the capital, and the old Mongol capital was renamed Beiping (Pei-p'ing; "Northern Peace"); the third Ming emperor, however, restored it as the imperial seat of the dynasty and gave it a new name, Beijing ("Northern Capital"). Beijing has remained the capital of China except for a brief period (1928–49) when the Nationalist government again made Nanjing the capital (although the capital was removed to Chongqing [Chungking] during World War II); during that time Beijing once again resumed the old name Beiping.

The city remained the most flourishing cultural centre in China despite the frequent political changes in the country throughout the early decades of the 20th century. Beijing's importance was fully realized, however, only when the city was chosen as the capital of the People's Republic in 1949, and this political status has added much vitality to it. Indeed, few cities have ever had such rapid growth in population and geographic area, as well as in industrial and other activities. Combining both historical relics of an ancient culture and new urban construction, ranging from fast-food franchises to plush hotels for foreign tourists and corporate travelers, it has become a showplace of modern China and one of the world's great cities. Renewed international attention focused on Beijing after it was chosen to host the 2008 Summer Olympic Games.

The area of the city is 1,763 square miles (4,567 square km), and that of the Beijing municipality is an estimated 6,500 square miles (16,800 square km). In 2006 the city had an estimated population of 8,580,376; a 2007 estimate for the urban agglomeration was 11,106,000, with the entire Beijing municipality numbering about 15,810,000.

CHARACTER OF THE CITY

Although much of Beijing's older and more picturesque character has been destroyed in the drive since 1949 to modernize and industrialize, some parts of the city are still redolent of the past. Many fine monumental buildings, old restaurants, and centres of traditional Chinese arts and crafts remain, and the central government has taken measures to prevent the city core from being further industrialized. Broad new boulevards, replete with even newer commercial ventures, have displaced the colourful stalls and markets for which the city was once famous, but the neighbourhood life of old Beijing can still be glimpsed in the narrow *hutong*s (residential alleys), with their tiny potted-plant gardens, enclosed courtyards, and (decreasingly) coal-burning stoves—some of which are still guarded by carved stone lions at their gates.

People in Beijing commute by subway, bus, automobile, or bicycle and on hot summer evenings sit outside their apartment blocks to catch cooling breezes and to chat. The citizenry has a wide range of leisure pursuits, particularly those considered good for health. The ancient art of tai chi chuan (*taijiquan*; Chinese boxing) is widely practiced, singly or in groups, along roadsides and in parks. Locals as well as tourists are attracted to the many nearby historical sites, such as the Summer Palace, the tombs of the Ming emperors, and the Great Wall. Older people, especially the men, like to huddle in tiny restaurants and tea shops. Young people are drawn to the city's many cafés and nightclubs, where the entertainment can range from DJ-run dance music to Chinese rock bands.

For all the vicissitudes of its history, Beijing continues to be a source of great pride for its inhabitants. Their obsessions are, as they have been for centuries, food and knowledge: they eat heartily when they have the means and read voraciously. Food stalls on the streets, selling a variety of cooked treats, are well patronized, as are newspaper and magazine kiosks. The ambition of most families is to provide their offspring with a higher education or, if not that, a good job.

LANDSCAPE

Beijing is situated at the northern apex of the roughly triangular North China Plain and lies at an elevation between about 100 and 130 feet (30 and 40 m) above sea level. The larger municipality is almost completely surrounded by Hebei province, except for two short stretches bordering Tianjin municipality to the southeast. The Yan Mountains lie along the municipality's northeastern side, and the Jundu Mountains occupy its entire western region; together these form a concave arc that circles the Beijing lowland from the northeast to the southwest to form what is known to geologists as the "Bay of Beijing."

CITY SITE

The city was built at the mouth of the embayment, which opens onto the great plain to the south and east, and between two rivers, the Yongding and the Chaobai, which eventually join to empty into the Bo Hai (Gulf of Chihli) in Tianjin municipality, some 100 miles (160 km) southeast

of Beijing. To the south of the city, the plain spreads out for about 400 miles (650 km) until it merges into the lower valley and the delta of the Yangtze River (Chang Jiang). On the east, the plain is bounded by the sea, except for the break caused by the Shandong Hills; on the west it is flanked by the Taihang Mountains, which constitute the eastern edge of the Loess Plateau.

Because Beijing stands at the apex of the triangle, it is a natural gateway on the long-distance land communication route between the North China Plain and the northern ranges, plains, and plateaus, and routes running across the great plain naturally converge on the city. In addition, since the dawn of Chinese history, the Yan range has constituted a formidable barrier between the North China Plain to the south, the Mongolian Plateau to the north, and the Liao River Plain in the southern region of the Northeast (historically Manchuria). A few passes, however, cut through the ranges—the most important being Juyong (northwest of Beijing), Gubei (northeast), and Shanhai (east in Hebei, on the Bo Hai)—and are so situated that all roads leading from Mongolia and the Northeast to the North China Plain are bound to converge on Beijing. For centuries, therefore, Beijing was an important terminus of the caravan routes leading to and from the vast Central Asian hinterland.

No large streams flow through the central city, although the municipality is drained by the Chaobai and Yongding rivers. East of the city, the Chaobai flows southward out of the Miyun Reservoir (itself formed by the combined inflows of the Chao and Bai rivers) in the northeastern corner of the municipality. The tumultuous Yongding, which drains the Shanxi uplands and northwestern Hubei before entering the municipality, is to the west. After following a twisting course through the mountains, it reaches the Beijing plain, passes under the Marco Polo Bridge, 9 miles (14 km) southwest of the central city, and then turns southward to meet the Grand Canal north of Tianjin. The flow of the Yongding is irregular; in the rainy season it rises rapidly, carrying with it large quantities of silt, which raise the level of the riverbed considerably. At the Marco Polo Bridge, it is 50 feet (15 m) above the level of the city, thus constituting a hazard when the river is in flood but also facilitating canalization and irrigation.

Since the early 15th century, the city of Beijing and its surrounding territories have been organized as a metropolitan district of enormous size, having a governor—formerly appointed by the emperor himself—equal in rank to a provincial governor. This special district organization was continued by the Qing (Manchu) dynasty (1644–1911/12) and, since 1949, in the People's Republic. The present metropolitan boundary was established in 1959. The metropolis may be divided into three concentric zones, based on urban functions. The central zone coincides with the central city; it is occupied mainly by old palaces, government buildings, commercial districts, and old residential areas and makes up roughly 1 percent of the total metropolitan area. The second zone, the near suburb, immediately surrounds the old walled city and is the site of the newer factories, schools, government buildings, and workers' dormitories. The outer fringe of this zone is intensively cultivated and supplies vegetables and fruits to the population of the central zone. The near suburb accounts for about 8 percent of the metropolitan area. The third zone, the far suburb, constitutes the remainder of the metropolitan area. This zone functions as the economic base—supplying coal, lumber, construction materials, vegetables and fruits, dairy products, water, and some grain crops to the urban population in the central zone and the near suburb.

CLIMATE

Though Beijing is a relatively short distance from the sea, the general air circulation in the region is mainly from the northwest throughout the year; maritime effects on the region's weather are meagre. The climate is clearly of the continental monsoon type that occurs in the temperate zone. Local topography also has a great effect on Beijing's climate. Because it lies in a lowland area and is protected by mountains, the city is a little warmer in winter than other areas of China located at the same latitude; nonetheless, the mean monthly temperature drops below 50 °F (10 °C) for five months out of the year. In addition, wind direction in Beijing is influenced by topography, with changes occurring from day to night. Generally, there are more southerly winds in the day but northerly or northwesterly winds at night.

The annual mean temperature of the city is 53 °F (12 °C). The coldest month is January, when the monthly mean is 24 °F (−4 °C), and the warmest month is July, when it is 79 °F (26 °C). In an average year, the city experiences 132 days of freezing temperatures between October and March; the mean annual precipitation is 25 inches (63.5 cm), with most of the total falling from June to August. July is ordinarily the wettest month of the year, with an average of 9 inches (23 cm).

One of the characteristics of the region's precipitation is its variability. In 1959—an extremely wet year for Beijing—the total precipitation amounted to 55 inches (140 cm), whereas in 1891—an extremely dry year—only 7 inches (18 cm) fell. The average number of rainy days per year is about 80, and the average relative humidity for the city is 57 percent.

Winter in Beijing is long and usually begins in late October, when northwesterly winds gradually gain strength. This seasonal wind system dominates the region until March; the Siberian air that passes southward over the Mongolian Plateau and into China proper is cold and dry, bringing little snow or other precipitation. The monthly mean temperature from December to February is below freezing. Spring, the windiest season, is short and rapidly becomes warm. The prevailing high spring winds produce an evaporation rate that averages about nine times the total precipitation for the period and frequently is sufficient to cause droughts that are harmful to agriculture. Dust storms in the region, exacerbated by increasing desertification in Inner Mongolia, are common in April and May. In addition to being the season of torrential rains, summer is rather hot, as warm and humid air from the southeast often penetrates into North China. Autumn begins in late September and is a pleasant, though short, season with clear skies and comfortable temperatures.

PLANT LIFE

Although the city of Beijing with its surrounding districts is one of the most densely populated parts of China, portions of the municipality (notably in the mountainous hinterland) are much more sparsely settled and support a wide variety of vegetation. The municipality's mountain areas are within the temperate deciduous forest zone, while the more southerly plains area is part of the wooded steppe zone. Continuous deforestation by humans for centuries, however, has stripped the woodlands in most sections of the metropolitan area. Mixed forests—composed mainly of pine, oak, and Manchurian birch—now cover only mountains in the northeast and the west. Distinct vertical forest zones can be seen at higher elevations. The lower slopes of many hills to the west of the city, being the most accessible to humans, have lost their original forest cover; only bushes and shrubs now dot the landscape there. A variety of species grow on sunny slopes between elevations of about 2,300 and 5,600 feet (700 and 1,700 m), including Manchurian birch, Dahurian birch, trembling poplar, Mongolian oak, and Liaotung oak. Between 5,600 and 6,250 feet (1,700 and 1,900 m), a mixed forest of truncated maple and trembling poplar replaces all other species. Above 6,250 feet, goat willow becomes the dominant tree.

The larger part of the lowland areas of Beijing has been either cultivated or occupied by various settlements, and, for the most part, it is bare of any natural vegetation. Occasionally, some small groves of planted trees may be seen in the vicinity of villages; these are composed mainly of mixed woods consisting of oil pine, Chinese juniper, Chinese cypress, willow, elm, and Chinese locust. In addition, the government has made a concerted and sustained effort to plant trees in and around the central city.

CITY LAYOUT

The traditional core of Beijing essentially consisted of two walled cities (the walls no longer stand), the northern inner city and the southern outer city. The inner city, also known conventionally as Tatar City, lay to the southwest of the site of the Mongol city of Dadu; it was in the form of a square, with walls having a perimeter of nearly 15 miles (24 km). The outer city, also known as the Chinese City, was added during the reign of the Ming emperor Jiajing (1521–66/67); it was in the form of an oblong adjoining the inner city, with walls that were 14 miles (23 km) in length, including 4 miles (6 km) of the southern wall of the inner city. Within the inner city was the Imperial City, also in the form of a square, which had red plastered walls 6.5 miles (10.5 km) in length. The only remaining portions of that wall are on either side of the Tiananmen (Tian'anmen; "Gate of Heavenly Peace"), the southern, and main, entrance to the Imperial City that stands at the northern end of Tiananmen Square. Within the Imperial City, in turn, was the moated Forbidden City, with walls 2.25 miles (3.6 km) long. The Forbidden City contains the former Imperial Palaces, which are now the Palace Museum.

Beijing represents, better than any other existing city, the heritage of Chinese architectural achievement. During each dynasty in which the city was the capital, care was consistently taken to preserve tradition when it was rebuilt or remodeled. Few cities in the world can thus rival Beijing in the regularity and harmony of its city plan.

The urban plan, based on traditional Chinese geomantic practices, was composed about a single straight line, drawn north and south through the centre of the Forbidden City, on which the internal

Forbidden City, imperial palace complex built by Yonglo, third emperor (1402–24) of the Ming dynasty, Beijing. Photograph, Palace Museum, Beijing/Wan-go Weng Inc. Archive

coherence of the city hinged. All the city walls, important city gates, main avenues and streets, religious buildings, and daily shopping markets were systematically arranged in relation to this central axis. Because the central axis has historically signified the authority of the ruling dynasty, many official buildings, public grounds, and city gates were located along this line. From north to south, this line passed through the Bell Tower (Zhonglou); the Drum Tower (Gulou); Jingshan Park; the Forbidden City, including the Imperial Palaces; Tiananmen Square; Qianmen (Front Gate); the Tianqiao neighbourhood; and (no longer standing) Yongding Gate.

The symmetrical layout of the city to the east and west of this line is quite striking. In front of the palaces, the Temple of the Imperial Ancestors (now in the People's Cultural Park) on the east side of the axis is balanced by the Altar of Earth and Harvests (now in Zhongshan Park) on the west. Farther away from the palaces, the market area of Dongdan to the east was balanced by the Xidan market to the west; these still form two of Beijing's main business districts. The Tiantan (Temple of Heaven) Park to the south of the inner city is counterbalanced by the Ditan (Altar of the Earth) Park to the north of the city. Of the sixteen city gates constructed in Ming times, seven were located on each side of the north-south line, and two were situated on the line itself. Only a few of the old gates still stand, but the city streets adjacent to their sites continue to carry their names.

The main avenues of the old city, whether running north-south or east-west, connected the gates on the opposite walls and divided the whole city into a rectangular grid. Within the walls, buildings were constructed around a courtyard or series of courtyards, with every important building facing south. Buildings often stood behind one another along the north-south line, with small courtyards in between. This prevailing southern orientation of buildings has a climatic functional basis, but it also appears to have been sanctified or conventionalized early in the Bronze Age in connection with ancestral ceremonies and with the worship of heaven and earth.

Since 1949 the greatest changes in Beijing's appearance have been the extension of its streets immediately outside the former old city walls and the accelerating pace of new construction throughout the city. On the west side of the old city, an area extending about 1 mile (1.6 km) from the spot where the Fuxing Gate stood has become an extension of the avenue Xichang'an Jie and is used primarily for government offices. Toward the Summer Palace, to the northwest, is the Haidian district, where the most important universities and research institutes of the country are located. To the north of the city, the outlying districts have been developed as a housing area adjoining the educational district in the northwest. The eastern suburb is an industrial district dominated by the manufacture of chemicals, automobiles, and agricultural machinery. Vegetable fields in the southern suburb are gradually being supplanted by industrial plants. More recently, the look of the central city, especially in the eastern sections, has been transformed by growing numbers of high-rise office and apartment buildings. This construction increased rapidly from 1995, reaching a fever pitch in the years leading up to the 2008 Olympic Games.

HOUSING

To cope with the rapid population growth, a number of housing projects have been constructed for office and factory workers since 1949. In the mid-1950s housing projects were concentrated in western areas of the city, where apartment buildings were erected near government offices outside the Fuxing Gate site. Subsequently, a large number of multi-unit housing estates were built in the northern districts between the Anding Gate site and Desheng Gate, centring on the residential neighbourhood of

Hepingli. The Hepingli housing development contains primary and secondary schools, nurseries, hotels, and recreational facilities, as well as scores of four- or five-story apartment buildings. In addition, there are many groups of single-family houses in the northern suburbs, with associated parks, theatres, and recreational centres. All these buildings were supplied with water and natural gas as they were constructed, in contrast with structures in the older parts of the city, where it took longer to provide such services.

In the area outside the Jianguo Gate site, to the east of the central city, apartment buildings accommodate the families of office workers employed in nearby government office buildings. This area has also become the diplomatic district, containing many foreign embassies and a number of Western-style houses for diplomatic representatives and their families, and a locus of high-rise construction.

Many dilapidated houses have been pulled down in the older districts inside the former city walls and have been replaced by multistory apartment buildings. Urban-renewal projects, however, have been unable to match population growth. As a consequence, many traditional living compounds—originally designed centuries ago to house the families of officials during the Qing dynasty—have been repaired or renovated and subdivided to provide quarters for three or four families per compound. Each family in a compound faces a public courtyard and shares a common front gate with other families.

Many factories in the eastern and southern outskirts of the city have erected apartment buildings to house workers as a way to reduce commuting traffic in the metropolis. These workers' residences constitute independent communities and are located so that they are easily accessible from the place of work yet are far enough away to minimize noise and smoke. Satellite towns also have been developed in the rural counties in an effort to disperse population and industries from the central city. Industries have been established in rural areas in order to absorb surplus labourers and to supplement farmers' incomes.

ARCHITECTURE

Beijing's heritage of Chinese architectural achievement is exemplified by both private housing and public buildings. The country's political and cultural centre for more than 700 years, Beijing has more buildings of historical and architectural significance than any other contemporary city in China. As the whole city was laid out in a rectangular street pattern symmetrically arranged around the palace compound, almost every dwelling in the city is also rectangular in form, with the four sides squarely facing the cardinal directions.

TRADITIONAL DWELLINGS

Most houses in the inner city were designed as residences for former officials and their families, and almost every dwelling compound is surrounded by high walls, with an open courtyard in the centre flanked by houses on the eastern, western, and northern sides, usually one story high. The former residences of high-ranking officials were composed of two or three compounds, interconnected along a north-south axis.

Just inside the high wooden sill of the front gate of a large compound was a brick screen wall, a structure that was supposed to shut off intruding evil spirits as well as prevent curious passersby from looking inside. Beyond the screen was the outer, or service, courtyard, flanked by houses to the east and west. In former days, these structures held the compound's kitchen and the living quarters for the gatekeeper, servants, and any visiting guests and relatives. A red-painted gate led through the north wall of the outer court into the main part of the house, built around three sides of the main courtyard; the courtyard, usually shaded by a large tree, was the centre of the family's life. All the windows looked inward to it, and a double door opened into it from each of the three wings. The windows extended from about three feet (one m) above the ground up to the deep, overhanging eaves. As they faced south, the rooms in the main building got the maximum possible sunshine in winter, and the eaves provided a pleasant shade in summer, when the sun was high. The wing at the northern end of the court was intended for the head of the family and his wife. It was divided into three compartments: the central one was the living or community room, and the smaller rooms at either side were the bedroom and study. The rooms facing east and west—three on each side of the court—were for married sons and their families. This was the basic plan of all the old houses in Beijing. Larger families built an extra courtyard behind the main house, because the traditional ideal was that all the existing generations should live together. Since 1949, however, a great many of the old-style houses have been adapted for use by several families.

PUBLIC AND COMMERCIAL BUILDINGS

While the style and architecture of private dwelling units are uniform throughout the city, the public buildings and temples are characterized by a variety of designs and structures. Since 1949 many new government and municipal buildings, combining both traditional and Western architecture, have been constructed.

The Imperial Palaces (Palace Museum) of the Forbidden City, with their golden roofs, white marble balustrades, and red pillars, stand in the heart of Beijing and are surrounded by a moat and walls with a tower on each of the four corners. The palaces, collectively designated a World Heritage site in 1987, consist of outer throne halls and an inner court. North of the three tunnel gates that form the Wu (Meridian) Gate (the southern entrance to the Forbidden City), a great courtyard lies beyond five marble bridges. Farther north is the massive, double-tiered Hall of Supreme Harmony (Taihedian), once the throne hall. A marble terrace rises above the marble balustrades that surround it, upon which stand beautiful ancient bronzes in the shapes of caldrons, cranes, turtles, compasses, and ancient measuring instruments. The Hall of Supreme Harmony is the largest wooden structure in China.

North of it, beyond another courtyard, is the Hall of Central (or Complete) Harmony (Zhonghedian), where the emperor paused to rest before going into the Hall of Supreme Harmony. Beyond the Hall of Central Harmony is the last hall, the Hall of Preserving Harmony (Baohedian), after which comes the Inner Court (Neiting). The Inner Court was used as the emperor's personal apartment. It contains three large halls, the Palace of Heavenly Purity (Qianqinggong), the Hall of Union (Jiaotaidian), and the Palace of Earthly Tranquillity (Kunninggong).

The Palace of Heavenly Purity is divided into three parts. The central part was used for family feasts and family

Palace of Heavenly Purity (Qianqinggong), Imperial City, Beijing, China. © liquidlibrary/ Jupiterimages

audiences, audiences for foreign envoys, and funeral services; the eastern section was used for mourning rites and the western section for state business. The other two palaces, one behind the other, were imperial family residences. The three throne halls in the Outer Court and the three main halls in the Inner Court lie along the central axis. On either side are smaller palaces, with their own courtyards and auxiliary buildings. Behind the buildings, before the northern gate of the Imperial Palaces is reached, lies the Imperial Garden. Each palace, its courtyard and side halls, forms an architectural whole.

Among the historical and religious structures in Beijing, the Temple of Heaven (Tiantan), located south of the palace compound in the old outer city, is unique both for its unusual geometric layout and because it represents the supreme achievement of traditional Chinese architecture. In 1998 it, too, was designated a World Heritage site. A path, shaded by ancient cypresses, runs about 1,600 feet (490 m) from the western gate of the temple to a raised passage about 1,000 feet (300 m) long. This broad walk connects the two sets of main buildings in the temple enclosure. To the north lies the Hall of Prayer for Good Harvests (Qiniandian) and to the south the Imperial Vault of Heaven (Huangqiongyu) and the Circular Mound Altar (Huanqiutan), all three built along a straight line. Seen from the air, the wall of the enclosure to the south is square, while the one to the north is semicircular. This pattern symbolizes the traditional Chinese belief that heaven is round and Earth square.

The Hall of Prayer for Good Harvests, built in 1420 as a place of heaven worship for the emperors, is a lofty, cone-shaped structure with triple eaves, the top of which is crowned with a gilded ball. The base of the structure is a large, triple-tiered circular stone terrace. Each ring has balustrades of carved white marble, which gives the effect of lace when seen from a distance. The roof of the hall is deep blue, resembling the colour of the sky. The entire structure, 125 feet (38 m) high and about 100 feet (30 m) in diameter, is supported by twenty-eight massive wooden pillars. The four central columns, called the "dragon-well pillars," represent the four seasons. There are also two rings of twelve columns each, the inner ring symbolizing the twelve months and the outer ring the twelve divisions of day and night, according to a traditional system. The centre of the stone-paved floor is a round marble slab that has a design of a dragon and a phoenix—traditional imperial symbols. The hall has no walls, only partitions of open latticework doors.

The Imperial Vault of Heaven, first erected in 1530 and rebuilt in 1752, is a smaller structure some 65 feet (20 m) high and about 50 feet (15 m) in diameter. The circular building has no crossbeam, and the dome is supported by complicated span work. Its decorative paintings still retain their fresh original colours.

South of the enclosure lies the Circular Mound Altar, built in 1530 and rebuilt in 1749. The triple-tiered white stone terrace is enclosed by two sets of walls that are square outside and round inside; thus, the whole structure forms an elaborate and integrated geometric pattern. The inner terrace is 16 feet (5 m) above the ground and about 100 feet (30 m) in diameter; the middle terrace is about 165 feet (50 m) across and the lowest terrace some 230 feet (70 m) across. Each terrace is encircled by nine rings of stones. Both the Imperial Vault of Heaven and the Circular Mound Altar were erected to portray the geometric structure of heaven, as conceived by the architects of the Ming dynasty. After 1949 the whole enclosure of the Temple of Heaven was repaired; it is now a public park.

To the east of Tiananmen Square within the People's Cultural Park is the Working People's Cultural Palace (formerly the Temple of the Imperial Ancestors), where the tablets of the emperors were displayed. The temple, like the Imperial Palaces in style, was built in three stonework tiers, each with double eaves. On either side are two rows of verandas surrounding a vast courtyard large enough to hold 10,000 people. Exhibitions of economic and cultural achievements, both of China and of other countries, are frequently mounted in the three halls. Lectures by leading scholars on science, literature, and the arts are also held there.

Perhaps the most imposing structure constructed in the heart of the city since 1949 is the Great Hall of the People. The Great Hall is located on the western side of Tiananmen Square and is an immense building with tall columns of gray marble set on red marble bases of floral design. It has a flat roof with a golden-yellow tile cornice over green eaves shaped like lotus petals. The base of the building is of pink granite, and its walls are apricot yellow. Its frontage is 1,100 feet (335 m) long—about the equivalent of two city blocks—and its floor space is some 1,850,000 square feet (172,000 square m). Inside the building, the ceiling and walls are rounded. The grand auditorium, with seating for 10,000, is where the National People's Congress holds its sessions; the focus of the room's lighting system is a red star in the ceiling surrounded by golden sunflower petals. Other components are a banquet hall that can hold 5,000 people, huge lobbies, and scores of meeting rooms and offices for the standing committee of the congress.

The extraordinary pace of building construction in Beijing since the mid-1990s produced a vast number of new and gleaming medium- and high-rise buildings. Many of these structures are commercial—banks, corporate headquarters, hotels, and apartment blocks—and, although most of them are fairly conventional towers, a number of them were built with innovative and eye-catching designs. Of note are the

China Central Television (CCTV) Building, designed by Dutch architect Rem Koolhaas; the National Centre for the Performing Arts complex, featuring an enormous egg-shaped dome that houses an opera house, a concert hall, and a theatre; the new National Stadium, built for the Olympics and popularly called the "Bird's Nest" because of its irregular interlocking outer framework; and the National Aquatics Center, also built for the Olympics and distinctive because its exterior resembles a giant cube of water.

PEOPLE

During the period when Beijing was the dynastic capital (mid-13th to the early 20th century), the city's population slowly fluctuated between 700,000 and 1,200,000. However, from the fall of the Qing in 1912 to the establishment of the People's Republic in 1949, the population rose sharply, from about 725,000 to more than 2,000,000. At least three factors contributed to this growth: the rural disorder on the North China Plain during that period, when much of China was ruled by warlords, caused large numbers of migrants to seek the relative safety of Beijing; the Japanese invasion of Manchuria in 1931 made Beijing a shelter for thousands of refugees from the northeastern provinces; and the civil war between the communists and Nationalists brought still more refugees to the city.

Beijing's population grew even more dramatically after the city resumed its role as the national capital. In 1949 Beijing was the fourth largest city in the country, and within a decade it had become the second largest, as thousands of government workers poured into the new capital, rapid industrial development in the municipality attracted thousands more workers, and the municipal boundary was extended in 1959 to include large rural areas. Growth slowed considerably in the 1960s and 1970s, initially because of the disruptions caused by the Great Leap Forward (1958–60) and the Cultural Revolution (1966–76) and later by the national government's rigorous birth-control policies. The city's population grew rapidly again in the early 1980s as China greatly expanded and globalized its economy, and Beijing again became a magnet for labour. Large numbers of these new migrants were farmers from China's rural hinterland. They tended to concentrate in residential communities with others from their home areas and to return to those areas for periods of time each year.

The overwhelming majority of Beijing's population is Han (Chinese). Hui (Chinese Muslims), Manchus, and Mongols constitute the largest minority groups. Beijing residents speak a dialect of Mandarin Chinese that forms the basis of Modern Standard Chinese (Guoyu), or *putonghua* ("common language"), which is commonly taught throughout the country.

Beijing has a small but growing community of foreign residents—mainly diplomats, journalists, business associates, teachers, and students—who have become an important aspect of the city's life. Government authorities have made great efforts to meet the special demands of foreigners. Foreigners generally send their children to Western-style schools (although the children are free to attend Chinese schools) and tend to live in the newer, more luxurious high-rise apartment buildings.

Since the late 1970s, efforts have been made to restore the ancient temples, churches, and seminaries of various religions (most prominently Buddhism) that were damaged during the Cultural Revolution. Some of the restored structures are again being used by worshipers, monks, and pupils.

ECONOMY

Beijing has a thriving and highly diversified economy, based largely on manufacturing, but also agriculture. However, the service sector has grown dramatically, especially with the significant increase in tourism to the city and surrounding region.

AGRICULTURE

Although Beijing has been the capital of China for hundreds of years, it is distant from the country's traditional key economic area, the productive Yangtze River valley. In the past the task of feeding the large urban population in Beijing was facilitated by transporting grain from the south through the Grand Canal or by sea. Since the first decade of the 20th century, railways have played an important role in transporting food supplies to the capital. The city, however, has become self-sufficient in secondary food supplies, such as vegetables, fruits, fish, and poultry, and in a number of construction materials. The expansion of municipal boundaries in the late 1950s was partially aimed at this goal, and the municipality has succeeded in maintaining an adequate supply of vegetables and fruits. Agricultural reforms since the early 1980s have given individual households greater freedom over what they can produce, providing the city with a greater and more varied food supply.

Thus, Beijing is unlike most of the world's major cities in that agriculture forms a significant part of its economy. Vegetables are grown in a belt that encircles the city and is covered by a network of irrigation channels supplied by reservoirs. However, the channels do not provide a sufficient amount of water and are supplemented by a large number of wells that draw considerable amounts of groundwater. Although these irrigation measures have made intensive farming possible in an area prone to frequent droughts, they have also caused the water table to drop significantly. Vegetables are grown in the winter months in hothouses. The municipality's farm belt is also one of the most highly mechanized agricultural areas in China. The government has encouraged farmers to expand cultivation of fruit and nut trees into large areas that were once wasteland north and east of the city. These orchards have reduced considerably the wind erosion of the soil. The hill areas produce large quantities of pears, persimmons, apples, chestnuts, and walnuts, and the reclaimed lowlands are covered with vineyards and peach orchards. Part of the Beijing fruit crop is exported to other Chinese cities.

INDUSTRY

One of the main differences between the imperial capital of former times and present-day Beijing is that the old city was a centre of consumption rather than production, receiving supplies of all kinds from other parts of the country. Since 1949, however, Beijing has emerged as one of China's most industrial cities, although a concern for the adverse effects of industrialization on the city's environment has, over time, curtailed expansion.

Among the large industrial establishments is the Shoudu Iron and Steel Works, located about 9 miles (14 km) west of the old city. The Shoudu plant was originally started in 1920 and made use of local deposits of iron ore and anthracite coal in the Western Hills; after the Japanese occupation of 1937, it produced a meagre amount of pig iron. In the late 1950s the plant was enlarged and grew to become one of the largest steel plants in China. Its high-quality steel production supplies such area industries as machine building, electrical engineering, and precision-instrument manufacturing. A number of smaller finishing mills have also been established to produce such items as cold-drawn bearing steel and flat spring steel for tractor and automobile accessories, seamless tubes for high-pressure boilers, and magnetic steel for machine tools and electronic devices. Beijing is also an important centre of machinery manufacturing. Most of these factories were built in the suburbs east and south of the central city, where extensive tracts of level land were available and where the prevailing northwest winds would carry industrial pollutants away from the densely populated areas. Beijing became one of China's major textile centres after cotton cultivation was expanded in Hebei province in the 1950s and 1960s; manufactured products include cotton and woolen fabrics and piece goods, serge, and several types of synthetic fabric. Beijing's petrochemical industry expanded rapidly when an oil pipeline was constructed in the mid-1970s to link the city with the Daqing oil field in the Northeast. The petrochemical industry is dominated by the Beijing Yanshan Petrochemical Company, Ltd., located southwest of the city.

Beijing, being a former imperial capital, was home to a variety of arts and handicraft industries that were intimately connected with court life and imperial needs. Much of the traditional handicraft industry has been reorganized and reequipped. Notable handicraft products produced in the city include rugs and carpets, porcelain and chinaware, jade and ivory sculpture, brassware, enamelware and lacquerware, lace, and embroidery.

COMMERCE AND FINANCE

The service sector, comprising both private companies and government agencies, has expanded significantly as the city's and region's industry and population have grown.

China has a nationwide and centralized system of banking, in which the state-owned People's Bank of China plays a key role. This institution, with its head office in the inner city, functions as the agent of the national treasury. All funds of state-owned industrial enterprises, as well as of national, provincial, and local governments, the People's Liberation Army, and the network of cooperatives, are deposited with the People's Bank. The bank uses the working capital at its disposal for the operations of the economy and the government and thus acts as cashier of the national budget and of a large part of the country's financial operations. Through its branch offices and savings account centres, the bank also serves the daily financial needs of people in the city and in the suburbs. Working in cooperation with the People's Bank and under its supervision are four other banking institutions: the People's Construction Bank, which finances and supervises all basic construction projects, such as new railways; the Agricultural Bank of China, which specializes in agricultural investment; the Bank of Commerce and Industry, which provides loans to industry; and the Bank of China, which handles most international trade and foreign exchange. In addition, several foreign-owned banks have representative offices in the city to assist foreign nationals doing business in China.

Because Beijing was originally an administrative centre with its layout focused on the Imperial City, it never developed the compact central business district that characterizes most of the world's major cities. Historically, the market areas of the city were situated at two street intersections to the southwest and southeast of the Imperial Palaces, and the Dongdan and Xidan neighbourhoods are still major shopping centres. Since 1990, however, Western-style shopping malls and department stores have been established in various parts of the city. One of the most vibrant retail areas is along Wangfujing Dajie, which is a few streets east of the Imperial Palaces. As part of a 20-year development plan for this shopping street that began in 1991, it was transformed in 1999 when storefronts were beautified and all vehicular traffic (except city buses) was banned. The Beijing Department Store, a state-owned enterprise, still operates there, but it has been overtaken by gigantic, privately owned shopping malls such as in Xindong'an Plaza, an enormous complex at the southern end of Wangfujing Dajie. Similar shopping districts can be found in other parts of the city, such as Jianguomenwai and Sanlitun, both of which are near diplomatic compounds. The Friendship Store still operates in Jianguomenwai. In the past, when it was the only place to buy Western goods, it mainly served foreign residents and visitors, although some Chinese—usually cadres or those who received foreign-currency remittances from relatives living abroad—were allowed to shop there. Although anyone can shop there now, it has been passed up by the newer commercial establishments.

Traditional markets that still serve a local function are spread around the city. They have a long history, and each has developed its own reputation for special commodities and services. The restored Liulichang Market is located just south of the Heping Gate in the old outer city. The

Agricultural produce market in northern Beijing, China. Zhang Shuyuan/Xinhua News Agency

area acquired its name (which means "Glazier's Shop") from the colourful glazed tiles that were made there during the Ming dynasty, but in the latter part of the 18th century it gradually became a market for curios, antiques, old books, paintings, works of ancient Chinese calligraphers, and paper. It is still a centre for traditional art shops. Dazhanlan, just west of Qianmen Dajie, was rebuilt in 1998, and many of the Qing period shops there were restored. Specialities sold there include silk, tea, herbal medicines, food, and clothing. The Panjiayuan neighbourhood, just east of Longtan Park—once popular with China's national minorities but now largely patronized by Han Chinese—sells numerous items, including a wide variety of metallic ornaments. Yabao Lu, near the Chaoyang Gate site, is popular with Russians and eastern Europeans. Most of the Chinese shop owners there speak at least some Russian, signs are written in Cyrillic, Russian food is served, and most of the products are Russian-made clothing and daily-use items. Yating Hua Niao Shichang, just outside the southeastern corner of Tiantan Park, is a market for flowers and birds and also sells kittens and Pekinese dogs, kites, and other items.

TOURISM

Tourism has become increasingly important to the Beijing economy. Visitors are drawn not only to the historical and cultural attractions of the central city but also to many sites in the rural areas of the municipality. Probably the best-known outlying attraction is the Great Wall, which can be viewed from designated places northwest and northeast of Beijing. Other popular locales include the tombs of the Ming emperors to the north of the city and the archaeological site at Zhoukoudian to the southwest, where prehistoric hominin fossils have been found. The tourist services provided in Beijing have improved steadily, especially since the 1980s. Many hotels and hostels have been built, and old ones have been renovated and enlarged to meet the growing demand. A major construction campaign was undertaken after the city was awarded the 2008 Summer Olympics. In addition to building facilities needed for the Games, the program has enhanced the city's infrastructure, notably public transportation.

TRANSPORTATION

Beijing is the railroad centre of China, forming the terminus of a number of lines in the national rail network. The major lines radiating from Beijing provide connections with Shenyang (Liaoning province), Shanghai municipality, Guangzhou (Guangdong province), Hong Kong, Baotou (Inner Mongolia Autonomous Region), and Taiyuan (Shanxi province). The local lines serve outlying districts within the metropolitan area. Beijing is linked by direct express with several other large urban centres,

Great Wall of China, near Beijing. © Digital Vision/Getty Images

and it is also connected by express train with Moscow; P'yŏngyang, North Korea; and Ulaanbaatar, Mongolia.

In addition to the rail system, Beijing has an increasingly dense network of highways radiating from the city, which are used by a growing number of privately owned automobiles as well as by trucks and long-distance bus services. Beijing's road-transportation system, though improving rapidly, is still inadequate and cannot keep up with the rapid increase in vehicles; traffic congestion is often severe. The once-ubiquitous bicycles and three-wheeled cycle carts continue to

be heavily used for short-distance transportation, despite the proliferation of automobiles. Ox- or horse-drawn carts are still sometimes used to transport goods in the rural areas of the municipality.

Beijing is also a centre of China's civil air transportation. The nation's major domestic air routes link Beijing to regional centres at Shanghai, Guangzhou, and Ürümqi (Urumchi; Uygur Autonomous Region of Xinjiang) as well as to other major cities, and international air carriers provide service to major overseas destinations. In 1999 a new terminal building was completed at Beijing's

Capital Airport, located northeast of the central city.

Beijing's intracity commuting services are provided primarily by a network of local and express buses. Taxis of various types are also an important means of getting around in the central city. In 1969 a subway line—the first in China—was opened, running east-west through the central area; this line was supplemented by a separate loop line opened in 1987 that follows the old limits of the inner city beneath the Second Ring Road. A third line, which extends eastward from the original east-west line, was completed in 1999 and connected to the existing line in 2000. The city's first north-south line (part of which is above ground) opened in 2007, and three more lines opened in 2008 in time for the Olympic Games: a line shaped like an inverted L situated farther out from and parallel to the eastern and northern sides of the central loop line; a northward spur from this new line to the main venues for the Games; and a line northeast from the inner loop to the airport. In addition, a system of light-rail lines extending into suburban areas has been under construction since 2000; the first portion of it, constituting a large semicircular loop through the northern suburbs, was fully operational by 2003.

ADMINISTRATION AND SOCIETY

Beijing is one of the four centrally administered (i.e., province-level) *shi* (municipalities) in China (the others being Chongqing, Shanghai, and Tianjin), and there is no governmental tier between it and the central government.

GOVERNMENT

The municipality is divided administratively into four urban and six suburban *chu* (districts) and eight *xian* (counties) in the peripheral areas. Beijing's municipal government is part of the hierarchical structure of the Chinese government that extends from the national organization, through the provincial apparatus, to the municipal and, ultimately, neighbourhood levels. Executive authority is formally assigned to the Beijing People's Government, the officers of which are elected by the Beijing Municipal People's Congress, the governmental decision-making body. The local government consists of a mayor, vice mayors, and numerous bureaus in charge of public security, the judicial system, and other civil, economic, social, and cultural affairs.

Paralleling this governmental structure is that of the Chinese Communist Party (CCP). As in all of China, real power in Beijing is held by the local CCP, but local government institutions perform various formal functions. The Beijing Municipal People's Congress follows the guidance of the local CCP in issuing administrative orders, collecting taxes, determining the budget, and implementing economic plans. Under the direction of the local CCP, a standing committee of the Municipal People's Congress recommends policy decisions and oversees the operation of municipal government.

The districts and townships, each a subdivision of the municipality, have their own mayors. Below the urban district level, police substations supervise the population, and subdistrict or neighbourhood offices handle civil affairs in their areas. Residents' committees help mediate disputes, conduct literacy campaigns, and promote sanitation, welfare, and family planning.

As the national capital, Beijing houses all the most important governmental and political institutions in the nation. These include the National People's Congress, constitutionally the supreme organ of state power; the State Council, the highest executive organ of the state; and the various administrative departments under the jurisdiction of the State Council, including the ministries and commissions in charge of foreign affairs, internal affairs, public security, national defense, justice, finance, culture, health, education, nationality affairs (concerning minority groups in the country), agriculture, and various branches in industry. Beijing is also the headquarters of the parallel CCP organizations—the National Party Congress, the Central Committee and Political Bureau (Politburo), and the Secretariat. In addition to the above, the highest organ of state concerned with the maintenance of law and order—the Supreme People's Court—is located in the capital.

MUNICIPAL SERVICES

Since the city of Beijing is not directly on a major river, most water for municipal consumption has to be brought into it from elsewhere. Some water, however, comes from shallow wells, which are common throughout much of the region. These provide some villages with drinking water and supply water for irrigation.

Since the earliest history of the city, local springs and rivers (such as the Chaobai and Yongding) have been used to supply water. Several springs rise at the foot of the Xiang (Fragrant) Hills and on Yuquan Hill, both to the northwest of the central city. During the Qing dynasty, these springs were tapped by means of an aqueduct that conveyed water for the city moat and for three lakes near the Imperial Palaces. The moat around the city walls became an important means of water distribution for the municipality.

Large-scale water-conservation projects were begun in the early 1950s to provide more water for the expanding urban area. Notable are the large Miyun Reservoir, northeast of the city, and the Guanting Reservoir, which impounds the Yongding in the northwestern mountains beyond the Great Wall. These regulate the flow of the rivers upstream, storing water at times of heavy discharge and then allowing it to be released when the rivers are low. Two lesser projects also have been carried out: the Ming Tombs Reservoir, whose waters feed a hydroelectric power station and irrigate the neighbouring countryside, and a hydro-electric power station near Moshikou, which uses the waters of the Yongding and feeds them back into the river through an ancient canal. The hydro-electric station at Guanting is the largest single source of electricity for the metropolitan area of Beijing.

Since the 1980s, however, demand for water typically has exceeded the supply available through the reservoir system. Shortages have been made up by pumping ever-larger quantities of groundwater, which has shrunk the underground reserves, lowered the water table, and reduced water quality. The municipal government has addressed this problem by enforcing water-saving measures and imposing quotas and has explored plans to carry water from the Yangtze to the city via a system of canals.

Beijing is rapidly developing a modern sewerage system. A system of underground pipes, eventually extending some 195 miles (315 km), was in operation as early as the 15th century, but it later became clogged and was abandoned. A new system was installed in the early 1950s, which, within the former walled area, was partly based on the rehabilitation of the old system. All open sewers, characteristic of many Chinese cities in the past, have been eliminated, and new pipes have been laid throughout the densely populated areas of the municipality. However, large quantities of industrial effluents and domestic sewage have continued to flow untreated into the municipality's waterways, causing varying levels of pollution.

Coal and charcoal were the traditional energy sources for domestic consumption, but, as Beijing's population soared in the late 20th century, the use of these fuels contributed to worsening air pollution in the city, especially during the winter. A major campaign has largely succeeded in replacing these with natural gas and liquefied petroleum gas, and this has reduced smoke emissions significantly. However, many of those gains have been offset by the tremendous increase in exhaust fumes from the city's large number of automobiles and trucks.

The headquarters of the Beijing General Post Office is located on the east side of Tiananmen Square. It provides more comprehensive services than do post offices in Western cities, handling mail, telegrams, long-distance telephone calls, and the distribution of newspapers and magazines. There are more than 350 branch offices and stations in the city and the suburbs, and the General Post Office also maintains several service centres at such busy traffic points as Qian Gate, Beijing Railway Station, and Wangfujing Dajie. The service centre on Wangfujing Dajie takes subscriptions to foreign newspapers and magazines and sells single issues.

Health

Chinese medical services employ both traditional Chinese and Western-style medical practices. Beijing has some of the best hospitals of both systems in the country.

The Peking Union Medical College Hospital, the first modern hospital in China, was founded in 1921 as an affiliate of the Peking Union Medical College (1906), which for years was supported by the China Medical Board of the Rockefeller Foundation. The hospital, the largest in Beijing, is a polyclinic facility combined with an institute of gynecology and pediatrics. Since 1949 many new hospitals, clinics, and sanitariums have been built. People's Friendship Hospital, a gift of the Soviet Union at the peak of Sino-Soviet friendship in the 1950s, is located in the Tianqiao neighbourhood in the outer city. Until 1960 the Soviet staff not only treated patients but also gave advanced training to Chinese medical personnel on the latest Soviet methods.

Many hospitals are clinical teaching facilities attached to medical schools. These include the Fuwai Hospital of the Chinese Academy of Medical Science, located outside the Fucheng Gate site; the First Affiliated Hospital of Beijing Medical University, just west of Bei Hai; and the Affiliated Hospital of the Research Institute of Chinese Medicine, located in the western suburban town of Xiaoyuan. The largest pediatrics facility in China, the Beijing Children's Hospital, is situated just outside the Fuxing Gate site and provides a homelike atmosphere for its young patients. A sanitarium in the traditional Chinese architectural style has been built in the hills west of the city for students from Asian

countries. The most specialized hospitals are located in the old residential districts of the city and include the Stomatological Hospital (dealing with diseases of the mouth), the Chest Surgery Hospital, the Hospital of Plastic Surgery, the Hospital of Chinese Medicine, and the Jisuidan Hospital, which focuses on traumatic (accident-related) and orthopedic surgery.

Chinese traditional medicine includes utilizing Chinese herb drugs and acupuncture treatments. Students in the Western-style medical schools are taught the essentials of Chinese traditional medicine, and Chinese traditional medical students are expected to be familiar with the essentials of Western medicine. Diagnoses of difficult cases are sometimes made only after consultations with specialists of both systems.

Each rural county in the municipality has a well-equipped hospital located in the county seat, but the basic unit for medical service there is the health centre in an individual work unit, which is equipped with complete clinical facilities. Medical teams of doctors, nurses, and public health personnel are sent frequently from the teaching centres in the city to the work units to assist in the general medical work and to keep local staff members in touch with the latest medical information and techniques.

EDUCATION

Before 1949 much of the education at all levels in Beijing was in the hands of private schools, many of which were run by missionaries. The government subsequently took steps to abolish private schools and put all education in the hands of the state. It was soon realized, however, that the government could not possibly provide enough schools for all who required education, and it reversed its policy to some degree. Local organizations, such as factories, business concerns, collectives, and communes, were encouraged to establish schools. The outbreak of the Cultural Revolution in 1966 stopped all regular classes in Beijing and throughout China, massively disrupting the education system; conditions did not return to pre-1966 levels until the late 1970s. A major part of the financing for elementary education is now met by sources other than the central government, though the government does provide considerable subsidies to schools in difficult financial situations.

There are now enough primary and secondary schools in Beijing to accommodate all students during their years of mandatory schooling, and essentially all primary-age children are enrolled. About three-fifths of the primary students move on to the secondary level, a rate that is considerably higher than the national average. For preschool-age children, kindergartens and nurseries are operated by factories, business enterprises, government offices, and city block cooperatives. Their main function is to permit mothers to work, and although some of these facilities are located in the residential neighbourhoods, many are on the premises of places of employment. In the suburban or rural areas, kindergartens are often temporarily set up during such events as the harvest.

There are three main types of secondary schools in Beijing: general middle schools, normal schools, and vocational and technical schools. The general middle school is of the academic type, with a curriculum designed to prepare students for college. The normal school trains teachers for primary schools. Vocational and technical schools, created to provide skilled workers in various fields, have developed rapidly in the city.

Since the end of the 19th century, when China began to adopt the Western educational system, Beijing has been the country's centre of higher education, a position that was only strengthened after 1949. The city is home to a number of the country's most prestigious institutions; many of them are located in the northwestern Haidian district, which is set against the background of Kunming Lake, the Summer Palace, and the Western Hills. Notable among these are Peking University and Tsinghua (Qinghua) University. Peking University (1898) is one of the largest comprehensive institutions in China. In 1953 the university moved from its old site at Shatan, in the inner city, to the present campus, which previously belonged to the missionary-established Yenching (Yanjing) University. The Haidian campus has been expanded considerably to the east and south. Tsinghua University (1911) is the country's most renowned facility for science and engineering. Other institutions of higher education within the academic district include the People's University of China, which offers ideological training; the Central Institute of Nationalities, enrolling students from the country's various autonomous regions and districts; Beijing Normal University, for teacher training; Beijing Medical University, which includes a large number of affiliated hospitals and institutes; the Central Conservatory of Music; and universities for specific disciplines, such as aeronautics and astronautics, geoscience, agriculture, and posts and telecommunications. The Chinese Academy of Sciences, the most prestigious research institute in the country, is also located in the district.

Beijing also has a number of foreign-language institutions where foreigners are employed to teach alongside their Chinese colleagues. The Beijing Foreign Studies University (1941), located in Haidian, is the largest facility of its kind in China. The Second Foreign Language Institute was set up in 1964 for training personnel for the New China News Agency. There are also a number of small institutes of language training run by the government and by the Beijing Radio Station. The Haidian Shangli Foreign Language School, at the secondary level, accepts children as young as eight years of age; most of them learn English, while others study French, German, Spanish, Arabic, Russian, and Japanese.

CULTURAL LIFE

Beijing has been the magnificent centre of traditional Chinese culture and learning since the Ming dynasty. Emperors and courtiers patronized the arts, especially painting and calligraphy. Precious objects from other parts of the empire and from foreign countries poured into the capital. This role of cultural centre was continued during the Qing dynasty, although the century of political and social upheaval that began in the mid-19th century led to an overall cultural decline in both Beijing and the whole of China. In the late 1940s, the Nationalists shipped a huge quantity of art treasures to Taiwan before their defeat by the communists. On the mainland, subsequently, many family heirlooms were purchased by the state for low prices and were then sold for export or used to enhance the country's museum holdings.

The communist government initially encouraged pursuit of traditional arts, crafts, and scholarship, but this policy abruptly ended with the onset of the Cultural Revolution. Art objects that were not deliberately smashed were confiscated, though some were returned to their former owners after 1980. Traditional Chinese scholarship was essentially put to an end, and many academics were sent to the countryside or imprisoned. Since that time the government has made a concerted effort to restore damaged treasures and to revive the work of traditional artists and scholars. Because much of this activity has taken place in Beijing, the capital has undergone something of a cultural renaissance and resumed its leading role in the country's cultural life.

The Arts

Traditional *jingxi* (Peking opera)—with its elaborate and stylized costumes and makeup, cacophonous music, and spectacular dance and acrobatic routines—has been revived, after an attempt during the Cultural Revolution to adapt the form to modern revolutionary themes. The opera has great appeal for older people but less for the young, who instead prefer movies, television, and popular music. A great variety of other performance styles are also found in Beijing. The city boasts a symphony orchestra, Western-style opera and ballet companies, and visits by foreign orchestras and performers. Concerts of traditional Chinese and Western-style popular music are common. A variety of plays by Chinese and Western dramatists are staged each year. Venues with high reputations include the Capital, Youth Art, and Tianqiao theatres. Also popular are acrobatic performances and musical revues.

Visual arts, notably calligraphy and Chinese-style painting, have had a major resurgence in the city, and there are many shops and galleries displaying these works as well as Western-style paintings. There is also a growing market for antiques, which can be found at Liulichang near the Qianmen site and the Panjiayuan area. In addition, the city has numerous well-stocked bookshops.

Museums and Libraries

The Palace Museum, housed in the main buildings of the former Imperial Palaces, contains the city's greatest collection of art treasures. Many of the halls are kept as they were in dynastic times, each constituting a museum in itself, and others are used to display some of the priceless treasures from China's past. Of special interest are its porcelains and enamels, works in embroidery and precious metals, and stone carvings and scrolls.

The Museum of Chinese History is located on the eastern side of Tiananmen Square. Thousands of historical relics and documents are on display, arranged chronologically from the appearance of the prehistoric Peking man some 770,000 years ago through the last 6,000 years of Chinese history. The Museum of the Chinese Revolution occupies a wing of the museum building and traces the country's history since the mid-19th century. The Capital Museum, in the northeast near the Anding Gate site and part of the Confucian Temple complex, has exhibits on the history of the city.

Notable art collections are housed in the China Art Gallery, just northeast of the Palace Museum, and in the Xu Beihong Museum in northwestern Beijing northeast of the Xizhi Gate site. Institutions devoted to the natural sciences include the Natural History

Museum, in the northwestern corner of Tiantan Park; the Geological Museum, just east of Bei Hai Park; and the Beijing Planetarium, west of the Xizhi Gate site and south of the Beijing Zoo. The former homes of such notable individuals as Song Qingling (Soong Ch'ing-ling), Guo Moruo, and Qi Baishi are preserved as museums.

The Beijing Library, which holds the collections of the National Library of China, is located in the southern Haidian district, just west of the zoo. The library inherited books and archives from the renowned Imperial Wenyuange library collection of the Qing dynasty that has existed for more than 500 years and that, in turn, included books and manuscripts from the library of the Southern Song dynasty, established some 700 years ago. Also in its holdings are other collections from imperial libraries of the Qing dynasty, imperial colleges, and private owners. Among them are rare copies of ancient manuscripts and books of five dynastic periods from the Song to the Qing, including a vast number of manuscript volumes on different subjects, copies of Buddhist sutras dating to the 6th century, old maps, diagrams, and rubbings from ancient inscriptions on metal and stone. In addition, it possesses the *Yongledadian* ("Great Canon of the Yongle Era") of the Ming dynasty and a copy of the *Sikuquanshu* ("Complete Library of the Four Branches of Literature"), dating from the Qing dynasty. In the late 1980s, most of the National Library's collections were moved to the present site from the Beijing Library's original building just west of Bei Hai; that facility is now a branch of the main library. Other important libraries include the Peking University Library, containing a large collection of documents on local history, and the Capital Library.

RECREATION

As the residence of the imperial families through several dynastic periods, Beijing is well known for its numerous parks and playgrounds; few cities in China have as large a proportion of land within the central city allocated for recreational uses. Among the most popular are Zhongshan Park, Bei Hai Park, Jingshan Park, the Summer Palace, and the Beijing Zoo.

Zhongshan (Sun Yat-sen) Park lies just southwest of the Forbidden City; it is the most centrally located park in Beijing and encloses the former Altar of Earth and Harvests (Shejitan), where the emperors made offerings to the gods of earth and agriculture. The altar consists of a square terrace in the centre of the park. To the north of the altar is the Hall of Worship (Baidian), now the Sun Yat-sen Memorial Hall, which dates to the early 15th century; its simple form, masterly design, and sturdy woodwork bear the characteristic marks of early Ming architecture. The Water Pavilion, built out over a lotus pond on three sides to provide a gathering place for scholars and poets, is in the southwest corner of the park. Scattered among the park's pools, goldfish enclosures, rocky hills, weeping willows, pines, cypresses, bamboos, and flowers are pavilions, kiosks, and towers, which are typical of Chinese garden landscape.

Bei Hai Park lies to the northwest of the Forbidden City. It covers some 170 acres (70 hectares), half of which is water. The focus is on Bei Hai, the most northerly of the three lakes—called "seas" (*hai*)—that lie roughly north-south along the western side of the Imperial City. Pleasure grounds, lakes, and buildings have existed on the site for eight centuries. As the lakes were deepened and dredged, the excavated earth was used to build hillocks and islands of great beauty. In 1651 a Qing emperor built the White Pagoda, the most striking landmark in the park, on the top of a hill. Bei Hai is crowded with rowboats in summer, and it freezes over to become a natural ice-skating rink in winter.

Jingshan (Prospect Hill) Park, also known as Meishan (Coal Hill) Park, is a man-made hill, more than a mile (1.6 km) in circumference, located north of the Forbidden City. The hill, offering a spectacular panorama of Beijing from its summit, has five ridges, with a pavilion on each. The hill was the scene of a historical tragedy when in 1644, at the end of the Ming dynasty, the defeated Ming emperor hanged himself on a locust tree on its east slope. In the northern part of the park is Beijing Children's Palace, with recreational, athletic, and educational facilities.

The Summer Palace—called Yiheyuan in Chinese ("Garden of Good Health and Harmony")—lies close to the Western Hills, about 6 miles (10 km) northwest of the Xizhi Gate site. Designated a World Heritage site in 1998, it is the largest park on the outskirts of Beijing and is noted for its artful landscaping, which provides an inimitable blend of woods, water, hills, and architecture. The park covers more than 800 acres (325 hectares), four-fifths of which consists of Kunming Lake and the remainder man-made hillocks. More than 100 buildings—halls, towers, pavilions, bridges, and pagodas—lie scattered throughout the park; a marble boat, two stories high and some 80 feet (24 m) long, is located at the northwestern corner of the lake and is one of the major attractions. A series of richly painted covered promenades connect the buildings and courts along the shore of the lake. Just east of the Summer Palace lie the ruins of the Former Summer Palace (Yuanmingyuan), destroyed in 1860 by foreign troops.

To the west of the Summer Palace, on the eastern edge of the Western Hills, is Xiangshan (Fragrant Hills) Park. Long an imperial retreat, it is now a popular area of rugged woodlands and scenic vistas. Nearby to the north is the Azure Clouds Temple (Biyunsi) complex, which contains a hall where the body of Nationalist leader Sun Yat-sen was kept after he died until he could be buried in Nanjing. Farther to the northeast is the Beijing Botanical Garden, within which is a

China's national Olympic Stadium, built in Beijing in 2008, is called the Bird's Nest.
Shutterstock.com

temple containing a large statue of a reclining Buddha.

The Beijing Zoo is located in the western part of the city. The zoo was established toward the end of the 19th century and was named the "Garden of Ten Thousand Animals" (Wanshengyuan). Its collection is actually about half that size, but it is the largest zoo in the country, with animals from all parts of China and the world; one of the zoo's most popular attractions is its collection of giant pandas.

Beijing hosted the 1990 Asian Games, and many of the facilities for that event were constructed in the far northern part of the city. That area became the nucleus of Olympic Green, the main location of competition venues and athlete housing for the 2008 Summer Games. Notable among its facilities is the new 80,000-seat National Stadium. In addition, existing facilities, such as the 72,000-seat Beijing Workers' Stadium on the city's east side and the Capital Indoor Stadium near the zoo, are being renovated for use during the Olympics.

Beijing's citizens have increasing access to leisure time. Movies remain a common form of entertainment, but teahouses, discos, nightclubs, and karaoke bars are popular among young people. Television viewing has also grown significantly, as have the number of Beijing households with colour television sets.

The Chinese love of good food is world-renowned, and Beijing is one of China's culinary showcases. All the regional cuisines are represented among the city's hundreds of restaurants, although the Beijing style predominates. The dish best known to foreigners is Peking duck, which is the specialty of several establishments. Among other local delicacies are various traditional snack foods (e.g., mutton shish kabobs, meat-filled pancakes, and rice balls) that can be enjoyed in restaurants or purchased from street vendors.

HISTORY

With but few interruptions, Beijing has been the capital of China for some eight centuries, and in number of years as the imperial capital it is exceeded only by Xi'an (Chang'an) in Shaanxi province and Luoyang in Henan province. In prehistoric times the area around Beijing was inhabited by some of the earliest-known human beings. Between 1918 and 1939, the fossil remains of Peking man (formerly *Sinanthropus pekinensis*; now known as *Homo erectus pekinensis*), who lived about 770,000 to 230,000 years ago, and of Upper Cave man, who lived about 50,000 years ago, were unearthed at the village of Zhoukoudian in Beijing municipality about 30 miles (50 km) southwest of the central city.

THE EARLY EMPIRES

While long periods in Beijing's early history remain blank, it is certain that some 3,000 years ago Neolithic communities settled on or near the site where the city now stands. During the Zhanguo (Warring States) period (475–256 BCE) of the Zhou dynasty (1046–256 BCE), one of the powerful feudal states—the kingdom of Yan—established its capital, named Ji, near the present city of Beijing; this was the first capital city to be associated with the site. The city was destroyed by the troops of Shihuangdi, founder of the Qin dynasty (221–207 BCE).

During the Qin, the Yan capital was incorporated into one of the thirty-six prefectures then established throughout the country. A new town was built during the succeeding Han dynasty (206 BCE–220 CE) that was also known as Yan. Throughout the Han period and the turbulent centuries that followed, however, the place remained a provincial town, most of the time caught in the fateful struggle between the Han Chinese to the south and the nomadic Xiongnu, or Huns, to the north.

From 220–280 CE, during the period of Sanguo (Three Kingdoms), the city was again called Yan. The northern border of ancient China ran close to the present city of Beijing, and northern nomadic tribes frequently broke in from across the border. Thus, the area that was to become Beijing emerged as an important strategic centre as well as a local political centre.

For nearly three centuries (from the end of the Xi [Western] Jin dynasty in 316/317 to the beginning of the Sui dynasty in 581), the northern territory, including the site where Beijing now stands, was largely under the control of invading nomads. It was not recovered by the Han people until the Tang dynasty (618–907), when it became known as Youzhou. By the middle of the Tang, measures were being taken to prevent the nomadic Tangut tribes of Tibet, such as the Xi Xia, and the Khitans (a Turco-Mongolian people from Manchuria) from raiding the borderlands and the local capital. The position of Youzhou consequently became increasingly important. A number of states emerged in North China after the fall of the Tang dynasty. One of these was established by the Khitans, who, after destroying Youzhou, founded the Liao kingdom (907–1125) and built one of their capitals on approximately the same site, calling it Nanjing ("Southern Capital") to distinguish it from other capitals in their Manchurian homeland. The Liao capital was bounded by a square wall with a perimeter of almost 14 miles (23 km) and a height of some 32 feet (10 m). It had eight gates and enclosed a fine imperial palace in the centre, which indicated the strong influence of Chinese city planning.

In the mid-12th century, when the Juchen, a Tungus people from eastern Manchuria, defeated the Liao and established the state of Jin, the Liao capital was rebuilt as the new Jin capital and renamed Zhongdu ("Central Capital"). Zhongdu under the rule of the Juchen was constructed on a larger scale, with splendidly decorated palaces and halls.

Between 1211 and 1215, the Mongols—under the leadership of Genghis Khan, one of the great conquerors of history and founder of the Yuan, or Mongol, dynasty (1206–1368)—repeatedly attacked and finally took the city from the Jin. In the battle the palaces of Zhongdu were set on fire and blazed for more than a month. When all China fell to the Mongol hordes, Kublai Khan (1215–94), a successor to Genghis Khan, determined to build a new capital at Beijing, abandoning the old city of Karakorum in Mongolia. In 1272 he named the new capital Dadu ("Great Capital"); under the Mongols it became for the first time the political centre of all China.

Dadu was larger than any of its forerunners and was rebuilt slightly northeast of the old site. The square of the outer wall measured about 18 miles (29 km) in length and enclosed an area of more than 20 square miles (50 square km). The city walls were built with pounded earth, and once each year labourers were called in to repair them with mud. The Imperial Palace, which was approximately to the west of the modern-day one, was situated in the southern half of the capital city. The chief palace architect at the time was an Arab, appointed by Kublai. The city of Dadu exemplified the imposing and variegated architecture of the Mongol period. The square walls and the twelve gates were all modeled on the Chinese plan, but the inner chambers and living quarters were often in the styles found in Mongolia or Central Asia. It was at that time that a waterway, the Tonghui Canal, was dug and connected to the Grand Canal, so that boats transporting tribute rice from the provinces south of the Yangtze could sail into one of the new lakes inside the city. Dadu, which had magnificent imperial palaces and treasures drawn from every corner of the country, was the scene of stupendous feasts given by the khan (ruler) on state occasions. These characteristics and the well-organized post stages on the roads leading to the city astounded the Venetian traveler Marco Polo, who visited Dadu in the 1280s.

The Ming and Qing Dynasties

In the mid-14th century, Zhu Yuanzhang headed a peasant revolt that overthrew the Mongol dynasty and, as the Hongwu emperor, established the Ming dynasty (1368–1644). He moved the capital to Jinling in Jiangsu province and called it Nanjing; Dadu was renamed Beiping ("Northern Peace") and was placed under his son's rule. On Zhu's death (1398) the throne passed to his grandson in Nanjing, but his son, Zhu Di (also called the Yongle emperor), who ruled Beiping, usurped the throne. In consequence, in 1403 the city was renamed Beijing ("Northern Capital"), and in 1421 it was officially made the capital city of the Ming dynasty.

Beijing in the Ming period grew on a grander scale than under the Mongols. The former city walls and the extant moats, palaces, and temples were built mainly in the 15th century. The old city of Dadu, including its palaces, was largely demolished. The new city was situated farther southwest, which left the northern part of the Mongol city derelict while at the same time slicing off one gate from the east and west walls, respectively. In 1553 an outer wall was begun, to include the increasing number of inhabitants living outside the city. However, when the entire construction was subsequently found to be too costly, the plan was abandoned on the completion of the south wall; thus emerged the present shape of the old city. Unlike the city wall of pounded earth of Mongol times, the walls of the Ming city were faced with a layer of bricks to prevent weathering.

In 1644 Beijing was taken over by Li Zicheng, who led a peasant uprising against the Ming regime. Li's army held it for only 40 days, for the Manchus were simultaneously preparing an incursion south of the Great Wall, and—thanks to the complicity of a Ming general who opened the gate in the wall at Shanhai Pass—they swept down on the city. Beijing fell intact and in the same year was declared the Manchu capital by Shunzhi, the first emperor of the Qing dynasty (1644–1911/12).

Beijing remained superficially the same throughout Qing times. The city plan was unaltered, though many palaces, temples, and pavilions were added outside the walls to the west, notably those that comprised the Old Summer Palace, built in the 17th century, and the Summer Palace, built in the late 19th century. The Old Summer Palace was completely destroyed by fire in 1860 by British and French troops during the Second Opium (or "Arrow") War (1856–60). In the same year, as a result of the treaties of Tianjin in 1858, a permanent British embassy was established in the city, and a legation quarter, situated to the southeast of the palace ground, was reserved for British and other embassies. The legation quarter was besieged for nearly two months by the Boxer rebels in 1900.

THE MODERN CITY

After the revolution of 1911, Beijing remained the political centre of the Republic of China until 1928, when the Nationalists moved the capital to Nanjing; Beijing was again called Beiping. The city came under increasing pressure from the Japanese, who established the puppet state of Manchukuo in Manchuria in 1931. In July 1937 fighting broke out between Chinese and Japanese troops near the Marco Polo Bridge, southwest of the city; Beiping was subsequently occupied by the Japanese until 1945. After World War II the city reverted to the Nationalists, who were defeated by the communists in the ensuing civil war. In 1949, with the establishment of the People's Republic of China, Beijing (with its old name restored) was chosen as the capital of the new regime. The city soon regained its position as the leading political, financial, and cultural centre of China.

In the 1950s and 1960s, urban-development projects widened the streets and established the functional districts that characterize the modern city, but political campaigns culminating in the Cultural Revolution (1966–76) delayed many of these projects. Beginning with the economic reforms of the early 1980s, the pace of change accelerated, and Beijing changed dramatically. New shopping centres and residential buildings appeared throughout the city, and high-tech industrial parks were established, especially in the suburbs. One such area, dubbed "Silicon Valley," was developed with government backing between Peking and Tsinghua universities. Another striking change, noticeable particularly in the newer shopping centres, has been the emergence of a consumption-oriented middle class similar to that found in Hong Kong, Singapore, Seoul (South Korea), and other Asian cities undergoing rapid economic growth. At the same time, Beijing, like other modern cities, has faced growing problems with air pollution, traffic congestion, and overcrowding.

Beijing's hosting of the 2008 Summer Olympic Games was a major impetus in modern construction projects, including sports venues and housing, as well as improving the city's transportation infrastructure. In addition to construction related to the Olympics, a host of other office and residential high-rise buildings mushroomed throughout Beijing, vastly transforming the look of the city.

CHAPTER 6

THE MAJOR CITIES OF NORTHERN CHINA

Although Beijing is by far the major city and cultural centre of northern China, the region, as one of the most populous in all of China, boasts several other large cities. Chief among these is the major industrial centre of Tianjin, the second largest urban complex in the region after Beijing and, like its larger neighbour, also a province-level municipality.

TIANJIN

Tianjin (Tientsin) is located adjacent to eastern Hebei province, at the northeastern extremity of the North China Plain. Central Tianjin (the municipality's urban core) lies about 75 miles (120 km) southeast of central Beijing and about 35 miles (55 km) inland from the Bo Hai (Gulf of Chihli), a shallow inlet of the Yellow Sea.

Tianjin ("Heavenly Ford") has been an important transportation and trading centre since the Yuan (Mongol) dynasty (1206–1368). It was famous as a cosmopolitan centre long before the arrival of the European trading community in the 19th century. Its maritime orientation and its role as the commercial gateway to Beijing fostered the growth of an ethnically diverse and commercially innovative population. The city is noted for its woven handicraft products, terra-cotta figurines, hand-painted woodblock prints, and extensive seafood cuisine.

The area of the Tianjin municipality is an estimated 4,540 square miles (11,760 square km). In 2006 the city had an estimated population of 5,332,140, while a 2007 estimate for the Tianjin municipality was 10,750,000.

LANDSCAPE

Central Tianjin is located where the Ziya and Yongding rivers and the north and south sections of the Grand Canal (Bei [North] Yunhe and Nan [South] Yunhe, respectively) meet before merging into the Hai River, which then flows eastward to the Bo Hai.

CITY SITE

The city stands at an elevation less than 15 feet (5 m) above sea level on a flat alluvial plain. Some low-lying areas east of the city are only about 6 feet (2 m) above sea level, and the majority of the built-up area is below 12 feet (4 m).

A couple rides an electric bicycle in the northern Chinese city of Tianjin. Frederic J. Brown/ AFP/Getty Images

The municipality borders on the Bo Hai to the east, Beijing municipality to the northwest, and Hebei province to the north, west, and south. Between 1958 and 1967, Tianjin was a subprovince-level city, which served as the capital of Hebei province. Its jurisdiction extended over the built-up urban core and eastward along the Hai River to include the port at Tanggu. At that time, Tianjin city was administratively separate from the Tianjin Special District, which had its seat at Yangliuqing, southwest of central Tianjin.

In 1967 Tianjin municipality was made a first-order, province-level administrative unit, and the area under its immediate control was expanded to include counties (*xian*) formerly under the special district. The city simultaneously became the special district seat but lost its position as provincial capital. Tianjin municipality is now composed of fifteen urban and suburban districts (*qu*) and three rural counties. The municipality is under direct jurisdiction of the central government in Beijing.

CLIMATE

Despite Tianjin's proximity to the sea, it has a distinctly continental climate with sharp daily and seasonal temperature fluctuations. It is subject to the full effects of the cool, dry Siberian high-pressure system during the winter (October to April), while in the summer (May to September) the high pressure system over the North Pacific Ocean brings hot and rainy weather. Winter precipitation is minimal, and the air is dry, with relative humidity averaging 50 percent. In summer, moist rain-bearing southerly winds prevail, and the average relative humidity exceeds 70 percent. The average annual temperature is 56 °F (13 °C), with a January average of 25 °F (–4 °C) and a July average of 81 °F (27 °C). Severe winter storms are common, but typhoons seldom occur.

DRAINAGE

The Hai River was long subject to frequent flooding. As the main outlet for the rivers of the North China Plain, it frequently became heavily silted during the spring and summer months; during the winter season its water level was often too low for navigation. Extensive water conservation began in 1897. The river was straightened to facilitate tidal action and to shorten the distance to the sea. Locks were constructed to regulate the flow of water from the river into its many canals, the river and the sand bars at its mouth were dredged, and silt-laden water was diverted into settling basins.

Since 1949 multipurpose flood-control, irrigation, and navigation improvements have been made. Construction of the Guanting Reservoir on the Yongding River near Beijing has helped alleviate flood damage within metropolitan Tianjin. New diversion channels have also been built to control the floodwaters of the Daqing and Ziya rivers to the southwest.

PLANT AND ANIMAL LIFE

The marshy lakes and floodplains around Tianjin abound with numerous varieties of reeds, bulrushes, and shrubs, such as tamarisk. Closer to the seashore, Russian thistle, glasswort, and artemisia can be found. Freshwater fish (including silver and golden carp) are raised in ponds and marshy depressions.

CITY LAYOUT

The urban core of Tianjin extends for about 7 miles (11 km) from east to west and about 9 miles (14 km) from north to south. Heping, the central district, is located on the west bank of the Hai River, just below the large bend of the Hai. It is the main commercial and financial centre, and its two main streets of Heping Lu (Heping Road) and Jiefang Lu have large department stores, restaurants, and hotels.

The old "Chinese" city is situated immediately to the northwest of Heping Lu. It is bounded by the four wide boulevards of Dong, Xi, Bei, and Nan Malu that follow the course of the old rectangular wall. The street pattern in the old city is winding and irregular, in contrast to the more regular gridded pattern in the foreign-developed zones to the south and west. The old city is subdivided into four smaller sections, each of which in traditional times had special marketing and commercial functions.

North and west of the old city and continuing across the Nan Yunhe is the mixed residential and industrial Hongqiao district. It extends to the confluence of the Ziya River, Bei Yunhe, and Nan Yunhe. The northern outskirts contain workers' housing developments, and the area is best known for its domestic handicrafts.

The southern and western neighbourhoods of Hexi and the Nankai district were built on what (until it was drained) was marshy, low-lying land. Nankai district in the west and southwest is given primarily to residential and recreational use. Nankai is also a major university and research centre. Hexi neighbourhood to the south is now one of the major industrial districts, with scores of large- and medium-sized enterprises located there.

The eastern districts of Hebei and Hedong, east of the Hai River, centre on industry and transportation. Hebei has a few technical and vocational educational institutions in addition to its residential quarters, while Hedong is mainly industrial.

HOUSING AND ARCHITECTURE

The provision of housing for Tianjin's workforce has been a major concern of the municipal authorities. The emphasis since 1949 has been on suburban development, although residential areas in the urban core have also been rehabilitated. Major new residential and commercial construction was undertaken in the early 1980s in central Tianjin as a result of damage incurred in the Tangshan earthquake of 1976. Before World War II many of the suburban residential areas were built on marshy, poorly drained land subject to flooding, and sanitary conditions were especially bad. Most of the modern complexes have been constructed near industrial zones on the outskirts of the city.

Many of the large commercial and administrative buildings in the central city were built by foreign concessionaires. They are typical of European and Japanese colonial architecture of the 1920s and 1930s, with buildings of contrasting architectural styles juxtaposed helter-skelter, without any plan. Some of the public buildings dating from the 1950s were built in imitation of the Soviet monolithic style, and housing complexes are usually standard multistory rectangular blocks. More recent commercial and residential construction follows modern design, with individual balconies and multicoloured facades.

PEOPLE

The majority of the population lives in the central city, where densities are probably in the range of 15,000 to 75,000 persons per square mile (6,000 to 29,000 persons per square km). Before 1949 most people were engaged in commercial or service occupations. Since then the occupational structure of the city has changed, and about half the population is employed by industry and only about one-fifth in commerce. The remainder are employed primarily in public services.

Ethnic minorities constitute a small proportion of the population; the largest groups are Hui (Chinese Muslims), Koreans, Manchus, and Mongolians. Most of them live in the central city in areas that have special historical associations. The largest single community of Hui is in the northern suburb of Tianmucun.

ECONOMY

Tianjin is one of the most important manufacturing centres in the country, and it is the leading port of northern China.

INDUSTRY

Since 1949 heavy industry has been developed and the existing industrial base consolidated for greater productivity. Major activities are the production of heavy machinery, chemicals, and iron and steel as well as shipbuilding and repair. The heavy-machine-building plant in the city is one of China's largest manufacturers of mining equipment. Other products include machinery for textile mills and agriculture, machine tools, electrical equipment, bicycles, tractors, elevators, precision instruments, trucks, and watches.

The chemical complexes at Dagu, Tanggu, and Hangu (north of Tanggu on the rail line to Tangshan) produce agricultural fertilizers and pesticides, pharmaceuticals, chemicals and petrochemical products, plastics, artificial fibres, dyestuffs, and paints. The Yongli (now Tianjin) alkali products plant at Tanggu accounts for much of China's total output of purified soda, some of which is exported to Japan.

Textiles are the chief light industry. Other such products include processed foods, hides, rubber goods, and paper. Since the 1980s dozens of the world's top companies have invested in Tianjin, following the city's adoption of economic reform policies.

FINANCE

Financial services include branches of the Bank of China, the Agricultural Bank of China, The People's Insurance Company of China, and other banks. Retail and wholesale trade is managed by commerce bureaus that are responsible to municipal and provincial authorities. Pricing and personnel matters are managed locally, while the distribution of commodities, long-range planning, and high-level financial management are handled by provincial-level bureaus responsible to Beijing. A municipality-run General Trade Corporation formed in the early 1980s helps coordinate and improve the efficiency of domestic and foreign trade by assuming functions previously performed by central government agencies.

TRANSPORTATION

Tianjin is North China's leading transportation centre. The Jing-Hu (former Jin-Pu) railway runs south from Beijing to Shanghai via Jinan, Shandong province, and Xuzhou, Jiangsu province. The Jing-Shan railway runs north from Beijing through Tianjin and Shanhaiguan on the Hebei-Liaoning border to Shenyang, Liaoning province. The lines are served in Tianjin by three railway stations, classification yards, and extensive maintenance and repair facilities.

Heavily traversed inland waterways radiate to the south and southwest along the Grand Canal and Ziya and Daqing rivers; they connect the city with Baoding, Cangzhou, and Hengshui in southern Hebei province. The Jing-Jin-Tang expressway from Beijing through Tianjin to Tanggu is the main all-weather freight road to the sea. Other main roads extend southward along the Jing-Hu railway into Shandong province, westward to Shanxi province, and northward to Qinhuangdao, northeastern Hebei, and the Northeast (formerly Manchuria).

Intraurban and suburban transportation is extensive. Several dozen intraurban trolley, electric trolleybus, and motor bus routes connect the city's light railway and subway stations and serve the near suburban districts. The first 7.5 miles (12 km) of Central Tianjin's subway line was in operation by mid-1983 and had been extended to 16 miles (26 km) by 2006; three more lines are under construction. In addition, about two dozen long-distance motor bus routes connect the urban core with more distant rural areas.

Tianjin is the main collection point and transshipment centre in North China for goods manufactured for export and is the chief port of entry for heavy machinery and other capital-intensive imports. Much of China's total foreign trade by value is handled through Tianjin's outport and fishing port of Tanggu.

ADMINISTRATION AND SOCIETY

Tianjin municipality, like Beijing, Chongqing, and Shanghai, is under direct control of the Chinese central government.

GOVERNMENT

The Tianjin People's Congress is the city's chief administrative body. Its predecessor, the Municipal Revolutionary Committee, was established in 1967 during the Cultural Revolution (1966–76). Prior to 1967, responsibility for the management of the city's affairs was shared by a number of bureaus under both party and governmental control.

The Tianjin Municipal Planning Commission plays a key role in managing industry and commerce. It controls the supply and distribution of industrial raw materials, sets production levels, allocates funds for capital investments, determines manpower needs, supervises product research and development, and coordinates transportation, public works, and environmental policy.

PUBLIC UTILITIES

Major public works projects since 1949 helped alleviate chronic flood damage and improved Tianjin's water supply and sewage disposal systems. Marshy, low-lying lands were drained and converted to agricultural and recreational use, new roads were constructed, and streetlights were installed.

The supply of fresh water has always been a problem because of the city's location near the sea at low elevation. Severe water shortages developed in the early 1980s because of industrialization, population growth, and drought that cut off the water supply from Miyun Reservoir northeast of Beijing. These shortages were temporarily alleviated by diverting water from the Huang He (Yellow River), to the south, but construction was also undertaken to divert water from the Luan River, to the northeast. The project began in late 1981, and its initial stage was completed in late 1983. Swampy lowlands to the southwest have been drained; one of the most extensive was converted into the large recreational area of the Shuishang Gongyuan (Park on the Water).

Electricity is generated by thermal power plants (fueled with coal), and the city is connected by a power grid with Beijing and Tangshan, Hebei province.

HEALTH

Tianjin has many Western-style and Chinese hospitals, with separate facilities for children, workers, and members of ethnic minorities. During the Cultural Revolution, Tianjin also developed one of China's earliest and most effective urban planned birth programs. In 1971 an Office of Planned Births was established by the municipality and was granted status and authority equal to the Department of Public Health.

EDUCATION

Before the Cultural Revolution, about one-sixth of Tianjin's population was enrolled in educational institutions. During the late 1960s and early 1970s, enrollments fell. By the late 1970s, to support China's modernization program, considerable investments had been made to improve and expand scientific and technical institutions, especially those supportive of petrochemical, iron and steel, and marine services and engineering industries. The general universities of Nankai and Tianjin are located in Nankai district, on the southwestern periphery of the city. Other higher educational institutions include the Polytechnic University, the University of Technology, the Academy of Fine Arts, the Conservatory of Music, a medical university, a normal university (which provides training for teachers), and other colleges and universities. Work-study schools attached to factories supplement formal educational programs.

CULTURAL LIFE

The city has several museums and a major library. The Fine Arts Museum is noted for its collection of Yuan, Ming, and Qing dynasty paintings, while the City Museum of History and the Tianjin Science Hall have more contemporary displays. The Tianjin Library is the municipality's largest library.

Special exhibits are held at the Industrial Exhibition Hall and the National Minorities' Cultural Palace, and the People's Festival Hall is used for operas, plays, and concerts. The largest movie house is the Peace Cinema. There is also an astronomical observatory.

There are several dozen parks and recreation centres. Victory Park and the Children's Park are in the centre of the city, and the Xigu, Nankai, People's, Changhong, Shuishang, and Beining parks are in the urbanized area. Recreational clubs have been built for industrial workers, and there are several stadiums—including the Tianjin Olympic Center Stadium, built to host preliminary football (soccer) matches during the 2008 Olympic Games.

HISTORY

The marshy, poorly drained area surrounding contemporary Tianjin was sparsely populated until the Song dynasty (960–1126), when the settlement of Sanchakou was built on the west bank of the Hai River. The original settlement was later joined by the larger town of Zhigu, built on high ground at the confluence of the Ziya and Hai rivers. Zhigu grew rapidly as a port and commercial centre, and it became the chief storage, transfer, and distribution point for grain and other foodstuffs from central and southern China.

In recognition of the importance of Zhigu (then called Haijin) as a shipping centre, the Yuan (Mongol) government (1206–1368) established offices for the regulation of navigation and customs and expanded the town's warehouse and harbour facilities. The city also became a major salt producer when salterns were constructed along the Hai River.

EVOLUTION OF THE CITY

The development of modern Tianjin began during the Ming dynasty (1368–1644), when the national capital was shifted from Nanjing to Beijing. In 1404 the settlement became a garrison town and was named Tianjinwei ("Defense of the Heavenly Ford"). A large military base was built and a rectangular wall constructed at that time. The town prospered as it became the main gateway to Beijing, and its population was swelled by immigrants from Shandong, Jiangsu, and Fujian provinces.

By the beginning of the Qing (Manchu) dynasty (1644–1911/12), Tianjin had become the leading economic centre of North China because of its location at the northern terminus of the Grand Canal (Da Yunhe). As better inland waterway connections were established, there was a steady increase in the city's volume of trade. Members of the first Dutch diplomatic mission to China in the mid-17th century commented favourably on the well-constructed 25-foot-high (7.6 m) high wall surrounding the city and noted the many temples and the large commercial and marketing area.

Economic prosperity declined temporarily during the mid-19th century when the European nations trading with China unremittingly pressed their demands for commercial and diplomatic privileges. The treaties of Tianjin (Tientsin), during the second Opium War (1856–60) against China, were signed by the British, French, and Chinese in 1858. They authorized, among other provisions, the establishment of British and French concessions in Tianjin. Between 1895 and 1902, concessions were given to Japan, Germany, Russia, Austria-Hungary, Italy, and Belgium. Hostilities were resumed in Tianjin in 1860, and the city was shelled by the British and French; the Convention of Beijing then declared Tianjin an open trading port. Ten years later, a violent expression of Chinese antiforeign feeling erupted in the city when the French Catholic orphanage and cathedral were attacked. In 1900, renewed antiforeign demonstrations led to the shelling and occupation of the city by Allied (Western) forces and the destruction of the old city wall.

By the end of the 19th century, Tianjin had grown to more than 200,000 people, with about half the population residing within the old "Chinese" city. Living conditions for the Chinese were in sharp contrast to those in the spacious, well-tended European quarters that were distributed to the southeast and along the riverbanks.

Tianjin became an important ocean shipping centre by 1900. The Huang He shifted its course, and the Grand Canal became silted up in the early 1850s, thereby restricting inland waterway traffic through the city, and shipping operations were shifted eastward along the banks of the Hai River. Facilities were also built at Dagu and Tanggu at the mouth of the Hai.

THE CONTEMPORARY CITY

Under the Republic of China (1911–49), Tianjin became a special municipality (*shi*) under the direct administration of the Nationalist government. In 1935 the Japanese attempted to extend their control over North China by establishing an autonomous area in eastern Hebei province, which was to be administered by Japanese military authorities in Tianjin. A year later they presented demands to the Chinese authorities that were designed to weaken Chinese control over the area. With the onset of the Sino-Japanese War (1937–45), the Japanese occupied Tianjin, and in 1939 they blockaded the British and French concessions in response to anti-Japanese demonstrations.

During the civil war period in China (1945–49), Tianjin remained under Nationalist control until mid-January 1949, when the city was captured by the communists. Since then, Tianjin's growth as a trading and manufacturing centre has been responsive to internal development needs. Despite its proximity to Beijing, the city retains a distinctive character, attributable to its functional and utilitarian origins. Tianjin was one of several cities outside Beijing selected to host events for the 2008 Olympic Games.

OTHER IMPORTANT NORTHERN CHINESE CITIES

Outside of the large urban complex of Beijing and Tianjin lie many other large, historically and economically important northern Chinese cities. These range from Harbin in the northeast—in what formerly was the heart of Manchuria—to Xi'an toward the centre of the country, the former capital of several historic dynasties.

HARBIN

The city of Harbin is the capital of Heilongjiang province, northeastern China. It is located on the south bank of the Sungari (Songhua) River. The site of the city is generally level to undulating, except near the river itself, where low bluffs lead down to the floodplain in places; low-lying areas are subject to flooding. The climate is cool, with cold winters that last four or five months; subzero overnight low temperatures are common and can reach -40 °F (-40 °C). A 2006 population estimate of the city was 3,075,326, while a 2007 estimate for the urban agglomeration was 3,621,000.

HISTORY

The city owes its origin to the construction of the Chinese Eastern Railway through Manchuria (Northeast China) by the Russians at the end of the 19th and the beginning of the 20th century. Before 1896 it was a small fishing village named Alejin ("Honour"; Harbin is derived from it) by the Juchen, the ancestors of the Manchu. Thereafter it became the construction centre for the railway, which by 1904 linked the Trans-Siberian Railroad from a point east of Lake Baikal in Siberia with the Russian port of Vladivostok on the Sea of Japan (East Sea). Harbin was a base for Russian military operations in Manchuria during the Russo-Japanese War (1904–05), and after the war it was temporarily under joint Chinese-Japanese administration. It became a haven for refugees from Russia after the Revolution of 1917 and for a time had the largest Russian population of any city outside the Soviet Union.

During the period of the Japanese-dominated state of Manchukuo (1932–45), Harbin was subordinated to Binjiang (Pinkiang) province. It was the site of a notorious Japanese biological warfare laboratory during World War II. Soviet

St. Sophia Russian Orthodox church, built in 1907, as seen through the arches of a nearby building, in the Daoliqu area, Harbin, Heilongjiang province, northeast China. Harbin has many examples of Russian-inspired architecture. Christian Kober/Robert Harding World Imagery/Getty Images

troops occupied the city in 1945, and a year later Chinese communist forces took it over and from it directed their conquest of Northeast China. Harbin's population subsequently grew rapidly, and the city became the region's chief industrial base.

THE CONTEMPORARY CITY

The city layout is centred on the main railway station, which is located somewhat away from the river. The rail lines radiating from it roughly form three districts: Daoli ("Inner Way"; northwest), Daowai ("Outer Way"; southeast), and Nangang ("South Mound"; west). More recently, urban development has spread north of the river. Much of the foreign-developed city has disappeared since 1950, although the city has maintained a Russian air and its nickname "Eastern Moscow." However, many of the Russian-built or Russian-influenced buildings have been replaced with contemporary ferroconcrete structures; a notable exception is the well-preserved St. Sophia Church in the Daoli district, the largest and most spectacular of several Russian Orthodox churches in the city.

Among Harbin's traditional food-processing industries are soybean-processing plants, sugar refineries (for sugar beets), and flour mills. There are also factories producing tobacco products, leather goods, and soap. Industries developed after 1950 include the production of machine tools, mining and metallurgical equipment, agricultural equipment, plastics, and electric power turbines, boilers, and generators. The city is also the outfitting centre for the Daqing oil fields to the northwest. More recently, Harbin has established a high-technology development zone. The surrounding agricultural region supports the cultivation of wheat, soybeans, sugar beets, corn (maize), flax, and kaoliang (a grain sorghum). Harbin is a shipping centre for agricultural and forest products sent to the rest of China. A trade fair held annually in the city has greatly promoted Sino-Russian business relations, as well as trade between China and countries in eastern Europe.

Harbin is the regional centre of land, water, and air transportation. A dense network of highways connects Harbin to neighbouring cities, and expressways stretch northwest to the Daqing area and east to the Yaboli winter skiing centre. Major rail lines radiate from the city south to Dalian in Liaoning province, southeast to Vladivostok, and northwest to Chita in southern Siberia. Ships can navigate the Sungari to Khabarovsk, Russia, during the warmer, ice-free months. The Harbin Taiping Airport, southwest of the city, is one of the largest air facilities in the country.

The city is home to numerous institutions of higher education, including the prestigious Harbin Institute of Technology and several research institutes. An annual winter festival features an ice-carving competition and is a popular tourist draw. Harbin also hosts a music festival each summer.

SHENYANG

Shenyang (conventional Mukden) is the capital of Liaoning province and the largest city of northeastern China, a region formerly known as Manchuria. It is one of China's greatest industrial centres. Shenyang is situated in the southern portion of the vast Northeast (Manchurian) Plain just north of the Hun River, a major tributary of the Liao River. The city site is a flat, low-lying alluvial plain, although the land rises to the east toward the forested slopes of the Changbai Mountains. A 2006 population estimate of the city was 4,101,197, while a 2007 estimate for the urban agglomeration was 4,787,000.

HISTORY

Since the time of the Han dynasty (206 BCE–220 CE), the lower Liao River basin has been known as the Chinese Pale, an area settled chiefly by Han Chinese immigrants from what are now the provinces of Hebei and Shandong. During the Xi (Western) Han period, a county called Houcheng was set up in the area of what is now Shenyang. The rest of Manchuria was long under the control of various nomadic and tribal peoples, of whom the Manchu became the most important. In later centuries the Pale was at least symbolically set off from the rest of Manchuria by a discontinuous barrier known as the Willow Palisade.

By the 10th century, Shenyang, known as Shenzhou at the time, had become a major frontier settlement of the Khitan kingdom; its dominant peoples, also known as the Khitan, founded the Liao dynasty (907–1125). Southern Manchuria was conquered by the Jin, or Juchen, peoples by 1122–23 and a century later by the Mongols, who by about 1280 had completed their conquest of all of China and established the Yuan dynasty (1206–1368). It was under the Mongols that the name of Shenyang was first applied to the city. By 1368 the Ming dynasty had displaced the Mongols.

In the early 17th century, the Manchu controlled all of Manchuria, and Shenyang, renamed Mukden (Manchu: "Magnificent Metropolis"; the equivalent Chinese name is Shengjing), proved an admirable organizing base for the conquest of China. In 1644, when the Manchu supplanted the Ming on the imperial throne and established the Qing dynasty (1644–1911/12), they transferred their capital to the former Ming capital at Beijing. However, Mukden retained its prestige as the older capital of the reigning dynasty; the tomb complexes of earlier Manchu rulers—Zhao (Beiling, or North) Tomb and Fu (Dongling, or East) Tomb—are among the most famous monuments of China; in 2004 both were added to an existing UNESCO World Heritage site protecting Ming- and Qing-era tombs.

Thereafter the city grew steadily, especially in the last half of the 19th century, when Chinese immigration to Manchuria reached flood proportions. For a time during the Qing dynasty, the city was called by the name Fengtian (for Fengtian prefecture, set up there in 1657). In 1929 the city's name changed back to Shenyang.

In the period of struggle between Russia and Japan for dominance in Manchuria after 1895, Mukden was inevitably one of the key positions. From that time, when the Russians gained rights to build railroads in Manchuria, Mukden was a Russian stronghold; during the Russo-Japanese War (1904–05), it was the scene of the Battle of Mukden, which lasted from February 19 to March 10, 1905, when the city was finally taken by the Japanese. In the early 1920s, the Chinese warlord Zhang Zuolin, a protégé of the Japanese, participated with other warlords in the struggle for control of Beijing. The last warlord to resist the advance of the Nationalist Party (Kuomintang) Army against Beijing in 1928, he was killed in his retreat with his defeated troops. Three years later, on September 18, 1931, an explosion touched off the Mukden Incident. A bomb, alleged to be Chinese, went off on the railway track near Mukden (Shenyang) and gave the signal for a surprise Japanese attack on the Chinese Nationalist garrison and arsenal in the city. After protracted fighting, the Chinese forces were driven out of Manchuria. During the Japanese occupation (until 1945), the name of the city was once again changed to Fengtian.

The Soviet Union declared war on Japan in early August 1945 and soon took Shenyang. Several months after the surrender of Japan on August 14, 1945, Shenyang was occupied by Chinese Nationalist troops (March 1946). During the ensuing civil war (1946–49), Shenyang was taken by Chinese communist forces on October 30, 1948. The city then served as a base for the subsequent communist conquest of the entire Chinese mainland.

THE CONTEMPORARY CITY

Since 1950, Shenyang has continued as the hub of the heavy industrial complex of the southern region of China's Northeast. The chief manufactures are machinery and fabricated metals. Rolling stock, machine tools, wire and cables, cement, electrical equipment, chemicals and chemical fertilizers, and pharmaceuticals are produced there. The complex also includes oil-seed-processing plants, flour mills, paper plants, soap and leather factories, textile mills, and glass factories. The smelting of metals such as copper, zinc, lead, and manganese also is an important part of the industrial mix of the city.

Shenyang remains one of the leading railway centres in China. In addition, a network of roads converges on the city, with expressways (completed in the 1990s) leading north to Changchun (Jilin province) and south to Dalian at the end of the Liaodong Peninsula. Taoxian International Airport, some 12 miles (20 km) south of the city, opened in 1989 and completed the first portion of a major expansion of its facilities in 2001. Within the city, construction began in 2005 on a multiple-line subway system.

Shenyang has long functioned as the education and cultural centre of the Northeast. The city houses more than twenty universities and colleges, including Liaoning University, Northeastern China Technical University, Northeastern Engineering College, Northeastern Institute of Finance and Economics, and two medical colleges. Dozens of scientific research institutes are located in the city as well. In addition to theatres and libraries, there are also music conservatories and an institute of fine arts.

Tourism has become increasingly significant in Shenyang. The central attraction is the city's Qing-era Imperial Palace complex, which in 2004 was added to an existing World Heritage site encompassing the Forbidden City in Beijing. In addition to this and the two tomb complexes, there are also numerous other historical monuments and sites and religious buildings in and around the city. Notable among Shenyang's many museums is the Liaoning Province Museum (formerly the Northeast Museum). The city is also noted for its many parks and lush greenery. Shenyang played host to several of the preliminary football (soccer) matches during the 2008 Olympic Games.

DALIAN

Dalian (Russian: Dalny; conventional and Japanese: Dairen; formerly Lüda) is a city and port in southern Liaoning province, northeastern China. It consists of the formerly independent cities of Dalian and Lüshun, which were amalgamated (as Lüda) in 1950; in 1981 the name Dalian was restored, and Lüshun became a district of the city.

Situated at the southern tip of the Liaodong Peninsula, Dalian has a good deepwater harbour that is ice-free throughout the year. It has an extremely important strategic position, commanding the entrance to the Bo Hai (Gulf of Chihli) and maritime access to Tianjin. A 2006 population estimate of the city was 2,407,345. A 2007 estimate of the urban agglomeration numbered 3,167,000 people.

HISTORY

LÜSHUN (PORT ARTHUR)

Lüshun, historically known in the West as Port Arthur, long was an important port of entry for southern Manchuria (Northeast China). It was used as a staging post in the 2nd century BCE by Chinese colonists of the Han dynasty (206 BCE–220 CE) in northern Korea and by the Tang dynasty (618–907) in campaigns in the 7th century. During the 15th and 16th centuries, under the Ming dynasty (1368–1644), it was a fortified port for Chinese settlements in the Liaodong area. It was captured by the Manchus in 1633 and became the headquarters of a coastal defense unit under the Qing dynasty (1644–1911/12). In 1878 it was chosen as

Chinese-built passenger steamer in the harbour at Dalian, Liaoning province, China. Sally Reston—Photo Researchers

the chief base for the Beiyang ("North Ocean") fleet, China's first modern naval force, and was again fortified.

Captured by the Japanese in the Sino-Japanese War of 1894–95, it was leased to Japan under the Treaty of Shimonoseki, which ended the war. However, after the intervention of the Western powers that followed, it was returned to China. Russia, which was eager to acquire an ice-free port on the Pacific, occupied the Liaodong Peninsula in 1897 after the Germans had taken Jiaozhou (Kiaochow) on the southern side of the

Shandong Peninsula. In 1898 Russia acquired a lease of the Liaodong Peninsula and the right to build a railway connecting it with the Chinese Eastern Railway at Harbin in Heilongjiang province—and thus with the Trans-Siberian Railroad. The Russians constructed a heavily fortified naval base for their Pacific fleet at Port Arthur, began the development of a commercial port in nearby Dalny (Dalian), and in 1903 completed the rail link to Harbin. During the Russo-Japanese War of 1904–05, Port Arthur was one of the principal Japanese objectives. In May 1904 the Japanese army cut off the Liaodong Peninsula from the mainland and seized the port of Dalian (called Dairen by the Japanese). The Russian forces withdrew to their supposedly impregnable base at Port Arthur, but it too was eventually taken by the Japanese.

The Treaty of Portsmouth (1905), which concluded the war, transferred Port Arthur to Japan. The Japanese renamed it Ryojun and made it the administrative and military headquarters of their Kwantung Provincial Government (later transferred to Dairen) and of the Kwantung army command (later transferred to Mukden [now Shenyang]). The naval base was strengthened and became a base for Japanese military operations not only in Manchuria but also in northern China.

The Yalta Conference (February 1945) had envisioned the return of the Liaodong territory to the Soviet Union after World War II. Under a treaty of friendship and alliance concluded in Moscow later that year between China and the Soviet Union, it was agreed that the Port Arthur naval base was to be used jointly by the two countries for 30 years; the Soviet Union would be responsible for its defense and the Russians would have control of the peninsula, apart from the port of Dairen.

The last Soviet forces finally withdrew from Lüshun (Port Arthur) in 1955, after which it became an important Chinese naval base. Present-day Lüshun district is a fine city laid out on Western lines. It consists of two separate parts: the old (eastern) town, which contains the port installations, and the new (western) town, which is largely residential.

DALIAN (DAIREN)

After the Russians took the lease of the Liaodong Peninsula in 1898, they initially focused much of their attention on building up the existing Chinese naval base at Port Arthur as the headquarters of their Pacific fleet. However, they also selected a minor nearby fishing village on the peninsula called Qingniwa to be developed as a major commercial port, which they called Dalny. They laid out a spacious Western-style city, dredged the harbour, and constructed wharves, piers, and breakwaters. Only the first stage had been completed by the outbreak of the Russo-Japanese War in 1904. After control of the Liaodong Peninsula was transferred to Japan in 1905, the Japanese (who renamed the port Dairen) completed the Russian plan, developing a fine modern city and an efficient modern port. By 1931 Dairen was a major Chinese port, exceeded in its volume of trade only by Shanghai.

Under the Japanese, Dairen became a major industrial centre. A chemical industry was established, and the city also became a centre of cotton-textile production; development of the latter, however, was hampered by the competition of Jinzhou (a short distance north on the Liaodong Peninsula) and by the depressed state of the Japanese cotton industry in the 1930s. Since the completion of the South Manchurian Railway in 1901, it had been the railway's headquarters; huge railway workshops were built to supply locomotives, rolling stock, and equipment to the railway and also to other rail lines in Korea and northern China. In the 1930s the machine-building industry was further developed with the construction of a large plant belonging to the Dairen Machinery Company. In addition, shipbuilding became important during that decade, and by 1941 the port was producing ships of 8,000 tons.

THE CONTEMPORARY CITY

During the postwar Soviet occupation of the Liaodong Peninsula, the city was less seriously damaged and looted than most of the other Manchurian cities. The merger with neighbouring Lüshun to form Lüda (the name derived by combining the first characters of Lüshun and Dalian) greatly expanded the area and population of the city. Further expansion occurred in 1981, when the name Dalian was restored to the city; the former city of Dalian became Zhongshan district, and Lüshun (under the name Lüshunkou) and Jinzhou were among the other districts created.

The amalgamated city experienced rapid economic growth from 1950. In 1984 Dalian was designated one of China's "open" cities in the country's liberalizing economic policy of inviting foreign investment, which further spurred its development. It is now a prosperous industrial centre, noted for the variety and quality of its products. In addition to its importance as a base for shipbuilding and the construction of locomotives, Dalian is a thriving manufacturer of machines, electronics, chemicals, petroleum products, and textiles; high-technology enterprises have become increasingly important. An annual clothing fair hosted by the city attracts large crowds of customers from China and abroad.

Dalian port is among the largest in China, and the city is also a fishing and marine centre. A new harbour, built some 19 miles (31 km) east of the original harbour, is large enough to accommodate vessels of up to 100,000 tons displacement. The city has continued as an important rail terminus and is connected by expressway to Shenyang and from there to other regional centres. Its international airport has regular flights to cities in Japan and Korea, as well as to other major Chinese cities.

Dalian has a number of institutions of higher education, including Dalian Maritime University (1909) and Dalian University of Technology (1949). The city's thriving fisheries have contributed to the development of a distinctive seafood-based cuisine, and restaurants and catering services are plentiful. Dalian's beautiful beaches and its unique scenery, which harmoniously combine both Eastern and Western styles of architecture, have contributed to making the city one of China's major tourist destinations.

QINGDAO

Qingdao (conventional Tsingtao) is a major port city of eastern Shandong province, eastern China. It is located on the south coast of the Shandong Peninsula at the eastern entrance to Jiaozhou (Kiaochow) Bay, one of the best natural harbours in northern China. Although the bay sometimes freezes in severe winters, it is always open for large ships.

Originally a minor fishing village, Qingdao developed a large junk trade in Qing times (1644–1911/12), when a customs station was established there. With the establishment of the Beiyang ("North Ocean") fleet in the 1880s, the Chinese government realized the strategic importance of Qingdao (at the time known as Jiao'ao) and set up a minor naval station and building fortifications there. In 1897 the German government, which had ambitions in this area, dispatched a force to occupy Qingdao; the next year it forced the Chinese government to pay an indemnity and to grant Germany a 99-year lease on Jiaozhou Bay and the surrounding territory, together with railway and mining rights in Shandong. Qingdao was declared a free port in 1899, and modern port facilities were installed; a railway was built to Jinan in 1904. A modern European-style city was laid out, and a variety of industries were founded. A branch of the Imperial Maritime Customs was established to control the trade of the coast as far south as the new port of Lianyungang in Jiangsu province.

In 1914, when Japan declared war on Germany, its prime purpose was the capture of Qingdao; the port capitulated after a blockade in November. The Japanese continued to occupy the city until the Washington Conference of 1922, when the port was returned to China. During that period, however, the Japanese had built up a strong position, both in Qingdao itself and in the Shandong hinterland.

Qingdao came under the effective control of the Nationalist government in 1929 and became a special municipality. Port development continued, and its trade overtook that of its rival, Tianjin, about 1930, after which it continued to expand at the expense of Tianjin. The Japanese occupied the city in 1938 and held it until 1945. During that period, considerable industrial development occurred. By 1941 Qingdao had major modern cotton mills, locomotive and railway car works and repair facilities, engineering shops, and factories manufacturing rubber, matches, chemicals, and dyestuffs. Its brewing industry produces one of the best-known beers of China. Since 1949 Qingdao has developed as a major base for heavy industry, and by the 1970s textiles, formerly the preeminent manufacture, were rivaled by the growth of the engineering sector. In the late 1950s, a major primary iron and steel industry was established there. The city is the terminus of an east-west railway line and is linked by rail with the ports of Yantai and Weihai. It is also a large fishing port and is renowned for its parks and beaches.

In 1984 Qingdao was designated one of China's "open" cities as part of a new policy inviting foreign investment. Since then the city has undergone rapid economic development. The region's zone of economic and high-technology development is located on the western shore of Jiaozhou Bay, opposite central Qingdao. Major enterprises headquartered in the city, such as the Haier Group, have gained in reputation in the country as well as abroad. An expressway rimming Jiaozhou Bay is connected with the others that link the city west to Jinan and northeast to Yantai and Weihai. The city's international airport, about 15 miles (24 km) to the north, provides scheduled flights to destinations in northeastern Asia, as well as to various cities in the country.

Qingdao, an important cultural centre, is the seat of Ocean University of China (1924), Qingdao University (1993), and other institutions of higher education. The city is also one of China's main centres for the pursuit of marine science and technology. The beautiful beaches and unique style of city construction make Qingdao a popular tourist destination in the country. The city was selected to host the yachting events during the 2008 Olympic Games. The 2006 population estimate of the city was 2,654,340 people, while a 2007 estimate for the urban agglomeration was 2,866,000 residents.

JINAN

The city of Jinan (conventional Tsinan) is the capital of Shandong province, eastern China. It lies in the northern foothills of the Mount Tai massif, on the high ground just south of the Huang He (Yellow River), which provides the major route along the north side of the Shandong Hills. A 2006 estimation placed the city population at 2,726,435 people, and a 2007 estimate of the urban agglomeration was 2,798,000.

HISTORY

Well-watered from natural springs, the area around modern-day Jinan was settled in early times. From the 8th century BCE, it was the site of Lixia, a major city of the state of Qi, which flourished in the Zhou period (1046–256 BCE). Later, in the 2nd century BCE, the town became the seat of Licheng county in the commandery (district controlled by a commander) of Jinan. The Chinese name Jinan ("South of the Ji") came from the Ji River, which formerly flowed along what is now the lower course of the Huang He. The seat of the commandery was shifted to the present city at the beginning of the 4th century CE.

Jinan remained an important centre of administration, under various names, during the next two centuries and also became a major religious centre. Nearby Mount Tai, to the south, has long been one of China's greatest holy mountains, and from the 4th to the 7th century, many Buddhist cave temples were built in the hills south of Jinan. During the Sui (581–618) and Tang (618–907) periods, it remained a major city, under the names Qi prefecture and Jinan commandery. In

1116 it became Jinan superior prefecture, a title that it retained until 1911. Marco Polo, the Venetian traveler to China in the 13th century, visited it and described it under the name Chingli. When the Ming dynasty (1368–1644) created Shandong province, Jinan became its capital. In 1911 it became a county (under its old name Licheng), but in 1929 it was made a municipality, incorporating the old city, the modern commercial area developed after 1906, and the northern suburb of Likou.

Jinan's modern growth began in 1852, when the Huang He shifted its course to the old riverbed of the Ji, just north of the city. Although the Huang He was not a major waterway, this shift provided a link, used by small craft, with the Grand Canal and the waterways of northern Shandong and southern Hebei provinces. The Xiaoqing River, flowing from Jinan to the sea south of the Huang He, was also a route for small craft. In 1904 Jinan's growing importance as a transportation centre was increased when a German-built railway was completed from Qingdao (Tsingtao), which opened the city for foreign trade. In 1912 the north-south railway from Tianjin to Pukou was completed, with a rail junction at Jinan. The city rapidly became a major commercial and collecting centre for the rich agricultural region to the north. A great market for cotton, grain, peanuts (groundnuts), and tobacco, it developed a textile-manufacturing industry, flour mills, oil presses, and paper, cement, and match factories, thus becoming Shandong's second largest industrial centre after Qingdao.

When Japanese influence replaced the German presence in Shandong after World War I, a sizable Japanese colony became established in Jinan. In 1928, during the Northern Expedition of the Nationalist Party (Kuomintang) armies, the Japanese army intervened—ostensibly to protect their own nationals—in what became known as the Jinan (Tsinan) Incident. A sizable arsenal in the city made Jinan the object of contention between rival forces throughout the pre-World War II period. It was occupied by the Japanese from 1937 to 1945.

THE CONTEMPORARY CITY

Jinan was taken by Chinese communist forces in 1948. It was then rapidly developed both as a major administrative and industrial hub. The existing textile and flour-milling plants were expanded, and an important machine-building industry was developed. By the early 1970s, Jinan had become one of the main centres of China's automotive industry, manufacturing a wide range of heavy trucks and earth-moving machinery. In the late 1950s, Jinan became the site of a major iron and steel industry, producing pig iron, ingot steel, and finished steel. It also developed a large chemicals industry.

Jinan is the chief cultural centre in Shandong, with agricultural, medical, and engineering colleges and several universities—notably Shandong University (1901). There are also many relics of

Jinan's historical importance. The surrounding area has many well-known sites of natural beauty. Mount Tai, designated a UNESCO World Heritage site in 1987, is one of China's main tourist attractions.

TAIYUAN

The city of Taiyuan is the capital of Shanxi province, north-central China. One of the greatest industrial cities in the country, it lies on the Fen River in the northern portion of the river's fertile upper basin. Taiyuan commands the north-south route through Shanxi, as well as important natural lines of communication through the mountains to Hebei province in the east and, via Fenyang, to northern Shaanxi province in the west. A 2006 estimate of the city population was 2,162,014 people, while a 2007 estimate of the urban agglomeration was 2,913,000.

HISTORY

The city was originally the site of Jinyang, a strategic centre for the ancient states of Jin and Zhao. After the Qin conquest of Zhao and other states in 221 BCE, it became the seat of the commandery (district under the control of a commander) of Taiyuan, which continued during the Han dynasty (206 BCE–220 CE) and after. In the Dong (Eastern) Han period (25–220 CE), it became the capital of the province (*zhou*) of Bing. In the 6th century it was for a time a secondary capital of the Dong Wei and Bei (Northern) Qi states, growing into a large city and also becoming a centre of Buddhism. From that time until the middle of the Tang dynasty (618–907), the construction of the cave temples at Tianlong Mountain, southwest of the city, continued. The dynastic founder of the Tang began his conquest of the empire with Taiyuan as a base and using the support of its local aristocracy. It was periodically designated as the Tang's northern capital and grew into a heavily fortified military base.

The Song reunified China in 960, but Taiyuan continued to resist, and it was destroyed during fighting in 979. A new city was set up on the banks of the Fen in 982, a short distance from the old site. The city became a superior prefecture in 1059 and the administrative capital of Hedong (northern Shanxi) in 1107. It retained this function, with various changes in its name and status, until the end of the Yuan (Mongol) period (1368). At the beginning of the Ming dynasty (1368–1644), it was renamed Taiyuan Fu (*fu* meaning "chief town"); it retained this name until 1912. During the Ming and Qing (1644–1911/12) periods, it was the capital of Shanxi. Under the republic (established in 1911), its name was changed to Yangqu, which it retained until 1927.

In 1907 the importance of Taiyuan was increased by the construction of a rail link to Shijiazhuang (in Hebei province), on the Beijing-to-Wuhan trunk line. Soon thereafter Taiyuan suffered a serious economic crisis. In the 19th century, the merchants and local banks of Shanxi had been of national importance, but the rise of modern banks and the Taiping Rebellion (1850–64) led to the rapid decline of this system—with disastrous effects upon Shanxi and its capital.

After 1911 Shanxi remained under a powerful warlord, Yan Xishan, who retained control from 1913 to 1948. Taiyuan flourished as the centre of his comparatively progressive province, and the city experienced extensive industrial development. It was linked by rail both to the far southwest of Shanxi and to Datong in the north.

After the Japanese invasion in 1937, Taiyuan's industries developed still further. In 1945 the Japanese army in Shanxi surrendered to Yan Xishan, and it continued to fight for him until 1948. Eventually, the Chinese communist armies captured Taiyuan, but only after a destructive battle.

THE CONTEMPORARY CITY

Since 1949 Taiyuan's industrial growth has been dramatic, and the city proper now covers an area a dozen times larger than what it was in the 1950s. Several industrial districts have been established on the outskirts of the city (particularly in the northern and western suburbs), including those with iron- and steel-making works, engineering and machine-making shops, and large chemical-industrial complexes. Local coal production is considerable and has

been used in large thermal-power-generating operations, although this activity also has produced heavy air pollution in the region. Taiyuan's role as a regional communication centre has been further strengthened by the construction of rail lines to Henan and southern Hebei provinces and expressways east to Shijiazhuang, north to Datong, and south to Yuncheng. The city's airport provides domestic and international flight services to a variety of destinations.

In addition to its position as an industrial giant, Taiyuan is also a centre of education and research, particularly in technology and applied science. Notable schools include Shanxi University (1902) and Taiyuan University of Technology, which originally was part of Shanxi University and became a separate institution in 1953. Jin Memorial Hall, a famous ancient structure 15 miles (25 km) southwest of the city, is under state protection and is a popular tourist attraction.

KAIFENG

Kaifeng is a major city of northern Henan province, north-central China. It was the provincial capital until 1954, when the capital was transferred to Zhengzhou, about 45 miles (75 km) to the west. Kaifeng is situated in the southern section of the North China Plain, to the south of the Huang He (Yellow River), in an area where a number of streams flow southeastward into the Huai River. A 2006 estimate of the city population was

591,303 people, while a 2007 estimate for the urban agglomeration was 872,000.

HISTORY

In the 4th century BCE (when it was known as Daliang), it became the capital of the Wei state. The Wei also built the first of many canals there—the Langtang Canal—joining the Huang He to the Qin River, flowing into northern Shandong province. At the end of the 3rd century BCE, however, Daliang was laid waste by the forces of the Qin dynasty (221–207 BCE), and, until the 5th century CE, Kaifeng was only a medium-sized market town. At the end of the 5th century, under the Bei (Northern) Wei dynasty (386–534/535), it became the seat of a commandery, and, in the 6th century, it became Bianzhou prefecture.

Under this name it again became one of the major commercial cities in China. Its new importance was based on the Grand Canal, built in 607–608 under the Sui dynasty (581–618), which linked the Huang He with the Huai River, the Yangtze River (Chang Jiang), and the region of what is now Hangzhou in Zhejiang province. All the revenues of southern China and a vast volume of private shipping passed through the city, which was the junction for another canal to western Shandong province built in the early 7th century. Its importance grew steadily throughout the Tang period (618–907), and after 756 it was made the seat of a military governor whose province was named Xuanwu. After 907 the various

regional regimes that successively controlled the North China Plain made it their eastern capital. When the Song (960–1126) reestablished a unified empire, they too made it their capital. The city was a cosmopolitan centre from early times and for many centuries had the only well-documented Jewish community in China.

Kaifeng was the first Chinese capital to be primarily a commercial metropolis. Under the Song it was probably the most important centre of trade in East Asia. The focus of four major canals, it drew in vast revenues in grain and commodities and also became the focus of an industrial complex, which included an iron industry. The city itself was surrounded by a triple ring of walls. It seems probable that in the 11th century Kaifeng's population was between about 600,000 and 700,000.

The city suffered a severe blow when the Juchen (Jin) overran North China, captured Kaifeng in 1127, and sacked it. Under Jin rule after 1127, Kaifeng was first known as Bianjing and later as the dynasty's southern capital. It remained an important administrative centre, as it also was under the Mongol occupation, which lasted from 1234 until 1368, during which period it was the seat of the provincial administration of Henan. After 1127 the outer walls were abandoned, and the city was confined to the old inner city of early Song times. In 1368 the first emperor of the Ming dynasty (1368–1644) made Kaifeng the capital of Henan province and built a new set of walls. Kaifeng suffered another disaster in 1642 when rebel forces diverted the Huang He to flood the city, which was temporarily abandoned and was not restored until 1662.

Although Kaifeng remained an important regional administrative centre throughout Ming and Qing (1644–1911/12) times, its commercial importance never regained its 11th-century peak. After the construction under the Mongols and the Ming of a new Grand Canal farther east, it was no longer a key point on the main north-south traffic artery. Neglect of the river works on the Huang He, moreover, made the river less useful as a waterway, while flood disasters became frequent.

THE CONTEMPORARY CITY

Kaifeng's position suffered still further in the 20th century when both the main north-south rail lines bypassed it, though it is linked to them by the east-west Longhai Railway. It has, however, undergone considerable industrial expansion. In addition to the old, established handicraft industries, such as cotton textiles and iron implements, it has become the centre of an engineering industry producing agricultural machinery, a zinc industry, and a large chemical industry. Some traces of the Song capital still remain. Expressways now provide quick access west to Zhengzhou and Luoyang and east to Xuzhou and Lianyungang in Jiangsu province.

As one of China's seven ancient capitals, Kaifeng was among the first historical and cultural cities to be so designated by the national government. The city has remained at the heart of Henan's cultural life even though it is no longer the provincial capital. Kaifeng is now one of the country's most popular tourist destinations. In addition to its many historical sites, it now has a new riverfront park that is modeled on a renowned 12th-century scroll painting by Zhang Zeduan depicting a prosperous Kaifeng during the Bei (Northern) Song period.

ZHENGZHOU

The city of Zhengzhou (formerly Zhengxian [1913–49]) is the capital of Henan province, east-central China. Located in the north-central part of the province, it is situated to the south of the Huang He (Yellow River) where its valley broadens into the great plain and at the eastern extremity of the Xiong'er Mountains. The city is at the crossing point of the north-south route skirting the Taihang Mountains and the mountains of western Henan and the east-west route along the southern bank of the Huang He. Zhengzhou, the provincial capital of Henan since 1954, forms a prefecture-level *shi* (municipality).

Since 1950, archaeological finds have shown that there were Neolithic settlements in the area and that the Shang Bronze Age culture, which flourished there from about 1500 BCE, was centred on a walled city. Outside this city, in addition to remains of large public buildings, a complex of small settlements has been discovered. The site is generally identified with the Shang capital of Ao. The Shang, who continually moved their capital, left Ao, perhaps in the 13th century BCE. The site, nevertheless, remained occupied; Zhou (post-1050 BCE) tombs have also been discovered. Traditionally it is held that in the Western Zhou period (1111–771 BCE) it became the fief of a family named Guan. From this derives the name borne by the county since the late 6th century BCE—Guancheng ("City of the Guan"). The city first became the seat of a prefectural administration in 587 CE, when it was named Guanzhou. In 605 it was first called Zhengzhou—a name by which it has been known virtually ever since. It achieved its greatest importance under the Sui (581–618 CE), Tang (618–907), and early Song (960–1127) dynasties, when it was the terminus of the New Bian Canal, which joined the Huang He to the northwest. There, at a place called Heyin, a vast granary complex was established to supply the capitals at Luoyang and Chang'an (present-day Xi'an) to the west and the frontier armies to the north. In the Song period, however, the transfer of the capital eastward to Kaifeng robbed Zhengzhou of much of its importance.

In 1903 the Beijing-Hankou railway arrived at Zhengzhou, and in 1909 the first stage of the Longhai Railway gave it an east-west link to Kaifeng and Luoyang; it was later extended eastward to the coast at Lianyungang, in Jiangsu province, and westward to Xi'an, in Shaanxi province, as well as to western Shaanxi. Zhengzhou thus became a major rail junction and a regional centre for cotton, grain, peanuts (groundnuts), and other agricultural produce. Early in 1923 a workers' strike began in Zhengzhou and spread along the rail line before it was suppressed; a 17-story double tower in the centre of the city commemorates the strike. In 1938, during the war with Japan, the retreating Chinese Nationalist Army blew up the dikes retaining the Huang He about 20 miles (32 km) northeast of the city, flooding a vast area. About the same time, in their drive to relocate industry in the interior far from the invading Japanese, the Chinese transferred all the local industrial plants to the west.

When the People's Republic was established in 1949, Zhengzhou was a commercial and administrative centre, but it had virtually no industry. Because it was the centre of a densely peopled cotton-growing district, it was developed into an industrial city, with industry concentrated on the west side so that the prevailing northeast winds would blow fumes away from the city. There are cotton-textile plants, spinning mills, textile-machinery works, flour mills, tobacco and cigarette factories, and various food-processing plants; coal is mined nearby. Zhengzhou also has a locomotive and rolling-stock repair plant, a tractor-assembly plant, and a thermal power-generating station. The city's industrial growth has resulted in a large increase in population, primarily of

Flood-control dam on the Huang He at Zhengzhou, Henan province, China. Paolo Koch—Rapho/Photo Researchers

industrial workers from the north. Trees have been planted throughout the city's metropolitan area, holding down the sand that formerly blew in thick gusts through the city. A water-diversion project and pumping station, built in 1972, provide irrigation for the surrounding countryside. Zhengzhou is Henan's cultural centre, with many colleges, universities, and research institutes located there. A 2006 estimate of the city population was 1,883,232 people, while a 2007 estimate for the urban agglomeration was 2,636,000.

LUOYANG

Luoyang (formerly Henanfu) is a city of northwestern Henan province, east-central China. It was important in history as the capital of nine ruling dynasties and as a Buddhist centre. The contemporary city is divided into an east town and a west town.

Luoyi (present-day Luoyang) was founded in the mid-11th century BCE at the beginning of the Zhou dynasty (1046–256 BCE), near the present-day west town, as the residence of the imperial kings. It became the Zhou capital in 771 BCE and was later moved to a site northeast of the present-day east town; it was named Luoyang because it was north (*yang*) of the Luo River, and its ruins are now distinguished as the ancient city of Luoyang.

The city of the Han period (206 BCE–220 CE) was located approximately on the site of the ancient Luoyi but was called Luoyang. This name alternated with the name Henanfu until contemporary times. Luoyang did not become the Han capital until the 1st century CE, at the beginning of the Dong (Eastern) Han period, though its economic importance had been recognized earlier. In 68 CE the Baima ("White Horse Temple"), one of the earliest Buddhist foundations in China, was built about 9 miles (14 km) east of the present-day east town.

During the 4th century, Luoyang changed hands several times between the rulers of Dong (Eastern) Jin, Hou (Later) Zhao, and Yan, and it did not prosper again until 495, when it was revived by the Xiaowendi emperor of the Bei (Northern) Wei dynasty (386–534/535). The Bei Wei emperors ordered the construction of cave temples at Longmen, south of the city. This inaugurated one of the greatest centres of Chinese Buddhism, the surviving sculptures of which are of prime importance to the history of Chinese art; the Longmen complex was designated a UNESCO World Heritage site in 2000.

As the eastern capital of the Tang dynasty (618–907), Luoyang was expanded, and the part now constituting the east town was created. After a rebellion in the mid-8th century, however, Luoyang fell into an economic decline that lasted until the mid-20th century. By 1949 Luoyang was so diminished that its population had dwindled to about 75,000.

However, Luoyang subsequently underwent substantial economic recovery. During the 1950s, with the assistance of the former Soviet Union, several large-scale industrial projects were launched in Luoyang, and it became one of China's major industrial cities. The city has experienced more rapid development since the 1980s. It now has flourishing metallurgical, petrochemical, textile, and food-processing industries. Luoyang is also an important local transportation hub. The east-west Longhai rail line, which connects Lianyungang with Lanzhou, and the north-south Jiaozuo-Zhicheng rail line cross at Luoyang. Luoyang airport has scheduled flights to Beijing and other major cities in China.

Luoyang is also a major cultural centre and is one of the nationally designated historical and cultural cities. Several institutions of higher education are located there, including the Henan University of Science and Technology (1952). The ruins of the former dynastic capitals around the city, as well as the Longmen cave complex and other historic Buddhist temples, are popular tourist attractions. The city is renowned for its peonies, and its annual spring peony exhibition draws many visitors. A

Stone sculptures in the Binyang cave, Longmen, Henan province, China, from the Northern Wei dynasty (386–534/535 CE). Jimbunkagaku Kenkyusho, Kyoto, Japan

2006 estimation places the city population at 1,065,137, while a 2007 estimate for the urban agglomeration was 1,715,000.

XI'AN

The city of Xi'an (also spelled Xian; conventional Sian; historically Chang'an) is the capital of Shaanxi province-central China. It is located in the south-central part of the province, at the southern limit of the Loess Plateau. The city site is on a low plain on the south bank of the Wei River. Just to the south, the Qin (Tsingling) Mountains rise dramatically above the plain. The Xi'an region is one of the most important in the history of China, both as the capital of several ruling dynasties and as a market and trade centre. Xi'an was the eastern terminus of the Silk Road, the ancient trade route that connected China with the Mediterranean. A 2006 estimate of the Xi'an population was 3,094,267, while a 2007 estimate for the Xi'an urban agglomeration was 4,009,000.

HISTORY

Cities have existed in the Xi'an area since the 11th century BCE. Chang'an Cheng ("Walled City of Chang'an"), built in 202 BCE just northwest of present-day Xi'an, was the capital of the Xi (Western) Han dynasty (206 BCE–25 CE) and was one of the greatest cities of the ancient world. It was largely destroyed during the disturbances that preceded the Xin interregnum

of the Han (9–25 CE) perpetrated by Wang Man. The Dong (Eastern) Han dynasty, established in 25, moved its capital east to Luoyang (now in Henan province).

For several centuries Chang'an declined, despite its strategic importance to the northwestern non-Chinese ("barbarian") principalities. It served briefly (311–316 CE) as the capital of the Xi Jin dynasty, but its capture and destruction by the Xiongnu marked the end of organized Chinese control of the region. Several small states made Chang'an their capital during the Sixteen Kingdoms (Shiliuguo) period (303–439), and it was adopted as the capital of the Xi Wei and Bei (Northern) Zhou states in the 6th century. It was revived by the Sui emperors (581–618), who also made it their capital.

As the capital of the much longer-lived Tang dynasty (618–907), Chang'an was expanded and divided into three parts—the Palace City; the Imperial City, for the officials; and the Outer City, for artisans and merchants. It soon became one of the most splendid and extravagant cities in the world. The city declined after the downfall of the Tang, though it continued as a market centre and broker of the Central Asian trade. In the 13th century the Venetian adventurer Marco Polo described the city as a thriving trade centre. The popular name Xi'an ("Western Peace"), adopted in 1369 after the Ming dynasty (1368–1644) was established, was later changed to Xijing in 1930 but was restored in 1943.

From the 1920s the city was the chief port of entry for communist ideology reaching China from the Soviet Union. In December 1936 the city was the site of the Xi'an (Sian) Incident, which marked the beginning of united Chinese Nationalist and communist resistance against the Japanese.

THE CONTEMPORARY CITY

Xi'an experienced some slow industrial development after the main east-west rail line reached the city in 1935, but this was curtailed by the Sino-Japanese War (1937–45). However, beginning in the mid-1950s, Xi'an was a primary focus of expenditures from the central government and since then has been one of China's major industrialized cities. Among the initial industries established were those manufacturing metallurgical products, chemicals, precision instruments, construction equipment, and processed foods. Subsequent development was directed toward creating regional centres dedicated to manufacturing specific products: the textile district is in the eastern suburban area, electrical machinery is made in the western suburbs, a research and production base for China's aerospace industry is in the northeastern suburbs, and at the southwestern outskirts of the city is an electronics sector. In addition, as the centre of an important farming region, Xi'an is engaged in agricultural processing, most notably of cotton, wheat, and tea.

Being located in the central part of the country, Xi'an has emerged as a railway and highway hub. The east-west Longhai rail line, passing through the city, extends from the eastern seaports along the coast to Gansu, Xinjiang, and the countries of Central Asia to the west. A dense highway network connects Xi'an with other cities within Shaanxi, as well as with those in the neighbouring provinces, and expressways link Xi'an with other major cities in the region. A regional international airport, northwest of the city, has service to most major mainland cities and Hong Kong, as well as to a number of foreign destinations.

Tourism—based on the city's many historical monuments and a plethora of ancient ruins and tombs in the vicinity—has become an important component of the local economy, and the Xi'an region is one of the country's most popular tourist destinations. Located in the city is the Shaanxi Provincial Museum, housed in a former Confucian temple; it is noted for its Forest of Stelae, an important collection of inscribed stelae and Buddhist sculpture. The Shaanxi History Museum preserves artifacts and art objects spanning Chinese history from Paleolithic times through the Qing dynasty. Other sites of interest in the city include the Little Wild Goose Pagoda, the Big Wild Goose Pagoda, and the Temple of Great Good Will, all constructed during the Tang dynasty; the Bell Tower and the Drum Tower, built during Ming times; the Great Mosque, founded in 742, its existing buildings dating from the 14th century; and three well-preserved 14th-century city gates in the wall that surrounds the old city.

Xi'an is a centre of higher education noted for its technological schools. In all, there are more than thirty universities and colleges in and around the city. Best known are Xi'an Jiaotong University, Northwest University, Xi'an Polytechnic University, a medical school, Xi'an University of Technology, Xi'an University of Architecture and Technology, and Xidian University, the latter specializing in electronics and information technology.

About 20 miles (32 km) northeast of Xi'an lies the tomb of Shihuangdi, the first emperor of the Qin dynasty (221–207 BCE) and the first to unify China. Known as the Qin tomb, it is world famous and is one of the most popular tourist destinations in the country. Excavation of it by archaeologists, begun in 1974, unearthed an army of about 6,000 life-size terracotta figures arrayed in battle formation. The Qin tomb complex was designated a UNESCO World Heritage site in 1987.

CHAPTER 7

THE THREE GREAT CITIES OF SOUTHEASTERN CHINA

Southeastern China, the most densely populated part of the country, is home to three of the most important Chinese cities: Shanghai, Guangzhou, and Nanjing. Shanghai, a province-level municipality, is China's largest city and is one of the most populous cities in the world.

SHANGHAI

The city of Shanghai, in east-central China, is one of the world's largest seaports and is a major industrial and commercial centre of the country. The city was one of the first Chinese ports to be opened to Western trade, and it long dominated the nation's commerce. Since the communist victory in 1949, however, it has become an industrial giant whose products supply China's growing domestic demands. The city has also undergone extensive physical changes with the establishment of industrial suburbs and housing complexes, the improvement of public works, and the provision of parks and other recreational facilities. Shanghai has attempted to eradicate the economic and psychological legacies of its exploited past through physical and social transformation to support its major role in the modernization of China. The area of the Shanghai municipality is 2,400 square miles (6,200 square km). The population estimate of

the city in 2006 was 11,283,714 people, and the 2007 estimate of the urban agglomeration was 14,987,000 with the Shanghai municipality at 18,150,000 people.

LANDSCAPE

Shanghai is located on the coast of the East China Sea between the mouth of the Yangtze River (Chang Jiang) to the north and the bay of Hangzhou to the south. The municipality's area includes the city itself, surrounding suburbs, and an agricultural hinterland; it is China's most populous urban area.

CITY SITE

Shanghai municipality is bordered by Jiangsu province to the north and west and Zhejiang province to the southwest. It includes the eighteen districts constituting the city of Shanghai and several islands in the mouth of the Yangtze and offshore to the southeast in the East China Sea. The largest island, Chongming, has an area of 489 square miles (1,267 square km) and extends more than 50 miles (80 km) upstream from the mouth of the Yangtze; it and the islands of Changxing and Hengsha administratively comprise a county under Shanghai municipality.

The mainland portion of the city lies on an almost level deltaic plain with an average elevation of 10 to 16 feet (3 to 5 m) above sea level. It is crisscrossed by an intricate network of canals and waterways that connect the municipality with the Lake Tai region to the west.

CLIMATE

The city's maritime location fosters a mild climate characterized by minimal seasonal contrast. The average annual temperature is about 61 °F (16 °C); the July maximum averages about 80 °F (27 °C), and the average January minimum is about 37 °F (3 °C). About 45 inches (1,140 mm) of precipitation fall annually, with the heaviest rainfall in June and the lightest in December.

LAYOUT

As China's main industrial centre, Shanghai has serious air, water, and noise pollution. Industrial relocation and construction in the suburbs since the 1950s initially helped alleviate central city air pollution, although high population density and mixed industrial-residential land use continued to cause problems. The Suzhou River (the lower reach of Wusong River) and the Huangpu River (a tributary of the Yangtze), which flow through the city, are severely polluted from industrial discharges, domestic sewage, and ships' wastes; nonetheless, the Huangpu is Shanghai's main water source. Environmental protection and urban cleanliness are enhanced by industrial and solid waste resource-recovery operations run by a municipal corporation. More than

The 88-story Jin Mao Tower in the Lujiazui section of the Pudong district, Shanghai, China.
© Photos.com/Jupiterimages

1,000 different materials are recycled, including plastic, chemical fibre and residues, machine components, oil and grease, rags, human hair, and animal bones.

The municipality radiates toward the north, west, and south from the confluence of the Suzhou and Huangpu rivers. Surrounding the central core is a transitional zone on both banks of the Huangpu, which encompasses a partially rural area of about 160 square miles (400 square km). The banks of the Suzhou River, an important inland waterway connection to the interior hinterland, are occupied by a westward arterial extension of the transitional zone. To the south, however, the transitional zone terminates abruptly a few miles south of the central Shanghai urban core, at the Huangpu. Pudong, directly east across the Huangpu from the central business district, was founded in 1870 as one of the earliest industrial areas; it was once notorious as the city's most extensive and appalling slum. The Lujiazui finance and trade zone as well as modern business complexes—including the 88-story Jin Mao Tower (completed 1999)—are now located there, and the Pudong New District was established in the area in 1993.

DOWNTOWN SHANGHAI

For some time before the late 1980s, the physical perspective of downtown Shanghai was much the same as in the precommunist period. Because of the policy of developing integrated residential and industrial complexes in suburban areas, central city development and renewal had been given low priority. Many of the pre-World War II buildings, which housed foreign commercial concerns and diplomatic missions, still dominated the area.

Extending southward and westward from the confluence of the Suzhou and Huangpu rivers, central Shanghai has a gridded street pattern and includes the area originally contained within the British concession. The area is bounded on the east along the Huangpu by Zhongshan Dong Lu (East Zhongshan Road); on the west by Xizang Zhong Lu; and on the south by Yan'an Dong Lu, which was built on the former Yangjingbang Canal that separated the British from the French concessions. Zhongshan Dong Lu has several hotels, the central administrative offices of Shanghai, and a residence for foreign seamen. On the main commercial artery, Nanjing Dong Lu, which runs westward from the eastern road, lies one of Shanghai's largest retail establishments—the Shanghai Number One Department Store—as well as restaurants, hotels, and the central communications building.

The Hongkou district lies to the north and east of the Suzhou River. It was originally developed by American and Japanese concessionaires and in 1863 was combined with the British concession to the south to create the International Settlement. It is an important industrial area, with shipyards and factories spread out along the bank of the Huangpu in the eastern section of the district. Its best-known building, the Shanghai Dasha

(Shanghai Mansions Hotel), overlooks the Huangpu.

The old Chinese city, which is now part of central Shanghai, is characterized by a random and labyrinthine street pattern. Until the early 20th century, the area was surrounded by a three-mile wall. It is now circumscribed by the two streets of Renmin Lu and Zhonghua Lu, which follow the course of the original wall; and it is bisected by the main north-south artery, Henan Nan Lu (South Henan Road).

Western Shanghai is primarily residential in character and is the site of the Shanghai Exhibition Center. To the southwest, the district of Xuhui, formerly Xujiahui, became a centre of Christian missionary activity in China in the 17th century. During the late 1800s, Jesuit priests established a major library, a printing establishment, an orphanage, and a meteorological observatory in the area.

Land use patterns in metropolitan Shanghai mirror pre-1949 real estate market conditions. Much of the high-value land given over to industrial plants, warehouses, and transportation facilities lies close to the Huangpu and Suzhou rivers. South of the Suzhou, which is traversed by about twenty bridges within the city, residential areas extend south from the industrial strip to the Huangpu. North of the Suzhou, residential areas are less clearly demarcated, and there is a more gradual merging of city and country in the transitional zone. Continuous urban settlement is bounded on the north by the two major east-west arteries of Zhongshan Bei Lu and Siping Lu.

Retail trade is concentrated in the old central business district, although the proportional volume of trade conducted there has diminished with the establishment of the industrial satellite towns and villages on the periphery of Shanghai.

HOUSING

Shanghai has made considerable progress since 1949 in providing housing for its growing population. Construction of self-sufficient residential complexes in conjunction with industrial, agricultural, and commercial development throughout metropolitan and suburban Shanghai has helped disperse population from the overcrowded central city and has led to dramatic changes in the urban and suburban landscape. A prolonged period of housing-complex construction has been under way since the 1980s to replace shanties, some of which still persist in some areas.

The concept of state-supported housing was introduced in 1951 with the development of Caoyang Xin Cun (Caoyang New Village) in an existing industrial zone on Shanghai's western periphery. Following the construction of the Caoyang Xin Cun, many other residential complexes were built. Some of them were constructed with the partial support of government bureaus or state-owned industrial enterprises to satisfy the needs of their employees. Two of the earliest complexes in this category were the Railroad Village and the Post and Telegraph Village.

Five major housing developments were built in the former slum area of Yangshupu. Other complexes are those at Pengpu, Zhenru, Yichuan, Rihui, and Jiangwan. Some of these are in relatively remote suburban locations in the transitional and hinterland zones near older rural marketing centres. The Pengpu workers' housing project is typical. Those who work in nearby factories live in a garden apartment complex that includes apartment buildings, administrative offices, workshops, clinics, and a nursery.

The adjacent fields supply wheat, clover, beans, cabbage, melons, and rapeseed (for cooking oil) for consumption by the inhabitants of the complex.

People

The greater municipality can be divided into three distinct population zones—the densely populated central city, the transitional zones, and the rural hinterland, which is one of the world's most densely settled agricultural areas.

Pedestrians strolling along the Huangpu River, central Shanghai, China. © Goodshoot/ Jupiterimages

Within metropolitan Shanghai there are few, if any, concentrations of ethnic minority groups. The majority of the population is of Han Chinese origin.

ECONOMY

For some time Shanghai has been the country's leading industrial and manufacturing centre because of a distinctive combination of factors. These include the availability of a large, highly skilled, and technologically innovative workforce; a well-grounded and broadly based scientific research establishment supportive of industry; a tradition of cooperation among producers; and excellent internal and external communication and supply facilities. In addition to serving as one of the country's major transportation hubs, the city is China's leading commercial and financial centre.

INDUSTRY

The iron and steel industry in Shanghai was one of the earliest to be established in China. In the 1950s the blast furnace capacity of the industry was enlarged, and attempts were made to integrate the operations of the iron and steel industry more closely with the machine-manufacturing industry. Iron and steel companies started to build new facilities north of the city in the Baoshan area in the late 1970s; one of these, the Baosteel Group Corporation, has been one of the world's largest enterprises since the beginning of the 21st century.

Shanghai's machine and machine tool industry has been especially important in China's modernization plans. Among the varieties of industrial equipment produced are multiple-use lathes, wire-drawing dies, and manufacturing equipment for assembling computers and other electronic devices, precision instruments, and polymer synthetics.

The chemical and petrochemical industries are almost fully integrated, and there is increasing cooperation among individual plants in the production and supply of chemical raw materials for plastics, synthetic fibres, dyes, paint, pharmaceuticals, agricultural pesticides, chemical fertilizers, synthetic detergents, and refined petroleum products. Heavy industry (especially metallurgical and chemical) predominated until the late 1970s. Light industry is now favoured in an effort to reduce pollution, alleviate transportation congestion, and compensate for energy and raw material shortages associated with heavy industry.

The textile industry has been reorganized to assure efficient utilization of the mills' productive capacity at all stages of the manufacturing process. The textile mills cooperate in their use of raw materials and have established cooperative relationships with plants that manufacture rubber shoes, tires, zippers, industrial abrasives, and conveyor belts.

Shanghai is a primary source of a wide variety of consumer goods such as watches, cameras, radios, fountain pens, glassware, stationery products, leather goods, and hardware.

COMMERCE

The retail trade in manufactured consumer goods was managed by the First Commercial Bureau until the bureau was disbanded in 1995; trade is now more market-directed. A number of commercial corporations under the bureau were responsible for the wholesaling, distribution, and warehousing of specific commodity groups; these operations also have been reorganized into independent business groups. A separate corporation manages the larger retail stores, while the smaller retail establishments and some specialized wholesaling organizations are controlled by local commerce bureaus in the various districts of the city.

FINANCE AND TRADE

Shanghai's two major banks—the People's Construction Bank and the Bank of China—function as administrative organs of the Ministry of Finance. They are responsible for the disbursement and management of capital investment funds for state enterprises. Two British banks, the Hong Kong and Shanghai Banking Corporation and the Chartered Bank, along with other foreign banks, maintain Shanghai branch offices that underwrite foreign trade transactions and exchange foreign currency in connection with trading operations. Remittances from Chinese living in Hong Kong and abroad (mainly in Southeast Asian countries) are managed and collected by several overseas Chinese banks. Since the 1980s many more banks, both domestic and foreign-owned, have established operations in Shanghai.

Industrial products are exported from Shanghai to all parts of China. Imports are mainly unprocessed food grains, petroleum and coal, construction materials, and such industrial raw materials as pig iron, salt, raw cotton, tobacco, and oils. In domestic trade, Shanghai still imports more than it exports. In foreign trade, however, the value of exported commodities exceeds that of imported goods, and the proportion of manufactured exports is steadily increasing.

TRANSPORTATION

Shanghai is one of China's major transportation centres. The central city is both a seaport and a river port, with the Huangpu River serving as an excellent harbour; at high tide, oceangoing vessels can sail up the river to the city.

In the early 1950s, the harbour was divided into a number of specialized sections. Pudong, on the east bank of the Huangpu and in the Huangpu district, is used for the storage of bulk commodities and for transportation maintenance and repair facilities. Puxi, in the Nanshi district on the west bank, and Fuxing Island are the sites of general cargo wharves. Since then, oceangoing terminals along the Huangpu have been constructed at Zhanghuabang, Jungong Lu, Gongqing, Longwu, and Zhujiamen. More terminals constructed at the southern bank of the Yangtze, including those at Baoshan, Luojing, and Waigaoqiao, have greatly increased the handling capacity of the city's port. A deepwater port operation off the coast at Hangzhou Bay started in 2005.

Heavily used inland waterway connections, via the Suzhou and Wusong rivers, and an extensive canal network are maintained with Suzhou, Wuxi, and Yangzhou in Jiangsu province and with Hangzhou in Zhejiang province.

The railway network reflects the efforts that have been made since 1949 to reorient the city's industrial economy to balance export and domestic development needs. Shanghai is the terminus of two major rail lines south of the Yangtze—the Hu-Ning line, from Shanghai to Nanjing, and the Hu-Hang-Yong line, from Shanghai via Hangzhou to the port of Ningbo in Zhejiang province. A short spur line also runs from Shanghai to Wusong. Additional spur lines built since 1949 connect the industrial districts to the main trunk routes.

Shanghai is served by two major airports. Hongqiao Airport, southwest of Shanghai, is now used mainly for domestic flights; Pudong International Airport, 19 miles (30 km) southeast of the city and on the bank of the Yangtze, has been in service since 1999 and has become one of China's busiest. Intraurban transportation by electric trolleybus, trolley, and motorbus has been substantially improved since 1949. In addition, a high-speed maglev (magnetic-levitation) train line between Pudong Airport and central Shanghai began operation in 2003.

ADMINISTRATION AND SOCIETY

As a first-order, province-level administrative unit, Shanghai municipality is, in theory, directly controlled by the central government in Beijing. It is difficult, however, to gauge the precise nature of this relationship. Since the Cultural Revolution of the late 1960s, China's administrative apparatus at all levels of the hierarchy has been in a process of readjustment so as to bring governmental organization in line with political reality.

GOVERNMENT

In 1967, early in the Cultural Revolution, the Shanghai Municipal Revolutionary Committee was established as the top governing body in the municipality after a chaotic period in which a number of popular-based revolutionary organizations seized control of the city for brief periods. The committee at that time was composed of representatives of the army, the mass revolutionary organizations, and some former Communist Party officials. By the mid-1970s this was replaced by a municipal government made up of commissions, offices, and bureaus responsible to the Shanghai People's

Congress, an elected body. These units serve both policy advisory and administrative functions and function as administrative links to both the national government in Beijing as well as the local governing bodies.

PUBLIC UTILITIES

Modern public works improvements include the installation and improvement of drainage and sewage-treatment facilities, public water supply systems, street lights, and public refuse bins. Roads have been widened and repaired, flood walls constructed in low-lying areas subject to tidal inundation, and housing built. The sea walls surrounding Shanghai have been strengthened and enlarged; two long sea walls extend east of the Huangpu for a total of more than 13 miles (21 km).

Shanghai is one of China's major electric power-generating centres. Electricity is produced mainly by coal-fired thermal plants, and the Shanghai area is linked via a major transmission network with Nanjing to the northwest and with Hangzhou and Xin'anjiang (the site of a hydroelectric generating facility) in Zhejiang province to the southwest. A large gasworks is located at Longhua. Increased energy demands for industry and domestic use beginning in the early 1980s led to a decision by the national authorities to construct one of China's first two nuclear power plants at Qinshan, in nearby Zhejiang province.

HEALTH

Shanghai's health care facilities range from thousands of small clinics associated with factories, schools, retail establishments, and government offices to numerous major research and teaching hospitals. Most hospitals have facilities for practicing and teaching both traditional Chinese and Western medicine. Medical schools had once concentrated on the training of "barefoot" doctors—practitioners with sufficient medical skills to supply basic care to people in rural areas—especially during the Cultural Revolution.

EDUCATION

Shanghai is China's leading centre of higher education and scientific research. There are numerous universities and other institutions of higher learning—including Fudan, Jiaotong, Tongji, and the Huadong Shifan Daxue—as well as technical and higher education institutes. At one time, many factories had affiliated work-study colleges to equip workers for more highly skilled jobs. Notable was the Shanghai Municipal Part-Work Part-Study Industrial University (1960), which was established through the cooperation of more than 1,000 industrial establishments. A large segment of the city's total workforce was once enrolled in one of these schools, but different, market-oriented types of higher-education institutions have become more typical since the late 1980s.

The Shanghai Branch of the Chinese Academy of Sciences, China's leading scientific research and development body, is located in Shanghai. During the Cultural Revolution, practical applications of scientific work in agriculture and industry were encouraged. Since the late 1970s, extensive research investments have been made in such high-technology areas as nuclear energy, computers, semiconductors, laser and infrared technology, and satellites.

CULTURAL LIFE

Shanghai's cultural attractions include museums, historical sites, and scenic gardens. The Shanghai Museum houses an extensive collection of bronzes, ceramics, and other artifacts dating over several thousand years. In 2000 the former Shanghai Revolutionary History Memorial Hall was combined with the former residence of revolutionary leader Chen Yun to create a new museum based on Chen's life. The Dashijie ("Great World"), founded in the 1920s, is Shanghai's leading theatrical centre and offers folk operas, dance performances, plays, story readings, and specialized entertainment forms typical of China's national minority groups. The city also has many workers' and children's recreational clubs and several large motion-picture theatres, including the Daguangming Theatre.

The old Chinese city houses the 16th-century Yuyuan Garden (Garden of the Mandarin Yu), an outstanding example of late Ming garden architecture, and the Temple of Confucius. Other points of attraction are the Longhua Pagoda of the Bei (Northern) Song dynasty, the Industrial Exhibition Hall, and the tomb and former residence of Lu Xun, a 20th-century revolutionary writer.

The major publishing houses of Shanghai are a branch of the People's Literature Publishing House (at Beijing), Shanghai Translation Publishing House, Shanghai Foreign Language Education Press, and the Shanghai Educational Publishing House. In addition to the large branch of the library of the Chinese Academy of Sciences, Shanghai has numerous other libraries. Shanghai's art and music schools include a branch of the Central Conservatory (relocated to Beijing in 1958), the Shanghai Conservatory, and the Shanghai Theatre Academy. There are a variety of professional performing arts troupes, including ballet and opera companies, symphonies, and puppet troupes.

Parks, open spaces, and playing fields were notably expanded after 1949. Two of the earliest to be opened for public use were People's Park in central Shanghai and Huangpu Park on the shore of the Huangpu River. Every section of the city has large parks and playing fields. Among the largest are the Hongkou Arboretum and Stadium in the north; Peace Park (Heping Park) and playing field in the northeast; Pudong Park in eastern Shanghai, Longhua and Fuxing parks in the south, and Zhongshan Park on the western periphery of the central city. Guangqi Park in Xuhui district contains the grave of the renowned Ming-dynasty statesman Xu Guangqi. The Shanghai Gymnasium, completed in 1975 and expanded in the late 1990s, is one of the largest of its kind in China.

HISTORY

As late as the 5th to 7th centuries CE, the Shanghai area—then known as Shen or Hudu—was sparsely populated and undeveloped. Despite the steady southward progression of Chinese settlement, the exposed deltaic position of the area retarded its economic growth.

EVOLUTION OF THE CITY

During the Song dynasty (960–1126) Shanghai emerged from its somnolent state as a small, isolated fishing village. The area to the west around Lake Tai had developed a self-sustaining agricultural economy on protected reclaimed land and was stimulated by an increase in population resulting from the southward migration of Chinese fleeing the invading Mongols in the north. The natural advantages of Shanghai as a deepwater port and shipping centre were recognized as coastal and inland shipping expanded rapidly. By the beginning of the 11th century, a customs office was established, and by the end of the 13th century Shanghai was designated as a county

seat and placed under the jurisdiction of Jiangsu province.

During the Ming dynasty (1368–1644) roughly 70 percent of the cultivated acreage around Shanghai was given to the production of cotton to feed the city's cotton- and silk-spinning industry. By the middle of the 18th century, there were more than 20,000 persons employed as cotton spinners.

After the 1850s the predominantly agricultural focus of the economy was quickly transformed. At this time the city became the major Chinese base for commercial imperialism by nations of the West. Following a humiliating defeat by Great Britain in 1842, the Chinese surrendered Shanghai and signed the Treaty of Nanjing, which opened the city to unrestricted foreign trade. The British, French, and Americans took possession of designated areas in the city within which they were granted special rights and privileges, and the Japanese received a concession in 1895 under the terms of the Treaty of Shimonoseki.

The opening of Shanghai to foreign business immediately led to the establishment of major European banks and multipurpose commercial houses. The city's prospects as a leading centre of foreign trade were further enhanced when Canton, a rival port in the southeastern coastal province of Guangdong, was cut off from its hinterland by the Taiping Rebellion (1850–64). Impelled by this potential threat to the uninterrupted expansion of their commercial operations in China, the British obtained rights of navigation on the Yangtze in 1857. As the natural outlet for the vast hinterland of the lower Yangtze, Shanghai rapidly grew to become China's leading port and by 1860 accounted for about 25 percent of the total shipping tonnage entering and departing the country.

Shanghai did not show promise of becoming a major industrial centre, however, until the 1890s. Except for the Jiangnan Arsenal organized by the Qing dynasty (1644–1911) in the early 1860s, most industrial enterprises were small-scale offshoots of the larger foreign trading houses. As the flow of foreign capital steadily increased after the Sino-Japanese War of 1894–95, light industries were established within the foreign concessions, which took advantage of Shanghai's ample and cheap labour supply, local raw materials, and inexpensive power.

THE CONTEMPORARY CITY

By contrast, local Chinese investment in Shanghai's industry was minimal until World War I diverted foreign capital from China. From 1914 through the early 1920s, Chinese investors were able to gain a tenuous foothold in the scramble to develop the industrial economy. This initial involvement was short-lived, however, as the post-World War I resurgence of Western and Japanese economic imperialism—followed closely by the Great Depression of the 1930s—overwhelmed many of the newly established

Chinese industries. Competition became difficult, as cheaper foreign goods were dumped on the Shanghai market, and labour was attracted to relatively higher paying jobs in foreign-owned factories. Prior to the Sino-Japanese War of 1937–45, the Japanese had gained control over about half of the city's yarn-spinning and textile-weaving capacity.

The 1920s was also a period of growing political awareness in Shanghai. Members of the working class, students, and intellectuals became increasingly politicized as foreign domination of the city's economic and political life became ever more oppressive. When the agreements signed by the United Kingdom, the United States, and Japan at the Washington Conference of 1922 failed to satisfy Chinese demands, boycotts of foreign goods were instituted. The Chinese Communist Party was founded in Shanghai in 1921, and four years later the Communist Party led the "May 30" uprising of students and workers. This massive political demonstration was directed against feudalism, capitalism, and official connivance in foreign imperialistic ventures. The student-worker coalition actively supported the Nationalist armies under Chiang Kai-shek, but the coalition and the Communist Party were violently suppressed by the Nationalists in 1927.

Shanghai was occupied by the Japanese during the Sino-Japanese War of 1937–45, and the city's industrial plants suffered extensive war damage. In the brief interim before the fall of Shanghai to the People's Liberation Army (PLA) in 1949, the city's economy suffered even greater dislocation through the haphazard proliferation of small, inefficient shop industries, rampant inflation, and the absence of any overall plan for industrial reconstruction.

After 1949 Shanghai's development was temporarily slowed because of the emphasis on internal regional development, especially during the period up to 1960 when close cooperation was maintained with the Soviet Union. With the cooling of relations after 1960, Shanghai resumed its key position as China's leading scientific and technological research centre, with the nation's most highly skilled labour force.

NANJING

The city of Nanjing (conventional Nanking) is the capital of Jiangsu province, east-central China. It is a port on the Yangtze River (Chang Jiang) and a major industrial and communications centre. Rich in history, it served seven times as the capital of regional empires, twice as the seat of revolutionary government, once (during the Sino-Japanese War of 1937–45) as the site of a puppet regime, and twice as the capital of a united China (the second time ending with the Japanese conquest of the city in 1937). The name Nanjing ("Southern Capital") was introduced in 1403, during the Ming dynasty. The area of the municipality is 2,547 square miles (6,598 square km). A 2005 population study estimated the urban

districts held 2,363,844; the urban and suburban districts held 5,133,771; and the muncipality held 5,957,992 people.

LANDSCAPE

The municipality (*shi*) of Nanjing includes territory extending to the border of Anhui province on the north, west, and south and to the borders of Yangzhou, Zhenjiang, and Changzhou municipalities on the east. Included in the municipality of Nanjing are two counties (*xian*) in the extreme south and both urban and rural districts on either side of the Yangtze.

CITY SITE

The central districts of Nanjing are situated on the southeastern bank of the Yangtze, some 160 miles (260 km) west of Shanghai. The city proper comprises the area encircled by a gigantic wall constructed during the Ming dynasty (1368–1644) and adjacent districts and outskirt suburbs. The city wall—of which about two-thirds is still standing—is 21 miles (34 km) long, has an average height of 40 feet (12 m), and originally included 13 gates (a few of which are still extant).

CLIMATE

Nanjing's four seasons are clearly distinguishable. The hot summer months are from July to September. Winter lasts from December until March. Spring and autumn are both mild and pleasant. January and July mean temperatures are about 37 °F (3 °C) and 82 °F (28 °C), respectively. The average annual rainfall is about 40 inches (100 cm), the bulk of it falling between June and August.

CITY LAYOUT

The central city of Nanjing, encircled by hills and rivers, resembles a gourd with its tip pointing northwest, toward Xiaguan district, on the south bank of the Yangtze. Xiaguan and Pukou district, which is opposite it on the north bank, house some of the harbour facilities of the huge Nanjing River Port. On the west and south, central Nanjing is bordered by the Qinhuai River, which runs along the outside of the city wall and is a tributary of the Yangtze. On the east are the foothills of the Zijin ("Purple-Gold") Mountains, and at the city's west side is Qingliang ("Clear-Cool") Hill. Outside of the city wall to the northeast is the extensive Xuanwu ("Mystic Martial") Lake, containing five islets linked by embankments, and on the other side of the Qinhuai River, to the southwest, is Mochou ("No Sorrow") Lake; both lake areas are city parks. The skyline suggests spaciousness and grandeur. Blue-glazed tiles adorning the old city gates, parklike scenery along the boulevards, lotus blossoms and tea pavilions on the lakes, and temples half-hidden in the green hills are all characteristic sights in Nanjing.

The old central city southeast of the Yangtze consisted of four districts (*qu*):
north, central, east, and west. These were subsumed into larger districts that encompassed central-city and suburban areas when the city was administratively reorganized in 1995. Of the six city districts, the largest is Xuanwu, named for Xuanwu Lake. It includes the old eastern district within the city wall and extends northeastward into an area formerly within the suburban Qixia district. Xuanwu district contains such landmarks as Beijige ("North Pole Pavilion") and Jimingsi ("Cockcrow Temple"), as well as city government offices and modern residential quarters. It is also a centre of the city's ancient culture; it includes the ruins of the former Ming dynasty palace as well as Nanjing Museum and scientific institutions. The northeastern portion of the district encompasses part of the magnificent forested Zijin range, and its cultural and historic sites include the Xiaoling tomb group of the Ming dynasty, notably the tomb of the Hongwu emperor (designated as part of a previously named UNESCO World Heritage site in 2003); the blue-tile-roofed mausoleum of the Chinese Nationalist Party leader Sun Yat-sen (Sun Zhongshan), the first provisional president of the Republic of China; the Linggu ("Valley of Spirits") Temple (first built in 514) and its nearby 200-foot- (60-m-) high pagoda; and the Zijinshan Astronomical Observatory.

West of Xuanwu district is Gulou district, named for the Gulou ("Drum Tower"), a city landmark built in 1382. Gulou encompasses the former northern and western districts of the old city. In addition to the provincial government offices, some major hotels and guest houses are located there. North of these two districts is the former suburban area of Xiaguan, now also one of the city districts. Alongside the Yangtze and known as the northern gate of Nanjing, Xiaguan is traditionally a collecting and distribution point for the city. South of Xuanwu district is the Baixia district. Surrounding the flourishing and crowded Xinjiekou ("New Crossroads"), it is both a shopping centre and the business hub of the city. Farther to the south is the district of Qinhuai. Named for the Qinhuai River, the district was historically famous for its entertainment venues. It is now once again a popular tourist destination, with its renowned Confucius Temple (Fuzi Miao; first built in 1034 and subsequently reconstructed) and the river cruise on the Qinhuai.

South of Gulou and west of Qinhuai is Jianye, the sixth city district. Situated west of the Qinhuai River and completely outside of the city wall (and thus with more vacant space available), it has been designated as a new city centre and includes a science and technology park. Scenic Mochou Lake is on its northeastern corner, and it also houses a memorial for victims of the Nanjing Massacre during the Sino-Japanese War of 1937–45.

Forming an integral part of the life of the city are its immediate outskirts. To the south is Yuhuatai ("Terrace of the Rain of Flowers") district, noted for its five-colour pebbles and a communist martyrs' memorial. To the northwest is Pukou, long a river port on the northern bank of the Yangtze and now also a rapidly developing industrial centre. Some other scenic spots located in the suburban districts include Yanziji ("Swallow's Bluff") in the north and Qixiashan ("Abode of Clouds Mountain") farther to the northeast.

PEOPLE

Despite much industrial growth, the city of Nanjing retains a traditional feature— the existence of a substantial rural population within the boundaries of the municipality. The people speak Mandarin with a marked local accent. Although a large number of the city's residents do not profess a religion, Nanjing has small communities of Christians, Buddhists, and Muslims.

ECONOMY

Nanjing, the economic capital of southwestern China, has a diversified economy focused on manufacturing, commerce, and trade. The city is also one of the main transportation and shipping hubs of the country.

AGRICULTURE

Much of the land in the municipality's rural districts and southern counties is under cultivation; the major agricultural products are rice, wheat, peanuts (groundnuts), and fruits and vegetables. In and around the many lakes and ponds, *baihe* (lily bulbs), water chestnuts, lotus roots, and other aquatic plants are grown. Both freshwater fishing and pig farming are important, and dairy production has increased significantly. Along the canals and creeks, farmers raise large flocks of ducks; the Nanjing duck, preserved in salt and pressed, is a delicacy of Chinese cuisine.

MANUFACTURING

Before 1949, Nanjing was noted chiefly for its traditional handicraft products, such as satins, velvets, and brocades. The city's industrial expansion has taken place since then, and Nanjing is now an important industrial centre. Hundreds of factories have been built to produce iron and steel, machine tools, motor vehicles, bicycles, clocks and watches, optical instruments, and building materials. Textiles, food processing, and other light industries are also important. In the outlying districts and southern counties, iron ore, manganese, copper, limestone, dolomite, lead, and zinc are mined. Its reserves of strontium are among the largest in China. Petrochemical and electronic plants, however, mark the city's greatest progress in industrial development. Its automobile production also ranks high in the country. A Nanjing Economic and Technological Development Zone, established by the national government and located northeast of the central city districts in suburban Qixia district, has facilities devoted to such areas as information technology, biomedical engineering, and the manufacture of light-industrial machinery and high-purity and precision chemicals.

TRANSPORTATION

Nanjing's major avenue of commerce is the Yangtze River, which connects the city with the Yangtze delta and with central China. The port of Nanjing is equipped with specialized coal, oil, container, and automobile roll-on/roll-off wharves. In addition to the major ports at Xiaguan and Pukou, there is a large port facility at Xinshengyu, some 6 miles (10 km) downstream from Xiaguan, that opened in the mid-1980s to directly handle foreign trade.

Nanjing is connected by rail to Shanghai to the southeast and to other major Chinese cities to the north. Intercity commuter rail service between Shanghai and Nanjing now takes less than 2 ½ hours one way. Another rail line, leading south and southwest, extends to Wuhu and Tongling in Anhui province; a loop line through the eastern suburban districts links it with the Shanghai-Nanjing line. In 1968 the rail ferry between Pukou and Xiaguan was replaced by the city's first bridge across the Yangtze. More than 20,000 feet (6,100 m) in length, it has a double-track railroad on its lower deck and a four-lane highway on the upper deck. Two more bridges have been built downstream of the first (opened in 2001 and 2005, respectively), the latter having a main span of 2,126 feet (648 m).

While bicycles and buses are still major means of transportation within Nanjing, the city streets have become increasingly crowded with cars and trucks that add significantly to traffic congestion in the downtown area. To help relieve this congestion, the city began construction of an extensive light-rail transit system, the first line of which opened in 2005. Major highways, including expressways, fan out from Nanjing to Shanghai and other cities in Jiangsu, Zhejiang, and Anhui provinces. Nanjing Lukou International Airport, located in a southern suburban district some 22 miles (35 km) from the city centre, has regular flights to other major cities in China and to some international destinations.

ADMINISTRATION AND SOCIETY

Nanjing's municipal government is part of the hierarchical structure of the Chinese government—and the parallel structure of the Chinese Communist Party—that extends from the national organization, through the provincial apparatus, to the municipal and, ultimately, neighbourhood levels.

GOVERNMENT

The principal responsibilities of the Nanjing Municipal People's Congress, the major decision-making body, include issuing administrative orders, collecting taxes, determining the budget, and implementing economic plans. A standing committee selected from its members recommends policy decisions and oversees the operation of the municipal government. Executive authority rests with the Nanjing People's Government, the officers of which are elected by the congress; it consists of a mayor, vice mayors, and numerous bureaus in charge of public security, the judicial system, and other civil, economic, social, and cultural affairs.

Following the municipal government reorganization of 1995, Nanjing was divided administratively into eleven districts (qu), and the municipality was given jurisdiction over the two counties (xian) to the far south. Below the district level, police substations supervise the population, while street mayoralties handle civil affairs in their areas. Neighbourhood associations help mediate disputes, carry out literacy campaigns, and promote sanitation, welfare, and family planning.

HEALTH

Nanjing made great progress in public health and medicine during the Nationalist period. Health conditions have continued to improve under the communist government, which has placed great emphasis on public health education. There are many general and specialized hospitals in Nanjing. However, many clinics and health stations previously maintained by neighbourhood associations, factories, and schools have been partially privatized since the 1990s. Nanjing is also a noted centre for training doctors in traditional Chinese medicine.

EDUCATION

Nanjing inherited from the Nationalist days an excellent school system that in 1949 included 300 primary and middle schools and some of the best universities and colleges in China. Since the 1950s there has been a considerable increase in the number of primary, middle, and technical secondary schools. In addition, much attention has been given to adult education, and many spare-time schools, university extensions, and other institutions that provide training in technical fields have been established. Nanjing University (1902), Southeast University (1902), Nanjing University of Aeronautics and Astronautics (1952), and Nanjing University of Science and Technology (1953) are among the leading institutions of higher education in the country, and colleges of hydraulic engineering, agricultural science, medical and pharmaceutical sciences, and meteorology are also of national significance.

CULTURAL LIFE

Nanjing's long history as a cultural centre is reflected in its many surviving monuments and buildings of historical significance. The Nanjing Museum, with its exhibits on Chinese history, the Historical Museum of the Taiping Heavenly Kingdom, and the Nanjing Municipal Museum (Chaotian Palace) are all housed in buildings constructed in traditional Chinese style. Among the city's numerous research agencies and scientific societies is the Nanjing branch of the Chinese Academy of Sciences.

Some of the leading artists of China have worked in the Jiangsu Institute of Traditional Chinese Painting, located in Nanjing. Troupes specializing in *jingxi* (Peking opera) and various forms of Jiangsu opera give performances of both traditional theatrical pieces and modern plays in the city. Sports grounds are found in all parts of Nanjing and its suburbs. The well-equipped Wutaishan Stadium, in Gulou district at the centre of the city, is used for major sports events and entertainment performances. The Nanjing Olympic Sports Centre (completed 2005) is just west of the city centre in Jianye district and has a capacity of 60,000 spectators. The public at large, however, finds its recreation in the many beautiful parks and resorts.

HISTORY

Nanjing's recorded history dates to the Warring States (Zhanguo; 475–221 BCE) period, when a castle near Yuhuatai was constructed by the Yue state in 472 BCE.

THE EARLY EMPIRES

After the Yue territory was taken over by the Chu state, another castle, under the name of Jinling, was built on Qingliang Hill to control the traffic between the Yangtze and the Qinhuai rivers. Under the Qin (221–206 BCE) and Han (206 BCE–220 CE) dynasties, Nanjing was successively under the jurisdiction of Moling and Danyang counties.

Nanjing—under the name of Jianye—emerged as the political and cultural centre of southeastern China during the period of the Three Kingdoms (Sanguo; 220–280 CE), when Sun Quan made it the capital of the kingdom of Wu from 229 to 280. In 317 the Dong (Eastern) Jin dynasty (317–420), fleeing foreign invaders in North China, again chose the city as a capital. Renamed Jiankang in 313, Nanjing became a haven for northern families in exile. After the fall of the Dong Jin, Nanjing under four successive dynasties—Liu-Song (420–479), Nan (Southern) Qi (479–502), Nan Liang (502–557), and Nan Chen (557–589)—was the seat of government of the regional empires south of the Yangtze.

These regimes were dominated by military men whose rivalries weakened the government. But in Nanjing progress was made in areas other than politics, and its population grew to one million during the Nan Liang. Bountiful harvests, coupled with tea, silk, papermaking, and pottery industries, supported a booming economy. Culturally, the Six Dynasties—as the dynasties that ruled from 220 to 589 are called—produced a galaxy of scholars, poets, artists, and philosophers. The works of Wang Xizhi and Gu Kaizhi set the canons of calligraphy and painting, respectively. Achievements of this period included the publication of *Wenxuan* ("Literary Selections") by Xiaotong (sometimes called *Zhaoming Wenxuan* to distinguish it from other similarly named anthologies) and of *Wenxin Diaolong* ("The Literary Mind and the Carving of Dragons"; a classic in literary criticism) by Liu Xie, the evolution of what has come to be known as the Six Dynasties essay style (a blending of poetry and prose), and the invention (reportedly by Shen Yue, a 6th-century courtier) of the system of determining the four tones of the Chinese language. In philosophy, the so-called *qingtan* ("pure discourse") movement, spiritually akin to a form of Daoism, found many adherents who held themselves aloof from politics. Hundreds of Buddhist temples were built, voluminous Buddhist scriptures were edited and transcribed, and thousands, including the emperor Wudi, founder of the Nan Liang dynasty, took monastic vows.

From 581 to 1368, under the successive unified empires of the Sui, Tang, Song, and Yuan dynasties, Nanjing reverted to the status of a prefectural city. Various names were given to the city: Jiangzhou and Danyang under the Sui; Jiangzhou, Jinling, and Baixia in the early Tang; Shengzhou in the late Tang; Jinling again under the Five Dynasties in the 10th century; Jiankang under the Song; and Jiqing under the Yuan. When the Nan Tang briefly maintained a regional regime in the city from 937 to 975, Nanjing enjoyed much intellectual creativity (the ruler Houzhu himself being a poet of consummate skill) and was the scene of new construction, notably the octagonal stone pagoda of the Qixia Temple and the crosstown channel of the Qinhuai River. Another period of prominence occurred during the Nan Song dynasty (1127–1279), when Yue Fei used the city as his base for resistance against the Juchen in North China.

In 1368 the Hongwu emperor, founder of the Ming dynasty, made Nanjing the capital of a united China. Naming the city Yingtianfu ("Responding to Heaven"), he built a grand imperial palace and the city wall. In addition, earth ramparts were prepared to form the basis for a larger outer wall. In 1421, however, Hongwu's son, the Yongle emperor, moved the capital to the newly named Beijing ("Northern Capital"), which he renamed from Beiping (its name after it was made a subsidiary capital to Nanjing in 1403). The city, which had been called Nanjing ("Southern Capital") since 1403, now became a subsidiary capital to Beijing.

However, the growth of trade and industry brought new wealth to Nanjing, especially to Xiaguan. Weaving, pottery, printing, and brocade making were the leading industries. Oceangoing vessels used by Zheng He in his famous 15th-century expeditions to the South Seas were built in the shipyards to the northwest of the city. An imperial college—the Guozijian—attracted students from throughout the empire, as well as from Japan, Korea, Okinawa, and Siam (Thailand). The scholars of this college helped compile the *Yongle Dadian* ("The Great Canon of the Yongle Era"); its printing plant issued fine editions of many classics, as well as such works as *Bencao Gangmu* ("Great Pharmacopoeia") by Li Shizhen and *Yuanshi* ("History of the Yuan [Dynasty]") by Song Lian.

In the Qing (Manchu) dynasty (1644–1911/12), Nanjing, renamed Jiangning, became the government seat of the viceroy of Jiangnan (who governed the provinces of Jiangsu and Jiangxi). In 1842 the Treaty of Nanjing, ending the first Opium War, was signed there. A decade later, in 1853, the city was taken by the revolutionary forces of the Taiping Rebellion under the leadership of Hong Xiuquan. As the capital of Taiping Tianguo ("Heavenly Kingdom of Great Peace"), Nanjing became a commune practicing universal brotherhood, equality of the sexes, and communal ownership of property. Numerous palaces for Hong and his lieutenants were built. When the Taipings were overthrown in 1864, there was widespread destruction of public buildings, temples, and the city wall by Qing troops, and the city was left nearly prostrate.

THE CONTEMPORARY CITY

Recovery from the Taiping period took decades. Foreign trade, although sanctioned by the treaties of Tianjin concluded with France in 1858, did not begin until 1899. By that time, modern industry and communication had reached the city. In 1908 the Shanghai-Nanjing railroad was opened, followed four years later by a railroad from the port city of Tianjin in Hebei province to Pukou. Such economic growth, however, was overshadowed by the Chinese Revolution of 1911–12. After the uprising had begun upstream at Wuhan in Hubei province, the revolutionary leaders proclaimed Nanjing the seat of the provisional government of the Republic of China. The democratic constitution of 1912 was adopted there

Chiang Kai-shek with his bride, Soong Meiling, in Nanjing, Jiangsu province, China, 1927. Encyclopædia Britannica, Inc.

before the first president, Yuan Shikai, moved the capital to Beijing.

Under the infant Republic of China, Nanjing was governed by warlords for more than a decade. Sun Yat-sen, leader of the Nationalist Party, embittered by politicians' intrigues centred in Beijing, vowed to make Nanjing the Nationalist capital. Accordingly, when his follower Chiang Kai-shek (Jiang Jieshi) achieved unified control of the country in 1928, the Nationalist government made Nanjing once more the capital of a united China. Progress was made in developing communications, industries, and natural resources. Physically, the city acquired a new look: modern boulevards and government buildings were constructed; new railroad stations and airfields were built; and the Sun Yat-sen Mausoleum was erected.

Such achievements were, however, cut short by the war against Japan. Nanjing fell in 1937. In the sack of the city that followed, great numbers of civilians were slaughtered (estimates vary widely, from as few as 40,000 to as many as 300,000). The city was then ruled by puppet governments until Japan's defeat in 1945. From 1946 to 1949, Nanjing resumed its status as the capital of Chiang Kai-shek's Nationalist government, but Chinese communist forces took the city in 1949. When the People's Republic of China was proclaimed on October 1, 1949, Nanjing was once again abandoned in favour of Beijing as the national capital. In 1952 it was made the provincial capital of Jiangsu, after which it was transformed into a modern industrialized city.

Despite the hardships suffered during the Great Leap Forward (1958–60) and the Cultural Revolution (1966–76)—especially during the latter, when many cultural and historical relics were damaged—the city has generally prospered during the communist period and has remained a major tourist destination. It has benefited greatly from its status as a leading city in the Yangtze delta regional economic plan. Nanjing has undergone rapid development since the 1980s, in the process emerging as a regional centre for business, finance, logistics, tourism, and information technology, in addition to manufacturing.

GUANGZHOU

The city of Guangzhou (conventional Canton, or Kwangchow) is the capital of Guangdong province, southeastern China. Its city centre lies near the head of the Pearl River (Zhu Jiang) Delta, more than 90 miles (145 km) inland from the South China Sea. Because of its position at the meeting point of inland rivers and the sea, it has long been one of China's main commercial and trading centres. It has served as a doorway for foreign influence since the 3rd century CE and was the first Chinese port to be regularly visited by European traders, who called it Canton. The city is a historic centre of learning. And as a centre of political activity for the Chinese Nationalist leader

Sun Yat-sen (Sun Zhongshan), it was one of the cradles of the Chinese Revolution of 1911–12. The area of Guangzhou's central city districts measures 108 square miles (280 square km); together, city districts measure 1,484 square miles (3,843 square km); and the entire municipality measures 2,870 square miles (7,434 square km). Its population according to a 2007 estimate numbered 3,461,100 in the central city districts; 6,367,700 in all city districts; and 7,734,800 people in the municipality.

LANDSCAPE

Located in the south-central part of Guangdong province, Guangzhou is a regional centre in southern China.

CITY SITE

The main part of the city is situated on the north bank of the Pearl River, which branches off the Xi (West) River before meeting with the Dong (East) River and forms the northern border of the immense Pearl River Delta to the south.

The central districts of the city lie to the south of Baiyun ("White Cloud") Mountain, which rises to 1,253 feet (382 m) above sea level about 4 miles (6 km) from the city centre. At the southern extension of Baiyun Mountain is Yuexiu Mountain, on which lived the earliest known inhabitants of the region. Archaeological work revealed that the site of the city during the Qin (221–206

A view of central Guangzhou, China at night. China, Photos/Getty Images

BCE) and the Han (206 BCE–220 CE) dynasties was slightly north of the modern urban centre. Later the city expanded southward as river-borne silt and sand were deposited and the Pearl gradually became narrower.

Old Guangzhou was a crowded city of narrow streets and winding alleys. A vigorous modernization program was carried out in the 1920s and '30s, during which wide streets were built, modern sewers introduced, arcades constructed for sidewalk shops, and numerous parks created.

New dikes built along the Pearl allowed the city to expand southward to its present waterfront. Until the 1980s, the hills to the north restricted growth there, and the numerous waterways to the west also were a barrier; and Guangzhou's subsequent expansion was mainly into the low plains to the east. However, with the influx of people after that, the city began to grow rapidly in all directions—notably to the north and south—though the core districts have remained concentrated around the old city site close to the riverbanks.

CLIMATE

Guangzhou has a subtropical monsoon (wet-dry) climate, which is typical of southeastern China. From May through early October, the summer season is long, wet, hot, and humid; south and southwest winds are often accompanied by typhoons (tropical cyclones), which are sometimes destructive. The July mean temperature is 83 °F (28 °C). The drier winter period lasts from November through early February and is mild and free of snow; the January mean temperature is 56 °F (13 °C). The third season, from February through April, is a period of transition that is marked by muggy weather. The average annual rainfall is about 64 inches (162 cm). Farmers in the Guangzhou area enjoy a year-round growing season. Flowers can be seen blooming throughout the year in Guangzhou, which has given rise to its nickname "city of flowers" (*huacheng*).

CITY LAYOUT

The central districts of Guangzhou stretch along a waterfront that runs south and then east along the Pearl River. The Old City (dating to the Ming dynasty and now mostly in the Yuexiu district), part of the district of Liwan to the west, and Tianhe district to the east are located on the north bank. On the south bank is the district of Haizhu, formerly largely industrial but now more given over to business offices, financial institutions, and other service-related activities. All these districts now comprise the core area of the city.

OLD CITY DISTRICTS

Yuexiu district is the commercial and financial centre of Guangzhou, as well as the site of provincial and municipal government offices. Included within it are the city's major hotels, department stores, and cinemas; traditional Chinese buildings are rarely found in this district, except in the hills to the north. Skyscrapers line the banks of the Pearl in the downtown area and ring Haizhu Square, a huge open space by the river. Yuexiu's original area, centred on the intersection of Guangzhou's two main thoroughfares—the north-south Jiefang Lu (Liberation Avenue) and the east-west Zhongshan Lu (Sun Yat-sen Avenue)—was enlarged with the addition in 2005 of the former Dongshan district to the east. The Peasant Movement Training Institute, which flourished in the mid-1920s under the leadership of Mao Zedong, is on Jiefang Lu just east of that intersection. Also located in the vicinity are the Huaisheng Mosque (built 627 CE), considered to be the oldest mosque in China; the Buddhist Temple of the Six Banyan Trees (Liurong Si), founded in the 5th century, and its nine-story Flower Pagoda (Huata); and, south of the intersection and west of Zhongshan Lu, the Gothic-style Roman Catholic cathedral of the Sacred Heart, built in the 1860s.

Yuexiu Park, in the northern part of the district, is one of the city's largest green spaces. Within the park are artificial lakes, a five-story red pagoda (built in 1380) that now houses the Guangzhou Municipal Museum, a flower exhibition hall, and sports and recreational facilities. Sun Yat-sen Memorial Hall (1931) is located immediately to its south. To the west of the park is the Guangzhou Foreign Trade Centre, which from the late 1950s to the early 21st century was the site of the China Import and Export Fair (also called the Guangzhou Trade Fair). The eastern (former Dongshan) portion of the district is home to two important sites— the Martyrs Memorial Park, dedicated to those killed in the uprising against the Nationalists (Kuomintang) in 1927, and a mausoleum for the 72 people killed during an unsuccessful revolt against the Qing dynasty in 1911. The area is also home to the Guangzhou Zoo.

The original Liwan district occupied the western part of the Old City, as well as a large island in the Pearl River to the west. It too was enlarged considerably in 2005, when it merged with Fangcun district, across the river to the southwest. The old part of the district has retained much traditional-style Chinese housing alongside a growing number of modern high-rise buildings. Liwan Park is located at the northern end of the district near the Pearl River Bridge, and northeast of there is Liuhua Park. To the southeast of Liwan Park, Shamian, a tiny island in the Pearl along the southern bank of the original district, was once an exclusive enclave of the British and French, and is noted for its Western-style mansions. The Fangcun area has long been known for its flower and tea markets.

OTHER DISTRICTS

Tianhe district, east of the Dongshan area, was created in 1985 from parts of the former eastern suburbs, and it is now considered to be one of the core districts of Guangzhou's central municipality. Its mixed urban and suburban landscapes now include business and shopping centres constructed along with high-rise office and residential buildings. Tianhe Science and Technology Park is home to many businesses engaged in the development of high technology and advanced software. In addition, many of the city's institutions of higher learning are located in Tianhe. It has been targeted as the city's new central business district for the 21st century, and, as part of that, a 103-story office tower (part of the Guangzhou International Finance Center, in the southwest part of the district, near the Pearl) has been under construction since 2005.

South of the Pearl is Haizhu district. It was long characterized by modern residential quarters and large industrial centres, but since the late 1980s a growing number of financial and business firms have established themselves there. Of great significance was the completion in the early 21st century of the first phase of the Guangzhou International Convention and Exhibition Center

(Pazhou Complex) on Pazhou Island in the Pearl River. One of the largest such venues in the world, it hosts Guangzhou's major trade shows (including the Guangzhou Trade Fair) and has spurred rapid development of Haizhu's commerce and tourism-related service sectors. Also located in the district are the south campus of Sun Yat-sen University (founded 1924) and the Pearl River (Zhujiang) Film Studio, one of the major film producers in China.

PEOPLE

Guangzhou is one of the most densely inhabited areas in China; most of its residents live in the central districts of the city. The local people, called Cantonese, speak the Cantonese language (Yueyu), which is distinctly different from the Mandarin spoken by most Chinese. However, with growing numbers of immigrants from northern and eastern China coming to live and work in the city, both Cantonese and Mandarin are now popularly used.

The earliest inhabitants, of Tai or Shan origin, were assimilated by the Chinese (Han) long ago. There are, however, small groups of Manchu and Chinese Muslims (Hui) in the city. A notable demographic feature is the large number of "overseas Chinese" who emigrated to Southeast Asia, the United States, Europe, and other parts of the world. Since the 1980s many of them returned and resettled in and around

Guangzhou. Another phenomenon that emerged since the 1980s is the presence of a large transient population of workers from other provinces or even overseas. These workers temporarily reside in the Guangzhou area to work in factories or at other jobs before returning to their home regions.

ECONOMY

Guangzhou has a mixed economy that is focused on a wide variety of manufacturing activities and on a broad array of services, notably the tourist trade.

MANUFACTURING AND TOURISM

Since 1950 there has been substantial expansion of the city's industries. The initial focus was on such light manufactures as electronics, textiles, newsprint, processed foods, and firecrackers. Smaller plants have also been developed to manufacture consumer goods. However, increasing investment has been made in heavy industries, including those producing machinery, chemicals (notably petrochemicals), iron and steel, and cement, as well as shipbuilding; in addition, automobile manufacturing has become important. The value of heavy manufactures now exceeds that of light industries. Since the late 1970s, much of the investment in the Guangzhou region has been by foreigners based in Hong Kong, Macao, and Taiwan. The result of all this growth is that the city has become one of the major industrial complexes of southern China.

Guangzhou is celebrated for its many handicraft products, including ivory carvings, jade objects, embroideries, fans, porcelain, and paper umbrellas. These, along with the city's famous cuisine and its many museums and other cultural attractions, have made Guangzhou one of China's principal tourist destinations. Considerable effort has been focused on improving tourist facilities, and tourism has become an important component of the local economy.

TRADE AND FINANCE

Guangzhou traditionally was the centre of trade for Guangdong, Guangxi, and adjacent provinces of southern China. Products such as sugar, fruits, silk, timber, tea, and herbs were exported, whereas manufactured goods and industrial equipment were transshipped via Guangzhou into the interior. However, since the 1980s, a growing quantity of manufactured goods and equipment (including mechanical, electrical, and electronic products) has been exported via the city to the world. The semiannual China Import and Export Fair, which began in 1957, has become an institution of world trade.

Large shopping centres and wholesale markets established in the central districts of the city include department stores and specialty shops. Banks, including state and provincial and local and foreign commercial establishments, now

have branches throughout the city area. Although the city does not have a stock exchange (such as those in nearby Shenzhen and Hong Kong), it does have several brokerage firms.

TRANSPORTATION

Buses and bicycles were once the principal means of transportation within the city. However, there has been a dramatic increase in the use of automobiles and motorcycles, and fewer bicycles are seen. As a result, the city has some of the worst traffic congestion in all of China. The traffic situation has been improved somewhat by widening streets, building more bridges across the Pearl River, and placing restrictions on motorcycle traffic at certain times of the day and in specific street zones downtown. More importantly, the city has been constructing an extensive subway network, several lines of which are now open. The system has come to play a major role in daily public transportation.

The Pearl River Delta is blessed with innumerable canals and creeks; the smaller canals are used by sampans (flat-bottomed boats propelled by oars) and the larger canals by steamers or motor launches. Guangzhou is a terminus of inland navigation and is also the focal point of coastal and ocean navigation for southern China. The Guangzhou Port Group, one of the largest port complexes in China, has its major facilities at Huangpu, which is 12 miles (19 km) downstream and now a district of the city;

at Xinsha, farther downstream along the Pearl estuary; and at Nansha, which is at the southern end of the municipality near Hong Kong and now also is a district of the city. All these and other ports under the group have been expanded to accommodate vessels with displacements of 10,000 or more tons.

Guangzhou is served by railroads linking it north to Beijing, south to Kowloon (Hong Kong), east to the coastal city of Shantou and into Fujian province, and west to the port city of Zhanjiang and into Guangxi province. Guangdong has one of the country's most advanced provincial highway systems. Major arterial roads and express highways link Guangzhou with other large cities in the province and with Macau and Hong Kong. The city's new Baiyun International Airport (opened 2004), some 18 miles (30 km) north of the city centre, is the largest in southern China.

ADMINISTRATION AND SOCIETY

Guangzhou's municipal government is part of the hierarchical structure of the Chinese government—and the parallel structure of the Chinese Communist Party—that extends from the national organization, through the provincial apparatus, to the municipal and, ultimately, neighbourhood levels.

GOVERNMENT

The principal responsibilities of the Guangzhou Municipal People's Congress,

the major decision-making body, include issuing administrative orders, determining the budget, and implementing economic plans. A standing committee selected from its members recommends policy decisions and oversees the operation of municipal government. Executive authority rests with the People's Government of Guangzhou Municipality, the officers of which are elected by the congress; it consists of a mayor, executive vice mayors, vice mayors, and numerous bureaus in charge of public security, the judicial system, and other civil, economic, social, and cultural affairs.

The municipality is now divided into ten districts (*qu*) and two county-level cities (*xianjishi*), each of which has a district or city mayoralty. Under a district there are police substations and street mayoralties. Neighbourhood associations have various functions, including mediating disputes, conducting literacy campaigns, supervising sanitation and welfare, and promoting family planning.

HEALTH

Health conditions improved dramatically during the 20th century, especially after 1950. Epidemics have been eliminated through the control of disease-carrying pests. Guangzhou has many high-quality hospitals with modern medical equipment. In addition, the city is a national hub of traditional Chinese medicine, centred around Guangzhou University of Chinese Medicine (established 1956) and its network of affiliated hospitals and clinics.

EDUCATION

Guangzhou is one of China's most progressive cities in regard to education. In addition to a large number of kindergartens, primary schools, and middle schools, it has dozens of institutions of higher learning. In addition to Sun Yat-sen University and the school of Chinese medicine, these include Jinan University (1906), South China University of Technology (1952), South China Normal University (1933), Southern Medical University (1951), South China Agricultural University (1909), and Guangzhou Academy of Fine Arts (1953). An ambitious project named Guangzhou University City was launched at the beginning of the 21st century, with the goal of creating a concentrated, multiple-campus college town on an island in the Pearl River south of the central city in Panyu district.

CULTURAL LIFE

Guangzhou is a vibrant city. Large tracts of parkland, many of them created since 1949, help give the city its characteristically lush appearance and provide the citizenry with a wide variety of recreational facilities. The colourful flower show held during the annual Spring Festival is a major highlight. Although the Cantonese share some aspects of the modern lifestyle of Hong Kong's residents, they also prize their own historical and cultural roots. Throngs of people are usually found visiting the city's many museums and monuments of historical importance, and productions of Yue opera and Chao opera and of musical performances are well attended. Guangzhou is noted for its puppet plays that feature large puppets with finely carved wooden heads.

The Sun Yat-sen (Sun Zhongshan) Library of Guangdong province has one of the largest holdings in China, including an extensive collection of vernacular-language works. Notable historic sites include the tomb of Zhao Mei, second ruler of Nanyue, a state that was incorporated into the Xi (Western) Han dynasty (206 BCE–25 CE); the restored campus of Huangpu (Whampoa) Military Academy; and the residence of Sun Yat-sen.

The vitality of the Cantonese people is exemplified by their passion for food. Cantonese cuisine is world-renowned, and the city's hundreds of restaurants offer a seemingly endless variety of dishes. Many feature fresh ingredients, including locally caught seafood, that are quickly cooked, often by stir-frying. Congees (porridges made from rice or millet) and soups are often part of the meal. Some unusual local dishes include fried snake, cooked fish maw (swim bladder), fried shark's fin, and fried chicken feet.

Modern recreational facilities have also enriched the city's cultural life. Sports facilities, including stadiums, natatoriums, tennis courts, and a rowing centre, have added to the leisure diversions available to city residents. A new television tower in Guangzhou has been under construction since 2005. When completed, it will have a total height of 2,000 feet (610 m) and will include an observation deck, restaurant, and other visitor facilities near the top of its 1,490-foot-tall (454 m) main structure.

HISTORY

The earliest known inhabitants of the Guangzhou area were the Baiyue, a Tai, or Shan, people.

THE EARLY PERIOD

During the Xi (Western) Zhou dynasty (1146–771 BCE), the local Baiyue people pledged allegiance to the feudal state of Chu to the northeast, giving rise to the name of Chuting for the area. Later, a walled town known as Nanwu Cheng, in the northern section of the present-day city, was built during the Spring and Autumn (Chunqiu) period (770–476 BCE). Between 339 and 329 BCE, the town was rebuilt and expanded and was known as Wuyang Cheng ("City of Five Goats")—named for the legend that gods riding five goats descended from heaven and saved the city from famine.

Under the Qin dynasty (221–207 BCE), what was by then a small city (known as Panyu for the twin hills of Pan and Yu located in the area) was made the capital of Nanhai prefecture. Upon the fall of the Qin, General Zhao Tuo (died 137 BCE) established an autonomous state known as Nanyue, which was annexed in 111 BCE by the Xi Han dynasty. For the next 300 years, Chinese assimilation of the Yue people proceeded, and the region was firmly integrated into the empire.

During the four centuries from the Three Kingdoms to the founding of the Tang dynasty in 618 CE, when North China was overrun by barbarian invaders, Guangzhou remained a part of the Chinese regimes. The city was first named Guangzhou in 226, when the Wu state of the Three Kingdoms (Sanguo) period set up a prefecture named Guangzhou there. During this period the city grew in wealth and population as an important trade port in southern China. Buddhist temples were erected, and a flourishing community was maintained by Arab and Hindu traders. Peace and prosperity were further augmented under the Tang (618–907). An auxiliary wall and settlement were built around the razed Yu Hill, but the city suffered much destruction during the civil strife at the end of the dynasty.

Under the Song dynasty (960–1279) the increase in Guangzhou's population and the growth of foreign trade made it necessary to enlarge the city. A second auxiliary wall and settlement were constructed near the razed Pan Hill in the late 11th century. Under the Nan (Southern) Song (1127–1279), Chinese seafarers and traders sailed to Southeast

Asia, thus opening the way for Chinese emigration abroad in subsequent ages. Also at that time, the rising port city of Quanzhou (in present-day Fujian province) replaced Guangzhou as the biggest trade port in China in terms of volume of trade. In the late 13th century and throughout the 14th, many Chinese families from North China moved into the Guangdong region in the wake of the Mongol conquest. Although the city suffered much destruction from the conquest, it subsequently experienced a booming economy under the Yuan (Mongol) dynasty (1206–1368), as the Yuan rulers encouraged maritime trade and kept Chinese-Mongol relations under control.

Under the Ming dynasty (1368–1644) the city underwent considerable rebuilding and expansion. In 1380 the old town and the two auxiliary districts were combined into one large walled city. In 1565 an outer wall was added on the south to incorporate the new commercial districts on the north bank of the Pearl. Meanwhile, the pattern of foreign trade changed as the supremacy of the Arabs ended with the coming of the Europeans. The Portuguese sent their first embassy to Guangzhou in the early 1500s, followed by the Dutch and the British in the 17th century.

Guangzhou next came under the rule of the Qing (Manchu) dynasty (1644–1911/12). Recognizing the importance of the city, in 1746 the government made it the capital of the Viceroyalty of Guangdong and Guangxi. The British East India Company established a "factory" (foreign traders' residences and business offices) in Guangzhou in 1685, and annual trading operations began in 1699. Throughout the 18th century, French, Dutch, American, and other foreign nationals also established trade relations with the city; what became known as the "13 factories" (*shisan hang* or *shisan yiguan*) were located on the waterfront.

Trade moved with little difficulty until friction began to mount in the 1820s. The foreigners found trade restrictions (through licensed Chinese merchants known as cohongs [*gonghangs*]) too irksome, while the Chinese authorities refused to open normal diplomatic relations. The Chinese seized and destroyed large quantities of illegal opium brought in by the British in 1839, and in retaliation the British attacked Chinese positions in the Pearl River Delta. The first Opium War (1839–42) ended in humiliating defeat for China, and the city saved itself from destruction only by paying a large ransom.

The Treaty of Nanjing (1842) with the United Kingdom negotiated at the conclusion of the war provided for Guangzhou to be opened as a treaty port. In 1844 the French and the Americans obtained similar treaties. However, antiforeign sentiment ran high in Guangdong province, and the city refused to open its gates until 1857. The coolie trade (the shipment of Chinese contract labourers overseas) and the use of foreign flags to protect pirates caused several crises. The second Opium War (the *Arrow* War) broke out between China and Britain and France in 1856. Guangzhou was occupied by Anglo-French forces until 1861, and Shamian Island was made an Anglo-French concession in 1859.

Amid the woes of foreign imperialism, Guangzhou was deeply shaken by the great antidynastic outbreak of the Taiping Rebellion (1850–64), the leader of which, Hong Xiuquan, was born in the city's northern suburb of Huaxian (now Huadu district). Many followers of Hong formed secret societies that kept his revolutionary ideals alive even after the failure of the rebellion. For the next 50 years, anti-Manchu agitation formed one of the twin forces that gripped Guangzhou; the other was the rise of nationalism. Starting from the late 1840s, Hong Kong and Shanghai gradually replaced Guangzhou as a leading centre of foreign trade.

THE CONTEMPORARY CITY

Guangzhou came under the spell of its most illustrious son, Sun Yat-sen, from 1895 to 1925. Sun made the city the testing ground for his campaign to overthrow the Manchu dynasty and to establish a Chinese republic. The Guangzhou Uprising of 1911 paved the way for the success of the Chinese Revolution of 1911–12. Guangzhou became the base of operations for action against the warlords between 1916 and 1925 and served as the headquarters of Sun's Nationalist Party (Kuomintang, or Guomindang). Besides completing his Three Principles of the People, Sun reorganized the party in 1924 to reactivate the Nationalist revolution. All manner of people flocked to Guangzhou—the right- and left-wing members of the Kuomintang, the members of the newly formed Chinese Communist Party, and Soviet advisers. Chiang Kai-shek (Jiang Jieshi), Mao Zedong, and Zhou Enlai began their careers in Guangzhou under Sun's tutelage.

Chiang gained power when he crushed an uprising by the Guangzhou Merchants' Volunteer Corps and defeated the disloyal local warlords (1924). With Sun's death in 1925, however, Guangzhou was embroiled in the power struggle between the communists and the Nationalists. In 1927 a communist-led coup attempted to set up a workers' government in the city, only to be crushed by Chiang. From 1928 to 1937, Guangzhou was officially under the control of the Nationalist government, but it was actually controlled by independent leaders, who criticized Chiang's dictatorship and threatened secession from the Nationalist government at Nanjing. In 1937, when war against the Japanese broke out, Guangzhou became a prime target of Japanese air raids. The city fell in 1938 and remained under Japanese occupation until 1945. Recovery did not begin until the communist government took control in 1949.

In 1921, during the Republican period, Guangzhou officially had been designated an administratively independent city under the Nationalist government, with the son of Sun Yat-sen being Guangzhou's first mayor. At first, under the new communist regime, it retained its status as a municipality directly under the national government, but in 1954 the city was placed under the administration of Guangdong province. Another significant administrative change occurred in 2005, when some urban districts were amalgamated and a number of what until then had been suburbs became city districts under a much-enlarged municipality.

The modernization of Guangzhou had begun in the 1920s but was interrupted by the Japanese occupation. It resumed after 1949, especially from the late 1950s, when heavy industries were introduced. The city developed into one of China's centres of foreign trade. Guangzhou benefited tremendously from China's adoption of economic reform policies beginning in the early 1980s, particularly with the establishment of special economic zones in nearby Shenzhen and Zhuhai. Guangzhou underwent a sustained period of economic growth that continued into the early 21st century and was marked by considerable building construction and infrastructure development. In the process, the city reemerged as a financial and economic hub of southern China.

CHAPTER 8

OTHER MAJOR CITIES OF SOUTHEASTERN CHINA

In addition to southeastern China's three great metropolises (Shanghai, Guangzhou, and Nanjing), there are numerous large urban centres scattered throughout the region, connected by a dense network of roads, rail lines, and waterways. These range from the beautiful garden city of Suzhou near Shanghai to the vast industrial and commercial conurbation of Wuhan in the interior. Some manufacturing cities, such as Wuxi in Jiangsu province, increasingly have focused on tourism in recent years.

WUXI

The city of Wuxi is in southern Jiangsu province, eastern China. It is situated along the Grand Canal at that waterway's junction with local rivers near the northeastern corner of Lake Tai. The city is the principal route focus of the dense network of canals and waterways that provides the basic transport system of southern Jiangsu.

Wuxi is one of the older cities in the Yangtze River (Chang Jiang) delta area. It was originally known as a source of tin, but, by the time the county was founded in 202 BCE under the Xi (Western) Han dynasty (206 BCE–25 CE), the deposits had been exhausted, and the county was named Wuxi ("Without

Tin"). From the end of the 3rd century, the city was subordinated to the commandery (district under the control of a commander) of Biling (later Changzhou) and remained so except for a brief interval under the rule of the Yuan (Mongol) dynasty (1206–1368), when it was made an independent prefecture.

Since early times the area around Lake Tai has been extremely fertile. After the completion of the Grand Canal in 609, Wuxi became a transshipment centre for tax grain destined for the capital. It thus became one of the greatest grain markets in China, handling vast quantities of rice annually, and was the seat of a complex commercial organization of extremely wealthy merchants and middlemen. When the Grand Canal fell into decay after 1850, Wuxi retained its importance as a rice market, exporting grain to Shanghai, 80 miles (130 km) to the southeast, for shipment by sea to Tianjin to the north. The trade in grain increased still further after the completion of a railway link to Shanghai and to Zhenjiang and Nanjing to the northwest, in 1908.

Wuxi has traditionally been a centre of the textile industry, being engaged in both cotton textiles and silk reeling. Textile mills were established there as long ago as 1894 and silk filatures (establishments for reeling silk) in 1904. This development was largely the work of Shanghai industrialists, many of whom were originally from Wuxi merchant families. The two cities have had unusually close links, and Wuxi was known colloquially before World War II as "Little

Shanghai." The cotton yarn produced was woven not only in the city itself but also in such nearby canal cities as Changzhou (northwest) and Suzhou (southeast), whereas the silk reeled in the city was mostly woven into cloth in Suzhou and (more recently) in Shanghai. Present-day Wuxi is one of the greatest silk-reeling centres in China. Cotton textile production is also important and is the city's largest single industry.

Other long-established industries include flour milling, rice polishing, and oil extraction. Industrial development has accelerated since the 1950s. The textile and food-processing industries have been modernized and expanded, and the city has become a centre for the engineering industry, particularly for the manufacturing of machine tools and diesel engines. Wuxi also manufactures electrical equipment and cables and boiler-plant and textile machinery of various types; more recently, manufacturing of chemicals and pharmaceuticals has become important.

Since 1949 the city's importance as a national commercial centre has declined, although its role as a distribution and collection hub for the Lake Tai area has continued. An expressway between Shanghai and Nanjing passes through the city area, with two branch roads in the province stretching from the city north to Jiangyin and southwest to Yixing. The local airport provides flight service to several major cities in the country.

Tourism has become increasingly important. Wuxi's surroundings include many well-known scenic spots that have been carefully preserved, together with city parks and historic sites, and the national government has designated it as one of China's historical and cultural cities. Industrial development has been closely restricted near the lake, the major scenic attraction, although an industrial park focused on science and technology was established there in 2006. Jiangnan University (founded 1902; reconstituted 2001) is the best-known institution of higher learning in the city. The 2002 population estimate of the city of Wuxi was 1,318,726; a 2007 estimate of the urban agglomeration was 1,749,000.

SUZHOU

Suzhou (conventional Soochow) is a major city of southern Jiangsu province, eastern China. It is situated on the southern section of the Grand Canal on a generally flat, low-lying plain between the renowned Lake Tai to the west and the vast Shanghai metropolis to the east. Surrounded by canals on all four sides and crisscrossed by minor canals, the city controls the Yangtze River (Chang Jiang) delta area north and northeast of Lake Tai. Suzhou is a place of great beauty, with lakes, rivers, ponds, world-famous gardens, and a string of scenic hills along the eastern shore of the lake. It also lies at the centre of some of the richest agricultural land in China. The population estimate of 2006 was 1,416,234; and the 2007 estimate of the urban agglomeration was 1,650,000.

HISTORY

The traditional founding date of Suzhou is 514 BCE, when a city with the approximate boundaries of the present-day Suzhou was established by the ruler of the state of Wu during the Spring and Autumn (Chunqiu) period (770–476 BCE) of the Dong (Eastern) Zhou dynasty. Under the Qin dynasty (221–207 BCE) it became the seat of a county, Wuxian, and of the Kuaiji commandery, which controlled most of present-day Jiangsu south of the Yangtze and Zhejiang province. The name Suzhou dates from 589 CE, when the Sui dynasty (581–618) conquered southern China.

With the building of the Grand Canal, Suzhou became an administrative and commercial centre for an area that rapidly developed into the major rice-surplus region of China. Under the Song (960–1279) and the Yuan (1206–1368) dynasties, Suzhou continued to flourish. In the 13th century, the Venetian traveler Marco Polo visited it and commented on its splendours. Wusong River and Suzhou Creek gave the city direct access to the sea, and for a while Suzhou was a port for foreign shipping, until the silting of the Yangtze River delta and the irrigation and reclamation works that went on continually impeded access. Under the Ming (1368–1644) and early Qing (1644–1911/12) dynasties, Suzhou reached the peak of its prosperity. The home of many wealthy landowning families, it became a centre for scholarship and the arts. Sources of the city's wealth included the silk industry and embroidery. It also served as an important source of commercial capital and a finance and banking centre.

From 1860 to 1863, during the Taiping Rebellion (1850–64), Suzhou was occupied by the Taiping leader Li Xiucheng. Although it was one of the few places in which Taiping reform policies seem to have been effectively carried out, the city was, nevertheless, largely destroyed. It was restored in the late 19th century, but its commercial supremacy was then challenged by nearby Shanghai. Under the Treaty of Shimonoseki (concluded between China and Japan in 1895), Suzhou was opened for foreign trade but without significant results. Before World War II the area was adversely affected by foreign competition, and the silk industry, most of which was on a small handicraft scale, was hard hit. At about that time some modern factories manufacturing satins and cotton fabrics were established, and a large electric-power-generating plant was set up; however, until the outbreak of the Sino-Japanese War in 1937, there was little modern industry. Suzhou was occupied by the Japanese from 1937 until the war's end in 1945.

THE CONTEMPORARY CITY

The silk and cotton textile industries, long a mainstay of Suzhou's economy, have been modernized considerably. In addition, factories producing metallurgical products, machinery, chemicals, pharmaceuticals, electronics, and processed foods have been established since the 1980s. A new high-technology industrial park, with joint investment from China and Singapore, has been set up in the eastern outskirts of the city.

The city's first railway, linking Suzhou with Shanghai and with Nanjing to the northwest, was opened in 1908. In 1936 a branchline was built joining this line to the main railway between Shanghai and Hangzhou at Jiaxing (both in northern Zhejiang), but it was dismantled by the retreating Japanese army in 1945. There are also expressways and highways to Kunshan and Changshu in the delta, as well as to Nanjing, Shanghai, and Hangzhou. In addition, a large amount of traffic still uses the region's network of waterways.

The city is a centre of learning; Suzhou University (formerly Dongwu University) and Suzhou School of Fine Arts were established in the early 20th century, and later more universities and colleges were established. Suzhou boasts some 150 exquisite gardens with temples, pavilions, and rock sculptures; a number of those dating from the 11th to the 19th century were collectively designated a UNESCO World Heritage site in 1997 (extended in 2000). The gardens, Suzhou's other cultural and historical sites, and nearby Lake Tai make the area a popular tourist destination. The Chinese Garden Society, reestablished in 1978, organizes international academic exchanges.

HANGZHOU

Hangzhou (conventional Hangchow) is the capital and largest city of Zhejiang province, southeastern China. The city is located in the northern part of the province on the north bank of the Qiantang River estuary at the head of Hangzhou Bay. It has water communications with the interior of Zhejiang to the south, is the southern terminus of the Grand Canal, and is linked to the network of canals and waterways that cover the Yangtze River (Chang Jiang) delta area to the north. The city stands at the eastern foot of a scenic range of hills, the Tianmu ("Eye of Heaven") Mountains, and on the shore of the famous Xi (West) Lake, celebrated in poetry and paintings for its beauty and a favourite imperial retreat. The 2006 population estimate was 2,455,584, and the 2007 estimate of the urban agglomeration was 3,007,000.

HISTORY

The county of Qiantang was first established at this site under the Qin dynasty (221–207 BCE) but did not start developing until the 4th and 5th centuries CE, when the Yangtze River delta area began to be settled. A prefecture named Hangzhou was created there in 589, during the Sui dynasty (581–618), which is the source of the city's name. It became a major local centre with the completion of the Jiangnan Canal (then the southern section of the Grand Canal) in 609. During the Ten Kingdoms (Shiguo) period (907–960), Hangzhou was the capital of the state of Wu-Yue. In the later Song period (960–1279), northern China fell to the Jin (Juchen) dynasty

(1115–1234); from 1127 the Song rulers were confined to southern China, and they made Hangzhou (then known as Lin'an) their capital. A centre of commerce, it was visited in the late 13th century by Marco Polo, who called it Kinsai, or Quinsay; it then had an estimated population of 1 million to 1.5 million.

Although it never again reached the peak of importance that it had achieved as capital of the Nan (Southern) Song, Hangzhou remained important. Under the Ming (1368–1644) and Qing (1644–1911/12) dynasties, it was a superior prefecture, in addition to being the provincial capital of Zhejiang. It became immensely wealthy, being at the centre of a fertile rice-growing area as well as being the site of the most important silk industries in China. It also was famous as a centre of culture, producing numerous writers, painters, and poets. Its importance as a port dwindled, however, as Hangzhou Bay gradually silted up and as its outport, Ganpu, became useless. From the 14th century, its trade gradually shifted to Ningbo to the southeast on the southern shore of the bay and, in the 19th century, to the new city of Shanghai, some 100 miles (160 km) to the northeast at the mouth of the Yangtze. In 1861, during the Taiping Rebellion (1850–64), the city fell to the rebels and suffered severe damage.

Subsequently, although no longer a major port, it remained a commercial centre for domestic trade and was opened to foreign trade in 1896. Its

Garden in Hangzhou, Zhejiang province, China. A. Topping—Rapho/Photo Researchers

commercial role was later augmented by the construction of a railway to Shanghai (1909), of another to Ningbo (1914), and of a main line to Jiangxi and Hunan provinces in 1936–38. Since the construction of railways in Fujian province in the 1950s, Hangzhou has become the focus of rail traffic from the southeastern provinces to Shanghai. It was also the focus of the earliest network of modern motor roads, constructed in the 1930s. Hangzhou was held by the Japanese from 1937 to 1945.

THE CONTEMPORARY CITY

Since 1949 Hangzhou, though it has been carefully preserved as a scenic district and tourist attraction, has also developed into an industrial centre. The textile industry, originally confined to silk production, now produces both silk and cottons. In addition to thermal electric-generating plants, the city is connected via the regional power grid to the large Xin'an River hydroelectric project to the southwest and to Shanghai and Nanjing. A chemical industry has also been established. In the late 1950s, a major tractor plant was built in Hangzhou, and a machine-tool industry subsequently developed. Electronics manufacturing has also become a major component of the city's economy.

Hangzhou is an economic centre of and export base for east-central China. A railway network connects Hangzhou to Shanghai and Ningbo, as well as to

Xuanzhou in Anhui province (northwest) and Nanchang in Jiangxi province (southwest). A Shanghai-Ningbo expressway via Hangzhou was completed in the 1990s, and a Nanjing-Hangzhou expressway opened in the early 21st century. There are scheduled flights to Singapore and to Hong Kong and other major cities in China from Hangzhou Xiaoshan International Airport (opened 2000), 17 miles (28 km) east of the city. With increased growth since the late 20th century, the city has spread to the southern bank of the Qiantang River in recent years, and its metropolitan area includes the city of Xiaoshan to the southeast.

Hangzhou's architecture and gardens are renowned, and it is situated among hills and valleys in which some of the most famous monasteries in China are located. Thus, the city, with its beautiful scenery and sites of historical interest, is among China's most popular tourist destinations. Notable are Xi Lake, nestled in hills, and, on a slope northwest of the lake, Lingyan Temple, considered one of the most famous Buddhist temples in China. Hangzhou is also a national centre of higher education. Zhejiang University (1897) is among the largest and most prestigious institutions in China; its size was expanded considerably in 1998 when it was reconstituted after amalgamating with the former Zhejiang Agricultural University (1910) and Hangzhou University (1952).

NINGBO

Ningbo is a major city of northeastern Zhejiang province, southeastern China. The city (its name meaning "Calm Waves") is situated in the low-lying coastal plain on the Yong River, some 16 miles (25 km) upstream from its mouth in Hangzhou Bay, at the confluence where two tributaries, the Yuyao and Fenghua rivers, join the main stream. Ningbo was from an early period itself a port, although the mouth of the river was masked by a mud bar. It has an outport, Zhenhai, on the western bank of the estuary, which originally had been a fishing port. The 2006 estimation of the city's population was 1,214,361. The 2007 estimation of the urban agglomeration was 1,923,000 people.

HISTORY

After Gouzhang county, a short distance to the east, was transferred to what is now Ningbo in 625, it became the seat of an independent Ming prefecture in 738. In 908 the county seat's name, which had been Mao Xian since 625, was changed to Yin Xian, which it has since retained. Under the Nan (Southern) Song (1127–1279), Ming prefecture was promoted in 1195 to a superior prefecture, Qingyuan. It kept this name through the Yuan (Mongol) period (1206–1368). In 1381 it became Ningbo superior prefecture, and it kept that name until 1912, when it was demoted to county status, taking the formal name of Yin Xian. It regained the name of Ningbo when the county seat was separated from the county to form a new city in 1949.

Ningbo first rose to importance during the latter part of the 5th century, when Korean shipping found it to be the most convenient port for contacts with the southern capital at Jiankang (present-day Nanjing). Under the Tang (618–907) this traffic continued. Although official relations lapsed after 838, private trade continued on a large scale. In the 11th century, Ningbo became a centre of the coastal trade. Its importance grew with the establishment of the Nan Song capital at Hangzhou in 1127, when overseas trade to and from the capital flowed through Ningbo. It grew rapidly during the Song (960–1279) and Yuan periods.

The early part of the Ming dynasty (1368–1644) was one of setbacks to Ningbo's development. Overseas trade was deliberately curtailed by the government; the building of oceangoing ships was prohibited; and even coastal trade was severely restricted. Ningbo was attacked by Japanese pirates, and it became a defensive base of some importance. Its growth seems to have stagnated, however, until the last quarter of the 15th century, when the rural prosperity of its hinterland began to recover.

This recovery was assisted when the Portuguese began trading in Ningbo in 1545, at first illicitly but later (after 1567) legally. Still later, Dutch and British merchants arrived, and the Ningbo merchants began to trade with the China coast from Manchuria (Northeast China) to Guangzhou (Canton), as well as with the

Philippines and Taiwan. Ningbo was the commercial centre of the coastal plain to the east of Shaoxing and an outport for the Yangtze River (Chang Jiang) delta area, to which it was linked by the Zhedong Canal leading to Shaoxing and the Qiantang River. As a result, in the 17th and 18th centuries, the Ningbo merchants became important in China's internal commerce and began to play a national role as bankers in the early 19th century. In 1843 Ningbo was opened to foreign trade as a treaty port, but later trade declined, and its place was taken by Shanghai to the north across Hangzhou Bay.

THE CONTEMPORARY CITY

Ningbo is now a local commercial centre and a busy port for northeastern Zhejiang. Ships of 3,000 tons can use the port, and there is regular passenger service to Shanghai. A large passenger terminal was built in 1979. A separate newer port, Beilun, east of the city on the southern coast of Hangzhou Bay, is now one of China's largest deep-water seaports with container-handling facilities. Established in 1985, Beilun is now a district of Ningbo. There are rail and expressway links with Shanghai via Hangzhou, and the new Hangzhou Bay Bridge (opened 2008) more directly links Ningbo to the Shanghai region; the bridge, 22 miles (36 km) in length, is one of the longest sea bridges in the world.

Ningbo is also the hub of a water-transportation network of coastal junk

Tianyige in Ningbo, the oldest library building in China. Shutterstock.com

traffic and canals. It is a collection centre for cotton and other agricultural produce of the plain, for the marine products of the local fisheries, and for timber from the mountains in the hinterland, and it is a major distribution centre for coal, oil, textiles, and consumer goods. In 1984 Ningbo was designated one of China's "open" cities in the new open-door policy inviting foreign investment.

Cotton-spinning mills, flour mills, textile plants, and tobacco factories were established before World War II, and from 1949 industrialization continued. The textile industry has expanded, with new textile plants, knitting factories, dyeing plants, and yarn-spinning mills. Food processing—flour milling, rice polishing, oil extraction, wine making, and particularly the canning of foodstuffs—has become a major economic activity. In addition, Ningbo supports a number of manufacturing concerns. A large shipbuilding industry constructs fishing vessels. Factories produce diesel engines, agricultural and other machinery, generators, machine tools, and petrochemicals. Thermal-power-generating stations there supply electricity to the entire region.

Ningbo was designated one of the national-level historical and cultural cities in China in 1986. The oldest library building in China—Tianyige—is in the western part of the city. Its collection of rare books and documents dates to the 11th century and includes many unique local chronicles of the Ming dynasty.

FUZHOU

The city of Fuzhou (conventional Foochow) is the capital of Fujian province, southeastern China. It is situated in the eastern part of the province on the north bank of the estuary of Fujian's largest river, the Min River, a short distance from its mouth on the East China Sea. The Min gives the city access to the interior and to the neighbouring provinces of Jiangxi and Zhejiang. The population of the city is 1,457,626 (2006 estimate), while the population of the Fuzhou urban agglomeration is 2,606,000 (2007 estimate).

HISTORY

Fuzhou was one of the first places in Fujian to be settled. At the beginning of the 2nd century BCE, it was called Ye, or Dongye, and it was once the capital of the kingdom of Min-Yue. After the Han dynasty emperor Wudi subjugated the area, it became the seat of Ye county. In the 2nd century CE, its name was changed to Houguan, and it became the military seat for the eastern coastal area. In 592, after the Sui conquest of southern China (581), it was renamed Min county, and under the Tang dynasty (618–907) it became the seat of Fuzhou prefecture. After the An Lushan rebellion of 755, it became the seat of the civil governor of Fujian, and in 789 the prefectural city was divided into two counties. In the 9th and 10th centuries, the population of Fujian as a whole rapidly increased.

Fuzhou was briefly the capital of the independent kingdom of Min (909–945) and has remained the capital of Fujian ever since. In Song times (960–1279) much overseas trade was concentrated at Fuzhou, which also became an important cultural centre for the empire as a whole.

Fuzhou prospered from the 16th to the 19th century, and its prosperity reached its height when it was opened as a treaty port after the first Opium War (1839–42). It subsequently became the chief port for the tea trade, being much nearer to the producing districts than Guangzhou (Canton), to which tea had to be shipped overland. The eclipse of the Guangzhou tea trade was completed when the Taiping Rebellion (1850–64) disrupted the overland route. However, with the decline of the tea trade, Fuzhou's export trade fell by half between 1874 and 1884; tea was gradually rivaled by exports of timber, paper, and foodstuffs.

In 1866 the port was the site of one of China's first major experiments with Western technology when the Fuzhou Navy Yard was established; a shipyard and an arsenal were built under French guidance, and a naval school was opened. A naval academy was also established at the shipyard, and it became a centre for the study of Western languages and technical sciences. The academy, which offered courses in English, French, engineering, and navigation, produced a generation of Western-trained officers, including the famous scholar-reformer Yan Fu (1854–1921).

The yard was established as part of a program to strengthen China in the wake of the country's disastrous defeat in the trading conflict known as the second Opium War (1856–60). But most talented students continued to pursue a traditional Confucian education, and by the mid-1870s the government had begun to lose interest in the shipyard; the facility had trouble securing funds and declined in importance. Fuzhou remained essentially a commercial centre and a port, with relatively little industry, until World War II. The port was occupied by the Japanese during 1940–45.

THE CONTEMPORARY CITY

Fuzhou has grown considerably since the establishment of the People's Republic of China in 1949. Its water communications have been improved by the clearing of the Min River for navigation by medium-sized craft upstream to Nanping in central Fujian. In 1956 a railway linking Fuzhou with the interior of the province and with the main Chinese railway system was opened. The port too has been improved; Fuzhou itself is no longer accessible to seagoing ships, but Mawei (Luoxingta) port and another outer harbour, at Guantou on the coast of the East China Sea, have been modernized and improved. An express highway connects the city with Xiamen (Amoy), another major coastal city in Fujian. Fuzhou's international airport has regular flights to Hong Kong and other major cities in China.

Two large power-generating facilities near Fuzhou—a thermal plant and the Shuikou hydroelectric station on the Min River—supply power to the city. The city is a centre for industrial chemicals and has food-processing, timber-working, engineering, electronics, papermaking, printing, and textile industries. In 1984 Fuzhou was designated one of China's "open" cities in the new open-door policy inviting foreign investments, and an economic and high-technology development zone in Mawei—together with other foreign investment districts—has been established.

Handicrafts remain important, and the city is famous for its lacquer and wood products. Among Fuzhou's institutions of higher learning are Fujian Medical University (1937), Fuzhou University (1958), Fujian Normal University (1907), Fujian Agriculture and Forestry University (1936), and a research institute of the Chinese Academy of Science. Fuzhou is a city two millennia old, known for its history and culture, and in 1986 the central government added it to the list of specially designated historical and cultural cities.

XIAMEN

Xiamen (conventional Amoy) is a major city and port of southeastern Fujian province, southeastern China. It is situated on the southwestern coast of Xiamen (Amoy) Island in Xiamen Harbour (an inlet of the Taiwan Strait), the estuary of the Jiulong River. Known as the "garden on the sea," it has an excellent harbour sheltered by a number of offshore islands, the most important of which, Quemoy (Chinese: Jinmen), in the mouth of the estuary, has remained a fortress in the hands of the government on Taiwan. The region has a warm and humid subtropical climate, with abundant precipitation falling mainly in the summer months. Xiamen's population according to the 2006 estimate is 961,758; the 2007 estimate of the urban agglomeration is 2,519,000 people.

HISTORY

During the Song (960–1279) and Yuan (1279–1368) dynasties, Xiamen was known as Jiahe Island and formed a part of Tong'an county. It was notable chiefly as a lair of pirates and a centre of contraband trade. The name Xiamen first appeared when the island was fortified as one of a series of measures taken against piracy in 1387. During the 1650s it was under the control of Zheng Chenggong, or Koxinga (1624–62), the ruler of Taiwan, at which time it was called Siming prefecture. In 1680 it was taken by the forces of the Qing dynasty (1644–1911/12), after which it became the headquarters of the Quanzhou naval defense force.

Foreign trade there had begun with the arrival of the Portuguese in 1544, but they were expelled shortly thereafter. The port became known to Europeans as Amoy, and, under Zheng Chenggong's rule, English and Dutch ships called there. British traders continued occasionally to visit Xiamen until 1757, when trade was restricted to Guangzhou (Canton). After the first Opium War (1839–42) between Britain and China, Xiamen was one of the first five ports to be opened to foreign trade and to residence by foreigners. A foreign settlement grew up on Gulang Island, in the harbour. Xiamen in the 19th century was preeminently a tea port, exporting teas from southeastern Fujian. The peak of this trade was reached in the 1870s but then declined, after which Xiamen became the chief market and shipping port for Taiwanese tea produced by local growers who had emigrated to that island.

In the latter decades of the 19th century, Xiamen was the base from which Taiwan was settled and exploited, and the port retained a close link with the island even after the Japanese conquest of Taiwan in 1895; it also was one of the chief ports of departure for Chinese emigrants (overseas Chinese) settling elsewhere in Southeast Asia. With the decline of the tea trade in the early 20th century, Xiamen continued to export canned fruits, canned fish, paper, sugar, and timber. From 1938 to 1945, the area was occupied by the Japanese, and it was a point of contention between communist and Nationalist forces during the subsequent civil war.

THE CONTEMPORARY CITY

After the communists had established the People's Republic of China on the mainland in 1949, the new government focused considerable attention on developing the city's infrastructure and economy. A causeway was built in 1956, linking the island to the mainland, and a railway line was constructed from Xiamen to the border of Jiangxi province, with a branch to Fuzhou. The railway was completed in 1956. Industrial development at that time consisted chiefly of light manufacturing, notably the canning of fruit and fish; the production of cod-liver oil, fish meal, and other fish products; and sisal processing, sugar refining, tanning, and tobacco curing. Sizable ship-repairing and engineering industries were also established.

However, the city's development was hampered at first by the high level of tension between the mainland and the Nationalist regime on Taiwan, which included periods of artillery shelling between Quemoy and Xiamen (notably an especially intense episode in 1958). Tensions between the two sides gradually diminished, and as China's new policies of economic reform and openness were instituted in the early 1980s, Xiamen was designated one of the country's special economic zones.

Prominent among the city's several institutions of higher education is Xiamen University, which was founded in 1921 by Tan Kah Kee (Chen Jiageng), a patriotic overseas Chinese entrepreneur. Gulang Island, with its beautiful scenery, fine beaches, and notable architecture, and the Jimei District on the mainland opposite Xiamen Island, known for its gardens and historic buildings, are popular destinations for tourists from throughout the country.

WUHAN

Wuhan is the capital and major industrial and commercial city of Hubei province, southeast-central China. It is located at the confluence of the Han and Yangtze rivers and consists of a conurbation of three adjacent former cities—Hankou (Hankow), Hanyang, and Wuchang. Hankou lies on the north bank of the Yangtze River (Chang Jiang) at the mouth of the Han River. Immediately across the Han from it is the older town of Hanyang, and across from these two, on the south bank of the Yangtze, is the ancient metropolis of Wuchang, which is the seat of the provincial government. In 1949 the government of the newly formed People's Republic of China merged the three cities into the single entity of Wuhan.

The triple city of Wuhan has a geographical centrality that gives its site immense strategic and commercial significance. Lying at the very heart of China, it is roughly equidistant from the cities of Beijing and Guangzhou (Canton) on a north-south axis and also is equidistant from Shanghai and Chongqing on an east-west line. The 2006 estimate of Wuhan's population was 4,593,410; the 2007 estimate of its urban agglomeration was 7,243,000.

HISTORY

The earliest settlement in the area, during the Xi (Western) Zhou period (1046–771 BCE), was to the southeast of Wuchang, which became a capital city of the Wu dynasty during the Three Kingdoms (Sanguo) period (220–280 CE). The primarily administrative role of Wuchang continued throughout the Yuan (1206–1368) and Ming (1368–1644) dynasties, when it served as a provincial capital.

Hanyang was founded during the Sui dynasty (581–618 CE) but was of minor commercial significance. In contrast, Hankou (then known as Xiakou) became known during the Song dynasty (960–1279) as one of China's four major commercial cities. The opening of Hankou to foreign trade under the terms of the treaties of Tianjin (1858) between China, France, and Great Britain gave added impetus to the commercial and industrial development of the three cities. Concessions in Hankou were granted between 1861 and 1896 to British, French, German, Japanese, and Russian interests, and a number of foreign commercial, trading, and shipping firms opened offices there during that period.

The three Wuhan cities played a prominent role in the 20th-century history of China. The Chinese Revolution of 1911–12, which toppled the Qing (Manchu) dynasty, broke out in the army barracks at Wuchang, and the line of heights overlooking the Han River there was the scene of the principal fighting between the imperial and revolutionary troops—the main objective being the government arsenal at Hanyang. Hankou's workers were in the forefront of the general strike of 1923, which was the first large-scale worker industrial action in China. The capture of Hankou by the Nationalist (Kuomintang) armies marching northward from Guangdong province in December 1926 marked the extension of Nationalist power to the middle Yangtze valley. It was followed by a serious mob onslaught on the British concession in

Hankou, after which an agreement was reached replacing the British municipal council there with one of mixed Chinese and British composition. The Wuhan cities soon afterward became a centre of conflict between the Nationalists and communists in their short-lived coalition government. After the split between the Nationalists and the communists in 1927, a left-wing faction of the Nationalists maintained its headquarters in Hankou. Mao Zedong, the future communist and national leader, ran a Peasant Movement Institute in Wuchang, where the Fifth Congress of the Chinese Communist Party was convened in 1927.

After the fall of the Nationalist capital of Nanjing to the invading Japanese in 1937, the Chinese government withdrew to Hankou, which temporarily became the base for Chinese resistance. Hankou fell to the Japanese in October 1938 after a defense that lasted more than four months, and the city was occupied by the Japanese until 1945, after which it reverted to Nationalist control. The three cities were taken by the Chinese communist forces in 1949.

THE CONTEMPORARY CITY

Hankou's development as a port in close contact with European commerce brought the three cities early under the influence of Western industrialism, and in the 1890s Hanyang became the site of the first modern steel plant in China. The Wuhan cities' steel industry declined during the Japanese occupation, and in

1938 the Nationalists dismantled the Hanyang steel plant and relocated it at Chongqing. Wuhan's steel industry was gradually revived in the 1950s, and by the late 20th century Wuhan had become the second most important metallurgical centre of China (after Anshan). It has several large iron- and steel-producing complexes, including a plant on the south bank of the Yangtze about 15 miles (25 km) east of Wuchang. Iron ore is obtained from the large mine at Daye, which is about 56 miles (90 km) southeast of Wuhan. Coal is shipped from the major Enan field, which lies to the south of the city.

The iron and steel base has attracted other industries producing chemicals, fertilizers, electrical equipment, glass, agricultural machinery, railroad cars, and trucks. Wuhan is also one of the largest manufacturers of heavy machine tools in China. Its consumer industries produce watches, bicycles, and radios and other electronic instruments. Older industries in Wuhan include rice, oil, and flour mills and factories making cotton and woolen fabrics and other textiles. Cement works, paper mills, distilleries, and soap factories are among Wuhan's other light industries. It is also the site of one of China's more important arsenals. The surrounding agricultural area produces wheat, tea, rice, and cotton.

Wuhan is crossed by converging maritime, river, rail, and road transportation routes from almost every direction. As the meeting point of these routes, the city has long been the chief collecting

Railway bridge (opened 1957) over the Yangtze River at Wuhan, Hubei province, China. Paolo Koch/Photo Researchers

and distribution point for the products of the middle Yangtze valley and for west and southwest China, particularly for tea, cotton, silk, timber, and tung oil and a variety of manufactured goods. The Yangtze, the greatest of China's arterial waterways, is navigable for large ocean-going vessels up to Wuhan—which can therefore be considered the head of ocean navigation on the river, although the city is some 600 miles (965 km) from the coast. The main north-south railroad linking Beijing and Guangzhou crosses the Yangtze on a bridge (completed 1957) at Wuhan. Several more rail and highway bridges across the Yangtze have been constructed at Wuhan since 1990, and work was completed on a highway tunnel under the river in 2008. Large bridges also span the Han River and connect Hankou with Hanyang. More railways east from Anhui and Jiangxi provinces and west from Shaanxi province plus major expressways from Beijing to Guangzhou and from Shanghai to Chengdu crisscross the region. The first line of an urban light-rail mass-transit system opened in 2004.

Wuhan is the seat of Wuhan University, which was founded as Ziqiang Institute in 1893 and designated a university in 1928; Huazhong (Central China) University of Science and Technology (1953), which merged with three other institutions in 2000; and dozens of other schools of higher learning. Among places of historic interest are the Changchunguan, a Daoist temple rebuilt east of Wuchang at the end of the 19th century; the Guqintai, an 8th-century pavilion in Hanyang; and a Yuan-dynasty temple and shrine in Wuchang. The Hubei Provincial Museum (1953), also in Wuchang, has notable displays of artifacts from the Spring and Autumn (Chunqiu; 770–476 BCE) and Warring States (Zhanguo; 475–221 BCE) periods.

CHANGSHA

The city of Changsha is the capital of Hunan province, southeast-central China. It is on the Xiang River 30 miles (50 km) south of Dongting Lake and has excellent water communications to southern and southwestern Hunan. The area has long been inhabited, and Neolithic sites have been discovered in the district since 1955. Changsha's population according to a 2006 estimate was 1,731,937; a 2007 estimate of the urban agglomeration was 2,604,000 people.

HISTORY

During the 1st millennium BCE, the area was the centre of the southern part of the Yangtze River (Chang Jiang) valley state of Chu. In 1935–36 some Chu graves excavated nearby produced important evidence of Chu culture. The city's most ancient name was Qingyang. Under the Qin dynasty (221–207 BCE) it became a staging post for Qin expeditions into Guangdong province. From Han times (206 BCE–220 CE) it was named Linxiang county and was the seat of the Changsha commandery. The county was renamed Changsha in 589, when it became the administrative seat of Tan prefecture. It lost some importance at that time, however, because traffic from Guangdong was mostly diverted up the Gan River valley in Jiangxi. After the fall of the Tang dynasty (618–907), it became the capital of the independent Chu state (927–951) that subsequently fell to other regional powers until being incorporated into the Song dynasty (960–1279). Between 750 and 1100, as Changsha became an important commercial city, the population of the area increased tenfold.

Under the Ming (1368–1644) and Qing (1644–1911/12) dynasties, it was made a superior prefecture, and from 1664 onward it was the capital of Hunan and prospered as one of China's chief rice markets. During the Taiping Rebellion, the city was besieged by the rebels (1854) but never fell; it then became the principal base for the suppression of the rebellion. Changsha was opened to foreign trade in 1904. It also became the seat of some Western schools, including a missionary medical college. Further development followed the opening of the railway to Hankou in Hubei province in 1918, which was extended to Guangzhou (Canton) in Guangdong province in 1936. Although Changsha's population grew, the city remained primarily commercial in character and before 1937 had little industry, apart from some small cotton-textile, glass, and nonferrous-metal plants and handicraft enterprises.

During the Sino-Japanese War (1937–45) Changsha was the site of three major battles. The city itself was virtually destroyed by fire in 1938–39, and it was captured by the Japanese in 1944.

THE CONTEMPORARY CITY

Changsha was rebuilt after 1949, and its population nearly tripled between the late 1940s and the early 1980s and essentially doubled again in the succeeding two decades. The city is now a major port, handling rice, cotton, timber, and livestock, and is also a collection and distribution point on the railway from Hankou to Guangzhou. It is a centre of rice milling and has oil-extraction, tea- and tobacco-curing, and meat-processing plants. Its textile industry produces cotton yarn and fabrics and engages in dyeing and printing. Agricultural chemicals and fertilizers, farm implements, and pumping machinery are also produced.

Changsha has a large thermal generating station linked by a power grid with the nearby industrial centres of Zhuzhou and Xiangtan; the three cities were designated in the 1970s as the nucleus of a major industrial complex. In the 1960s there was some development of heavy industry. The manufacturing of machinery, especially machine tools and precision tools, became important, and Changsha emerged as a centre of China's aluminum industry. The city also has cement, rubber, ceramic, and papermaking plants and is known for many types of traditional handicrafts, producing *xiang* embroidery, leather goods, umbrellas, and buttons. Coal is mined in the vicinity.

Changsha was the seat of many ancient schools and academies. It is the site of Hunan Medical University (1914) and has several colleges and institutes of higher learning. The Hunan Provincial Museum houses artifacts from the many ancient tombs in the vicinity, including the well-known Changsha Mawangdui Tomb of the Hsi (Western) Han period (206 BCE–25 CE), discovered in the 1970s. Among the many renowned scenic spots in the vicinity are Orange Isle (Juzi Zhou) in the Xiang River and the Yuele Hills on the river's western bank.

CHAPTER 9

THE MAJOR CITIES OF SOUTHERN AND WESTERN CHINA

The southern and western regions of China encompass vast areas of the country's territory but, overall, contain only a small proportion of the national population. Southern China has a fairly high population density, especially in the region centred on Chongqing and Chengdu. However, the great, largely dry expanses in the western parts of the country generally are sparsely populated, with nodes of settlement typically arrayed along ancient trade routes like the Silk Road.

CHONGQING

The province-level municipality of Chongqing (conventional Chungking) is the great metropolis of southwest-central China. The leading river port, transportation hub, and commercial and industrial centre of the upper Yangtze River (Chang Jiang) basin, the city is located some 1,400 miles (2,250 km) from the sea, at the confluence of the Yangtze and Jialing rivers. During the Sino-Japanese War (1937–45) it was the capital of Nationalist China. The city was named Chongqing ("Double-Blessed") in 1189 under the Nan (Southern) Song dynasty (1127–1279 CE). At that time the city occupied a commanding position between the prefectures of Shunqing (centred on modern Nanchong) to the north and Shaoqing (centred on modern Pengshui) to the east.

Chongqing city was under the administration of Sichuan province from 1954, but in 1997 it was separated from the province and designated a provincial-level municipality under the direct administration of the central government. At that time the entire eastern portion of Sichuan was incorporated into the municipality, which greatly expanded Chongqing's overall land area and population. Both the city and municipality have experienced quick development since then.

The area of the Chongqing municipality is approximately 31,700 square miles (82,000 square km). The population according to a 2006 estimate was 4,776,027; a 2007 estimate placed the urban agglomeration at 6,461,000; and the estimate of the Chongqing municipality was 28,080,000.

LANDSCAPE

In addition to Sichuan to the west, the municipality is bordered by the provinces of Shaanxi to the north, Hubei to the east, Hunan to the southeast, and Guizhou to the south.

CITY SITE

Chongqing municipality consists of three lobes of unequal size extending southwest, northeast, and southeast. The districts of central Chongqing city occupy the southwestern lobe and are ringed by suburban districts. From there the northeastern arm spreads along the Yangtze valley. The southeastern lobe,

stretching southeastward from the Yangtze valley, consists of a series of hills and valleys between Hunan and Guizhou; the Wu River (another tributary of the Yangtze) runs roughly along the southwestern side of the lobe until it veers south into Guizhou.

The western and southwestern portions of the municipality lie in the Sichuan Basin and consist of relatively level to hilly terrain. The Daba Mountains run along the northern border with Shaanxi, and in the northeast the Wu Mountains demarcate the Yangtze's entry into Hubei, in the river's Three Gorges region. The Fangdou Mountains occupy the eastern portion of the municipality, and in the south the Dalou Mountains extend northward from Guizhou.

CLIMATE

Chongqing is noted for its mild and intensely humid climate. It is shielded from the cold northern winds by the Qin (Tsinling) Mountains in Shaanxi and has little or no frost or ice in winter; the mean temperatures in January and February, the only cool months, are about 47 °F (8 °C) and 50 °F (10 °C), respectively. Summer, which lasts from May through September, is hot and humid; the August mean temperature is 84 °F (29 °C), and on many days the high temperature exceeds 100 °F (38 °C). The remaining months are warm, with annual mean temperatures ranging between 64 and 67 °F (18 and 19 °C).

The bulk of the municipality's precipitation (all as rain) falls from April through October; the average annual total ranges from 43 to 55 inches (about 1,100 to 1,400 mm). Because of the high humidity, fog and mist are particularly heavy. From October to April, the city is perpetually blanketed by fog, which hampers inland navigation, aviation, and local traffic. Chongqing's climate has earned the city the nickname "fog capital" (*wudu*). The aptness of this name has only increased under present-day conditions; contaminated by soot, carbon dioxide, and acid rain, the atmosphere of Chongqing is among the most polluted in China.

CITY LAYOUT

The central part of Chongqing city is built on and around a hilly promontory of red sandstone and shale that constitutes the southern limit of the relatively low Huaying Mountains, which reach southward from Sichuan. The promontory is bounded on the north by the Jialing River and on the east and south by the Yangtze, effectively forming a peninsula projecting between the two rivers. Other hills, some also offshoots of the Huaying, rise in the city's outskirts and suburban districts.

CENTRAL DISTRICTS

The Old City of Chongqing (formerly surrounded by a city wall and gates, of which only two gates now remain) occupies the eastern third of the rocky promontory and covers an area of about 28 square miles (73 square km). The southern and eastern slopes, facing the waterfront, form the "lower city," while the remainder is the "upper city." An east-west avenue runs through the middle of each of these areas, and a third runs atop the spine of the promontory's ridge. Prior to the city's modernization, its cross streets were narrow and often winding; following the topography of the hill, some of them went up and down in flights of hundreds of steps. However, few of these picturesque lanes now remain.

Newer sections of the city on the western part of the promontory spread far along the banks of the two rivers, covering an area considerably larger than that of the Old City. During the Sino-Japanese War (1937–45) the offices of the Nationalist government were located there, and they are now the sites of government office buildings and of museums and exhibition halls, notably the Great Hall of the People (completed 1954). The city has grown so much that the incorporation of numerous industrial towns and suburban communities has extended the city limits to Jiangbei in the north and to Baishiyi in the west. Equally important are the former suburban areas on the south shore of the Yangtze. In former times, ferries were the only means by which the rivers could be crossed; later they could also be crossed by way of the Jialing Bridge (1966) to the northwest and the Chongqing Yangtze Bridge (1980) to the south. Since then, some dozen more bridges have been constructed across the Yangtze and Jialing, notably the Chaotianmen Bridge over the Yangtze, which had the world's longest steel-arch span at its completion in 2008. In addition, cableways across the Jialing and Yangtze link the Old City with adjacent districts. The spacious gardens and beautiful residences of the surrounding districts contribute much to relieving the crowded conditions of the central part of the city.

SUBURBAN AND OUTLYING DISTRICTS

In contrast to the congested conditions in the central city and the industrial districts, the suburban districts of Chongqing have a number of delightful resorts and spas. Among the scenic spots on the south shore are the temple in honour of the empress Yu, consort of the Yu (or Da Yu) emperor (the legendary founder of the Xia dynasty), on Mount Tu; the wooded summer resorts of Qingshuixi ("Clear Water Creek") on Mount Huang; and Nanwenquan ("South Hot Springs"), which has delightful retreats at Huaxi ("Flower Creek") and Huxiaokou ("Tiger Roar Gap"). A short distance north of the city are the springs of Geleshan. Farther up the Jialing River at Beipei are the Jinyun Temple, the celebrated retreat of the Song dynasty savant Feng Jinyun, and Beiwenquan ("North Hot Springs"), reputedly superior to Nanwenquan because its water is warmer in winter and cooler in summer.

With the establishment of the larger provincial-level municipality, the administrative area under the city expanded significantly to the northeast and southeast. The area of the Old City was renamed Yuzhong district; Yuzhong continues to function as the political, economic, and commercial hub of the municipality, focused on the district's main business centre, located around the Liberation Monument (Jiefangbei) in the centre of the Old City.

Areas surrounding Yuzhong, including some former suburbs, are now the municipality's core districts, including Jiangbei, Nan'an, Shapingba, Jiulongpo, and Dadukou. These districts have developed into major shopping and commercial centres. Shapingba also has emerged as a regional cultural centre, home to several of the municipality's major institutions of higher learning. Jiangbei district is a centre of automobile and machinery production, as well as a distribution hub for goods and materials, and Nan'an district has developed light industries and supportive commercial services.

Farther to the northeast, Chongqing municipality is included in the western portion of the Three Gorges Dam project along the Yangtze, which required that large numbers of residents in areas flooded by the reservoir be relocated. Wanzhou district (formerly Wanxian city), at the western end of the reservoir, has become one of the major ports along the Yangtze and has emerged as a regional hub of water, rail, road, and air transportation with the construction of deepwater berths, rail lines, express highways, and an airport.

HOUSING

Before the Sino-Japanese War, Chongqing was a city of narrow streets and crowded housing. Streets and lanes followed the contours of the hills. The houses were constructed of bamboo, wood, or thatch in the poorer residential areas and of brick in the wealthier areas. In all areas there was a high degree of congestion. A vigorous modernization program was introduced when the city became the seat of the Nationalist government. Most of the city wall was demolished to make way for new streets, and existing streets were graded and widened. The tremendous demand for housing created by an influx of government workers and refugees led to the rapid expansion of the sections west of the Old City.

From 1938 to 1942, Chongqing was heavily bombarded by the Japanese, causing massive destruction in the city. Parts of the remaining wall and virtually all of the city's historic monuments and temples were damaged or destroyed. Because of the destruction, the new communist government (which came to power in 1949) had little difficulty in carrying forward the tasks of modernization and expansion after the war. Modern buildings now stand throughout the city, with skyscrapers dotting the sky in the newer commercial centres. In the northern suburban districts and adjacent areas, large buildings were erected to provide living quarters for workers and accommodations for factories and workshops. More recently, the completion of the Three Gorges Dam and the subsequent relocation or resettlement of some one million inhabitants in the municipality precipitated an economic boom, as massive government investment was used to build new towns, business enterprises, and communications and transportation infrastructure in the affected areas.

PEOPLE

Before the war with Japan, Chongqing had fewer than 250,000 inhabitants. From 1938 onward, people from the Japanese-occupied coastal provinces flocked to the wartime capital at an astonishing rate. A part of Chongqing's population increase since 1938 consisted of government workers, factory personnel, and refugees from other provinces. In the late 1940s, however, the city's population decreased temporarily with the return of people to the coastal provinces. The influx of people from downriver contributed to turning formerly parochial Chongqing into a cosmopolitan city. The population generally has continued to grow since the early 1950s, especially after the establishment of the municipality in 1997. The number of people living in the city's core districts is now some twenty times greater than the population of the Old City before the war.

The Southern Mandarin dialect of Chinese is the most commonly spoken language in the municipality. Despite its heavy accent and many regional slang words, it is quite intelligible to speakers of standard Mandarin. There are more than one million people of the Tujia minority group and some half million Miao (Hmong) living in four autonomous counties and in Qianjiang district in the eastern and southeastern parts of the municipality.

ECONOMY

Chongqing is the main manufacturing and commercial centre of southwest-central China, and it is the principal hub of regional transportation.

MANUFACTURING

As early as the middle of the Ming dynasty (1368–1644), workshops for spinning, weaving, silk reeling, and brewing were established in Chongqing. The city was opened to foreign trade in 1890, and two metal mills were set up a year later. By 1905 Chongqing had spinning and weaving mills, silk-reeling mills, and glass-making and cigarette plants.

The foundations of Chongqing's modern industry were laid between 1938 and 1945, when factories transplanted from the coastal provinces began production under the aegis of the Nationalist government. Because coal, iron, and other resources were in such close proximity, industry rapidly expanded. Considerable industrial development was undertaken by the communist government after 1949. During the 1960s and early '70s, some military-related industries were moved to or established in the city and vicinity or transferred there from other parts of

China as part of a program to increase industrial production at inland locations; this provided a strong foundation for the city's machinery industry. By the late 20th century, Chongqing was one of the largest and fastest-growing industrial centres in southwestern China.

The city's enormous complex of integrated iron and steel plants is among China's largest facilities. Ore is mined at Qijiang (in the southern part of the municipality) and at Weiyuan (a short distance west of Neijiang) in neighbouring Sichuan province. In addition, there is now a large iron ore mine in the northeastern corner of the municipality at Wushan. Rich bauxite deposits have made Chongqing a major manufacturer of aluminum products in China. It is also a major producer of strontium carbonate, which is widely used in the production of colour television tubes and optical glass.

Coal is mined at several locations in the municipality, and Chongqing is an important coal-mining base of southwestern China. The municipality also has rich reserves of natural gas, notably the large Wolonghe natural gas field at Dianjiang. Gas pipelines and production facilities have been developed, including a major natural gas purification plant at Changshou. Chongqing's power-generating capacity was greatly enlarged with the completion of the Shizitan hydroelectric station on the Longxi River, northeast of the city. A large new hydropower plant at Pengshui, on the Wu River, started operation in early 2008. In addition, a large thermal power station was constructed southwest of the city, near the Yangtze River. However, more hydroelectric and thermal capacity is being added to satisfy the municipality's increasing power supply needs.

Other important heavy industries include machine, farm tool, and munitions factories; truck and motor-coach manufacturing plants; and chemical and fertilizer plants that manufacture soap, candles, acid and caustic soda, fertilizers, plastics, and chemical fibres. Since the late 1980s, several well-known Chinese automobile manufacturers have established production lines in Chongqing, making trucks, a variety of car models, and motorcycles. Petrochemical and pharmaceutical industries developed quickly after 1980, and the manufacture of precision instruments has also become important.

Chongqing's light industrial manufacturing leads the entire southwest of China. Noteworthy are the production of cotton, silk, paper, and leather goods, as well as flour mills, dyeing factories, and vegetable-oil and food-processing plants. Chongqing is also noted for its handicrafts, especially lacquerware. A high-technology industrial development zone was established in Chongqing in the early 1990s, and hundreds of scientific and technological enterprises—concentrating on electronic information, bioengineering, pollution control, optoelectronic integration, and new and advanced materials—are now located there.

TRADE

Chongqing is the focal point of trade and transportation not only of the municipality and neighbouring Sichuan province but also of the hinterland provinces of Shaanxi, Yunnan, and Guizhou and of the autonomous region of Tibet. Since 1979 its port—along with several others on the Yangtze—has been open for direct foreign trade, increasing the city's importance as an international trade centre. Before the early 1950s, especially before the Sino-Japanese War, Chongqing imported large quantities of consumer goods from downriver or from abroad, but rapid industrialization brought self-sufficiency in consumer goods to the region and to the southwestern provinces. Chongqing is now the major commodity-distribution centre for southwestern China.

Trading and financial sectors have been established in the city, with national and foreign banks, insurance companies, and even stock-trading firms opening offices there. In addition, leading Chinese and international retailers have set up both retail stores and wholesale distribution channels in the municipality. The central business district at the Liberation Monument in the Old City remains the most prosperous business centre in the city, while the wholesale market at Chaotianmen (at the confluence point of the Yangtze and Jialing rivers) is among the largest of its kind for daily-use manufactured goods in the upper course of the Yangtze region.

TRANSPORTATION

After 1949, bicycles, buses, and motorbikes gradually replaced chairs on bamboo poles and rickshaws as the principal means of transportation in Chongqing. Cable tramways have long provided cheap and convenient transport over the steep hills. The municipality's rapid economic development has been accompanied by considerable improvements in its transportation infrastructure. By the early 21st century, the ubiquity of bicycles on the streets had given way to a dramatic increase in automobile and motorcycle traffic. The city also began developing a rail transit system, the first line of which opened in 2005.

Chongqing is served by two great rivers, the Yangtze and the Jialing, and is the leading port of southwestern China. As a result of extensive work carried out in the 1950s—including dredging, clearing shoals, and installing buoys and signals—navigation through the Yangtze Gorges was rendered easy and safe. Completion of the Three Gorges Dam, which created a large reservoir in the gorges region, now makes it possible for 3,000-ton oceangoing ships to sail directly up the Yangtze to ports in Chongqing municipality. The port of Chongqing itself has been equipped with large container docks and automobile roll-on and roll-off wharves. Above Chongqing, smaller steamers are able to sail into Sichuan province, up to Yibin on the Yangtze and up to Nanchong on the Jialing. Above these points, junks can navigate beyond Chengdu to Guanxian and Maoxian on the Min River and to Lüeyang in southern Shaanxi on the Jialing. Chongqing is also a major embarking point for excursion boats to the Three Gorges area.

Chongqing's railroad system developed rapidly after 1949. A line between Chongqing and Chengdu, completed in 1952, is the vital link between the Chengdu Plain and the Yangtze; a southern spur extends through Zigong and Yibin. The Chengdu-Baoji line, completed four years later and electrified in 1975, connects the city with the Longhai Railroad and the entirety of northwestern China, as well as with Wuhan in Hubei province and a major north-south line; the Chongqing-Xiangfan (Hubei) railway also directly links the city with Wuhan. The line between Chongqing and Guiyang not only connects Chongqing with the province of Guizhou to the south but also joins other lines in Yunnan and Guangxi running to the Vietnamese border. More recent construction includes a line from Chongqing to Huaihua (completed 2007), which provides direct access from the city to Hunan province and connects with a line to Liuzhou (the capital of Guangxi province); and a spur line from Suining, east of Chengdu to Chongqing (completed 2006) that shortens the distance from Chongqing to Chengdu.

The first roads for wheeled traffic in the city were built in 1933. As a result of work begun during the Sino-Japanese War, Chongqing is now the hub of an extensive network of highways. Major arterials lead south to Guiyang, northeast to Wanzhou, and northwest to Chengdu. The riverside boulevards and numerous bridges across the Yangtze and Jialing rivers have become the main traffic arteries within the central city area.

Jiangbei International Airport, opened in 1990 and expanded in the early 21st century, is located about 20 miles (32 km) north of the central city. It provides regular flights to major cities throughout China and to some international Asian destinations such as Bangkok, Seoul, and Singapore. Another airport, completed in 2003, is located at Wuqiao, some 10 miles (16 km) southeast of the northeastern municipality of Wanzhou; it provides convenient air service for travelers to the Three Gorges area.

ADMINISTRATION AND SOCIETY

Chongqing's municipal government is part of the hierarchical structure of the Chinese government—and the parallel structure of the Chinese Communist Party—that extends from the national organization, through the provincial-municipal apparatus, to the district and, ultimately, neighbourhood levels.

GOVERNMENT

The principal responsibilities of the Chongqing Municipal People's Congress, the major decision-making body, include issuing administrative orders, collecting taxes, determining the budget, and implementing economic plans. A standing committee selected from its members recommends policy decisions and oversees the operation of municipal government. Executive authority rests with the Chongqing People's Government, the officers of which are elected by the Chongqing Municipal People's Congress; it consists of a mayor, vice mayors, and numerous bureaus in charge of public security, the judicial system, and other civil, economic, social, and cultural affairs.

Administratively, the city is divided into a number of districts (*shixiaqu*), counties (*xian*), and autonomous counties (*zizhixian*). Grassroots administrative units are organized as villages in rural areas and as neighbourhood street committees in urban districts. Neighbourhood street committees perform the auxiliary functions of mediating disputes, propagating legal orders, and promoting sanitation and welfare. These committees are quasi-official administrations, covering blocks of streets of varying sizes. Chongqing municipality has considerably extended the territorial limits of the municipal area to include a series of urban-rural units surrounding the city proper. Since 1980 the municipal government has allowed farmers to engage in industry, commerce, and transportation in addition to cultivation.

PUBLIC UTILITIES

Although an electric-light plant was established in the early 1900s, it was not until the late 1920s and early 1930s that a modernization drive was launched by local leaders in Chongqing to improve living conditions. Demolition of the city walls was initiated, streets were widened, and a piped-water system and a telephone exchange were introduced. Yet, even during the 1940s, sanitation and public hygiene were still poor. The city had a large rat population, opium smoking in homes and inns was widespread, and lice-ridden waifs and beggars were a familiar sight. But because of energetic measures carried out since 1949, including the installation of a modern sewer system with sewage-treatment plants and the building of garbage-disposal facilities, these conditions belong to the past. Chongqing has achieved a high degree of cleanliness, the capacity of the water-supply system has been enhanced, and the general living conditions of residential districts have improved. However, air pollution has become a serious problem.

HEALTH

Chongqing has a considerable number of hospitals and health care facilities. By the early 21st century, there were some 2,500 medical and health care institutions in the municipality, staffed with a workforce of about 80,000 people. Most of them are equipped with enough beds and with modern instruments and equipment for diagnosis and treatment. However, the adoption of commercialized medical facilities in the early 1990s made it more difficult for ordinary residents to afford good health care services. Western-style medicine is combined with traditional herbal medicine and acupuncture. Family planning is practiced, and contraceptives usually are distributed free. Physical fitness is emphasized by the government.

EDUCATION

Since 1949 the number of schools at all levels—kindergartens, primary schools, middle schools, and secondary schools—has increased. The growth of kindergartens, which were little known before 1940, has enabled many women to obtain proper care for their children and thus become part of the workforce. The government has attached great importance to the establishment of teacher-training schools, vocational-technical schools, and part-time agricultural middle schools.

Chongqing is a national centre of higher education, with some three dozen universities and colleges. Several of the major institutions are in Shapingba district, including Chongqing University (founded in 1929), Southwest University (1906), Southwest University of Political Science and Law (1950), and Chongqing Normal University (1954). Other schools include Chongqing Medical University (1956) in Yuzhong district, Sichuan Fine Arts Institute (1940) in Jiulongpo district, and Chongqing Jiaotong University (1951) in Nan'an district.

CULTURAL LIFE

Chongqing Library and Chongqing Municipal Museum are among the leading cultural centres in the city. The latter institution was merged into a new venue, the China Three Gorges Museum, that opened in central Chongqing in 2005; among the many historical and cultural artifacts displayed there are large numbers of items collected from areas that were submerged by the Three Gorges reservoir. The Great Hall of the People, with its large, traditionally styled dome, is another popular attraction. The city has maintained a number of locations associated with the wartime Nationalist government period, including the residences of Nationalist leader Chiang Kai-shek, Song Qingling (wife of Sun Yat-sen), and U.S. General Joseph W. Stilwell. In addition, Chongqing municipality has numerous acting and acrobatic troupes, including those performing Sichuan opera.

Sports and recreation are dominant features of Chongqing's cultural life. Datianwan Stadium in Yuzhong district, the city's main sports centre, offers a football (soccer) field; volleyball, basketball, and tennis courts; a track-and-field venue; and a parachute tower. Sports centres

Ethnic Tujia musicians perform during the Qianjiang Culture Week in Chongqing, China. China Photos/Getty Images

and stadiums have also been constructed in the other districts, including the Chongqing Olympic Sports Center (opened 2004) in Jiupongpo district. Numerous parks, both in the Old City districts and in outlying areas, attract large numbers of visitors. Of particular appeal are the hot springs, which are open year-round. South of the city, among well-kept gardens with lakes and pavilions, are the sulfurous springs of Nanwenquan Park. Some 30 miles (50 km) northwest of the city centre are the well-known hot springs of Beiwenquan Park, along the Jialing River. Visitors come to relax, often soaking for hours in one of the numerous baths filled with warm mineral water, or they swim in one of the three Olympic-sized pools, which are also fed by the hot springs.

Chongqing municipality boasts two UNESCO World Heritage sites: the Dazu Rock Carvings (designated 1999), located on steep hillsides west of the central city; and the Wulong karst area to the southeast, which is part of a larger karst region of southern China (designated 2007). Other notable scenic areas in the municipality include the magnificent Three Gorges area along the Yangtze in the northeast; the White Emperor Town (Baidicheng), a strategic fort during the Three Kingdoms (Sanguo) period (220–280 CE), east of Fengjie in the northeast; the historic Zhang Fei Temple (between Wanzhou and Fengjie), a memorial to Zhang Fei, a renowned general of the Shu-Han kingdom (one of the Three Kingdoms); and the "Ghost Town" of Fengdu, on the Yangtze some 100 miles (160 km) east of the central city.

A noteworthy feature of Chongqing's cultural life is its distinctive Sichuan cuisine. This highly spiced food is characterized mainly by the use of hot peppers as well as by such delicacies as tree ears (a type of mushroom), black mushrooms, and fresh bamboo shoots and peanuts. Chongqing is renowned for its distinctive *huoguo* ("hotpot"), a style of cooking in which portions of vegetables and meat are cooked at the table in a chafing dish filled with a spicy soup base.

HISTORY

Chongqing, with its strategic location, has been settled for thousands of years. According to ancient accounts, the area was the birthplace of the consort of the legendary Yu emperor, founder of the Xia dynasty, about 4,000 years ago.

THE EARLY PERIOD

In the 11th century BCE, under the Xi (Western) Zhou dynasty, the region surrounding Chongqing became a feudal state known as Ba. In the 5th century BCE, Ba established relations with the mid-Yangtze kingdom of Chu. It was later incorporated into the Qin empire. By the mid-3rd century BCE, the region was part of the kingdom of Shu and was totally independent of northern and central China.

The swing of the historical pendulum—in which the city and its surrounding area's status alternated between forming part of an empire in northern and central China and detaching itself to become independent of both northern and central China—continued throughout subsequent centuries. The city became an integral part of the unified Chinese empire first under the Ming dynasty (1368–1644) and then under the Qing, or Manchu, dynasty (1644–1911/12).

The first substantial city wall was constructed about 250 BCE. It was repaired and expanded during the 3rd century CE and about 1240, and was rebuilt with solid stone early in the Ming period. In the 1630s, near the end of the Ming, the rebellion of Zhang Xianzhong subjected Chongqing to plunder, slaughter, and destruction. The city wall was restored in 1663. Some 5 miles (8 km) in circumference, it had a total of seventeen gates: eight gates remained closed on the advice of geomancers (practitioners of divination by means of figures or lines), while nine were open to traffic. Additional work was done to strengthen the city wall in 1760.

THE MODERN PERIOD

Chongqing was opened to British trade in 1890, but navigational difficulties on the Yangtze delayed steamer traffic for more than a decade. Meanwhile, the Treaty of Shimonoseki (1895), which concluded the first Sino-Japanese War (1894–95), gave Japan the right to access the wharves of Chongqing as well. Accordingly, in 1901, when British trade opened, a Japanese concession also was established at Wangjiatuo, on the south shore of the Yangtze. This concession lasted until 1937, when it was abandoned by Japan on the outbreak of the second Sino-Japanese War (1937–45).

In 1911, on the eve of the Chinese Revolution, Chongqing—along with the Sichuan provincial capital, Chengdu—played a major role in bringing about the overthrow of the Manchus; many patriots of the region joined the revolutionary party of the Chinese Nationalist leader Sun Yat-sen (Sun Zhongshan). Despite such progressive trends and a nominal allegiance to the central government, Chongqing was unable to break away from the grip of regional separatism.

Yet in 1938, a year after war had again broken out with Japan, Chongqing became the capital of the Nationalist government. Hundreds of government offices were moved to the city from Nanjing, along with the diplomatic missions of foreign countries. Tens of thousands of people came from coastal provinces, bringing with them arsenals, factories, and schools. Friendly powers at the time also rushed supplies to Chongqing to bolster its war effort. Despite the Japanese bombings, the morale of the population—which had grown to more than 1,000,000 from a prewar total of less than 250,000—was high. Chiang Kai-shek's failure to control inflation and corruption, however, caused the war effort to falter from 1942 onward. In 1946, on the eve of the renewed civil war against the communists, the Nationalist capital returned to Nanjing. Three years later, in April 1949, communist forces took Nanjing. The Nationalist government fled to Guangzhou (Canton) and then once again—for less than two months—to Chongqing (October to late November 1949). When the Nationalists fled to Taiwan in December, the communist victory on the mainland was complete.

More than a decade of warfare had devastated the city, but repair of the war damage began shortly after the communist takeover. The new regime also vigorously pursued restoring and expanding the city's industrial base, which had been established in the early 20th century. Even though energies were temporarily deflected during the periods of the Great Leap Forward (1958–60) and the Cultural Revolution (1966–76), the city nonetheless succeeded in carrying out extensive modernization projects and significantly raised the standard of living.

Chongqing had been an independent municipality during the Nationalist period, but from 1954 to 1996 it was a city under the administration of Sichuan province. In 1997 it was separated from the province to become a provincial-level municipality directly under the central government. At that time, jurisdiction for the entire eastern portion of Sichuan was transferred to the new municipality, thereby greatly expanding Chongqing's area and population. Chongqing's population grew dramatically and its economy boomed after that.

OTHER IMPORTANT SOUTHERN AND WESTERN CHINESE CITIES

The cities of southern and western China outside of Chongqing tend to be smaller than those found in other regions of China, although several of them have populations of at least one million. In addition, comparatively larger proportions of the populations of these cities consist of minority groups, since many of them are located in autonomous regions or in provinces with significant numbers of minority peoples.

YAN'AN

The city of Yan'an is in northern Shaanxi province, north-central China. It became famous as the wartime stronghold of the Chinese communists from the mid-1930s to 1949. Yan'an is on the heavily dissected Loess Plateau, which consists of loess (windblown soil) that is deeply etched by gullies. The city stands on the south bank of the Yan River in a basin surrounded by hills. It is a road junction for northeast Shaanxi and was a strategic town in historical times, being located near the border between the part of Shaanxi where agriculture is practicable and the arid lands to the north that merge into the Ordos Plateau.

The name Yan'an was first given to the commandery (district controlled by a commander) set up there in 607 CE by the Sui dynasty (581–618). It was a vital frontier post under the Tang dynasty (618–907). It served as part of the defenses of the Song dynasty (960–1279) against the northwestern Xi (Western) Xia dynasty (1038–1227) and was the scene of a crucial victory by Mongol armies over the forces of the Jin (Juchen) dynasty in 1221. Since the 15th century, the importance of the area has declined. It was badly affected by Muslim uprisings of 1864–75; by droughts and famines of the 1870s, which decimated the population; and by the almost equally disastrous droughts of the 1920s and '30s, which depopulated whole counties in the area.

The communist armies, driven from their bases in the Jiangxi Soviet areas by the Chinese Nationalist Party (Kuomintang) in 1934, eventually reached Yan'an after their epic 6,000-mile (9,600-km) Long March (1934–35). They made the town their headquarters during the Sino-Japanese War (1937–45) and during the subsequent civil war that brought communist victory in 1949. Yan'an has thus come to represent a symbol of the heroic phase of the Chinese communist revolution, when the leadership of Mao Zedong was firmly established and the communists mastered both guerrilla warfare and the peasant-based reform policies that were to bring them to power in 1949. Remote Yan'an stands as a national shrine for the communist government, which recalls the spirit and example of its pioneer period.

The contemporary city itself is a relatively minor place. The original walled settlement was ruined by Japanese bombing in 1938–39. Yan'an is at the centre of a district that has suffered seriously from soil erosion but which has begun to be reclaimed as part of the vast scheme for the development of the Huang He (Yellow River) drainage region. The surrounding area has been increasingly devoted to livestock, and the town has a long-established woolen textile industry.

The whole area lies in a rich coal- and oil-bearing plain. Oil was discovered at Yanchang about 22 miles (35 km) to the east early in the 20th century, and a small amount was produced in the 1930s. The oil field has been further developed since 1949 but still remains small. Nonetheless, oil production and coal mining have become mainstays of the city's economy, along with cigarette making and the generation of electric power.

Yan'an has become the communications centre of northern Shaanxi. A rail line from the city south to Xi'an (the provincial capital) has been extended to Shenmu in the northern part of Shaanxi and from there eastward into Shanxi province and northward into the Inner Mongolia Autonomous Region. The airport provides regular flights to Xi'an, Beijing, and other Chinese cities. There is a good network of highways in the region; an expressway from Xi'an has reached the city and also has been extended northward into Inner Mongolia. There are some 100 historical sites north of the old walled town that are related to the communists' wartime presence there, and the area is a popular tourist destination.

The Yan'an 2006 population estimate recorded 196,049 people.

YINCHUAN

The city of Yinchuan (conventional Yinchwan) is the capital of the Hui Autonomous Region of Ningxia, north-central China. It is located in northern Ningxia in the south-central section of the Helan Mountains (which define the western extent of the Ordos Desert), near the western end of the Great Wall of China. The city lies west of the upper course of the Huang He (Yellow River), where the river makes its great bend to flow north along the western edge of the Ordos Plateau.

Yinchuan originally was a county under the name of Lian in 119 BCE; its name was changed to Huaiyuan in the 6th century CE. After the fall of the Tang dynasty in 907, it was occupied by Tangut tribespeople in the 10th century; they later established the Xi (Western) Xia dynasty (1038–1227), of which Yinchuan was the capital. After the destruction of the Xi Xia dynasty by the Mongols in 1227, Yinchuan came under the rule of the Yuan (Mongol) dynasty. Under the Ming (1368–1644) and Qing (1644–1911) dynasties, it was the seat of the prefecture of Ningxia. In 1929, when the province of Ningxia was formed from parts of Gansu and Inner Mongolia, it became the capital city. In 1954, when Ningxia province was abolished, the city was put in Gansu province; but, with the establishment of the Hui Autonomous Region of Ningxia in 1958, Yinchuan once again became the capital.

Traditionally, Yinchuan was an administrative and commercial centre. In the 1950s it had many commercial enterprises, and there were some handicrafts but no modern industry. However, the city subsequently grew considerably. Beginning in the late 1950s, some of the factories located in the eastern provinces along the coast were moved to Yinchuan, which initiated the development of a local machine-building industry. In addition, extensive coal deposits were discovered near Shizuishan, about 60 miles (100 km) to the north, making Shizuishan a coal-mining centre. Exploitation of these coal deposits led to the growth of a chemical industry and the construction of thermal power-generating plants in Yinchuan. The production of building materials has become an important component of the local economy. West of the old town and close to the railway station, a new residential district was built with all-new infrastructure.

The immediate plains area around Yinchuan, intensively irrigated by a system developed as long ago as the Han (206 BCE–220 CE) and Tang (618–907) dynasties, is extremely productive. Yinchuan is the chief agricultural market and distribution centre for this area and also deals in agricultural and animal products from the farms and ranches and from the herds tended by nomads in the surrounding grasslands. It is a market for grain and has flour mills as well as rice-hulling and oil-extraction plants. The wool produced in the surrounding plains supplies a woolen textile mill. Other farm-derived industries include sugar refining, flax spinning, tanning, and food processing. In addition to wool, local specialties include the fruit of the Chinese wolfberry and *facai* (black moss), a kind of fungus served in Chinese cuisine, notably at the New Year.

Until the 1950s the Huang He (navigable downstream as far as Baotou [northeast] in the Inner Mongolia Autonomous Region and upstream to Zhongwei and Zhongning in Ningxia) was Yinchuan's chief communication link. Since then, highways have been built to Baotou, to Lanzhou (southwest) and Wuwei (west) in Gansu, and to Xi'an (southeast) in Shaanxi province. Since 1958 the city has been on the railway from Lanzhou to Baotou and is thus linked to other parts of China by rail. Yinchuan's airport, opened in the late 1990s west of the city, provides regular flights to major

Hui Chinese Muslims exit Yinchuan Central Mosque following afternoon prayers in Yinchuan, China. Frederic J. Brown/AFP/Getty Images

cities in the country. Expressways north to Shizuishan and south to Zhongwei also have been completed.

Yinchuan is a centre for the country's Hui (Chinese Muslim) minority peoples, who constitute one-third of the population, and it thus has extensive cultural and economic relations with Islamic countries. Located 22 miles (35 km) east of the city are several imperial mausoleums and many more tombs of princes and dukes of the Xi Xia dynasty; the area has been an archaeological dig site since the early 1970s. Ningxia University (founded 1958; established as a university 1962) and other institutions of higher learning are located in the city. In 2006, Yinchuan's estimated city population was 663,655; a 2007 estimate of the urban agglomeration was 991,000 people.

LANZHOU

The city of Lanzhou (conventional Lanchow) is the capital of Gansu province, west-central China. It is situated in the southeastern portion of the province on the upper course of the Huang He (Yellow River), where the river emerges from the mountains. Lanzhou has been a transportation centre since early times, being at the southern end of the route leading via the Gansu (Hexi) Corridor across Central Asia; it also commands the approaches to the ancient capital area of Chang'an (modern Xi'an) in Shaanxi province from both the west and the northwest, as well as from the area of Koko Nor (Qinghai Hu) via the upper waters of the Huang He and its tributaries. The 2006 population estimate of the city was 1,708,168; the 2007 estimate of the urban agglomeration was 2,561,000.

HISTORY

Originally in the territory of the Xi (Western) Qiang peoples, Lanzhou became part of the territory of Qin in the 6th century BCE. Under the Han dynasty (206 BCE–220 CE), it became the seat of Jincheng *xian* (county) in 81 BCE and later of Jincheng *jun* (commandery); the county was renamed Yunwu. In the 4th century, it was briefly the capital of the independent state of Qian (Former) Liang. The Bei (Northern) Wei dynasty (386–534/535) reestablished Jincheng commandery and renamed the county Zicheng.

Under the Sui dynasty (581–618) the city became the seat of Lanzhou prefecture for the first time, retaining this name under the Tang dynasty (618–907). In 763 the area was overrun by the Tibetans, and it was then recovered by the Tang in 843. Later it fell into the hands of the Xi (Western) Xia (Tangut) dynasty (which flourished in Ningxia from 1038 to 1227) and was subsequently recovered by the Song dynasty (960–1127) in 1041, who reestablished the name Lanzhou. After 1127 it fell into the hands of the Jin (Juchen) dynasty (1115–1234), and after 1235 it came into the possession of the

Mongols. Under the Ming dynasty (1368–1644) the prefecture was demoted to the status of a county and placed under the administration of Lintao superior prefecture, but in 1477 Lanzhou was reestablished as a political unit. In 1739 the seat of Lintao was transferred to Lanzhou, which was later made a superior prefecture also called Lanzhou. When Gansu became a separate province in 1666, Lanzhou became its capital.

The city was badly damaged during the rising of Gansu Muslims in 1864–75; in the 1920s and '30s, it became a centre of Soviet influence in northwestern China. During the Sino-Japanese War (1937–45) Lanzhou, linked with Xi'an by highway in 1935, became the terminus of the 2,000-mile (3,200-km) Chinese-Soviet highway, used as a route for Soviet supplies destined for the Xi'an area. This highway remained the chief traffic artery of northwestern China until the completion of a railway from Lanzhou to Ürümqi in the Uygur Autonomous Region of Xinjiang. During the war Lanzhou was heavily bombed by the Japanese.

THE CONTEMPORARY CITY

Since 1949 Lanzhou has been transformed from the capital of a poverty-stricken province into the centre of a major industrial area. It has become a centre of the country's petrochemical industry and has a large refinery linked by pipeline to the oil fields at Yumen in western Gansu; it also manufactures equipment for the oil industry. In addition, the city produces locomotives and rolling stock for the northwestern railways, as well as machine tools and mining equipment. Aluminum products, industrial chemicals, and fertilizers are produced on a large scale, as are rubber products. Copper is mined in nearby Gaolan.

Lanzhou remains the collecting centre and market for agricultural produce and livestock from a wide area. It has a textile industry, particularly noted for the production of woolens. Leather goods are also produced. In addition, since the 1960s Lanzhou has been the centre of China's nuclear power industry. There is a thermal-power-generating plant supplied with coal from fields in Qinghai, and there are several hydroelectric-power stations in the Lanzhou area, including the installation at the Liujiaxia Gorge on the Huang He, above the city.

Lanzhou, one of the major points on the ancient Silk Road, is situated near China's geographical centre and is an important hub of land communications. The Longhai Railway line had been extended northwestward to Lanzhou from Tianshui by 1953. Later, Lanzhou was linked with Beijing via Baotou in Inner Mongolia. Lines have also been constructed northwest to Ürümqi and westward into Qinghai province via Xining and Haiyan (on Koko Nor) to Golmud and (since 2006) from there southward to Lhasa in the Tibet Autonomous Region. In addition, expressways have been built to Xining and northeast to Yinchuan in the Hui Autonomous Region of Ningxia. Lanzhou's airport, located north of the city, has service to a number of Chinese cities.

The city is the cultural centre of Gansu and the seat of Lanzhou University (founded 1909). The Northwest Minorities University, the Northwest Normal University, and a number of scientific institutes are also located there. The caves and grottoes of Bingling Temple, southwest of the city, are filled with Buddhist statuary, and the site is a popular tourist destination.

GUILIN

The city of Guilin (formerly Lingui) is in northeastern Zhuang Autonomous Region of Guangxi, southern China. The natural route centre of the Gui River basin, Guilin lies along the easiest of all the routes leading from central China to Guangdong province—that between the headwaters of the Xiang River in Hunan province and the upper waters of the Gui River (there called the Li River). The two streams were linked in early times by the remarkable Ling Canal, which thereby made it possible for small craft to pass between the Yangtze (north) and Xi (south) river systems.

When the first emperor of the Qin dynasty (221–207 BCE) undertook his great campaign against the state of Nanyue in Guangdong, his forces arrived by this route and are said to have set up the first administration in the area. In the

1st century BCE, the Han dynasty (206 BCE–220 CE) established a county seat there, called Shi'an. The former county name, Lingui, was first given during the Tang dynasty (618–907). Under the Ming (1368–1644) and Qing (1644–1911/12) dynasties, it became Guilin superior prefecture; under the Qing it was also the provincial capital of Guangxi. In 1912 it reverted to county status as Guilin, and the provincial capital was moved to Nanning. It again became the provincial capital in 1936 but was replaced for a second time by Nanning in 1949.

Guilin has long been an important centre of trade and administration because of its location on an agriculturally rich valley floor that is also the easiest route south from Hunan. In 1939 the Hunan-Guangxi railway was extended through Guilin to Liuzhou via this corridor.

Guilin has always been a handicraft centre, but until 1949 the only signs of modern industry were a thermal power plant, a cement works, and some small textile mills. Since the 1950s Guilin has developed industries engaged in the manufacturing of electronics, engineering and agricultural equipment, medicine, rubber, and buses, and it also has textile and cotton yarn factories. Food processing, including the processing of local agricultural produce, remains the most important industry.

Guilin is also a cultural centre. As a major centre of Buddhism in the 7th century, it had many famous monasteries.

Today the city has more than ten colleges and universities. Guilin (its name means "Forest of Sweet Osmanthus") is set in a landscape of outstanding natural beauty and is renowned for its karst formations. Deep erosion of the limestone plateau has left a multitude of tall needle-shaped pinnacles out of whose steep sides trees sprout improbably. These fantastical mountains have long been memorialized in Chinese painting and poetry. The city also has many caves, the largest and most spectacular of which is Ludiyan ("Reed Flute Cave"). Guilin is listed as a state-level historical and cultural city. There are scheduled flights to major cities in China and to Japan and the countries of Southeast Asia. The 2006 population estimate was 573,828; and the 2007 estimate of the urban agglomeration was 987,000.

NANNING

The city of Nanning (formerly Yongning [1913–45]) is the capital of the Zhuang Autonomous Region of Guangxi, China. The city is located in the south-central part of Guangxi on the north bank of the Yong River (the chief southern tributary of the Xi River system) and lies some 19 miles (30 km) below the confluence of the You and the Zuo rivers. The Yong River (which later becomes the Yu River) affords a good route to Guangzhou (Canton) and is navigable by shallow-draft junks and motor launches, even though it is obstructed by rapids and sandbanks. Nanning's estimated city population in 2006 was 1,277,300, while its 2007 estimated urban agglomeration total was 2,167,000.

HISTORY

A county seat, called Jinxing, was first established at the site in 318 CE; it also became the administrative seat of a commandery. In 589 the commandery was suppressed, and the county was renamed Xuanhua. Under the Tang dynasty (618–907) the prefecture of Yong was established there; it was garrisoned to control the non-Chinese districts in Guangxi and on the border between Yunnan and Guizhou provinces. In the mid-9th century, the Tang and the Tai state of Nanzhao (in what is now western Yunnan) fought over the region, and after 861 it was briefly occupied by Nanzhao. It remained a frontier prefecture throughout the Song dynasty (960–1279), being the scene of a rebellion led by Nong Zhigao in 1052 and thereafter a garrison town. Under the Ming (1368–1644) and Qing (1644–1911/12) dynasties, it was a superior prefecture: Nanning.

Opened to foreign trade by Qing authorities in 1907, Nanning grew rapidly. From 1912 to 1936, it was the provincial capital of Guangxi, replacing Guilin. Earlier in the 20th century, the city had spilled over from the old walled city into a southern suburban area. In the 1930s Nanning became the centre of a "model provincial government," under the warlord Li Zongren, and a spacious modern city was laid out. During the Sino-Japanese War (1937–45), Nanning was temporarily occupied in 1940 by the Japanese. It subsequently became an important U.S. air base supporting the Chinese armies in Guangxi, but during 1944–45 it was again under Japanese occupation.

In 1949 Nanning again became the provincial capital, first of Guangxi province and then of the Zhuang Autonomous Region of Guangxi, which replaced it in 1958. Until then Nanning had essentially been a commercial centre dependent on Guangzhou and on the Xi River system. In the late 1930s, a railway was begun, joining Hengyang in southern Hunan province with Guilin, Liuzhou, Nanning, and the Vietnam border, while another was begun from Liuzhou to Guiyang in Guizhou. The construction of the Nanning section of this line was halted in 1940 by the Japanese advances, however, and was not completed until 1951, after

Riverside scene in the ancient town of Yangmei on the outskirts of Nanning city, Guangxi province, China. Yangmei, founded during the Song dynasty (960–1279 CE), retains much of its historic character. Guang Niu/Getty Images

which Nanning was directly linked with central China; completion of a branch line to the port of Zhanjiang (in Guangdong) in 1957 gave it a direct outlet to the sea. During the French Indochina War (1946–54), Nanning was the chief support base in China for Vietnamese forces, and, during the ensuing Vietnam War in the 1960s and early 1970s, it again became a staging post for sending supplies southward to what was then North Vietnam. It was also an important military supply centre during the Sino-Vietnam confrontation in 1979.

THE CONTEMPORARY CITY

Beginning in 1949, Nanning's economy began developing beyond its former role as essentially a commercial and administrative centre, as it underwent sustained industrial growth. The city is surrounded by a fertile agricultural region producing subtropical fruits and sugarcane; food processing, flour milling, sugar refining, meatpacking, and leather manufacturing are important in the city. Nanning is a centre for printing and papermaking, and heavy industry is also important—as is the production of building materials, especially cement. In the 1990s the completion of a rail line between Nanning and Kunming (west) in Yunnan province and of railways from Nanning and the port cities of Fangchenggang and Beihai on the Gulf of Tonkin provided the shortest rail transport for southern China to the sea. Nanning subsequently became the railway hub of southern Guangxi.

After the Chinese government officially recognized the Tai-speaking Zhuang ethnic minority in 1958, Nanning became the chief centre for the training of Zhuang leaders. Guangxi University, a large medical school, and a school of agriculture, all in the city, date from the 1920s.

A cavern at Yiling, 12 miles (19 km) northwest of Nanning, has a 3,600-foot (1,100-m) passage through picturesque stalactites. In the 1970s coloured lights were installed, and the cavern was developed as a tourist attraction.

CHENGDU

The city of Chengdu is the capital of Sichuan province, southwest-central China. The city, in central Sichuan, is situated on the fertile Chengdu Plain, the site of Dujiangyan, one of China's most ancient and successful irrigation systems, watered by the Min River. The system and nearby Mount Qingcheng, an early centre of Daoism, were collectively designated a UNESCO World Heritage site in 2000. The irrigation system, first set up during the Qin dynasty (221–207 BCE), diverted half the waters of the Min River eastward to irrigate the plain through a dense network of channels. This system has survived basically in its original form and enables the area to support what has been claimed to be one of the densest agrarian populations anywhere in the world. Chengdu's 2006 estimated population was 3,582,019; its estimated 2007 urban agglomeration total was 4,123,000 people.

HISTORY

The city of Chengdu is said to have been founded by the Qin before they achieved control of all China during the 3rd century BCE. Under their imperial regime, the county of Chengdu was established; the name dates from that period. First under the Qin and then under the Han dynasty (206 BCE–220 CE), it was the seat of the commandery of Shu, and in 221 it became capital of the independent dynasty of Shu. Under the Tang dynasty (618–907) it was known as Yizhou, one of the empire's greatest commercial cities. In the late 8th century, it became a secondary capital. After 907 it again became capital of two short-lived independent regimes—the Qian (Former) and Hou (Later) Shu (respectively, 907–925 and 934–965). During that time it was immensely prosperous, and its merchants introduced the use of paper money, which rapidly spread throughout China under the Song dynasty (960–1279).

Chengdu became famous for its fine brocades and satins. The city was also notable for its refined culture and display of luxury. Throughout history it has remained a great city and a major administrative centre, and it has been the capital of Sichuan since 1368. Chengdu developed rapidly during World War II, when many refugees from eastern China, fleeing the Japanese, settled there. The influx of refugees to the city stimulated trade and commerce, and several universities and institutes of higher learning were also moved there. In 2008 a strong earthquake in Sichuan (centred near Chengdu) killed some 4,300 people in the city and nearby vicinity and injured more than 26,000 others, but it caused relatively little damage to the city's buildings and infrastructure.

THE CONTEMPORARY CITY

From 1949 Chengdu's growth was rapid. The city has always been an important communication centre, initially with waterways (the Yangtze River [Chang Jiang] and its tributaries, the Min and Tuo rivers) extending throughout the Sichuan Basin and beyond. Railways were built to Chongqing in 1952, to Baoji and extended to Xi'an (both in Shaanxi) in 1955, to Kunming (Yunnan) in the late 1960s, and via Ankang to Xiangfan (Hubei) in 1978—making Chengdu the rail hub for all southeastern China. Highways stretch north to Lanzhou in Gansu province, northeast to Xi'an, southeast and south to Guizhou and Yunnan provinces, southwest and west into the Tibet Autonomous Region, and northwest into Qinghai province. In addition, express highways have been built to such major cities as Shanghai and Chongqing. Chengdu's airport is one of China's air hubs, with flights to several international destinations as well as to most major Chinese cities. Work began in the early 21st century on a multiple-line subway system for the city.

The city is also a major industrial centre. In the 1950s a large thermal power-generating station was built, and two important radio and electronics plants were installed by Soviet experts. A precision-tool and measuring-instrument plant was also established to serve the southwestern region. In addition, there are important engineering shops manufacturing railway equipment and power machinery and, more recently, aircraft. In the 1960s Chengdu became an important centre of China's national defense industry. A chemical industry—producing fertilizers, industrial chemicals, and pharmaceutical products—was also developed. The city's oldest industry—textiles—remains important in the production not only of traditional silks but also of cotton and woolen textiles. Since 1990 the economic reforms enacted in China have encouraged the development of Chengdu's electronic and high-technology industries, including the establishment of a large industrial park in the region.

Chengdu continues to be a major cultural centre. In addition to Sichuan University (1905), there are other universities; higher institutes of medicine, science, geology, and economics; normal colleges; a fine museum; and a variety of specialist technical schools, several connected with the radio and electronics industries. There is a minorities institute for the training of Tibetan students. The city also has many historical monuments and buildings, including the cottage of the Tang-era poet Du Fu. Sichuan is home

to much of the world's giant panda population, and Chengdu has a panda-breeding facility. To the west of the city is Wolong Nature Preserve, one of several sanctuaries for giant pandas in the province that together were designated a UNESCO World Heritage site in 2006.

KUNMING

The city of Kunming is the capital of Yunnan province, southwestern China. It is situated in the east-central part of the province in a fertile lake basin on the northern shore of Lake Dian, surrounded by mountains to the north, west, and east. Kunming has always been a focus of communications in southwestern China. The population of the city as of 2006 was 1,700,210; the 2007 estimate of the urban agglomeration was 2,931,000.

HISTORY

Kunming boasts a long history. As early as 30,000 years ago, ancient tribes inhabited the area around Lake Dian. During the 3rd century BCE, Zhuangqiao of the Chu (in the middle reaches of the Yangtze River [Chang Jiang]) led his men to the area around Lake Dian and established the Dian Kingdom. In 109 BCE, during the reign (141–87 BCE) of the Xi (Western) Han emperor Wudi, the Dian Kingdom became part of the Han territory and was named Yizhou prefecture, with Dianchi county as its seat. It was then an important traffic centre, connecting China's hinterland with the southern branch of the ancient Silk Road to the west. Via Yunnan, it also connected present-day Sichuan to Vietnam. During the Sui dynasty (581–618), it was renamed Kunzhou.

From the 8th century onward, it was known to the Chinese as Tuodong city in the independent states of Nanzhao and Dali. It then came under the control of the Chinese central government with the Yuan (Mongol) invasion of the southwest in 1253. In 1276 it was founded as Kunming county and became the provincial capital of Yunnan. It is considered by scholars to have been the city of Yachi, described by the 13th-century Venetian traveler Marco Polo. During the Ming (1368–1644) and Qing (1644–1911/12) dynasties, it was the seat of the superior prefecture of Yunnan. It reverted to county status in 1912, under the name Kunming, and became a municipality in 1928.

Kunming was a communications centre in early times and a junction of two major trading routes, one westward via Dali and Tengchong into Myanmar (Burma) and the other southward through Mengzi to the Red River in peninsular Southeast Asia. Eastward, a difficult mountain route led to Guiyang in Guizhou province and thence to Hunan province. To the northeast was a well-established trade trail to Yibin in Sichuan province on the Yangtze River. However, these trails were all extremely difficult, passable only by mule trains or pack-carrying porters.

The opening of the Kunming area began in earnest with the completion in 1906–10 of the railway to the Vietnamese city of Haiphong in what was then French Indochina. Kunming became a treaty port open to foreign trade in 1908 and soon became a commercial centre. In the 1930s its importance grew still further when the first highways were built, linking Kunming with Chongqing (then in Sichuan) and Guiyang to the east.

Kunming's transformation into a modern city resulted from the outbreak of the Sino-Japanese War in 1937. In the face of the advancing Japanese forces, great numbers of Chinese flooded into southwestern China and took with them dismantled industrial plants, which were then reerected beyond the range of Japanese bombers. In addition, a number of universities and institutes of higher education were evacuated there. When the Japanese occupied French Indochina in 1940, the links of Kunming with the west, both via the newly constructed Burma Road and by air, grew increasingly vital. Industry became important in Kunming during World War II. The large state-owned Central Machine Works was transferred there from Hunan, while the manufacturing of electrical products, copper, cement, steel, paper, and textiles expanded.

THE CONTEMPORARY CITY

After 1949, Kunming developed rapidly into an industrial metropolis, second only to Chongqing in the southwest. Its chief industries are the production of copper, lead, and zinc; its iron and steel industry is also significant. In addition, Kunming is a centre of the engineering industry, manufacturing machine tools, electrical machinery and equipment, and automobiles. It has major factories that manufacture chemicals, cement, and textiles. Its many processing plants, which include tanneries and woodworking and papermaking factories, use local agricultural products. Beginning in the 1980s, the city's principal industries also came to include food and tobacco processing and the manufacturing of construction equipment and machines.

Since the 1950s, railways connecting Kunming with Guiyang, Chengdu (Sichuan), Nanning (Guanxi), and Vietnam have been built. The city is also a hub for major national highways in southwestern China. Kunming's airport has daily flights to Beijing, Hong Kong, and Macau, as well as international service to Southeast Asia and Japan.

Kunming remains a major cultural centre. Notable among the city's numerous universities, medical and teacher-training colleges, technical schools, and scientific research institutes are Yunnan University (1922), Kunming University of Science and Technology (1925), and Yunnan Agricultural University (established in 1938 as part of Yunnan University; made separate in 1958). Kunming hosted the 1999 World Horticulture Exposition, and the grounds of that, just north of the city,

have been converted into a large park. Some 60 miles (100 km) southeast of the city is the Shilin ("Stone Forest") karst formation, consisting of rock caves, arches, and pavilions; a popular tourist destination, it and other karst areas in the region were collectively designated a UNESCO World Heritage site in 2007.

LHASA

The city of Lhasa (Chinese: Lasa) is the capital of the Tibet Autonomous Region, southwestern China. It is located at an elevation of 11,975 feet (3,650 m) in the Nyainqêntanglha Mountains of southern Tibet near the Lhasa River, a tributary of the Yarlung Zangbo (Tsangpo) River (the name of the Brahmaputra River in Tibet). Tibetan Buddhists consider Lhasa a holy land, and it is a state-level historical and cultural city in China.

Lhasa had been designated as the capital of Tibet by the 9th century CE. However, national power became decentralized following the assassination of the Tibetan king in 842, and Lhasa lost its position as the country's capital, though it gained in religious importance in succeeding centuries. It served as the national religious centre of Tibet, and much of its population was composed of Buddhist monks and laypeople. In 1642 Lhasa was again the seat of the central government, a position it held into the 20th century. Although Chinese troops moved into Lhasa and Tibet in 1951, both remained under the Tibetan authority until 1959, when direct Chinese administration was imposed. Lhasa was established as a city in 1960.

The centre of the city is occupied by the four-story Tsuglagkhang, or Gtsug-lag-khang (Jokhang), Temple, built in the mid-7th century CE and considered the holiest place in Tibet. It was temporarily converted into a guesthouse by the Chinese after 1951, but restoration of its artistic and architectural heritage began in 1972–75, and its religious functions were restored in 1979. Other city landmarks include Klu-khang (Lukhang) Temple; Potala Palace, once the winter residence of the Dalai Lama; and the former summer palace of the Dalai Lama, the Norbuglingka (Nor-bu-gling-ka; Jewel Palace), which is now called the People's Pleasure Park. The monasteries of 'Bras-spungs (Drepung) and Se-ra, two of the largest in Tibet, have received renovation.

Before 1951 the city's economy was based on the historic trade routes that converged on Lhasa from China, India, Nepal, and Bhutan. Except for handicrafts, the only industries were those of a munitions factory and a mint. The Chinese administration reopened Lhasa to foreign trade in the 1980s and has established experimental farms outside the city and encouraged the scientific breeding of livestock. Small-scale industries include chemical production, electric-motor manufacturing, tanning, wool processing, pharmaceutical and fertilizer production, motor-vehicle maintenance and repair, tractor assembly, rug and carpet making, and cement production.

Lhasa is connected by road with the major cities of Sichuan and Qinghai provinces and the Uygur Autonomous Region of Xinjiang. A large modern airport offers passenger service to Beijing and other major Chinese cities and also to Kathmandu, Nepal. A railway line connecting Lhasa and Golmud in Qinghai province was opened in 2006.

Tourism has become an increasingly important component of the local economy, and Lhasa has been designated one of the country's historic and cultural cities. In addition, Potala Palace was designated a UNESCO World Heritage site in 1994; Jokhang Temple and the Norbuglingka were added to the site in 2000 and 2001, respectively. The main institution of higher learning in the city is the University of Tibet, which was founded in 1951 and reorganized in 1985. Lhasa's population according to an estimate in 2006 was 156,096.

ÜRÜMQI

The city of Ürümqi (Chinese: Wulumuqi; Uighur: Ürümchi) is the capital of the Uygur Autonomous Region of Xinjiang, northwestern China. The city (whose name in Uighur means "fine pasture") is situated in a fertile belt of oases along the northern slope of the eastern Tien (Tian) Shan range. Ürümqi commands the northern end of a gap leading from the Tarim Basin into the Junggar (Dzungarian) Basin. In 2006, its population was an estimated 1,504,252; in 2007, the estimated urban agglomeration was 2,151,000 people.

HISTORY

The area first came under full Chinese control in the 7th and 8th centuries, when the Chinese established the protectorate general of Beiting some 80 miles (130 km) to the east. A county named Luntai had earlier been founded at Ürümqi in 640, which became an important centre for caravans traveling into the Ili River valley from the main route across Turkistan. After the withdrawal of the Tang dynasty (618–907) from the area in the 750s, Ürümqi came under the control of the Uighurs. It again came under Chinese rule during the campaigns of the Qing dynasty against the Dzungars in the 18th century. In 1760 military colonies were established in the surrounding oases, and in 1763 a Chinese city called Dihua was founded there.

The city became an important Manchu garrison for northwestern China. When Muslim rebellion broke out in Xinjiang in the 1860s, Ürümqi was taken by the rebels in 1864, but it was eventually recaptured in 1876 by Qing forces under Zuo Zongtang. When the province of Xinjiang was set up in 1884, Ürümqi (Dihua) became its capital. It grew rapidly into the greatest city and centre of trade in Central Asia. Its commercial importance was matched in the last days of the Qing dynasty (1644–1911/12) by its growing strategic and international significance as the British and Russians each attempted to establish influence in Xinjiang.

THE CONTEMPORARY CITY

Since 1949 Ürümqi has been developed not only as the regional capital and cultural centre of Xinjiang but also as a major industrial base. In addition, efforts have been made to extend the irrigated farmlands in the vicinity (along the foot of the Tien Shan) and to improve the region's agricultural productivity by mechanization. Ürümqi's prosperity has come largely from its mineral resources. In 1955 a large petroleum field was discovered at Karamay, to the north in the Junggar Basin; it was brought into production in 1958–59 and has since become one of China's major domestic sources of oil. Extensive coal deposits were found along the foot of the Tien Shan, and there are major mining centres near Ürümqi and at Liudaowan. A large thermal power station, ironworks and steelworks, an engineering sector (producing agricultural machinery), a cement works, chemical and fertilizer plants, an oil refinery, and cotton textile mills have been built. Southeast of Ürümqi, in Chaiwopu, is a large windmill power station, the first of its kind in China.

A railway extending northwestward from Lanzhou (Gansu province) that links Ürümqi to the Chinese rail network was completed in the early 1960s. A highway was built following the same route, and other highways have been built across the Junggar and Tarim basins, greatly improving Ürümqi's communications. The rail line has been extended northwestward from Ürümqi to the Dzungarian (Junggar) Gate (Chinese: Alataw Shankou)—a pass through the Zhongghar Alataū (Alataw) Mountains into Kazakhstan. Another rail line, completed in 1999, follows the route of the ancient Silk Road along the northern edge of the Tarim Basin and gives the city convenient access to Kashgar (Kashi), in southwestern Xinjiang. The city's international airport is just to the northwest. The great expansion of and improvements in Ürümqi's transportation infrastructure have transformed the city into a major communications centre for northwestern China.

Culturally, Ürümqi largely remains a Uighur city, in spite of the fact that Han Chinese constitute the great majority of the population—especially with the increased influx of Han since the 1990s.

Uighur is widely spoken, and most Uighurs are Muslim. There are Kazakh, Dungan, and Manchu minorities. Although much effort has been devoted to building a Uighur cultural base, there also has been a certain level of ethnic tension between the Uighur and Han populations in the region. Periodically, this tension has precipitated protests and violence, notably in July 2009, when scores of people were killed and hundreds more wounded during disturbances in the city.

The city has many schools and institutes of higher education, including several universities, colleges offering special courses for minorities, and institutions for studying medicine, agricultural science, and the Russian language. Notable among these is Xinjiang University, founded in 1924 and reorganized in 2000 following its merger with Xinjiang Engineering Institute. Tian Lake, formed in a crater of the Bogd Mountains (the eastern extension of the Tien Shan) about 70 miles (110 km) east of Ürümqi, is a scenic spot and popular tourist destination.

CHAPTER 10

SPECIAL ADMINISTRATIVE REGIONS

At the end of the 1990s, China created the new jurisdictional category of special administrative region (*tebie xingzhengqu*) when two foreign-controlled territories—the British crown colony of Hong Kong (Chinese: Xianggang) and the Portuguese colony of Macau (Chinese: Aomen) reverted to Chinese control. Although these two regions are under the direct jurisdiction of the central government in Beijing, each has been granted a certain degree of economic and (to a lesser degree) administrative autonomy.

HONG KONG

The special administrative region of Hong Kong is located to the east of the Pearl River (Xu Jiang) estuary on the south coast of China. The region is bordered by Guangdong province to the north and the South China Sea to the east, south, and west. It consists of Hong Kong Island, originally ceded by China to Great Britain in 1842, the southern part of the Kowloon Peninsula and Stonecutters (Ngong Shuen) Island (now joined to the mainland), ceded in 1860, and the New Territories, which include the mainland area lying largely to the north, together with 230 large and small offshore islands—all of which were leased from China for 99 years from 1898 to 1997. The Chinese-British joint declaration signed on

December 19, 1984, paved the way for the entire territory to be returned to China, which occurred July 1, 1997.

Hong Kong developed initially on the basis of its excellent natural harbour (its Chinese name means "fragrant harbour") and the lucrative China trade, particularly opium dealing. It was the expansion of its territory, however, that provided labour and other resources necessary for sustained commercial growth that led to its becoming one of the world's major trade and financial centres. The community remains limited in space and natural resources, and it faces persistent problems of overcrowding, trade fluctuations, and social and political unrest. Nevertheless, Hong Kong has emerged strong and prosperous, albeit with a changed role, as an entrepôt, a manufacturing and financial centre, and a vital agent in the trade and modernization of China. Its limited area measures 426 square miles (1,104 square km), while its population measured 6,864,346 in 2006.

Hong Kong skyline at night, including the Convention and Exhibition Center (centre). © Digital Vision/Getty Images

LAND

The area of Hong Kong has expanded over the years, and it has continued to grow as more land has been reclaimed from the surrounding sea. Hong Kong Island and its adjacent islets have an area of only about 31 square miles (81 square km), while urban Kowloon, which includes the Kowloon Peninsula south of Boundary Street, and Stonecutters Island measure about 18 square miles (47 square km). The New Territories account for the rest of the area—more than 90 percent of the total. The Victoria urban district located on the barren rocks of the north-western coast of Hong Kong Island is the place where the British first landed in 1841, and it has since been the centre of administrative and economic activities.

RELIEF

Hong Kong has rugged relief and marked variations in topography, which is in sharp contrast to the low-lying areas of

Kowloon street at night, Hong Kong. Photos.com/Jupiterimages

the Pearl River Delta region but conforms geologically and structurally to the well-eroded upland region of the great South China massif. Structurally, the area is an upfold, running northeast-southwest, that was formed about 150 million years ago toward the latter part of the Jurassic Period. Lava poured into this structure and formed volcanic rocks that were later intruded by an extensive granitic dome. The harbour of Hong Kong was formed by the drowning of the denuded centre of the dome. The surrounding hills on the mainland and on Hong Kong Island are partly capped by volcanic rocks, and steep, scarplike concave slopes lead to the inner harbour.

The area is a partially submerged, dissected upland terrain that rises abruptly to heights above 2,950 feet (900 m); its backbone is made up of a series of ridges, running northeast to southwest, that tie in closely with the structural trend in South China. This trend is clearly observable from the alignment of Lantau Island and the Tolo Channel. From Mount Tai Mo—at 3,140 feet (957 m) the highest peak in the territory—the series of ridges extends southwestward to Lantau Island, where the terrain rises to 3,064 feet (934 m) on Lantau Peak and 2,851 feet (869 m) on Sunset Peak. Extending southeastward from Mount Tai Mo, the Kowloon Peak attains an elevation of 1,975 feet (602 m), but there is an abrupt drop to about 650 feet (198 m) at Devil's Peak. Victoria (Hong Kong) Harbour is well protected by mountains on Hong Kong Island that include Victoria Peak in the west, which rises to 1,810 feet (552 m), and Mount Parker in the east, which reaches a height of about 1,742 feet (531 m).

Lowlands of the Hong Kong region, including floodplains, river valleys, and reclaimed land, occupy less than one-fifth of the land. Extensive lowland regions are found only north of Mount Tai Mo, in the Yuen Long and Sheung Shui plains. The urban area that spans the two sides of the harbour, with ongoing reclamation, takes up only about one-tenth of the level area.

DRAINAGE

Hong Kong lacks a river system of any scope, the only exception being in the north where the Sham Chun (Shenzhen) River, which forms the boundary between Guangdong and Hong Kong, flows into Deep Bay after collecting a number of small tributaries. Most of the streams are small, and they generally run perpendicular to the northeast-southwest trend of the terrain. The construction of reservoirs and their catchment systems has reduced the amount of fresh water available downstream.

SOILS

In general, Hong Kong's soils are acidic and of low fertility. An exception is the alluvial soils, which are found mainly in the Deep Bay area, where the sediment-laden waters of the Pearl River estuary meet saline waters at high tide and slow down to deposit their sediments to form mudflats. Paddy rice farming and, more recently, intensive vegetable cultivation have modified the alluvial soils. Elsewhere, hill soils, classified as red-yellow podzolic and krasnozem, abound. Under forest, these hill soils have a well-developed profile, with rich topsoil, but, when they are exposed, as is mostly the case, they tend to be thin and lacking in nutrients. Under tropical conditions, sheet and gully erosion is extensive and drastic.

CLIMATE

Hong Kong lies at the northern fringe of the tropical zone. Its monsoonal (wet-dry) seasonal changes are well marked, however, with hot, humid summers and cool, dry winters. The climate is largely controlled by the atmospheric pressure systems over the adjacent great Asian landmass and ocean surface. Thus, relatively dry monsoonal winds blow from the northeast in winter as a result of the cooling of the landmass and the development of a large thermal anticyclone over Inner Mongolia Autonomous Region. Warm, wet southeasterly winds develop in summer when the North Pacific Ocean heats up more slowly through solar radiation and becomes a high-pressure area.

The mean January and July temperatures are about 60 °F (16 °C) and 84 °F (29 °C), respectively. The lowest recorded temperature was 32 °F (0 °C) in January 1893, and the highest was 97 °F (36 °C) in August 1900. Frost occasionally occurs on hilltops in winter. The average annual rainfall amounts to about 88 inches (2,220 mm), more than half of which falls during the summer months of June, July, and August; only about 10 percent falls from November to March. Tropical cyclones, or typhoons, generally occur between June and October, and, of the twenty to thirty typhoons formed over the western North Pacific and South China Sea each year, an average of five or six may affect Hong Kong. The torrential downpours and strong winds that frequently accompany the typhoons sometimes devastate life and property in Hong Kong and in adjacent areas of Guangdong.

PLANT AND ANIMAL LIFE

Hong Kong is noted for the lushness and great diversity of its plant life. The transitional climate between humid subtropical and warm temperate maritime excludes the most sensitive humid tropical genera due to the cool, dry winter conditions, but many tropical as well as temperate-zone families are represented. Most of the land, except for the heavily eroded badlands, is under tropical herbaceous growth, including mangrove and other swamp cover. The most common forest genus today is *Pinus*, represented by native South China red pines and by slash pines, introduced from Australia. Some of the oldest areas of woodland are in the feng-shui wood, or "sacred groves," found in many New Territories villages. These woods consist essentially of native forest trees, some of which are of potential value to the villagers. Centuries of cutting and burning, however, have destroyed much of Hong Kong's original vegetation, leaving only about one-sixth of the land forested. A large portion of Hong Kong's present-day forest cover owes its origin to afforestation programs undertaken since World War II, which have restored some of the stands of pine, eucalyptus, banyan, casuarina, and palm trees.

Hong Kong's animal life consists of a mixture of mammals adapted to the subtropical environment. Among the few arboreal mammals are two species of nonnative monkeys that flourish in forests of the New Territories, the rhesus macaque and the long-tailed macaque. Tigers are reputed to have once roamed the area, but they are no longer in evidence. The largest remaining carnivores are rare and include the South China red fox, the Chinese leopard cat, the seven-banded civet, and the masked palm civet. Some rat and mouse species typically inhabit scrubland and grassland areas. Birdlife is abundant, and there are numerous species of snakes, lizards, and frogs.

PEOPLE

Hong Kong is renowned as one of the world's great cosmopolitan cities. It is one of the most densely populated places on Earth, its entire population being classified as urban.

ETHNIC GROUPS

The great majority of the population is Chinese by place of origin, the non-Chinese making up only a tiny fraction of the total. Non-Chinese groups consist largely of Asians (primarily Filipinos, Indonesians, and South Asians), with small numbers of non-Asians (mainly Americans, Canadians, and Australians). An overwhelming majority of the Chinese are from Guangdong province and from Hong Kong itself, with smaller numbers coming from other parts of China.

LANGUAGES

Chinese and English are both official languages. Chinese, especially Cantonese in the spoken form, is the common language, however, and is almost universally understood. A variety of dialects and other languages are used among the ethnic minorities. Apart from Cantonese, common dialects such as Teochew, Hakka, and Tanka are used within separate communities of the Guangdong and Hong Kong Chinese. Groups from other parts of China are also likely to use their own native dialects, and, similarly, the non-Chinese are likely to use their own native languages among themselves. The use of Mandarin Chinese has risen as Hong Kong has reintegrated with China.

RELIGION

The majority of Hong Kong's population does not profess a religion. Those that do

Woman lighting incense at a Buddhist temple, Hong Kong. © Corbis

practice a wide variety of beliefs. Among the Chinese, followers of Buddhism and Daoism far outnumber other groups; a large number also follow Confucianist beliefs. The numerous Buddhist and Daoist temples and monasteries, some centuries old, play an important role in the daily life of the average Chinese. Although each temple is generally dedicated to one or two deities, it is not unusual to find images of a number of other gods or goddesses inside. For a fishing and trading port, the most significant deities are those associated with the ocean and the weather, such as Dian Hau, the goddess of heaven and protector of seafarers, who is honoured by temples at virtually every fishing harbour. Other leading deities include Guanyin (Avalokitesvara), the Buddhist bodhisattva of mercy; Hong Shing, god of the South Seas and a weather prophet; and Wong Daisin, a Daoist saint and deity. A small but significant proportion of the people are Christians, with somewhat more Protestants than Roman Catholics; there are dozens of Protestant denominations and sects such as Baptist, Lutheran, Anglican, and Methodist. There are also small numbers of Muslims, Hindus, Sikhs, and Jews.

Settlement Patterns

The predominantly urban settlements of Hong Kong are typically distributed linearly, following the irregular coastline and transportation routes. The principal urban areas are established on Hong Kong Island and the Kowloon Peninsula, where roughly half of the total population lives. There, most of the population is concentrated around Victoria Harbour, living on the limited flatland that is being continuously extended by reclamation. Many major streets, especially those on the northern shore of Hong Kong Island, as well as the entire industrial district of Kwun Tong and much of the southern tip of the Kowloon Peninsula, have been built on reclaimed land.

In the New Territories north of the Kowloon hills, rural settlements vary from hamlets to small towns. Most of the villages, compactly built and often walled, follow the alignment of the river systems in the low-lying but fertile alluvial floodplains or the major route corridors. Villages of the Cantonese people are located mainly in the flat alluvial regions,

Street scene, Hong Kong. © Goodshoot/Jupiterimages

whereas villages of the Hakka people usually are found in narrow valleys or on foothills. The feng-shui grove and pond are characteristic of both the Cantonese and Hakka villages: the grove is generally planted on the upslope, or back side, of a village for shade and protection, and the pond is for fish-farming.

A number of new towns have sprung up in the New Territories as a result of the tremendous increase in population there. Among these are Tsuen Wan, Tuen Mun (Castle Peak before 1973), and Sha Tin, which were established in the 1960s and designed to have populations of between about 500,000 and 850,000 each. Others, including Tai Po, Fanling, Yuen Long, and, more recently, Tseung Kwon O (Junk Bay), were designated as new towns in the 1970s, with population goals ranging from about 200,000 to 450,000. Thus, the New Territories, where only one-eighth of the population resided in 1961, accounted for more than half of the total by 2005; the bulk of the New Territories population is now concentrated in the new towns.

True to its original character as a fishing port, Hong Kong has a sizable, though rapidly dwindling, marine settlement. The "boat people," or Tanka as they are locally known, are essentially fisherfolk living on junks and boats, as their ancestors did for centuries before them. They inhabit fishing towns, such as Aberdeen, Shau Kei Wan, and Cheung Chau, and typhoon shelters in the harbour areas. With the advance of urbanization and the decline of fishing activity, increasing numbers of them are working ashore.

DEMOGRAPHIC TRENDS

As in many large urban centres of the world, Hong Kong's population has increased in the late 20th century. Since the 1950s the average annual rate of growth has fluctuated between about 2 and 4 percent, the variations based in some degree on the sporadic flow of immigrants from China. Immigration has been a chief cause of population increase, but it was slowed through changes in immigration policy in 1980 and 1982, and emigration rose from the late 1980s. Birth rates have steadily declined since the late 1950s, the rate of natural increase falling below 1 percent by the 1980s. Life expectancy, however, has been showing a gradual increase. Since the 1950s, the proportion of the population under 15 has decreased rapidly, while that between 15 and 64 has shown a marked increase and the group over 65 has more than doubled. Hong Kong is one of the world's most densely populated places.

ECONOMY

With its limited natural resources, Hong Kong depends on imports for virtually all of its requirements, including raw materials, food and other consumer goods, capital goods, and fuel. Under its unique status as an international free

"Boat people" (Tanka) in Hong Kong Harbour. © Goodshoot/Jupiterimages

port, entrepôt trade, mainly with China, flourished until 1951, when a United Nations embargo on trade with China and North Korea drastically curtailed it. This situation, combined with the need to export and with the availability of cheap labour, led to the establishment of competitive light industries and a transformation of the economy in the early 1960s. The market economy and the laissez-faire policy of the British colonial government provided flexibility for further industrialization and the incentive and freedom, from the late 1960s, to attract foreign investment and financial transactions. In succeeding years, with China adopting a more open foreign policy, entrepôt trade rapidly revived, while Hong Kong–China trade surged. Hong Kong developed not only in manufacturing, trade, and shipping but also as a regional financial centre and as an agent in China's pursuit of modernization. The tertiary (services) sector of the economy now makes up some four-fifths of the gross domestic product (GDP).

AGRICULTURE AND FISHING

Only 6 percent of Hong Kong's land area is arable, and another 2 percent is under fishponds. Since the 1950s about one-third of the agricultural land has been lost to other uses. The growing season is year-round, however, and several crops per year are possible. Paddy rice cultivation once dominated agricultural land use, but it has practically disappeared, having been surpassed by vegetable and pond fish farming. Other minor uses include the production of fruits, flowers, and crops such as sweet potatoes, taro, yams, and sugarcane. There also is some livestock farming, mainly of chickens and pigs.

Marine fishing in the adjacent waters is one of Hong Kong's most important primary activities. Apart from pond fish, a marine fish culture has shown signs of development, notably in the eastern New Territories.

RESOURCES AND POWER

Hong Kong is practically devoid of any significant mineral resources. The mining for graphite and lead at Cham ("Needle") Hill and iron ore at Mount Ma On stopped long ago. The small-scale mining of feldspar, feldspar sand, and kaolin clay ceased by 1990. Some stone is quarried for use in construction. Hong Kong is similarly poorly endowed in other natural resources: no commercial timber is produced from its sparse forest cover, and there is no hydroelectric potential from the small and short streams. Indeed, even water has been in serious short supply as a consequence of the limited areal extent, the steep terrain, and the lack of catchment areas. In spite of the many reservoirs, which were built mostly before World War II, and several giant projects, such as the water desalinization plant at Castle Peak and the Plover Cove and the High Island reservoirs, which are enclosed sea areas, the bulk of water consumed is piped in from Guangdong province.

Hong Kong must import all of the fossil fuel it consumes. It produces most of its electric-power needs at thermal generating plants. The rest of its power requirements are imported from Guangdong province.

MANUFACTURING

The rapid development of manufacturing in the 1950s was made possible by immigrant Chinese industrialists, mainly from Shanghai, who brought with them technology and capital. Foreign investments soon began to flow in to tap the huge supply of cheap labour and relatively cheap raw materials available in the surrounding region. Most industry has been confined to the urban areas, especially in the densely populated districts of Kowloon. With the development of industrial and other new towns, manufacturing began to disperse into Kwun Tong, Tsuen Wan, Tuen Mun, and other areas. In 1977 the Hong Kong Industrial Estates Corporation was established to develop and manage industrial estates that would accommodate high-technology industries, first on reclaimed land in Tai Po and later in Yuen Long.

Manufacturing, once the most important sector of the Hong Kong economy, has been overshadowed by the vast service sector; manufacturing now constitutes only a tiny fraction of the gross domestic product and employs only a slightly higher proportion of the labour force. Textile and clothing production is the leading manufacturing activity and contributes about one-third of the value of domestic exports. The electronics industry is the second largest export earner. There are some heavy industries such as shipbuilding and repair and aircraft engineering. Steel rolling, production of machine parts and plastics, and cement manufacturing serve local needs.

FINANCE

Since 1969 Hong Kong has emerged as one of the major financial centres of the Asia-Pacific region, despite the fact that it is without the services of a central bank. The regional government delegates the functions of such an institution to the Hong Kong Monetary Authority and to selected commercial banks. In addition to the licensed banks in the region, there are representative offices of foreign banks, including registered deposit-taking companies.

Domestic and international currencies are traded at the Hong Kong foreign-exchange market. The stock market attracts investment from both foreign and domestic sources. Some of its major shares are also traded on the London stock market. A gold bullion market, once the world's largest, is operated by the Chinese Gold and Silver Exchange Society. The lack of exchange controls has contributed to the success of Hong Kong as a financial centre.

TRADE AND TOURISM

Hong Kong's free-trade policy has made the territory one of the world's great centres of trade. There is no tariff on imports, except for some luxury items, such as perfumes, motor vehicles, alcoholic beverages, and tobacco. Hong Kong is dependent upon imported products, which make up about half of the total amount of external trade, the rest being divided between exports and reexports. Apart from trade with other regions of China, Japan supplies the largest percentage of imports, and other major suppliers include Taiwan, the countries of the European Union (EU), and Singapore. Capital and consumer goods such as electrical machinery and apparatus, clothing, radios, television sets, stereos, and computers represent the largest group of imports. The second largest group includes mineral fuels, raw materials, semi-manufactured goods (such as synthetic and natural textiles, chemicals, and electronic components), and foodstuffs.

China became the main market for Hong Kong's products prior to 1997, and this trade remained predominant after the territory's reintegration. Other major export destinations include the United States, the countries of the EU, and Japan. Textiles and clothing are the leading exports. Also important are electrical machinery and appliances, office machinery, photographic apparatus, and a variety of other manufactured items. Reexports constitute a major portion of the goods shipped out of Hong Kong.

Wholesale and retail trade also are major components of the service sector, as is tourism. The tourist trade, which is highly promoted by the government and well catered to by the huge service sector, now constitutes a significant component of the economy. The largest number of tourist arrivals are from the mainland. In addition, a large number of business and tourist travelers from Taiwan pass through Hong Kong on their way to and from destinations on the mainland.

TRANSPORTATION AND TELECOMMUNICATIONS

With roadways limited relative to the population, the government has enforced strict limitations on automobile ownership and placed heavy emphasis on the development of public transportation. As a result, the rate of car ownership is low, although it is steadily rising. The majority of the populace makes its daily trips by public transportation. Apart from the bus, tram (streetcar), and ferry, the public is also served by a unique minibus service, a rapid transit system, and an electric railway. Buses are the largest road carrier, responsible for roughly one-third of the daily public-transport trips excluding those by taxi, followed by the combined minibus and maxicab (a regulated form of minibus) service. Commuter rail service also accounts for about one-third of overall ridership. The precipitous Victoria Peak area is served by one of the oldest transportation companies, which operates a cable-car system between the peak and the Central District.

International traffic is served by Hong Kong's international airport and its magnificent harbour, and there are good overland linkages with Guangdong province. The Hong Kong International Airport was located at Kai Tak, on the eastern fringe of Kowloon, until 1998, when it was relocated to a new, larger facility on Chek Lap Kok Island. Designed by British architect Sir Norman Foster, the airport's passenger terminal is among the world's largest enclosed spaces, covering some 133 acres (54 hectares). The port of Hong Kong, based at one of the world's finest natural harbours, is renowned for its efficiency and capacity. The capacity of its container terminals at Kwai Chung ranks Hong Kong among the world's largest container ports. Speedy ferry service between Hong Kong and Macau and parts of Guangdong is provided by various craft, including hydrofoils and hovercraft.

Passenger and freight rail services are provided by the Kowloon-Canton Railway (in operation since 1910). Electrification and double-tracking of the railway and the growth along its lines of the new towns of Sha Tin, Tai Po, Fanling, and others caused a considerable increase in passenger traffic. The railway's commuter services expanded considerably with its merger in 2007 with MTR Corporation, which had been established in 1975 to develop and operate Hong Kong's mass-transit system. Hong Kong's rail system is connected by a line running to nearby Shenzhen and, to the northwest, Guangzhou (Canton) in Guangdong province; the line carries millions of tons of freight annually, as well as passenger traffic between Hong Kong and Guangdong.

Hong Kong has one of the world's most advanced and technologically sophisticated telecommunications systems, and it is one of the principal centres of the global telecommunications network. Hong Kong is a leader in integrating multiple-platform communication modes (e.g., land-line and mobile telephony) and implementing the most cutting-edge technology. Land-line telephones are nearly ubiquitous among Hong Kong households, and mobile-phone subscriptions exceed considerably the total number of inhabitants. Internet use is widespread, a large proportion of it using broadband.

Government and Society

As a colony, Hong Kong was administered by a governor, who was appointed by and represented the monarch of the United Kingdom, directed the government, served as the commander in chief, and presided over the two main organs of government, the Executive Council and the Legislative Council.

With the resumption of Chinese sovereignty over the territory in July 1997, the Basic Law of the Hong Kong Special Administrative Region (promulgated by the National People's Congress of China in 1990) went into effect.

Legislative Council Building (centre) at night, Hong Kong. © Digital Vision/Getty Images

CONSTITUTIONAL FRAMEWORK

The guiding principle of the Basic Law of the Hong Kong Special Administrative Region was the concept of "one country, two systems," under which Hong Kong was allowed to maintain its capitalist economy and to retain a large degree of political autonomy (except in matters of foreign policy and defense) for a period of 50 years.

The Basic Law vests executive authority in a chief executive, who is under the jurisdiction of the central government in Beijing and serves a five-year term.

Legislative authority rests with a Legislative Council, whose sixty members serve a four-year term; the chief executive, however, can dissolve the council before the end of a term.

According to the Basic Law, the chief executive for the second term was appointed by the central government, following election by an 800-member Election Committee in Hong Kong. The constituencies for council members were then defined during their second and third terms, and by the third term half were directly elected from geographic constituencies and half were selected from "functional constituencies" drawn from business and professional circles. The Basic Law further states, however, that the chief executive and council members ultimately were to be elected by universal suffrage. These electoral procedures were to have been determined by 2007, but in that year the Standing Committee of the National People's Congress in Beijing ruled that universal suffrage would not be implemented before 2012.

Civil and criminal law is derived generally from that of the United Kingdom, and the Basic Law states that this system is to be maintained. The highest court in the judiciary is the Court of Final Appeal, headed by a chief justice. This is followed by the High Court (headed by a chief judge) and by district, magistrate, and special courts. The chief executive appoints all judges, although judges of the Court of Final Appeal and the chief judge of the High Court also must be confirmed by the Legislative Council and reported to the Standing Committee of the National People's Congress.

HEALTH AND WELFARE

The health of the populace is generally good, the result, in part, of an aggressive program of public measures, including the promotion of preventive medicine and personal health services, and a relatively high quality of life. Improving health indexes and a downward trend in the occurrence of major communicable diseases are leading indicators of the state of health in Hong Kong. Most deaths are caused by cancer, heart disease, and respiratory diseases. Hospitals are divided into three groups: government, government-assisted, and private. These hospitals are under great pressure to meet the needs of the people. Clinics, some operated by the government, supplement other medical facilities. Boat-borne clinics provide services to some outlying villages.

The social security system long was largely limited to emergency relief programs. However, since the mid-1990s, spending on social welfare has increased significantly. There are assistance programs for the unemployed, the elderly, and people with disabilities. The aging of the population, coupled with the extreme crowding in the city, has been one of the main issues with elder care. More recent programs have included those focused on family welfare (including day care), counseling services, and accident compensation.

HOUSING

Historically, housing has been a major problem in Hong Kong, where space is limited and the number of occupants ever-growing. Changes in the residential environment between the establishment of the colony in 1842 and the Japanese occupation in 1941 were moderate, compared to those that took place in the postwar years. There was no planning in the earlier days of development, except that generally the British lived on the Peak (the area around Victoria Peak), other nationalities in the Mid-Levels (below the Peak), and the wealthy on somewhat higher ground, where the grand garden houses and large mansions remain as landmarks. Most of the Chinese lived on the lowlands surrounding the harbour, where the streets were narrow and the houses made of wood, bricks, and mortar. The houses lacked not only good natural lighting and ventilation but also piped water and flush toilets. Frequently urban development was the result of plagues, fires, and typhoons rather than of comprehensive city planning. However, the government has made efforts to construct public housing and to reduce the number of squatters and street sleepers in the region.

The limited housing supply was further reduced by the ravages of World War II. In the early postwar years, more than half of all families shared accommodations with others, living in cubicles, bed spaces, and attics and on roofs and verandas and in similar quarters. The colonial government's reluctant involvement in housing provision began with the building of resettlement blocks for fire victims in 1953, but it took real impetus in the early 1960s when the great demand for urban land resulted in the relocation of large numbers of squatters and urban poor. Public housing came to accommodate more than half of the population, most of them living far from the urban core, though by the early 21st century the proportion of the populace in public units was about one-third. Large numbers of people have settled into the new towns, and the design capacity for most of these areas has been increased.

EDUCATION

Most of the schools from kindergarten to secondary are either subsidized or aided by public funds, although there also are a large number of private schools. The number of public schools in Hong Kong is quite small though increasing. Education is compulsory through the junior secondary level. Students finishing primary, junior secondary, and senior secondary education take examinations for allocation of school places at the next higher level.

Postsecondary schools, mostly subsidized, are strained by their small size, although efforts are being made to increase the size and number of institutions. The combined enrollment of the two universities, the University of Hong Kong (1911) and the Chinese University of Hong Kong (1963), has risen dramatically since the mid-1980s. The Hong Kong Polytechnic (1972), with mainly technical and vocational courses, and the Hong Kong Baptist University (1956), a private institution, offer degree courses in selected subjects. Colleges of education train teachers, mainly for primary schools, while responsibility for teacher training for secondary education rests with the two universities. In 1984 the City Polytechnic of Hong Kong (now the City University of Hong Kong) accepted its first students. Numerous other vocational, technical, and industrial-training institutions operate throughout Hong Kong, and thousands of students are also enrolled in extension programs. Nonetheless, thousands also travel overseas each year for study. Nearly all of Hong Kong's people have at least a primary school education.

CULTURAL LIFE

Hong Kong's culture is a true mix of many influences. Though these are primarily of Chinese origin, many Western components are also present.

CULTURAL MILIEU AND THE ARTS

The territory of Hong Kong not only celebrates festivals and holidays of the East but also those of the West, such as the Dragon Boat Festival, the Mid-Autumn Festival, the Lunar (Chinese) New Year, Christmas, the Western New Year, and others. In addition, it also enjoys hundreds of annual cultural events ranging from traditional Cantonese and other Chinese regional operas and puppet shows to performances of ballet, theatre, and music and exhibitions of paintings and sculptures by nationally and internationally renowned performers and artists. The Hong Kong Arts Festival has become one of Asia's major cultural events, and the Hong Kong Philharmonic Orchestra, the

Hong Kong Chinese Orchestra, the Chung Ying Theatre Company, and the City Contemporary Dance Company are among the best-known local artistic groups. The Hong Kong Conservatory of Music and the Hong Kong Academy of Ballet have been combined into the Hong Kong Academy for Performing Arts, offering full-time diploma courses in dance, drama, music, and technical arts.

Scores of motion pictures are produced every year in Hong Kong, many of which attain international fame; some have even started new trends in the art, such as the so-called kung fu films, and some of their stars (notably Jackie Chan) have achieved international celebrity. The Hong Kong International Film Festival, inaugurated in 1977, is a major event, especially for the display of Asian films. Hong Kong is also a regional as well as an international centre in fashion design and in the cutting and design of ornamental diamonds.

RECREATION

Hong Kong's country park system covers some two-fifths of the land area, and outdoor recreation in parks is a part of the way of life for many of the people. City dwellers use park areas on the urban fringe for walking, running, and practicing tai chi chuan, among other activities, while remoter locations are used for kite flying, picnicking, hiking, cycling, and camping. There are well-organized programs of recreation and sports at the community level. The Ocean Park, one of the world's largest oceanariums; the Hong Kong Coliseum, a 12,500-seat indoor stadium that is among the largest in Asia; and the 40,000-seat outdoor Hong Kong Stadium are among the best venues for local and international sports events and for musical, cultural, and entertainment programs. For those who can afford it, the many inlets and bays in Hong Kong provide a superb setting for pleasure sailing, waterskiing, canoeing, and other aquatic sports; the Hong Kong Yacht Club is one of the most active in the South China Sea region.

CULTURAL INSTITUTIONS

Apart from the libraries of the major educational institutions, Hong Kong has a system of several dozen public libraries, including mobile ones, focused on the Hong Kong Central Library (opened 2001). Of the museums, major ones include those specializing in history, art, science and technology, and space. The Hong Kong City Hall (a cultural centre), Hong Kong Cultural Centre, and Hong Kong Arts Centre—each a multifunctional facility with several venues—provide the major gallery, theatrical, and concert facilities. In addition, town halls have been established in the new towns and cultural centres in some districts to serve local communities.

PRESS AND BROADCASTING

A wide-ranging and sophisticated communications network has developed in Hong Kong, reflecting its thriving commerce and international importance. There are several dozen newspapers (in various languages, but mostly Chinese), and the numbers of periodicals run into the hundreds. The territory is in addition the East and Southeast Asian headquarters for most of the major international news services. Broadcast news is provided by several television and radio companies, one of which is government-run. Under the British administration, the press developed largely free from government censorship. Television provides the major source of news and entertainment for the average family, and the Chinese television programs produced are not only for local consumption but also for overseas markets. Both cable and satellite television reception are growing in popularity. Hong Kong also ranks as an important centre of publishing and printing: numerous books are published yearly for local and overseas consumption, several leading foreign publishers have their regional offices in Hong Kong, and many international magazines are printed in the territory.

HISTORY

Archaeological remains of pottery, stone implements, rings, and bronzes found on more than twenty sites in Hong Kong are evidence of settlements in the region during Neolithic times. Thousands of years later, Hong Kong became known as a refuge for mainland Chinese.

Early Settlement

The earliest modern peoples in Hong Kong are thought to have come from North China in the 2nd millennium BCE. The Cantonese began to settle in the area about 100 BCE; later came the Hakka, and by the mid-17th century the Hoklo had arrived. Hong Kong was the scene of the last struggles between the declining Ming dynasty and the rising Qing, led by the Manchu.

Before the British arrived in the mid-19th century, Hong Kong Island was inhabited only by a small fishing population, with few features to recommend it for settlement. It lacked fertile soil and fresh water, was mountainous, and was reputed to be a notorious haunt of pirates. But it was a relatively safe and undisturbed base for the British merchants who in 1821 began to use the fine harbour to anchor opium-carrying vessels. The great commercial and strategic significance of this deep, sheltered harbour, possessing east and west entrances and lying on the main trade routes of the Far East, was quickly realized.

After the first Opium War (1839–42), Hong Kong Island was ceded to Britain by the Treaty of Nanjing. The British were never satisfied with an incomplete control of the harbour, however. Less than 20 years later, after the second Opium War (1856–60), China was forced to cede the Kowloon Peninsula south of what is now Boundary Street and Stonecutters Island by the Convention of Beijing (1860). By the Convention of 1898, the New Territories together with 235 islands were leased to Britain for 99 years from July 1, 1898. With this expansion of territory, Hong Kong's population leaped to 120,000 in 1861 and to more than 300,000 by the end of the century.

Events Before and During World War II

Almost since its establishment, Hong Kong, more than any other treaty port, afforded a refuge for runaway persons and capital from China as well as an interim abode for rural emigrants destined for Southeast Asia and beyond. Such movements of Chinese people between China and Hong Kong were free and were highly responsive to the political and economic conditions in China. After the establishment of the Republic of China in 1912, proponents of emerging nationalism sought to abolish all foreign treaty privileges in China. A boycott against foreign goods particularly hurt Britain, which was well established in China. The campaign soon spread to Hong Kong, where strikes in the 1920s caused agitation.

When the Sino-Japanese War broke out in 1937, Hong Kong was once more a refuge, with thousands of Chinese fleeing to it before the advancing Japanese. With the outbreak of war in Europe in 1939, the position of the colony became more precarious, as it was now a target; the Japanese attacked and occupied Hong

Kong in December 1941. During the war years, Hong Kong's commerce was drastically impaired; food was scarce, and many residents fled to inland China. The population, which had numbered 1,600,000 in 1941, was reduced to about 650,000 by 1945 when the Japanese surrendered.

CONTEMPORARY HONG KONG

British troops returned to the city on August 30, 1945, and civil government was reestablished in May 1946. Meanwhile, hundreds of thousands of Chinese and foreigners returned, and they were soon joined by economic and political refugees from China, who were fleeing the civil war between the Nationalist and communist armies.

The United Nations embargo in 1951 on trade with China and North Korea during the Korean War seriously curtailed the entrepôt trade, the lifeline of the colony, and for several years conditions were depressed. Hong Kong began its revival on the basis of light industries such as textiles, which were set up by immigrant capitalists and provided needed employment. These soon assumed their importance in the economy, providing as well the basis for further industrialization. But it was because much of the development depended on cheap labour, which toiled under extremely poor working conditions, that labour disputes and social discontent began to spread in the early 1960s. Severe riots broke out in Hong Kong and Kowloon in May 1967 following a labour dispute in a plastic-flower factory. The economic and social unrest was immediately turned into violent political demonstrations, largely inspired by followers of the Cultural Revolution (1966–76) in China. When the situation stabilized toward the end of the 1960s, general working and living conditions were notably improved by labour legislation, large government housing projects, and extensive public works programs. Simultaneously, high-technology industries such as electronics were developed, and the property and financial markets prospered until early 1973, when the stock market collapsed as billions of dollars were drained out of Hong Kong. From the mid-1970s the economy resumed its upward trend as relations with China improved.

In the late 1970s, concern about the future of Hong Kong began to loom large, as British jurisdiction over the leased areas of the New Territories neared the 1997 expiration date. Although the lease applied only to the New Territories, the Chinese government had consistently maintained that the whole of Hong Kong was Chinese territory and considered that the question of the earlier Hong Kong–British agreements came under the category of unequal treaties and also required resolution. Initial contacts between the two governments on the matter were made from March 1979, but formal negotiations did not start until after the visit of the British prime minister to Beijing in September 1982. Negotiations continued for 2 years. Finally, the Chinese-British joint declaration on the question of Hong Kong was formally signed by the heads of the two governments in Beijing on December 19, 1984. The agreement stipulated that Hong Kong (including Hong Kong Island, Kowloon, and the New Territories) would be recovered by China from July 1, 1997. There ensued a period of often difficult negotiations between Hong Kong and Beijing on the final wording of the document by which Hong Kong would be governed under Chinese sovereignty. Despite some reservations from Hong Kong, the National People's Congress formally ratified the Basic Law on April 4, 1990, which took effect on July 1, 1997, and established the Hong Kong Special Administrative Region directly under the Chinese central government.

The years after reunification generally were prosperous, as Hong Kong's economy experienced steady growth, despite its heavy dependence on global economic conditions. The already significant economic ties with the mainland increased even more dramatically than before reunification. In addition, major resources were devoted to improving the region's transportation infrastructure, which included new bridges and roadways in addition to the new airport. Politically, there were sustained calls for democratic reforms to the Basic Law that, at times, included large demonstrations and pressure from opposition-party

members in the Legislative Council. Beijing eventually stated its intention to allow the direct election of council members in 2012.

Hong Kong was hit hard by an outbreak of severe acute respiratory syndrome (SARS) in 2003, which killed some 300 people there and 350 more on the mainland and, for a time, significantly reduced tourism in the region. However, the crisis soon passed, and tourism rebounded. Hong Kong was the venue for the equestrian events during the 2008 Olympic Games, and it was chosen to host the 2009 East Asian Games.

MACAU

The special administrative region of Macau (or Macao) is located on China's southern coast, on the southwestern corner of the Pearl River (Zhu Jiang) estuary (at the head of which is the port of Guangzhou [Canton]). It stands opposite the Hong Kong Special Administrative Region, which is some 25 miles (40 km) away on the eastern side of the estuary. Macau comprises a small, narrow peninsula projecting from the mainland province of Guangdong and includes the islands of Taipa and Coloane. Extending up a hillside is the city of Macau, which occupies almost the entire peninsula. The name Macau is derived from the Chinese Ama-gao, or "Bay of Ama," for Ama, the patron goddess of sailors. Macau's area measures 11 square miles (29 square km), while its population in 2008 was an estimated 549,000.

LAND

Macau Peninsula connects to Taipa by bridge, and Taipa and Coloane are linked by a causeway, which traverses Duck Channel, a distributary of the Xi River estuary. Both the peninsula and the islands consist of small granite hills surrounded by limited areas of flatland, which is used for agriculture. The original natural vegetation was evergreen tropical forest before the hills were stripped for firewood and construction. No part of Macau reaches any great elevation; the highest point, 565 feet (172 m), is at Coloane Peak (Coloane Alto) on Coloane. There are no permanent rivers, and water is either collected during rains or piped in from the mainland.

Macau lies just within the tropics, and it has a monsoonal (wet-dry) climate. Four-fifths of its total average annual rainfall of 83 inches (210 cm) falls within the summer rainy season (April–September), when the southwest monsoon blows. Temperatures reach 84 °F (29 °C) in the summer and fall to 59 °F (15 °C) in winter. Besides being rainy, the summer months are also hot and humid. Winters, on the other hand, are somewhat cooler and less humid.

PEOPLE

Nearly all the population, of which a great majority live on the Macau Peninsula, are ethnic Chinese; there are also small groups of other Asians (mainly Filipinos) and people of mixed Chinese and Portuguese ancestry (often called Macanese). However, the once-significant Portuguese minority has been reduced to only a small proportion of the population. Of the ethnic Chinese, the vast majority are Cantonese speakers, and a few speak Hakka. Chinese (Cantonese) and Portuguese are both official languages; English is also commonly spoken. A large number of the people in Macau profess no religious affiliation. Of those practicing a religion, the Chinese are primarily Buddhist, while others adhere to Daoism and Confucianism or combinations of the three; among the small number of Christians the great majority are Roman Catholics. Virtually the entire population is classed as urban, and Macau is one of the most densely populated places in the world.

ECONOMY

The service sector dominates the economy, employing about three-fourths of the total labour force. There are few natural resources, an exception being fish in the Pearl River estuary, which are used for local needs. Agriculture is minimal; small quantities of vegetables are grown, and there is some poultry raising (chickens and eggs). However, Macau is a free port, and trade is vital. The mainland is of major importance as a supplier of food and inexpensive consumer goods, and a 2004 agreement with China that eliminated tariffs on many of Macau's goods has helped increase exports to the mainland. Much of Macau's imports consist of raw materials or semifinished goods for manufacturing purposes. Other imports include machinery and apparatuses, and imported petroleum provides most of the power for domestic electric generation; however, some two-thirds of Macau's power requirements must be imported from Guangdong. Apparel and textile fabrics are the primary exports, and reexports constitute a small but significant proportion of the total value of exports. China is Macau's principal trading partner; trade with the United States and Hong Kong is also significant. In 1991 Macau became a member of the General Agreement on Trade and Tariffs, now the World Trade Organization.

In 1989 the Monetary and Foreign Exchange Authority of Macau replaced the Instituto Emissor de Macau as regulator of the currency, the Macau pataca, which is pegged to the Hong Kong dollar. Commercial and foreign banks, as well as banks of issue and a banking association, constitute Macau's banking and financial system. Since the mid-1990s the government has made efforts to attract foreign investors and thus diversify the economy away from its heavy reliance on tourism.

Nonetheless, tourism and gambling are the most important components of Macau's overall economy, and the region in effect serves as the playground of nearby Hong Kong and, increasingly, the Chinese mainland. High-speed hydrofoils, as well as some traditional but slower river ferries, carry tourists from Hong Kong and Shenzhen (just north of

Hong Kong) to Macau's numerous gambling casinos, bars, hotels, and other attractions. Internal transportation is good, and there are local ferries between the peninsula and the islands. Following the December 1999 transfer of administrative status from Portugal to China, Macau remained a free and open port. An international airport became operational in Macau in 1995.

GOVERNMENT AND SOCIETY

Before it became a special administrative region of China in 1999, Macau followed the colonial constitution promulgated in 1976; it was administered by a governor, who in agreement with the Legislative Assembly was appointed by the Portuguese president. With the transfer of sovereignty over the territory to China, the Basic Law of the Macau Special Administrative Region, which outlined a policy of "one country, two systems," went into effect. For a period of 50 years, Macau will thus retain its capitalist economy and some political autonomy, but foreign policy and defense matters will remain under Chinese administration.

According to the Basic Law, the chief executive, who serves a five-year term, holds executive authority but is under the jurisdiction of the central government in Beijing. An election committee of 300 members, who serve 5-year terms, selects the chief executive, who can serve up to two consecutive 5-year terms. The chief executive appoints an executive council, which consists of seven to eleven members, to assist in policy making. The legislature is a single-chamber Legislative Assembly, headed by an elected president and vice president; the assembly has twenty-nine members, who serve 4-year terms and are selected by a combination of direct popular election (twelve), indirect election by a committee of special-interest groups (ten), and appointment by the chief executive (seven).

Law is based on the Portuguese system. The judicial system was completely administered from Portugal until 1993, when a high court of justice was established in Macau. A new penal code was authorized in 1996 in response to a rise in crime. The Basic Law states that the judicial system remains intact with the transfer of sovereignty and that all judges are appointed by the chief executive. The highest court is the Court of Final Appeal, headed by a chief justice. There are also lower primary courts, intermediate courts, and administrative courts. Macau has a small security force, but defense is the responsibility of the central government in Beijing.

Primary and secondary education in Macau is overwhelmingly at private schools, although the great majority of these schools receive government subsidies. Five years of primary education are officially compulsory, and education is free for children from ages 6 to 15. Most receive instruction in Chinese (Cantonese), while the remainder are taught in either English or Portuguese. The University of Macau, formerly the University of East Asia, opened in the early 1990s. Literacy

is now nearly universal in Macau; although a larger proportion of males than females is literate, the gap between them is narrowing.

There are medical centres and hospitals in Macau, and traditional Chinese medicine is also practiced. The elderly receive medications free of charge. The average life expectancy is about 80 years, and the birth and infant mortality rates are both low. The government has constructed low-income housing units, and the private sector has introduced social housing with controlled prices.

CULTURAL LIFE

Chinese culture predominates, overlaid by a veneer of Portuguese architecture (notably churches and cathedrals) and customs. Chinese temples and shrines coexist with restored villas from the colonial period. Barrier Gate, which links Macau Peninsula to the mainland, is a popular spot for tourists, as are such early 17th-century structures as Monte Fort and the nearby ruined facade of St. Paul's Cathedral (destroyed 1835). The historic buildings on the peninsula collectively were designated a UNESCO World Heritage site in 2005.

As is the case in Hong Kong, Cantonese pop ("canto-pop") is a popular form of music. Spectator sports include both dog and horse racing. The Macau Grand Prix attracts numerous international competitors and fans of motor racing. Macau's major sports complexes include the Macau Olympic Complex

Facade of the ruined St. Paul's Cathedral, Macau. Brand X/Jupiterimages

and the Macau East Asian Games Dome; the latter was built for the 2005 East Asian Games, hosted by Macau. Football (soccer), track and field, volleyball, and roller hockey are popular team and individual sports. In the 1990s Macau hosted several roller hockey world championships.

The former Luís de Camões Museum, named for the Portuguese poet and writer of the epic *Os Lusíadas*, was in a 17th-century house that once was used by the British East India Company; its collections are now part of the Macau Museum of Art (opened 1999) and feature Chinese pottery, paintings, and artifacts. Adjacent to the art museum is the Macau Cultural Centre (opened 1999), with several performance and exhibition venues. Also of note is the Museum of Macau (opened 1998) in the Monte Fort compound, which has exhibits on the history of the region.

Local radio stations in Macau (one state-run) and a state-run television station broadcast programs in Chinese (Cantonese) and Portuguese. In addition, cable and satellite television broadcasting is available, and television and radio broadcasts also come from Hong Kong. Several daily newspapers are circulated; most are published in Chinese, but a handful are in Portuguese and English. Internet use is widespread, and mobile-telephone usage is ubiquitous.

HISTORY

The first Portuguese ship anchored in the Pearl River estuary in 1513, and further Portuguese visits followed regularly. Trade with China commenced in 1553. Four years later Portuguese paying tribute to China settled in Macau, which became the official and principal entrepôt for all international trade with China and Japan and an intermediary port for ships traveling from Lisbon to Nagasaki (at the time, Japan's only outport for trade); China, nonetheless, still refused to recognize Portuguese sovereignty over the territory. The first governor was appointed in the 17th century, but the Portuguese remained largely under the control of the Chinese. Missionaries carried over on Portuguese ships transformed Macau into an East Asian centre of Christianity. Even though China's trade with the outside world was gradually centralized in Guangzhou (Canton) toward the end of the 18th century, merchants were allowed into Guangzhou only during the trading season—from November to May—and the international merchant community established itself at Macau. By the mid-19th century, the British colony of Hong

Kong had surpassed Macau in trade, and within a few years the merchants had largely deserted the Portuguese possession, which never again was a major entrepôt.

In the 1930s and '40s, Macau—declared a neutral territory during the Sino-Japanese War and World War II—became a refuge for both Chinese and Europeans. The Chinese population in the territory continued to grow when the communist government assumed power in China in 1949. In 1951 Portugal officially made Macau an overseas province. Following a military coup in Portugal in 1974, the government allotted more administrative autonomy and economic independence to the territory. The constitution promulgated in 1976 established the Legislative Assembly, which was dominated by the minority Portuguese. Until diplomatic relations were solidified between Portugal and the communist government in China in 1979, discussions on transferring Macau to Chinese control were fruitless.

In March 1984 the Portuguese governor dissolved the assembly in response to opposition within the government to extend the right to vote to the Chinese majority. A few months later, new elections, which included Chinese suffrage, finally brought a significant number of Chinese deputies into the government. In April 1987 Portugal and China reached an agreement to return Macau to Chinese rule in 1999, using the Hong Kong Joint Declaration between Britain and China as a model. They agreed to provisions under the Basic Law that would ensure the autonomy of Macau for 50 years after the start of Chinese rule. These included Macau's right to elect local leaders, the right of its residents to travel freely, and the right to maintain its way of life, both economically and socially. Defense and foreign policy matters were to be administered by China, and those living in Macau without Portuguese passports would become Chinese citizens. Elections continued to turn out record numbers of voters and a Chinese majority legislature. On December 20, 1999, Macau became a special administrative region under Chinese sovereignty, as Hong Kong had in 1997.

The period since reunification has been peaceful and marked by increasing prosperity. Much of the region's economic growth has come from the tremendous expansion in gambling and gaming since 2000, which transformed Macau into one of the world's largest gambling centres (in terms of revenue). Tourism also has risen sharply from levels in the 1990s. Major infrastructure projects have included continued land reclamation throughout the region and a third bridge (opened 2005) between Macau Peninsula and Taipa Island. The political situation has been stable, with orderly legislative elections. Ho Hau Wah (Edmund Ho) was named Macau's first chief executive at reunification in 1999; he was reelected to a second term in 2004.

CHAPTER 11

SELECTED AUTONOMOUS REGIONS

China has established five province-level autonomous regions (*zizhiqu*) within the country, each of which encompasses an area in which a minority people constitute at least a significant proportion of the population. This chapter highlights two of those regions—Tibet and Xinjiang—which are both the largest and most remote political subdivisions in the country.

TIBET

Tibet (Tibetan: Bod; Chinese: Xizang) is a historic region and an autonomous region of China that is often called "the roof of the world." It occupies a vast area of plateaus and mountains in Central Asia, including Mount Everest (Qomolangma [or Zhumulangma] Feng; Tibetan: Chomolungma). Lhasa, in the southern part of the region, is the capital city. The name Tibet is derived from the Mongolian Thubet, the Chinese Tufan, the Tai Thibet, and the Arabic Tubbat.

Before the 1950s Tibet was largely isolated from the rest of the world. It constituted a unique cultural and religious community, marked by the Tibetan language and Tibetan Buddhism. Little effort was made to facilitate communication with outsiders, and economic development was minimal.

Tibet's incorporation into the People's Republic of China began in 1950 and has remained a highly charged and controversial issue, both within Tibet and worldwide. Many Tibetans (especially those outside China) consider China's action to be an invasion of a sovereign country, and the continued Chinese presence in Tibet is deemed an occupation by a foreign power. The Chinese, on the other hand, believe that Tibet has been a rightful part of China for centuries and that they liberated Tibet from a repressive regime in which much of the population lived in serfdom. There is truth in both assertions, although public opinion outside China (especially in the West) has tended to take the side of Tibet as an independent (or at least highly autonomous) entity. There is no question, though, that the fourteenth Dalai Lama, Tibet's exiled spiritual and temporal leader, has become one of the world's most recognizable and highly regarded individuals.

Tibet's area is estimated at about 471,700 square miles (1,221,600 square km). Its population according to a 2007 estimate was 2,810,000.

LAND

Tibet is bordered by the Chinese provinces of Qinghai to the northeast, Sichuan to the east, and Yunnan to the southeast; by Myanmar (Burma), India, Bhutan, and Nepal to the south; by the disputed Kashmir region to the west; and by the Uygur Autonomous Region of Xinjiang to the northwest.

RELIEF

Tibet is on a high plateau—the Plateau of Tibet—surrounded by enormous mountain masses. The relatively level northern part of the plateau is called the Qiangtang; it extends more than 800 miles (1,300 km) from west to east at an average elevation of 16,500 feet (5,000 m) above sea level. The Qiangtang is dotted with brackish lakes, the largest being Lakes Siling (Seling) and Nam (Namu). There are, however, no river systems there. In the east the Qiangtang begins to descend in elevation. The mountain ranges in southeastern Tibet cut across the land from north to south, creating meridional barriers to travel and communication. In central and western Tibet, the ranges run from northwest to southeast, with deep or shallow valleys forming innumerable furrows.

The Qiangtang is bordered on the north by the Kunlun Mountains, with the highest peak, Mount Muztag (Muztagh; on the Tibet-Xinjiang border), reaching 25,338 feet (7,723 m). The western and southern border of the Plateau of Tibet is formed by the great mass of the Himalayas; the highest peak is Mount Everest, which rises to 29,035 feet (8,850 m) on the Tibet-Nepal border. North of Lake Mapam (conventional: Manasarowar) and stretching eastward is the Kailas (Gangdisi) Range, with clusters of peaks, several exceeding 20,000 feet (6,100 m). This range is separated from the Himalayas by the upper course of the Brahmaputra River (in Tibet called the Yarlung Zangbo or the Tsangpo), which flows across southern Tibet and cuts south through the mountains to India and Bangladesh.

DRAINAGE AND SOILS

The Plateau of Tibet is the principal source of the rivers of East, Southeast, and South Asia. The Indus River, known in Tibet as the Sêngê Zangbo ("Lion Spring"; Chinese: Shiquan He), has its source in western Tibet near Mount Kailas, a mountain sacred to Buddhists and Hindus; it then flows westward across the Kashmir region to Pakistan. Three other rivers also begin in the west: the Xiangquan River (Tibetan: Langqên Kanbab, "Elephant Spring") flows west to become the Sutlej River in northwestern India and eastern Pakistan; the Mabja Zangbo River flows into the Ghaghara (Nepali: Kauriala) River to eventually join the Ganges (Ganga) River; and the Maquan River (Tibetan: Damqog Kanbab, "Horse Spring") flows east and, after joining the Lhasa River south of Lhasa, forms the Brahmaputra.

The Salween (Nu) River has its source in east-central Tibet, from where it flows through eastern Tibet and Yunnan and then enters Myanmar. The Mekong River begins in southern Qinghai as two rivers—the Ang and Zha—which join near the Tibet border; the river then flows through eastern Tibet and western Yunnan and enters Laos and Thailand. The source of the Yangtze River (Chang Jiang) rises in southern Qinghai, near the Tibet border; after flowing through southern Qinghai, the Yangtze turns south to form most of the Tibet-Sichuan border.

Tibet's three largest lakes are centrally located, northwest of Lhasa: Lakes Dangre Yong (Tibetan: Tangra Yum), Nam, and Siling. South of Lhasa lie two other large lakes, Yamzho Yun (Yangzho Yong) and Puma Yung (Pumo). In western Tibet two adjoining lakes are located near the Nepal border—Lake Mapam, sacred to both Buddhists and Hindus, and Lake La'nga.

Soils are alluvial and are often composed of sand that is blown by the wind to form a layer above gravels and shingles. Colour varies from light brown to gray, according to the humus content, which is generally poor.

CLIMATE

Although Tibetans refer to their land as Gangs-ljongs or Kha-ba-can ("Land of Snows"), the climate is generally dry. Most of Tibet receives only 18 inches (46 cm) of precipitation (both rain and snow) annually, with much of that falling during the summer months. The Himalayas act as a barrier to the monsoon (rain-bearing) winds from the south, and precipitation decreases from south to north. The perpetual snow line lies at some 16,000 feet (4,800 m) in the Himalayas but rises to about 20,000 feet (6,100 m) in the northern mountains. Humidity is low, and fog is practically nonexistent.

Temperatures in the higher elevations are cold, but the lower valleys and the southeast are mild and pleasant. Seasonal variation is minimal, and the greatest temperature differences occur diurnally (i.e., during a 24-hour period). Lhasa, which lies at an elevation of 11,975 feet (3,650 m), has a daily maximum temperature of 85 °F (30 °C) and a minimum of -2 °F (-19 °C). The bitterly cold temperatures of the early morning and night are aggravated by the gale winds that blow throughout the area most of the year. Because of the cool dry air, grain can be safely stored for 50 to 60 years, dried raw meat and butter can be preserved for more than one year, and epidemics are rare.

PLANT AND ANIMAL LIFE

The windswept Qiangtang is devoid of trees and larger forms of vegetation. Its arid climate supports little except grasses, and grasslands cover some two-thirds of Tibet's total area. The varied plant life of Tibet—in excess of 6,400 species, of which more than 1,000 are of economic value—is found mainly in the river valleys and in the lower, wetter regions of the south and southeast. Common plants include willows, poplars, several types of conifers, teak, rhododendrons, oaks, birches, elms, bamboo, sugarcane, babul

trees, thorn trees, tea bushes, *gro-ba* (small white trees that grow mainly in hilly regions), *'om-bu* (bushlike trees with red flowers that grow near water), *khres-pa* (strong durable forest trees used to make food containers), *glang-ma* (a willow tree used for basketry), and *rtsi-shings* (the seeds of which are used for making varnish). Fruit-bearing trees and certain roots are used for food, as are the leaves of the *lca-wa*, *khumag*, and *sre-ral*, all of which grow in the low, wet regions. Both wild and domestic flowers flourish in Tibet. Among the wildflowers are blue poppies, lotuses, wild pansies, oleanders, orchids, *tsi-tog* (light pink flowers that grow at high elevations), *shang-dril*s (bell-shaped flowers, either white, yellow, or maroon, that also grow at high elevations), and *ogchu* (red flowers that grow in sandy regions).

Tibet has more than 100 species of mammals, forty species of reptiles, and fifty species of amphibians. Mammal life in the forest regions includes tigers, leopards, bears, wild boars, wild goats, stone martens (a kind of cat), langurs (long-tailed monkeys), lynx, jackals, wild buffaloes, *pha-ra* (small members of the jackal family), and *gsa's* (spotted cats that are smaller than leopards). In the high grasslands and dry bush areas, there are brown bears, wild and bighorn sheep, mountain antelope, musk deer, wild asses, wild yaks, snakes, scorpions, lizards, and *dre-tse* (members of the wolf family). Aquatic life includes various types of fishes, frogs, crabs, otters, and turtles.

Undisturbed by aircraft or hunters, Tibet's some 400 species of birds reign supreme in the sky. Among the many kinds to be seen are black-necked cranes (*Grus nigricollus*), Himalayan monal (or Impeyan) pheasants (*Lophophorus impejanus*), jungle fowl, ptarmigans, spotted tinamous, mynahs, hawks, and hoopoes. Others include gulls, sheldrakes, cinnamon teals, *sing-bya* (tiny owl-like birds), *khra* (crow-sized, hawklike birds), *byalong* (birds about the size of a duck), and *skya-ka* (black-and-white crow-sized birds). The calls of the *rmos-'debs*—a small gray bird that inhabits agricultural regions—signal the opening of the planting season.

PEOPLE

Vast stretches of Tibet are virtually devoid of people, and the region has the smallest population and the lowest population density of any Chinese political subdivision.

POPULATION COMPOSITION

The population found in Tibet is almost entirely Tibetan, with Han (Chinese), Hui (Chinese Muslims), Monba, Lhoba, and other minority nationalities. Thus, the majority of the people of Tibet have the same ethnic origin, have traditionally practiced the same religion, and speak the same language.

The Tibetan and Burmese languages are related, although they are mutually unintelligible in their modern forms.

Spoken Tibetan has developed a pattern of regional dialects and subdialects, which can be mutually understood. The dialect of Lhasa is used as a lingua franca. There are two social levels of speech—*zhe-sa* (honorific) and *phal-skad* (ordinary); their use depends upon the relative social status of the speaker and the listener. The use of Chinese has become more common in the region since the 1960s.

Tibetan is written in a script derived from that of Indian Gupta about 600 CE. It has a syllabary of thirty consonants and five vowels; six additional symbols are used in writing Sanskrit words. The script itself has four variations—*dbu-can* (primarily for Buddhist textbooks), *dbu-med* and *'Khyug-yig* (for general use), and *'bru-tsha* (for decorative writing).

Bon is considered to be the first known religion in Tibet, although there is some argument as to the time of its establishment. It is a form of shamanism, encompassing a belief in gods, demons, and ancestral spirits who are responsive to priests, or shamans. With the rise of Buddhism, Bon adopted certain Buddhist rituals and concepts, and the Buddhists also adopted certain features of Bon, so that the two religions came to have many points of resemblance.

Although Chinese Buddhism was introduced in ancient times, the mainstream of Buddhist teachings came to Tibet from India. The first Buddhist scripture may have arrived in the 3rd century CE, but active promulgation did not begin until the 8th century. In later centuries numerous Buddhist sects were formed, including the Dge-lugs-pa, which emphasizes monastic discipline; also known as the Yellow Hat sect, in the 17th century it gained political supremacy that lasted until 1959.

The overwhelming majority of Tibetans traditionally have been Buddhists. Before the 1950s, prayer flags flew from every home and adorned the mountain slopes. Monasteries were established throughout the country, and the Dalai Lama, the spiritual head of Tibetan Buddhism, was the supreme political head of the nation. A minority, however, were adherents of Islam, Hinduism, Bon, or Christianity. The Dalai Lama went into exile in 1959 after the outbreak in Tibet of an armed rebellion against Chinese authorities that was suppressed by the Chinese army. Since then the Chinese at times have attempted to eliminate the influence of religion in Tibetan life.

SETTLEMENT PATTERNS

Tibet was traditionally divided into three regions, called the Chol-kha-gsum (*chol-kha,* "region," and *gsum,* "three"). The Dbus-Gtsang region stretches from Mnga'-ris skor-gsum at the border of the Kashmir region to Sog-la skya-bo near the town of Sog. The Khams, or Mdo-stod, region consists of the territory between Sog-la skya-bo and the upper bend of the Huang He (Yellow River), now located in Qinghai province. The A-mdo, or

Mdo-smad, region reaches from the Huang He to Mchod-rten dkar-po in Gansu province, comprising most of present-day Qinghai. Traditionally, Tibetans have said that the best religion comes from Dbus-Gtsang, the best men from Khams, and the best horses from A-mdo. Within the Chol-kha-gsum approximately one-third of the area is uninhabitable, about one-fifth is roamed by nomads, and the rest is occupied by seminomads and agriculturalists, with a small percentage claimed by trappers in the forest belt.

The main agricultural region is the great valley of southern Tibet, stretching some 1,000 miles (1,600 km) from the upper Indus River valley in the west to the valley of the upper Brahmaputra. Most of the agriculture, animal husbandry, and industry of Tibet is concentrated in this valley, which includes the main cities of Lhasa, Xigazê (Shigatse, or Rikaze), and Gyangzê (Jiangzi).

ECONOMY

Tibet's economy has largely remained underdeveloped. In fact, there were no banks before 1951. Small loans to be paid with interest could be obtained from local merchants, and the Tibetan government loaned public funds at interest as a means of collecting revenue. Since then—and especially since the 1980s—banks have established branches in the region and have also extended agricultural and commercial credit and introduced Chinese and foreign currency-exchange services.

Little of the region's territory is suitable for agriculture, and large areas have remained remote and inaccessible, making it difficult to exploit its rich mineral resources or to develop industry there.

RESOURCES AND POWER

Surveys of the Kailas and Mapam districts in western Tibet conducted in the 1930s and '40s discovered extensive goldfields and large deposits of borax, as well as reserves of radium, iron, titanium, lead, and arsenic. Subsequent investigative teams dispatched from the 1950s onward reported the existence of a huge variety of minerals and ores. The most significant of these include large copper deposits around Qulong, east of Lhasa, and Yulong, some 85 miles (140 km) east of Changdu, near the border with Sichuan province; graphite obtained from Ningjin and coal reported to be plentiful around Changdu; deposits of iron ore in concentrated seams of high quality and extractable depth found in the Tanggula Mountains on the Tibet-Qinghai border; and oil-bearing formations, a reserve of oil shales, and chromite (chromium ore), lithium, lead, zinc, and manganese deposits.

Considerable effort has been directed toward improving Tibet's power-generating capacity, which was virtually nonexistent before 1950. Several thermal generating plants have been built, including those at Lhasa and Xigazê. Tibet's swift-flowing rivers and mountain streams have enormous hydroelectric power potential, constituting a significant proportion of China's overall estimated hydroelectric resources. Much effort has been focused on developing promising sites, especially on the Brahmaputra, Mekong, Lhasa, and Nyang Qu rivers. The first such project—actually the repair of an earlier small hydroelectric power station at Lhasa—was undertaken in the 1950s. Since then a number of small and medium-size hydropower plants have been developed, including the Jinhe station near Changdu, on the upper course of the Mekong, and the Zhikong station on the Lhasa River, about 60 miles (100 km) northeast of Lhasa.

In addition to thermal and hydroelectric power, there are vast opportunities for geothermal, solar, and wind power production. A major geothermal power plant, one of the largest in China, has been constructed at Yangbajing, some 55 miles (90 km) northwest of Lhasa, and small stations utilizing both wind and solar energy also have been developed for local towns and villages.

AGRICULTURE AND FORESTRY

The staple crops are barley (notably a variety developed for high-elevation cultivation), wheat, corn (maize), and pulses (legumes); other important crops include millet, buckwheat, *rgya-bra* (a grain similar to buckwheat), beans, hemp, and mustard. Butter from the yak (a large long-haired ox) or the *mdzo-mo* (a crossbreed of the yak and the cow) is the main dairy product. The diet is supplemented by a variety of garden vegetables. Some rice is raised in the southeast, but most must be imported, along with tea and sugar. The cultivation of fruits, vegetables, and flowers in greenhouse facilities has become important. Most farmers keep domestic animals such as yaks, horses, mules, donkeys, and goats, and meat is obtained from cows, sheep, pigs, and chickens.

The mountain areas along the middle and lower reaches of the upper Brahmaputra River are the main forest areas in southwestern China. However, because of the inaccessibility of those areas, forestry has developed slowly. The forest dwellers derive their main income from the production of such wood products as planks, beams, printing blocks, and kitchen utensils.

MANUFACTURING

Before the 1950s Tibet had no modern industries. There were small handicraft centres that were owned either individually or collectively and that produced scroll paintings, metal images, wooden block prints, and religious images. For these crafts the *lag-shes-pa*, or craftsmen, had to be well versed in literature and mathematics. There were also carpet weavers, tanners, potters, gold- and silversmiths, carpenters, tailors, and incense-stick makers—all of whom learned their trade through apprenticeship. Because the government rewarded outstanding artists and craftsmen with official titles, estates, and money, the arts and crafts of Tibet were well preserved.

The initial steps toward industrial development came in 1952, when an iron- and woodwork factory was opened in Lhasa. This was followed by an automobile repair shop in 1957 and a tannery in 1958. Modern industries began emerging in the early 1980s. At first, emphasis was placed on agricultural processing enterprises. This was followed by such sectors as metallurgy, machinery, textiles, chemicals, building materials, forest products, and light industries. Pharmaceutical production based on Tibetan medicinal plants also became important, and production of traditional handicrafts (notably of woolen fabrics, boots, blankets, and wooden bowls—all well-known products in China) was expanded.

TOURISM

Tibet is one of the world's best-known tourist destinations, renowned as a mecca for mountaineering and adventurism, cultural and scientific exploration, and religious pilgrimage. Considerable effort has been made to expand tourist services in Lhasa and other localities, and tourism has become a pillar of the Tibetan economy. Most notable is the historic Potala Palace complex in Lhasa, designated a UNESCO World Heritage site in 1994.

Also popular with tourists are the Tsuglagkhang, or Gtsug-lag-khang (Jokhang), Temple and the Norbuglingka (Nor-bu-gling-ka; Jewel Palace), both at Lhasa; the Tashihlungbo Monastery in Xigazê; and the Palcho (Baiju) Monastery in Gyangzê.

Tibet is the staging area for mountaineering in the northern Himalayas, particularly for expeditions to the North Face of Mount Everest. Another popular scenic area is the "Grand Canyon" of the Yarlung Zangbo (Brahmaputra) River in southeastern Tibet, a gorge nearly 300 miles (500 km) long; in its deepest stretch, south of Namjagbarwa (Namcha Barwa) Peak, the gorge has an average depth of some 16,500 feet (5,000 m).

TRANSPORTATION

Before 1951, traveling in Tibet was done either on foot or on the backs of animals. Coracles (small boats made of wicker and hides) were used to cross the larger rivers. The Tibetan government obstructed the development of modern transportation to make access to the country difficult for outsiders. For trading, the Tibetans relied on the centuries-old caravan routes leading to Lhasa, of which the most important were from Qinghai (via Nagqu, or Naqu) and Sichuan (via Changdu), India (via Kalimpong, West Bengal state, and Yadong in Tibet), Nepal (via Skyid-grong and Nyalam), and the Kashmir region (via Leh and Gar).

Since the early 1950s, a network of roads has been constructed, notably highways to Qinghai and Sichuan. Additional trunk roads that connect Tibet to Xinjiang, Yunnan, and Nepal have been built. A main railway line from Xining (capital of Qinghai) to Lhasa opened in 2006.

The first air link between Tibet and Beijing was inaugurated in 1956. Airports in Lhasa, Changdu, and Linzi now provide commercial air service to travelers. The first telegraph line was strung between Kalimpong (India) and Gyangzê by the British in 1904, and the line was extended to Lhasa in the 1920s; this was the only telegraph system in use in Tibet until the Chinese took over in 1951. Postal and telecommunication stations, including mobile units, serve remote border areas and geological, hydrological, and construction teams. Radio and television stations have also been constructed.

GOVERNMENT AND SOCIETY

Prior to 1951, Tibet had a theocratic government of which the Dalai Lama was the supreme religious and temporal head. After that the newly installed Chinese administrators relied on military control and a gradual establishment of civilian regional autonomy.

CONSTITUTIONAL FRAMEWORK

Tibet was formally designated an autonomous region in 1965, as part of the separation of religion and civil administration. It is now divided into the *dijishi* (prefecture-level municipality) of Lhasa, directly under the jurisdiction of the regional government, and six *diqu* (prefectures), which are subdivided into *shixiaqu* (districts), *xian* (counties), and *xianjishi* (county-level municipalities).

The army consists of regular Chinese troops under a Chinese military commander, who is stationed at Lhasa. There are military cantonments in major towns along the borders with India, Nepal, and Bhutan. Local people have also been recruited into some militia regiments.

HEALTH AND WELFARE

The former Tibetan government is said to have had programs for providing medical assistance to expectant mothers and for care of the kinless aged and handicapped persons—in addition to projects for constructing and maintaining proper drainage systems, wells, and canals to improve sanitation. The Chinese refute these assertions and point to their own efforts to improve the health and welfare of the populace. It is true that since the 1950s modern hospitals have been built, drainage systems have been improved, and mobile health units have been placed at key locations. In addition, the average life expectancy in Tibet has improved dramatically since 1950.

EDUCATION

There were a few secular schools in Tibet before the Chinese established control. The monasteries were the main seats of learning, and some of the larger ones were similar in operation to theological universities. Secular facilities, including government-run primary schools, community primary schools, and secondary technical and tertiary schools, were established in the 1950s. Institutions of higher learning include Tibet University (1951) and Tibetan Traditional Medical College (1989).

CULTURAL LIFE

Tibet's rich and ancient culture is largely based on religion, and many Tibetan cultural elements have become well-known throughout the world.

THE ARTS

Tibet is most renowned for its religious scroll paintings (*thang-ka*), metal images, and wooden block prints. There are three categories of images, representing the peaceful, moderate, and angry deities, and three schools of painting, the Sman-thang, Gong-dkar Mkhan-bris, and Kar-ma sgar-bris, which are differentiated by colour tones and depicted facial expressions.

The *gar* and the *'cham* (Chinese: *qamo*) are stylistic dances performed by monks; they reenact the behaviour, attitudes, and gestures of the deities. Ancient legendary tales, historical events, classical solo songs, and musical debates are elaborately staged in the open air in the form of operas, operettas, and dramas. The folk songs and dances of local regions abound with colour, joy, and simplicity: the *bro* of the Khams region, the *sgor-gzhas* of the *dbus-gtsang* peasants, and the *kadra* of the A-mdo area are spectacles that are performed in groups; on festive occasions they continue for several days. These cheerful performances tell of the people's loves and celebrate their faith in their religion, the beauty of their land, and the brave deeds of their ancestors.

CUSTOMS

Traditional marriage ceremonies involved consultations with both a lama and an astrologer in order to predict the compatibility of a couple. The signing of a marriage contract was followed by an official ceremony at the home of the bridegroom. Appearance in a temple or before a civil authority was not required.

It is now more common for couples to meet at public gatherings and to then seek permission from their respective families to marry. After a couple is officially wedded (typically at the bridegroom's house), prayer flags are hoisted from the bride's side of the family upon the rooftop of the house, and all participate in the wedding feast. Although polygamy was once practiced on a limited scale, monogamy is now predominant.

When a death occurs, the family members make charitable contributions in the hope of ensuring a better reincarnation for the deceased. In the case of the death of an important religious figure, his corpse is preserved in a tomb or stupa (Buddhist commemorative monument).

Otherwise, tradition calls for the corpse to be fed to the vultures, a practice named sky burial or celestial burial. Water burial (i.e., sending the body downstream in a river) is also practiced in some areas. The customs of interment and cremation exist but are seldom practiced. Traditional Tibetan funerary practices are described in the *Bardo Thödol* (Tibetan "Book of the Dead").

A white scarf (*kha-btags*, or *hada*) is offered during greetings, visits to shrines, marriage and death ceremonies, and other occasions. The tradition was derived from the ancient custom of offering clothes to adorn the statues of deities. Gradually, it evolved into a form of greeting, and the white scarf offering, symbolizing purity, became customary. Another tradition is the hoisting of prayer flags on rooftops, tents, hilltops, and almost anywhere a Tibetan can be found. These flags signify fortune and good luck. The use of prayer wheels (Tibetan *mani chos 'khor*), which are spun during prayers in lieu of orally reciting mantras, is also common among the Tibetans. The wheels are of different sizes and types, though small handheld ones are the most common.

FOOD AND DRINK

The staple Tibetan food is flour dough (*rtsam-pa*, or *zanba*) made of roasted barley, which is consumed daily. Other major dishes include baked goods made from wheat flour, yak meat, mutton, and pork. Dairy products such as butter, milk, and cheese are also popular. The people at higher elevations generally consume more meat than those of the lower regions, where a variety of vegetables are available. Rice is generally restricted in consumption to the well-to-do families, southern border farmers, and monks.

Two beverages—tea and barley beer (*chang*, or *chhaang*)—are particularly noteworthy. Brick tea from elsewhere in China and local Tibetan tea leaves are boiled in soda water. The tea is then strained and poured into a churn, and salt and butter are added before the mixture is churned. The resulting tea is light reddish white and has a thick buttery surface. *Chang*, which is mildly intoxicating, is thick and white and has a sweet and pungent taste.

FESTIVALS

Festivals are both national and local in character. The many local celebrations are varied; national festivals, though fewer, are marked with a spirit of unity and lavishness.

The first day of the first month of the Tibetan calendar (February or March of the Gregorian calendar) is marked by New Year (Losar) celebrations throughout Tibet. Monasteries, temples, stupas (outdoor shrines), and home chapels are visited at dawn, and offerings are made before statues and relics of deities and saints. A special fried cookie known as *kha-zas* is prepared in every home. Either a real or an artificial head of a horned sheep

adorns the offerings. A colourful container filled with barley flour and wheat grain and another container of *chang* are presented to all visitors, who take a pinch of the contents and make an offering to the deities by throwing it in the air.

The New Year celebrations are almost immediately followed by the Smom-lam ("Prayer") festival, which begins 3 days after the New Year and generally is celebrated for 15 days, though the length of the festival varies from place to place. The festival marks the victory of the Buddha over his six religious opponents through debates and the performance of miracles. During this festival, special prayers are offered daily. Prayers, fasting, and charitable donations mark Sa-ga zla-ba (or Saga dawa), the celebration of the anniversary of Buddha's birth, enlightenment, and death—three events that all occurred on the fifteenth day of the fourth month of the Tibetan calendar.

The anniversary of the death of Tsong-kha-pa, founder of the Dge-lugs-pa sect, is observed on the twenty-fifth day of the tenth month by the burning of butter lamps on the roofs and windowsills of every house. This festival is known as Lnga-mchod. The Dgu-gtor festival, or festival of the banishment of evil spirits, takes place on the twenty-ninth day of the last month of the Tibetan year. At night a bowl of flour soup and a bunch of burning straws are taken into every room of every house, and the evil spirits are called out. Outside, on a distant path, the soup and straws are thrown and left to burn.

SUPERSTITIONS

Superstition is prominent in Tibet. A traveler who encounters either a funeral procession, the source of running water, or a passerby carrying a pitcher of water is considered to have good fortune awaiting. If a vulture or an owl perches on a rooftop, it is believed that death or misfortune will soon befall the household. If snow falls during a marriage procession, it is believed that the newlyweds will face many misfortunes or difficulties. A snowfall during a funeral, however, symbolizes an impediment to death in the family for a long period of time.

HISTORY

Ruins in eastern Tibet near Qamdo indicate that humans inhabited the region some 4,000 to 5,000 years ago. According to Tibetan legend, the Tibetan people originated from the union of a monkey and a female demon. The Chinese Tang dynasty annals (10th century CE) place the Tibetans' origin among the nomadic pastoral Qiang tribes recorded about 200 BCE as inhabiting the great steppe northwest of China. That region, where diverse ethnic elements met and mingled for centuries, may be accepted as the original homeland of the present-day Tibetans, but until at least the 7th century CE they continued to mix, by conquest or alliance, with other peoples. From that heritage two groups in particular stand out: those who predominate in the cultivated valleys and may have derived from the Huang He (Yellow River) basin and be akin to the early Chinese and Burmese; and those, found mainly among the nomads of the north and in the noble families of Lhasa, who seem to have affinities with the Turkic peoples and whose early wandering grounds were farther to the north. In addition, there are Dardic and Indian influences in the west, and along the eastern Himalayan border there are connections with a complex of tribal peoples known to the Tibetans as Mon.

From the 7th to the 9th century, the Tibetan kingdom was a significant power in Central Asia. When that kingdom disintegrated, Tibetans figured there from the 10th to the 13th century only casually as traders and raiders. The patronage of Tibetan Buddhism by the Yuan (Mongol) dynasty of China made it a potential spiritual focus for the disunited tribes of Mongolia. This religious significance became of practical importance only in the 18th century when the Oyrat, who professed Tibetan Buddhism, threatened the authority of the Qing dynasty throughout Mongolia. In the 19th century, Tibet was a buffer between Russian imperial expansion and India's frontier defense policy.

EARLY HISTORY TO THE 9TH CENTURY

Credible history begins late in the 6th century, when three discontented vassals of one of the princes among whom Tibet was then divided conspired to support the neighbouring lord of Yarlung, whose title was Spu-rgyal btsan-po. *Btsan-po* ("mighty") became the designation of all kings of Tibet (*rgyal* means "king"; and *spu*, the meaning of which is uncertain, may refer to a sacral quality of the princes of Yar-lung as divine manifestations). Their new master, Gnam-ri srong-brtsan (*c.* 570–*c.* 619 CE), was transformed from a princeling in a small valley into the ruler of a vigorously expanding military empire.

Gnam-ri srong-brtsan imposed his authority over several Qiang tribes on the Chinese border and became known to the Sui dynasty (581–618) as the commander of 100,000 warriors. But it was his son, Srong-brtsan-sgam-po (*c.* 617–650), who brought Tibet forcibly to the notice of the Taizong emperor (reigned 626–649), of the Tang dynasty. To pacify him, Taizong granted him a princess as his bride. Srong-brtsan-sgam-po is famed as the first *chos-rgyal* ("religious king") and for his all-important influence on Tibetan culture, the introduction of writing for which he borrowed a script from India, enabling the texts of the new religion to be translated. He extended his empire over Nepal, western Tibet, the Tuyuhun, and other tribes on China's border; and he invaded north India.

In 670, 20 years after Srong-brtsan-sgam-po's death, peace with China was broken and for two centuries Tibetan armies in Qinghai and Xinjiang kept the frontier in a state of war. In alliance with the western Turks, the Tibetans challenged Chinese control of the trade routes through Central Asia.

The reign of Khri-srong-lde-brtsan (755–797) marked the peak of Tibetan military success, including the exaction of tribute from China and the brief capture of its capital, Chang'an, in 763. But it was as the second religious king and champion of Buddhism that Khri-srong-lde-brtsan was immortalized by posterity. He initially had prohibited Buddhism, but that restriction was lifted in 761. In 763, when he was 21, he invited Buddhist teachers from India and China to Tibet, and about 779 he established the great temple of Bsam-yas, where Tibetans were trained as monks.

Buddhism foreshadowed the end of "Spu-rgyal's Tibet." The kings did not fully appreciate that its spiritual authority endangered their own supernatural prestige or that its philosophy was irreconcilable with belief in personal survival. They patronized Buddhist foundations but retained their claims as divine manifestations.

DISUNITY, 9TH TO 14TH CENTURY

In the 9th century, Buddhist tradition records a contested succession, but there are many inconsistencies; contemporary Chinese histories indicate that Tibetan unity and strength were destroyed by rivalry between generals commanding the frontier armies. Early in the 9th century, a scion of the old royal family migrated to western Tibet and founded successor kingdoms there, and by 889 Tibet was a mere congeries of separate lordships. In 843, during that period,

Glandar-ma (reigned 841–846) ordered the suppression of Buddhism, and Tibet's Buddhist traditions were disrupted for more than a century.

Tibetan generals and chieftains on the eastern border established themselves in separate territories. The acknowledged successors of the religious kings prospered in their migration to the west and maintained contact with Indian Buddhist universities through Tibetan scholars, notably the famous translator Rin-chen bzang-po (died 1055). In central Tibet, Buddhism suffered an eclipse. A missionary journey by the renowned Indian pandit Atisha in 1042 rekindled the faith through central Tibet, and from then onward Buddhism increasingly spread its influence over every aspect of Tibetan life.

Inspired by Atisha and by other pandits whom they visited in India, Tibetan religious men formed small communities and expounded different aspects of doctrine. Atisha's own teaching became the basis of the austere Bka'-gdams-pa sect. The Tibetan scholar Dkon-mchog rgyal-po established the monastery of Sa-skya (1073), and a series of lamas (Tibetan priests) founded several monasteries of what is generally called the Bka'-brgyud-pa sect.

Hermits such as Mi-la ras-pa (1040–1123) shunned material things; but the systematized sects became prosperous through the support of local lords, often kinsmen of the founding lama, and, except for the Bka'-gdams-pa, each developed its own system of keeping the hierarchical succession within a noble family. In some sects the principle of succession through reincarnation was evolved. Although lamas of different schools studied amicably together, their supporters inevitably indulged in worldly competition. This tendency was intensified by the intervention of a new Asian power, the Mongols.

Although it has been widely stated that the Tibetans submitted about 1207 to Genghis (Chinggis) Khan to avert an invasion, evidence indicates that the first military contact with the Mongols came in 1240, when they marched on central Tibet and attacked the monastery of Ra-sgreng and others. In 1247, Köden, younger brother of the khan Güyük, symbolically invested the Sa-skya lama with temporal authority over Tibet. Later Kublai Khan appointed the lama 'Phags-pa as his "imperial preceptor" (*dishi*), and the politico-religious relationship between Tibet and the Mongol empire is stated as a personal bond between the emperor as patron and the lama as priest (*yon-mchod*).

A series of Sa-skya lamas, living at the Mongol court, thus became viceroys of Tibet on behalf of the Mongol emperors. The Mongols prescribed a reorganization of the many small estates into thirteen myriarchies (administrative districts each comprising, theoretically, 10,000 families). The ideal was a single authority, but other monasteries, especially 'Bri-gung and Phag-mo-gru of the Bka'-brgyud-pa sect, whose supporters controlled several myriarchies, actively contested Sa-skya's supremacy.

The collapse of the Yuan dynasty in 1368 also brought down Sa-skya after 80 years of power. Consequently, when the native Chinese Ming dynasty (1368–1644) evicted the Mongols, Tibet regained its independence; for more than 100 years the Phag-mo-gru-pa line governed in its own right.

A proliferation of scholars, preachers, mystics, hermits, and eccentrics, as well as monastic administrators and warriors, accompanied the subsequent revival of Buddhism. Literary activity was intense. Sanskrit works were translated with the help of visiting Indian pandits; the earliest codifiers, classifiers, biographers, and historians appeared. In an outburst of monastic building, the characteristic Tibetan style acquired greater extent, mass, and dignity. Chinese workmen were imported for decorative work. Temple walls were covered with fine frescoes; huge carved and painted wooden pillars were hung with silk and with painted banners (tankas). Chapels abounded in images of gold, gilded copper, or painted and gilded clay; some were decorated with stucco scenes in high relief; in others the remains of deceased lamas were enshrined in silver or gilded stupas. Under Nepalese influence, images were cast and ritual vessels and musical instruments made in a style blending exuberant power and sophisticated craftsmanship; wood-carvers produced beautiful shrines and book covers, and from India came palm-leaf books, ancient images, and bell-metal stupas of all sizes.

Tibet, 14th to 19th Century

For 70 peaceful years, Byang-chub rgyal-mtshan (died 1364) and his two successors ruled a domain wider than that of the Sa-skya-pa. Thereafter, although the Phag-mo-gru Gong-ma (as the ruler was called) remained nominally supreme, violent dissension erupted again. In 1435 the lay princes of Rin-spungs, ministers of Gong-ma and patrons of the increasingly influential Karma-pa sect, rebelled and by 1481 had seized control of the Phag-mo-gru court.

The Dge-lugs-pa (Yellow Hat Sect)

Already a new political factor had appeared in the Dge-lugs-pa sect. Its founder was a saintly scholar, Blo-bzang grags-pa (died 1419), known as Tsong-kha-pa for his supposed birthplace of Tsong-kha in eastern A-mdo. After studying with leading teachers of the day, he formulated his own doctrine, emphasizing the moral and philosophical ideas of Atisha rather than the magic and mysticism of Sa-skya—though he did not discard the latter entirely. In 1409 he founded his own monastery at Dga'-ldan, devoted to the restoration of strict monastic discipline. Tsong-kha-pa's disciplinary reform appealed to people weary of rivalry and strife between wealthy monasteries. Tsong-kha-pa probably did not imagine that his disciples would form a new sect and join in that rivalry, but, after his death, devoted and ambitious followers built around his teaching and prestige what became the Dge-lugs-pa, or Yellow Hat sect, which was gradually drawn into the political arena.

In 1578 the Dge-lugs-pa took a step destined to bring foreign interference once more into Tibetan affairs. The third Dge-lugs-pa hierarch, Bsod-nams-rgya-mtsho, was invited to visit the powerful Tümed Mongol leader Altan Khan, with whom he revived the patron-priest relationship that had existed between Kublai Khan and 'Phags-pa. From this time dates the title of Dalai ("Oceanwide") Lama, conferred by Altan and applied retrospectively to the two previous hierarchs. The holder is regarded as the embodiment of a spiritual emanation of the bodhisattva Avalokiteshvara (Tibetan: Spyan-ras-gzigs; Chinese: Guanyin)—and hence of the mythic monkey demon and progenitor of the Tibetans. The succession is maintained by the discovery of a child, born soon after the death of a Dalai Lama, into whom the spirit of the deceased is believed to have entered. Until 1642 the Dalai Lamas were principal abbots of the Dge-lugs-pa, and in that year they acquired temporal and spiritual rule of Tibet. With Altan's help virtually all the Mongols became Dge-lugs-pa adherents, and on Bsod-nams-rgya-mtsho's death they acquired a proprietary interest in the order and some claims on Tibet itself when the fourth Dalai Lama was conveniently discovered in the Tümed royal family.

To support their protégé, the Mongols sent armed bands into Tibet. Their opponents were the Red Hat Lama, head of a Karma-pa subsect, and his patron the Gtsang king. That phase of rivalry ended inconclusively with the early death of the fourth Dalai Lama and the decline of Tümed Mongol authority in Mongolia. The next came when Güüshi Khan, leader of the Khoshut tribe, which had displaced the Tümed, appeared as champion of the Dge-lugs-pa. In 1640 he invaded Tibet, defeating the Gtsang king and his Karma-pa supporters.

THE UNIFICATION OF TIBET

In 1642 with exemplary devotion, Güüshi enthroned the Dalai Lama as ruler of Tibet, appointing Bsod-nams chos-'phel as minister for administrative affairs and himself taking the title of king and the role of military protector. These three forceful personalities methodically and efficiently consolidated the religious and temporal authority of the Dge-lugs-pa, establishing a unique joint control over the region by both Mongols and Tibetans. Lhasa, long the spiritual heart of Tibet, now became the political capital as well. Dge-lugs-pa supremacy was imposed on all other orders, with special severity toward the Karma-pa. A reorganized district administration reduced the power of the lay nobility.

The grandeur and prestige of the regime were enhanced by reviving ceremonies attributed to the religious kings, by enlarging the nearby monasteries of 'Bras-spungs, Sera, and Dga'-Idan, and by building the superb Potala Palace, completed by another great figure, Sangs-rgyas-rgya-mtsho, who in 1679 succeeded as minister regent just before the death of his patron the fifth Dalai Lama. By then a soundly based and unified government had been established over a wider extent than any for eight centuries.

The installations of the fifth Dalai Lama (the "Great Fifth") at Lhasa (1642) and the Qing, or Manchu, dynasty in China (1644) were almost synchronous. In 1652 the fifth Dalai Lama went to Beijing to meet with the Qing emperor Shunzhi. Prior to the Dalai Lama's return to Tibet the following year, the Shunzhi emperor conferred upon him a golden album and a golden seal and formally proclaimed him the Dalai Lama (which, to the Qing, was an honorific title). In addition, a Qing envoy accompanied the Dalai Lama back to Tibet and conferred Qing legitimacy to the Güüshi Khan on behalf of the emperor. Good relations with Tibet were important to the Manchu because of the Dalai Lama's prestige among the Mongols, from whom a new threat was taking shape in the ambitions of the powerful Oyrat of western Mongolia. The Dalai Lama also expected more support from the Qing government to confirm his political power over Tibet, as Mongolian control there gradually weakened.

Elsewhere, Lhasa's expanding authority with both Mongolian and Tibetan martial forces brought disagreements with Bhutan, which held its own against Tibetan incursions in 1646 and 1657, and with Ladakh, where a campaign ended in 1684 in Tibetan withdrawal to an accepted frontier when the Ladakhǐ king appealed for help to the Muslim governor of Kashmir.

TIBET UNDER MANCHU OVERLORDSHIP

The Dalai Lama's death in 1682 and the discovery of his five-year-old reincarnation in 1688 were concealed by Sangs-rgyas-rgya-mtsho, who was intent on continuing the administration without disturbance. He informed the Manchu only in 1694 or 1696 (sources disagree). The Kangxi emperor (reigned 1661–1722) was incensed at the deception. In 1703 he discovered an ally in Tibet and an antagonist to Sangs-rgyas-rgya-mtsho when Lha-bzang Khan, fourth successor of Güüshi, sought to assert rights as king that had atrophied under his immediate predecessors. The behaviour of the sixth Dalai Lama, Tshangs-dbyangs-rgya-mtsho, who preferred poetry and libertine amusements to religion, gave Lha-bzang his opportunity. In 1705, with the emperor's approval, he attacked and killed Sangs-rgyas-rgya-mtsho and deposed Tshangs-dbyangs-rgya-mtsho as a spurious reincarnation. The Tibetans angrily rejected him and soon recognized in eastern Tibet the infant reincarnation of the dead Tshangs-dbyangs-rgya-mtsho.

In 1717 the Oyrat, nominally Dge-lugs-pa supporters, took advantage of Tibetan discontent to intervene in a sudden raid, defeating and killing Lha-bzang. Fear of hostile Mongol domination of Tibet compelled the emperor to send troops against the Oyrat. After an initial reverse, his armies drove them out in 1720 and were welcomed at Lhasa as deliverers, all the more because they brought with them the new Dalai Lama, Bskal-bzang-rgya-mtsho. For the next 200 years, there was no fighting between Tibetans and Chinese. However, after evicting the Oyrat, the emperor decided to safeguard Manchu interests by appointing representatives—generally known as *ambans*—at Lhasa, with a small garrison in support. The Tibetans, interpreting this as another patron-priest relationship, accepted the situation, which generally left them to manage their own affairs. It was only in recurring crises that Manchu participation became, briefly, energetic. Imperial troops quelled a civil war in Tibet in 1728, restored order after the political leader was assassinated in 1750, and drove out the Gurkhas, who had invaded from Nepal in 1792. As Manchu energy declined, the Tibetans became increasingly independent, though still recognizing the formal suzerainty of the emperor, behind which it sometimes suited them to shelter. At no time did the *ambans* have administrative power, and after 1792, when Tibet was involved in wars with Ladakh (1842) and Nepal (1858), the Manchu were unable to help or protect them.

ADMINISTRATION AND CULTURE UNDER THE MANCHU

No Dalai Lama until the thirteenth approached the personal authority of the Great Fifth. The seventh incarnation was overshadowed by Pho-lha, a lay nobleman appointed ruler by the Manchu. The eighth was diffident and retiring. But after the Pho-lha family's regime, Dge-lugs-pa clerics resumed power and held onto it through a series of monk regents for about 145 years.

Chinese contacts affected Tibetan culture less than might be expected. They helped shape the administrative machinery, army, and mail service, which were based on existing institutions and run by Tibetans. Chinese customs influenced dress, food, and manners; china and chopsticks were widely used by the upper classes. The arts of painting, wood carving, and casting figures continued on traditional lines, with much technical skill but few signs of innovation. An important effect of Manchu supremacy was the exclusion of foreigners after 1792. That ended the hopes of Christian missionaries and the diplomatic visits from British India, which had been started in 1774. Tibet was now closed, and mutual ignorance enshrouded future exchanges with its British neighbours in India.

TIBET SINCE 1900

In the mid-19th century, the Tibetans repeatedly rebuffed overtures from the British, who saw Tibet at first as a trade route to China and later as countenancing Russian advances that might endanger India. Eventually, in 1903, after failure to get China to control its unruly vassal, a political mission was dispatched from India to secure understandings on frontier and trade relations. Tibetan resistance was overcome by force, the Dalai Lama fled to China, and the rough wooing ended in a treaty at Lhasa in 1904 between Britain and Tibet without Chinese adherence. In 1906, however, the Chinese achieved a treaty with Britain, without Tibetan participation, that recognized their suzerainty over Tibet. That success emboldened the Chinese to seek direct control of Tibet by using force against the Tibetans for the first time in ten centuries. In 1910 the Dalai Lama again was forced to flee, this time to India.

That dying burst by the Qing dynasty converted Tibetan indifference into enmity, and, after the start of the Chinese Revolution of 1911–12, the Tibetans rose up against and expelled the Chinese; the Dalai Lama returned to Tibet in mid-1912. Tibet subsequently functioned as a de facto independent government until 1951 and defended its frontier against China in occasional fighting as late as 1931. Of note was the Shimla Conference (1913–14), in which Tibet and Great Britain, with Chinese participation, negotiated the status of Tibet and of the Tibet-India frontier (the McMahon Line). However, China refused to ratify the conference's agreement (including the demarcated border), nor would it recognize Tibet as an independent entity.

In 1949, after the communist takeover in China, the Chinese heralded the "liberation" of Tibet, and in October 1950 Chinese troops entered and took control of eastern Tibet, overwhelming the poorly equipped Tibetan troops. An appeal by the fourteenth Dalai Lama to the United Nations was denied, and support from India and Britain was not forthcoming. A Tibetan delegation summoned to Beijing in 1951 had to sign a treaty dictated by Chinese authorities. It professed to guarantee Tibetan autonomy and religion but also allowed the establishment at Lhasa of Chinese civil and military headquarters.

Smoldering resentment at the strain on the country's resources from the influx of Chinese soldiery and civilians was inflamed in 1956 by reports of fighting and oppression in districts east of the upper Yangtze River, which were outside the administration of Lhasa but bound to it by ethnicity, language, and religion. Refugees from the fighting in the east carried guerrilla warfare against the Chinese into central Tibet, creating tensions that exploded in a popular rising at Lhasa in March 1959. The Dalai Lama, most of his ministers, and many followers escaped across the Himalayas, and the rising was suppressed.

The events of 1959 intensified China's disagreements with India, which had given asylum to the Dalai Lama. In 1962 Chinese forces proved the efficiency of the new communications they had established in Tibet by invading northeastern Assam, although they soon withdrew.

In 1966 and 1967, the Chinese position in Tibet was shaken by the excesses of the early Cultural Revolution (1966–76), as the upheavals it unleashed reached Lhasa. Military control was restored by

1969, and in 1971 a new local government committee was announced. Between 1963 and 1971, no foreign visitor was allowed to enter Tibet. Repression in Tibet generally abated in the late 1970s with the end of the Cultural Revolution. However, repressive measures resumed periodically during times of civil disturbance, as when riots broke out in Tibet in the late 1980s or after protests erupted in 2008 before the Beijing Summer Olympic Games.

Meanwhile, China invested heavily in the economic development of Tibet, notably in its mineral and power-generating resources. Considerable effort also was directed at improving Tibet's transportation infrastructure—for example, through highway and railroad construction. Tourism generally has been encouraged. In addition, both China and the Dalai Lama have made diplomatic overtures toward the other side, though the two camps remained far apart. For his part, the Dalai Lama since the 1980s has stated his desire for what he described as "autonomy" for Tibet and regions adjacent to Tibet. Chinese authorities have viewed such calls for autonomy as a continuation

The fourteenth Dalai Lama, Tibet's spiritual leader, has lived in exile from his homeland since 1959. Diptendu Dutta/AFP/Getty Images

of the exiled Tibetan community's desire for Tibet's independence from China. During that time the Dalai Lama—winner of the 1989 Nobel Prize for Peace—became a renowned figure throughout the world.

XINJIANG

Xinjiang (conventional Sinkiang; officially Uygur Autonomous Region of Xinjiang) occupies the northwestern corner of the country. It is China's largest political unit, occupying some one-sixth of the country's total area. The capital is at Ürümqi (Wulumuqi) in the north-central part of the region.

Known to the Chinese as Xiyu ("Western Regions") for centuries, the area became Xinjiang ("New Borders") upon its annexation under the Qing (Manchu) dynasty in the 18th century. Westerners long called it Chinese Turkistan to distinguish it from Russian Turkistan. Xinjiang is an area of lonely, rugged mountains and vast desert basins. Its indigenous population of agriculturalists and pastoralists (principally Uighurs) inhabit oases strung out along the mountain foothills or wander the arid plains in search of pasturage. Since the establishment of firm Chinese control in 1949, serious efforts have been made to integrate the regional economy into that of the country, and these efforts have been accompanied by a great increase in the Han (Chinese) population there. The policy of the Chinese government is to allow the ethnic groups to develop and maintain their own cultural identities. However, the extent to which that policy has been successful in Xinjiang has been interpreted variously; ethnic tensions exist, especially between Uighurs and Han. Xinjiang's area is about 635,900 square miles (1,646,900 square km). Its population numbered about 20,500,000 as of 2007.

LAND

Xinjiang is bordered by the Chinese provinces of Qinghai and Gansu to the east, the Tibet Autonomous Region to the south, Afghanistan and the disputed territory of Kashmir to the southwest, Kyrgyzstan and Tajikistan to the west, Kazakhstan to the northwest, Russia to the north, and Mongolia to the northeast.

RELIEF

Xinjiang can be divided into five physiographic regions: the Northern Highlands, the Junggar (Dzungarian) Basin, the Tien (Tian) Shan ("Celestial Mountains"), the Tarim Basin, and the Kunlun Mountains. These regions run roughly from east to west, the high mountains alternating with large basins.

In the north the Northern Highlands extend in a semicircle along the Mongolian border. The major range in this area is the Altai Mountains, with average heights of approximately 4,500 feet (1,400 m) above sea level. The slopes of the Altai Mountains on the

Chinese (western) side are relatively gentle, with numerous rolling and dome-shaped hills.

The triangular-shaped Junggar Basin, or Dzungaria, with an area of some 147,000 square miles (380,000 square km), is bordered by the Altai Mountains on the northeast, the Tien Shan on the south, and the Zhongghar (Dzungarian) Alatau (Alataw) Mountains (principally of Kazakhstan) on the northwest. The basin is open on both the east and west. It contains a ring of oases at the foot of the enclosing mountains and a steppe and desert belt in the centre of the depression.

The Tien Shan occupies nearly one-fourth of the area of Xinjiang. The mountains stretch into the region from Kazakhstan, Kyrgyzstan, and Tajikistan and run eastward from the border for about 1,000 miles (1,600 km). They are highest in the west and taper off slightly to the east. The highest mountains are Khan Tängiri (Hantengri) Peak on the Kazakh border, which rises to an

Satellite image of a river's large alluvial fan between the Kunlun and Altun ranges, Uygur Autonomous Region of Xinjiang, western China. Image provided by the USGS EROS Data Center

elevation of 22,949 feet (6,995 m); and Victory Peak (Russian Pik Pobedy) on the Kyrgyz border, which attains 24,406 feet (7,439 m). They are found in a cluster of mountains, from which ridges extend southwestward along the boundary between China and Kyrgyzstan. The Tien Shan is perpetually covered by snow, and numerous long glaciers descend its slopes from extensive snowfields.

The Tarim Basin is surrounded by the Tien Shan to the north, the Pamirs range to the west, and the Kunlun Mountains to the south. It occupies about half of Xinjiang, extending some 850 miles (1,370 km) from west to east and about 350 (560 km) miles from north to south. The basin consists of a central desert, alluvial fans at the foot of the mountains, and isolated oases. The desert—the Takla Makan—covers an area of approximately 123,550 square miles (320,000 square km) and is nearly barren. The core of the basin has an elevation ranging from about 4,000 feet (1,200 m) above sea level in the west to about 2,500 feet (760 m) in the east. However, the Turfan (Tulufan) Depression—northeast of the Takla Makan and between the Bogda and Qoltag mountain ranges to the north and south, respectively—is 505 feet (154 m) below sea level.

The Kunlun Mountains form the northern rampart of the Plateau of Tibet. With its tallest peaks surpassing 24,000 feet (7,300 m), the central part of the range forms an almost impenetrable barrier to movement from north to south. There are passes on the west and east, such as the Karakoram in the Kashmir region and the Korgan in Xinjiang. In the east the Altun Mountains turn northeast and eventually merge with the Qilian Mountains in Gansu province.

DRAINAGE

The drainage pattern of Xinjiang is unique within China. The only stream whose waters reach the sea is the Irtysh River, which rises in north-central Xinjiang (as the Ertix River), flows west and crosses into Kazakhstan (where it is called the Ertis), and, as the Irtysh, flows through Russia into the Ob River, which then empties into the Arctic Ocean. Other streams in Xinjiang issue from the mountains and disappear into inland deserts or salt lakes. The principal river of the region, the Tarim, is fed by largely intermittent streams that rise in the Kunlun Mountains and in the Tien Shan. It flows generally eastward across the Tarim Basin, becoming intermittent in its lower reaches.

CLIMATE

Remote from the ocean and enclosed by high mountains, Xinjiang is cut off from marine climatic influences. It therefore has a continental, dry climate. The Tien Shan separates the dry south from the slightly less arid north, so the northern slopes of the Tien Shan are more humid than those of the south.

Precipitation not only is scanty but also fluctuates widely from year to year. On the average, the annual rainfall is about 6.5 inches (16.5 cm). Average January temperatures in the Tarim Basin are about 20 °F (-7 °C), compared with 5 °F (-15 °C) in many parts of the Junggar Basin. In the summer, average temperatures north of the Tien Shan are lower than they are south of the mountains. In the Junggar Basin, July averages vary from 70 °F (21 °C) in the north to 75 °F (24 °C) in the south. In the Tarim Basin, July temperatures average about 80 °F (27 °C). The hottest part of Xinjiang is the Turfan Depression, where a maximum of 120 °F (49 °C) and a July mean of 90 °F (32 °C) were recorded.

PLANT AND ANIMAL LIFE

Because of the great expanses of desert, the plant life of much of Xinjiang is

Bactrian camel near Huoyan ("Flaming") Mountain, Uygur Autonomous Region of Xinjiang, China. © Corbis

monotonous. There are pine forests in the Tien Shan and stands of drought-tolerant trees in many places on the edge of the Takla Makan Desert. Apart from these trees, the most common are varieties of poplar and willow. In the Tien Shan and other mountains, there is a great assortment of plants and wildflowers, many of which have never been classified. Nonetheless, more than 3,000 plant species have been identified in Xinjiang, of which some 300 have economic or medicinal value.

Animal life is of greater interest, and big-game hunting is an attraction of the Tien Shan. The mountains are inhabited by antelopes, ibex (wild goats), wapiti (elks), various wild sheep, leopards, wolves, bears, lynx, and marmots. There are wild horses in the north, wild camels in the southern and eastern fringes of the Takla Makan Desert, and wild yaks (large, long-haired oxen) and wild asses on the Tibetan frontier. Birdlife is concentrated in wetter areas. The few varieties of fish are mostly of the carp family. Snakes are not numerous and appear to be harmless. Scorpions and centipedes, however, abound. During the summer, horseflies, mosquitoes, flies, and midges are thick in the woods. A great variety of butterflies are found in the mountains.

People

Large areas of the desert and mountains are uninhabitable (or nearly so). Because of this, Xinjiang has one of the lowest population densities of any Chinese administrative unit.

Population Composition

Xinjiang is inhabited by more than forty different ethnic groups, the largest of which are the Uighurs and the Han (Chinese). In addition to Hui (Chinese Muslims), other groups include Mongolians, Khalkha, Kazakhs, Uzbeks, Tungusic-speaking Manchu and Sibos, Tajiks, Tatars, Russians, and Tahurs.

The Han migration altered the pattern of population distribution and ethnic composition of Xinjiang. In 1953 about three-fourths of the population lived south of the mountains in the Tarim Basin. The Han influx was directed mainly to the Junggar Basin because of its resource potential. The Kazakhs, the third largest minority group in the region, are nomadic herders in the steppes of the Junggar Basin; they are especially concentrated in the upper Ili (Yili) River valley.

There are two major language groups besides Chinese in the region. The Mongolians speak languages of the Mongolian branch of the Altaic group, and the Uighurs, Kazakhs, and Uzbeks speak the Turkic branch of the Altaic group. The Tajiks, however, belong to the Iranian branch of the Indo-European language group. Mongolian, Uighur, and Kazakh are written languages in everyday use; Mongolian has its own script, while Uighur and Kazakh are written in the Arabic script.

The largest Muslim groups in China are the Uighurs and the Hui. The Kazakhs and Tajiks also follow Islam, while the Mongolians are adherents of Buddhism.

SETTLEMENT PATTERNS

There are many differences in rural settlement patterns in the north and the south. Oasis agriculture in the Tarim Basin occupies a large part of the population, and only a small percentage is engaged in animal husbandry. North of the Tien Shan the grasslands support many of the inhabitants, who are pastoralists.

Xinjiang has some major cities. Ürümqi, the regional capital, was once an agricultural centre for the Junggar Basin; it subsequently underwent considerable industrial and commercial development. Karamay, also in the Junggar Basin, was developed in the late 1950s as a centre of the petroleum industry. Shihezi, near the southern edge of the Junggar Basin, is a significant agricultural processing centre. Kuldja (Yining), located in the upper Ili River valley near Kazakhstan, is an administrative town with a growing food-processing industry. Kashgar (Kashi), the largest city of the Tarim Basin, is an ancient centre for the manufacture of handicrafts such as textiles, rugs, and tanned leather. Turfan, a vital highway and railway communication centre in northeastern Xinjiang, has growing petrochemical and cotton textile industries.

ECONOMY

Xinjiang's economy has grown significantly since 1950. This has been in large measure because of improvements to the region's transportation infrastructure, which have made it possible to exploit the rich mineral resources and to develop industry there.

AGRICULTURE

Because of the dry climate, most of the cultivated land in Xinjiang depends entirely on irrigation. The various ethnic groups in the region have had rich experience in water conservancy techniques, of which the wells of the *qanāt* system in the Turfan and Hami depressions are a fine example. Since the 1950s these have been greatly supplemented with canals and reservoirs, and the amount of arable land has almost tripled.

Xinjiang is self-sufficient in food grains. About half of the total crop area produces winter and spring wheat. Corn (maize), another important crop, is grown more in the south than in the north. Rice, kaoliang (a variety of grain sorghum), and millet are also produced in large quantities. Significant crops of long-staple cotton are produced in the Turfan Depression and the greater Tarim Basin, and cotton has become an important cash crop. Xinjiang is one of China's main fruit-producing regions; its sweet Hami melons, seedless Turpan grapes, fragrant Korla pears, and crisp Ili apples are well known. Sugar beets support an important sugar-refining industry in north-western China. Hops and silkworm cocoons are increasingly produced on a large scale for national markets and for export. Livestock raising has been given renewed attention, particularly north of the Tien Shan.

RESOURCES AND MANUFACTURING

Mineral resources include deposits of coal, iron, zinc, chrome, nickel, and copper, as well as molybdenum and tungsten (used in strengthening steel). Gold is produced from placer and lode deposits on the southern slopes of the Altai Mountains. Xinjiang's products of national significance include petroleum and natural gas. Since the first oil well was developed at Karamay in 1955, that region has been extensively developed; subsequently, a second region has been exploited, at Dushanzi to the south. The exploitation of both petroleum and natural gas in the Tarim and Hami basins (the Tu-Ha Oil Field) also has expanded significantly since the late 1980s, with major fields being developed in both basins. West-east pipelines were built to transport natural gas from Xinjiang to cities on China's east coast.

Xinjiang's heavy industry includes iron and steel works and a cement factory at Ürümqi and a farm-tool plant at Kashgar. Petrochemical plants have been established at Karamay, Dushanzi, Ürümqi, Korla (in the northeastern Tarim Basin), and Zepu (at the western edge of the basin). Thermal power generation is also important for the region. Industries processing agricultural and animal products have been established near the sources of raw materials and include several textile mills and beet sugar mills.

TRANSPORTATION

A system of roads encircles the Tarim Basin along the foothills of the surrounding mountain ranges, and roads run along the northern foothills of the Tien Shan in the Junggar Basin. The two basins are connected by roads that cross the Tien Shan near Ürümqi and west of Ürümqi. There are roads leading to Kazakhstan in the north, through passes in the Junggar Basin, and to Tajikistan in the south, through a pass near Kashgar, which was the historic gateway of the Silk Road that long facilitated trade between Asia and Europe. The region is also connected by road to Gansu and Qinghai in the southeast.

A railway crosses Xinjiang from Gansu through Hami, Ürümqi, and the Dzungarian (Junggar) Gate (Chinese: Alataw Shankou; a pass through the Zhongghar Alatau range), connecting with the railway system of Kazakhstan. The northern and southern sectors of the province have also been linked by a railway constructed across the Tien Shan, from Turfan to Korla and further to Aksu and Kashgar. There are some dozen airports scattered in different cities of the

Pagoda along the Silk Road, Uygur Autonomous Region of Xinjiang, China. © Corbis

region, with Ürümqi being the centre of civil aviation services.

GOVERNMENT AND SOCIETY

The administrative structure of Xinjiang reflects the policies of recognition of ethnic minorities and self-administration, in which local leaders are appointed to governmental positions.

CONSTITUTIONAL FRAMEWORK

The Uygur Autonomous Region of Xinjiang is divided on the subregional level into three types of administrative units. There are two prefecture-level municipalities (*dijishi*), five autonomous prefectures (*zizhizhou*), and seven prefectures (*diqu*). The region is further subdivided into districts under municipalities (*shixiaqu*), county-level municipalities (*xianjishi*), counties (*xian*), and autonomous counties (*zizhixian*).

EDUCATION

Before World War II the educational system in the region was minimal. Since 1949, educational facilities have been broadened, and the literacy rate is better than the national average. Institutions of higher learning, concentrated in Ürümqi, include Xinjiang University (1924); Xinjiang Agricultural University (1952; the former Xinjiang "August First" Institute of Agriculture); Xinjiang Medical University (1956); Xinjiang Petroleum Institute (1958);

and Xinjiang Normal University (1978). Standard education is supplemented by instruction broadcast over radio and television. The provincial library and museum are also in Ürümqi.

CULTURAL LIFE

The indigenous peoples of Xinjiang practice a variety of cultural traditions. The dominant Uighur are sedentary farmers whose social organization is centred upon the village. Many of the important Uighur cultural forms are rooted in Islam. Spoken Uighur predominates despite the popularization of Mandarin Chinese. Islam itself has revived since the onslaught of the Cultural Revolution during the 1960s and '70s, and there are now numerous mosques and a training academy for clergy. The popular Uighur performing arts tradition called *muqam* emphasizes ancient songs and dances accompanied by traditional instrumental groups. Professional troupes, first organized in the 1950s, are dominated by Uighur balladeers and dancers, although administrative duties are often performed by Han troupe members.

The Kazakhs are pastoralists related to the people of Kazakhstan. They migrate seasonally in search of pasturage and live in dome-shaped, portable tents known as *gers*, or yurts. Livestock includes sheep, goats, and some cattle; horses are kept for prestige. The basic social unit is the extended family. Political organization extends through a hierarchy of chiefs.

Although there is a concept of national origin, the chiefs are seldom united politically.

Like the Kazakhs, the Mongolians traditionally have been pastoralists who live in yurts, but their society is more firmly organized. The basic social unit is the nuclear family. As part of their traditions, there was an established political hierarchy of groups, the smallest of which was a group of several households known as a *bag*. The average person, or free nomad (*arat*), owed allegiance to nobles (*taiji*) and princes (*noyan* or *wang*). However, this system has diminished in importance as larger numbers of Mongolians become settled on farms or in urban areas.

Xinjiang possesses unique scenic sites and renowned cultural relics in addition to its colourful ethnic features. The ancient Silk Road traverses the whole region, roughly along an east-west line, and there are numerous temples and ancient towns along the route. Areas of special note include Tian ("Heavenly")

Kyrgyz mosque in the Pamirs, western Uygur Autonomous Region of Xinjiang, China. Dugald Bremner/Stone

Lake in the Bogda Mountains (an eastern extension of the Tien Shan), the Kizil caves on the northern edge of the Tarim Basin near the ancient Buddhist centre of Kucha, and the site of the ancient capital city of the Gaochang state and the Bezeklik Thousand Buddha caves on Huoyan ("Flaming") Mountain, both near Turfan. Noted local handicrafts are rugs, small swords, musical instruments of the different minority groups, jade ware, and small felt hats, all of which are popular with tourists.

History

Far to the northwest of the heartland of Chinese civilization, the Xinjiang region was thinly populated by herders and oasis farmers organized into small kingdoms and tribal alliances. A military command-ery (*duhufu*) named Xiyu was set up for the region under the Xi (Western) Han dynasty in 60 BCE, with its headquarters at Wulei (now Luntai, in the northern Tarim Basin). Later, an extension of the Great Wall was built 300 miles (480 km) west of the present Gansu-Xinjiang bor-der. The Han capital of Chang'an (near present-day Xi'an), in Shaanxi province, came into contact with the Roman Empire over the Silk Road, a trade route that passed through a series of oasis settle-ments south of the Tien Shan. This route carried Chinese silk to the Roman world in exchange for precious metals, glass-ware, and woolen cloth.

With the decline of Han power in the 3rd century CE, the area passed under the control of local Uighur leaders. The resur-gence of imperial power during the Tang period (618–907) increased Chinese influ-ence in the region, though many elements of western Asian culture were transmitted along the trade routes. The Tang dynasty set up two military commanderies—Anxi (640) and Beiting (702)—for the areas north and south of the Tien Shan, respec-tively. As Tang power decreased in the late 9th and early 10th centuries, Arab influence increased, and Islam gained many converts. The Turkic language came to be spoken in the oases, while Mongolian remained the language of the steppes.

Xinjiang was again incorporated into the Chinese empire when it was con-quered by the Mongol leader Genghis (Chinggis) Khan in the 13th century. The Qing (Manchu) dynasty (1644–1911/12) successfully asserted control over the Xinjiang region, defeating the resistance of stubborn tribes in the north and send-ing loyal Muslims from Gansu to settle in the oases of northern Xinjiang in the 17th and 18th centuries. In 1884 the Qing gov-ernment created a new Xinjiang province.

After the Chinese Revolution of 1911–12, Yang Zengxin, a Han commander of native Turkic troops, seized control of Xinjiang and later was appointed gover-nor by the Beijing government. He maintained control until his assassina-tion in 1928, which was followed by a series of rulers and shifting allegiances, mainly under Jin Shuren (governed 1928-33) and Sheng Shicai (1933-44). Following the communist victory in 1949, the central government implemented moderate policies toward the local minorities, and Xinjiang was established as an autonomous region in 1955. About that time, the quasi-military Xinjiang Production and Construction Corps, consisting mainly of veterans from the People's Liberation Army and of educated urban youths, started setting up plantations, and these played an important role in the region's stability and economic development.

Radical policies established elsewhere in China during the Great Leap Forward (1958–60) and the Cultural Revolution (1966–76) were also implemented in Xinjiang, however. The food shortages caused by these disruptions, as well as the break in Sino-Soviet relations in the early 1960s, sparked a mass exodus of Kazakh people in 1962 into Kazakhstan (which then was part of the Soviet Union). This caused massive political instability and heightened ethnic tensions along the border area. After the Cultural Revolution, political and economic policies were moderated, leading to widespread improvement in the livelihood of farmers and pastoralists and to relative stability and economic growth in the region. This was accompanied—especially from the late 1990s—by increased economic investment in Xinjiang, as well as by an influx of Han from other parts of China. While the overall economic situation of the region improved as a result, inequities between the Uighur and Han populations became more pronounced. These economic disparities, along with ethnic tensions between Uighurs and Han, have precipitated occasional Uighur protests and disturbances. A notable outbreak of violence occurred in July 2009 (mainly in Ürümqi), during which scores of people were killed and hundreds were injured.

CHAPTER 12

SELECTED PROVINCES

Central to China's long-enduring identity as a unitary country are its provinces, which are traceable in their current form to the Tang dynasty (618–907). Over the centuries, provinces gained in importance as centres of political and economic authority and increasingly became the focus of regional identification and loyalty. Provincial power reached its peak in the first two decades of the 20th century, but, since the establishment of the People's Republic, that power has been curtailed by a strong central leadership in Beijing. Nonetheless, while the Chinese state has remained unitary in form, the vast size and population of China's provinces dictate their continuing importance as a level of subnational administration.

This chapter highlights three of the most prominent provinces—Shandong, Guangdong, and Sichuan—each of which would rank among the top fifteen most populous countries of the world.

SHANDONG

Shandong (conventional Shantung) is the major northern coastal province of China, lying across the Yellow Sea from the Korean peninsula. The name Shandong, which means "East of Mountains," was first officially used during the Jin dynasty in the 12th century. The capital is Jinan, located in the northwest-central part of the province. Shandong's area measures 59,200 square miles (153,300 square km), and its population was an estimated 93,090,000 in 2007.

LAND

The province consists of two distinct segments. The first is an inland zone bounded by the provinces of Hebei to the north and west, Henan to the southwest, and Anhui and Jiangsu to the south. The second is the Shandong Peninsula, extending some 200 miles (320 km) seaward from the Wei and Jiaolai river plains, with the Bo Hai (Gulf of Chihli) to the north and the Yellow Sea to the south; the peninsula accounts for a large share of the province's coastline of some 1,575 miles (2,535 km).

The inland zone, covering roughly two-thirds of the province's total area, includes a hilly central region, centred on the famous Mount Tai complex, and a fertile and intensively farmed agricultural area on the north, west, and south, which forms part of the Huang He (Yellow River) basin and the North China Plain. Jinan is situated just northwest of Mount Tai and about 3 miles (5 km) south of the Huang He, which flows from southwest to northeast through the province before emptying into the Bo Hai.

The Shandong Peninsula, by contrast, is entirely an upland area and, with its seaward orientation and indented coastline, has traditionally depended on fishing, mining, and port-related activities. Long a focal area in the evolution of Chinese civilization and institutions, the province's natural inland-peninsular division is paralleled by a dual orientation in its past and present political and economic configurations. The eastern peninsula historically had coveted autonomy, whereas the inland portion was closely tied to the inward-facing empire.

RELIEF

Shandong is dominated by two hill masses to the east-northeast of the Grand Canal and to the south-southwest of the present course of the Huang He. These hills are formed mainly of ancient crystalline shales and sedimentary rocks on their flanks and of hard, very ancient rocks with granitic intrusions in their core. Both masses are detached remnants of China's most ancient geologic core. The easternmost (peninsular) mass is connected to the Liaodong Peninsula (Liaoning province) by a submerged ridge that extends northward from the Penglai area of the Shandong Peninsula and emerges periodically between the Bo Hai and Yellow Sea as the Miaodao Archipelago. In fairly recent geologic times, the Shandong hill masses stood as islands in an inland sea that separated them from the Taihang Mountains of Shanxi province to the west.

A broad, marshy depression—the Jiaolai Plain—extends for about 100 miles (160 km) from Laizhou Bay in the Bo Hai,

Visitors can walk up 7,200 stone steps to reach the top of Mount Tai, Shandong province, China. Martin Gray/National Geographic/Getty Images

south to Jiaozhou Bay in the Yellow Sea, near Qingdao (Tsingtao), and westward into the North China Plain. The generally flat surface of the plain is interrupted occasionally by bedrock-derived monadnocks, or residual rocks or hills, that have resisted erosion. Another depression, part of the inland zone of western Shandong, forms the central segment of the North China Plain. It slopes eastward into a northwest-southeast trough skirting the western perimeter of the central Shandong hill mass and is filled with a mixture of loess (windblown silt) and alluvial materials (sand, clay, and gravel), along with more recently deposited alluvium, resulting from the building up of the Huang He floodplain. Four narrow lakes forming part of the Grand Canal system stretch out along this depression and are also linked to a series of saline marshes that separate the fertile margin at the western edge of the central hills from the main sections of the North China Plain to the south and west.

Of the two main hill masses, the westernmost (inland) complex is the most extensive. It consists of a northern series of three parallel faulted ranges—the Yi, Lu, and Tai, which stretch northeastward for more than 200 miles (320 km)—and a more diversified, lower, and more exposed southern portion. The granitic Tai massif, dominated by Mount Tai, the most famous of China's five sacred mountains, attains a maximum elevation of 5,000 feet (1,534 m) at Tianzhu Peak. The mountains of the peninsular mass to the east seldom rise above 700 feet (210 m). There surface erosion has etched irregular and deeply cut valleys, and rounded hills contrast sharply with small intermontane basins. Both the north and south coasts of the peninsula are rocky, with hills dropping precipitously to the sea and separating a series of intensively cultivated crescent-shaped plains.

DRAINAGE

Shandong's drainage is predominantly radial and subject to the prevailing configuration of the mountains. The only navigable river (other than portions of the Huang He) is the Xiaoqing River, which emerges from a small spring-fed lake in a limestone outcrop zone near Jinan and flows parallel to the Huang He before emptying into Laizhou Bay. The southern hills, in contrast, are drained by several rivers in arable valleys and eventually terminate in the marshy plain east of the Grand Canal in Jiangsu province.

SOILS

The soils of Shandong fall into two broad categories associated with upland or lowland distributions. The so-called Shandong brown soils are found over most of the two major hill masses and include a variety of brown forest and cinnamon-coloured soils formed through clay accumulations and sod processes.

A distinctive variant of the typical Shandong brown soil is the recalcified soil (soil that has been made hard or stony by the deposit of calcium salts) found on the northern perimeter of the central hill mass. Calcareous alluvial soils predominate in both lowlands and plains. They are usually quite fertile, depending on both the length of time they have been cultivated and their proximity to urban centres, where heavier fertilization with human and animal wastes results in rich, dark-coloured soils. Silty alluvium covers most portions of the North China Plain area of the province.

Another distinctive soil type found in central and western Shandong on the North China Plain is the subsurface *shajiang tu*, or "sandy ginger soil." This soil appears at the lowest elevations of alluvial plains where surface water remains unevaporated for several months until the dry season and also in sections of the plains subject to annual alluvial inundation. Such soils are always covered with alluvium or redeposited loess. Their name derives from the appearance of lime concretions that resemble the shape of ginger roots. Other *shajiang tu* soils develop impervious layers of limestone hardpan.

CLIMATE

Shandong falls within the North China climatic region, which extends from the Huai River in the south to the Hebei-Liaoning border in the north. It is characterized by a continental climate with cold winters and hot, dry summers.

Climatic variation prevails, however, between the peninsular and inland zones of the province.

The inland zone, especially in its northern sections, is subject to the full effect of the winter monsoon, when cold, northwesterly winds continue through December. The wind direction gradually reverses by March, and warmer, south-easterly winds prevail throughout the summer. In the inland zone, annual precipitation ranges from about 20 inches (50 cm) in northwest Shandong to 40 inches (101 cm) as one approaches the mouth of the Huang He. Of the total annual precipitation, 70 to 80 percent falls in summer. The interior areas of Shandong are also subject to severe winter and spring dust storms, sometimes followed by droughts, and frequent summer floods. Temperatures in the inland zone range from a mean January reading of 25 °F (–4 °C) in the northern interior to a mean of 82 °F (28 °C) in July. This area is subject to freezing temperatures during one to three months, with frosts common from late October to April. Rivers often freeze over for extended periods during the winter months. In the interior zone, the annual growing season extends from 200 to 250 days.

The maritime orientation of the Shandong Peninsula tends to modify the climatic extremes of the inland zone. The northern half of the peninsula is subject to winter snow and rainstorms and to extensive coastal ice from the mouth of the Huang He to Weihai and

Yantai (Chefoo); the southern half is somewhat warmer. Mean January temperatures range from 25 °F (-4 °C) on the northern coast of the peninsula to 32 °F (0 °C) in the south. There is less temperature difference during the hot summer months, when the mean July temperature is 79 °F (26 °C), but the ports of Yantai and Qingdao are cooler than interior stations. Maximum summer temperature in these ports rarely exceeds 77 °F (25 °C). Sea fog is common along the north and south coasts of the peninsula. Because of the high relative humidity, annual mean precipitation over the peninsula reaches 31 inches (78 cm), with less seasonal contrast than in the interior of the province. The heaviest precipitation occurs on the south-facing slopes of the central and peninsular hill masses.

PLANT AND ANIMAL LIFE

The limited natural vegetation that remains in the intensively cultivated inland zone of Shandong is found in minor depressions in the flat, alluvial landscape. Species there include reeds, grassy legumes, and several varieties of shrubs, notably tamarisk. Halophytic (salt-tolerant) vegetation is common in alkaline and saline soil areas along the coasts of the Bo Hai and southern Shandong near the Jiangsu border. Many of the halophytic shrubs are harvested for fuel and are used for salt manufacturing. *Lianliu*, a shrub with long willowy branches, is used for basket weaving, while other plants are woven into thatch mattings and sunshades. Poplars, pines, and arborvitae (an aromatic evergreen tree of the cypress family) are planted around settlements, along roads, and on the coasts.

The mountainous zones of Shandong are almost completely deforested, with only a small part of the area covered by scattered deciduous and coniferous forests interspersed among barren, eroded hills. Several types of pine grow at higher elevations on rocky, shallow soils in association with alpine meadow species. On the lower slopes and in the valleys, mixed oak, elm, cedar, linden, ash, maple, and chestnut forests appear along with such economically important fruit trees as apple, pear, apricot, and peach. Other deciduous species found at the lower elevations include pagoda (or Chinese scholar) trees (*Sophora japonica*), white mulberries, Persian walnuts, silk trees, and acacia. For centuries Shandong forests were overharvested for fuel and timber, and natural regeneration became extremely difficult. Since 1949, aggressive reforestation efforts and closer regulation of timber harvesting have resulted in extensive growth.

Despite the obliteration of much of Shandong's natural vegetation cover, the peninsular zone still exhibits an interesting mixture of northern and southern vegetation. Along with common northern plants, uniquely southern varieties such as wing nuts (trees of the walnut family), magnolias, and species of the genus

Styrax are common. Some special plants found in the area, such as the Qingdao lily (*Lilium tsingtauense*), have been listed as endangered and have been protected.

Through long periods of human settlement, intensive cultivation, and destruction of forests, Shandong's animal life has suffered drastic decline. Among the mammals found there today are roe deer and field and harvest mice; birds include mandarin ducks, dollar birds (belonging to the roller group), and large owls. Even with the attempts at reforestation since the 1950s, formerly extensive populations of native birds and mammals have almost vanished. Species of insects, beetles, and moths, however, are still unusually diverse and varied.

PEOPLE

Shandong is China's third most populous province, its population exceeded only by that of Henan and of Guangdong. It also has one of the highest population densities of the provinces.

POPULATION COMPOSITION

Shandong's population is predominantly Northern Mandarin-speaking and of Han (Chinese) origin, but there are small concentrations of Hui (Chinese Muslims) in Jinan, Zhoucun (near Zibo), Tai'an (south of Jinan), and Jining and Linqing (trading centres on the Grand Canal in western Shandong). The population, more than half of which is classified as rural, is fairly evenly distributed over the level, cultivated areas of the province.

SETTLEMENT PATTERNS

The two largest cities are Qingdao and Jinan, followed by the Zibo conurbation, a leading mining and industrial zone at the northern edge of the central hill mass, about 50 miles (80 km) east of Jinan. Other major cities include Yantai and Weihai, ports and fishing centres on the northeast coast of the peninsula; Weifang, an industrial and commercial town on the central Jiaolai Plain; and Dezhou, a rail and highway hub and major supplier of electric power for the northern provinces.

The greatest rural population densities are found in three areas. The first is one of the earliest settled places in the province, where irrigation works were constructed as long ago as the Han dynasty (206 BCE–220 CE); it lies along the foothills of the central hill mass. The second, the southwestern Heze-Qingdao-Jining area, is bounded on the northwest by the Huang He and on the southwest by the former course of the Huang He. This area was frequently subject to flooding but, because of its fertility and level terrain, gradually became densely settled. The third area comprises a fertile, irrigated strip along the north coast of the Shandong Peninsula.

ECONOMY

Shandong has a diversified agricultural and industrial economy. A broad range of food and cash crops are grown for internal consumption and export to other provinces and overseas. The province's industrial base has expanded since 1949. Before World War II, light industrial enterprises produced limited quantities of goods. Although the province often suffered a food deficit, agricultural products were continuously exported along with salt, coal, iron ore, and bauxite. Since 1949 relatively greater emphasis has been given to the development of industry, mining, and electric-power generation, although the overall level of agricultural output continued to rise. Shandong attained food self-sufficiency in 1970 while still increasing cash crop production.

AGRICULTURE AND FISHING

The success of agriculture in Shandong since 1949 is attributable to extensive investment in irrigation, flood control, and soil-conservation measures; drainage of alkalinized and salinized land; and increased mechanization. Some two-thirds of the province's wasteland has been reclaimed and cultivated, and in most irrigated areas the productivity ratio has improved from three crops in two years to two crops in one year. The leading food crops—wheat, corn (maize), soybeans, kaoliang (a variety of grain sorghum), spiked millet, and sweet potatoes—account for most of the total cultivated acreage of the province. The remaining arable land is given over to cash crops, which contribute substantially to agricultural earnings.

Peanuts (groundnuts), the leading cash crop, are grown primarily in the peninsular uplands and in the south-central sector. The large size of the peanuts grown in Shandong is especially well suited for oil pressing, and Shandong is a leading manufacturer of peanut oil for cooking. Shandong's other major cash crop, cotton, is grown throughout the province but is concentrated in the western and northern sections on the intensively irrigated lands near the mouth of the Huang He. Other cash crops include tobacco, grown chiefly on irrigated land in the vicinity of Yishui and Weifang; hemp, produced on low ground in the southwest; and fruit, formerly grown only on lower slopes of the central and peninsular hill masses but now cultivated over a wider area.

Animal husbandry plays an important role. The most common animals are pigs, yellow oxen, and donkeys. Sheep are raised in the uplands. Sericulture (silkworm raising), another important subsidiary activity, has been carried out in Shandong for hundreds of years. The popular fabric known as shantung was originally a rough-textured tussah, or wild-silk cloth, made in the province. Silkworm raising is most common in the central hills near Yishui, Linqu, Zichuan, and Laiwu, and most of the raw silk is sent to other provinces for processing and spinning.

Shandong's seaward orientation and its excellent harbours, as well as the convergence of cold and warm currents in offshore waters, have fostered a thriving ocean-fishing industry, complemented by the intensive development of pisciculture in the province's western lake region. Trawlers and smaller fishing craft operate from ports around the peninsula and off the Huang He delta. The ocean catch consists mainly of eels, herring, gizzard shad, fish roe, and several varieties of shrimp and crab. Catches of prawns, scallops, abalone, and sea urchins are among the largest in the country. Freshwater varieties raised through aquaculture are chiefly carp and crucian carp.

RESOURCES AND POWER

Shandong's industrial base is supported by extensive mining activities, principally coal mining, which was originally developed by German concessionaires in the early 20th century. Considerable mechanization of coal-mining operations has taken place since 1949. The coal field around Yanzhou and Tengzhou in southern Shandong has some of the largest coal reserves in China. There are also major iron ore deposits located near Zibo and Laiwu (southwest of Zibo), and some bauxite is mined near Nanding (Zibo). Gold is scattered throughout the peninsular hills, but the ore in many of the mines has been exhausted. Edible salt is produced on both the north and south coasts of the Shandong Peninsula.

Petroleum and petroleum products have exerted an increasing influence on the economy of the province. The Shengli oil field, one of China's largest oil-production areas, is located in northern Shandong on the mouth of the Huang He in the Bo Hai. The field yields a type of oil especially suitable for fuel. The province also shares part of the Zhongyuan oil field, on the Shandong-Henan border. A pipeline completed in 1978 connects the Shengli oil field with those of the North China Plain in Hebei and the ports and refineries of the lower Yangtze River (Chang Jiang) area.

Major emphasis since the late 1970s has been given to increasing electric-power generation. High-voltage transmission lines and feeder lines to rural areas extend throughout the province and have substantially increased the supply of rural electric power, as well as the amount of electrically irrigated and drained acreage.

MANUFACTURING

The province is still especially well known for its light industrial products, despite post-1949 gains in heavy industry. Qingdao, the major manufacturing centre, has a large textile industry, a locomotive works, and chemical, tire, and machine-tool factories. Pre–World War II oil pressing (peanut oil), cigarette making, flour milling, brewing, and beverage installations are still important; of note is the world-renowned Tsingtao brewery. Other enterprises produce a wide range of household electrical appliances as well as some petrochemicals and pharmaceuticals, and a high-technology sector has been set up. Jinan—long famous for its silks, precious stones, and handicrafts—also manufactures trucks and automobiles, motorcycles, agricultural machinery, machine tools, precision instruments, chemicals, fertilizers, and paper. Zibo is now a major industrial municipality in the province; in addition to its traditional manufactures of glass, porcelain and ceramics, and textiles, more recent production includes thermal power generation and the manufacturing of petrochemicals and electrical equipment. Weifang is an important food-processing centre, and it also manufactures machinery, chemicals, electronics, pharmaceuticals, and textiles. The coal-mining city of Zaozhuang in southern Shandong now also produces chemicals and mining machine tools. Dongying, on Laizhou Bay, home to the Shengli oil field, is a newly rising city with petrochemicals, paper, rubber products, textiles, and food processing as its mainstays. Some of Shandong's better-known handicraft goods are embroidered tablecloths from Yantai and Linzi, straw braids for hat weaving from Pingdu (east of Weifang), poplins, pottery, and ceramics.

TRANSPORTATION

Shandong's earliest railways were built in the first decade of the 20th century during the time of the German concession. One of the lines traverses the province from north to south, and another line crosses from east to west, connecting Qingdao and Jinan. Since 1949, new lines have been built, including a major trunk line from Qingdao northeast to Yantai. The new trunk line between Beijing and Hong Kong, completed in 1996, runs across the western part of the province.

Shandong's highways connect every district in the province. An extensive system of express highways has been developed since the mid-1990s. Truck traffic accounts for a majority of the total annual vehicular movement over Shandong's highways.

Except for portions of the Huang He and of the Xiaoqing River in northern Shandong, part of the Grand Canal in the west, and the Yi River in the southeast, inland waterway transportation is limited. The chief route—for shallow-draft craft only—extends upstream from Lijin, about 50 miles (80 km) inland from the mouth of the Huang He, to Qihe, the main Huang He river port in Shandong and just northwest of Jinan. The Grand Canal was long navigable only to a limited extent south of the Huang He, but channel-improvement projects since 2000 have made it possible for ships up to 1,000-tons displacement to travel from Jining directly to the Yangtze River (Chang Jiang).

Shandong has a number of excellent seaports. Qingdao is the largest in terms of tonnage handled, although Yantai, Weihai, and Longkou on the north coast of the peninsula also handle a considerable amount of shipping. Coastal shipping plays an important role in Shandong's economy. Qingdao alone handles more than one-third of the province's intraprovince trade. Trade between Qingdao and Shanghai to the south and Qingdao and Dalian (Liaoning) to the north is particularly heavy. A new seaport was constructed in the 1990s at Rizhao, southwest of Qingdao, on the coast of Yellow Sea, to export coal from Yanzhou (northeast of Jining) via a newly built railway.

The province's major cities have airports for domestic flights, with those at Jinan, Qingdao, and Yantai providing international service.

GOVERNMENT AND SOCIETY

Shandong is divided into seventeen prefecture-level municipalities (*dijishi*). At the next lower administrative level, there are districts under municipalities (*shixiaqu*), counties (*xian*), and county-level municipalities (*xianjishi*).

CONSTITUTIONAL FRAMEWORK

The Shandong Provincial Revolutionary Committee, the chief provincial administrative body from 1967, was replaced in 1980 by the People's Government, which is the administrative arm of the People's Congress. Until the early 1980s, the rural "people's communes," made up of production teams and brigades, served as the lowest administrative units. With the institution of family farms as the primary production units, commune labour allocation, production, and marketing have virtually ceased to be important. In many areas, county seats operate as

coordinating centres for the production and distribution of commodities produced in the areas under their administrative jurisdiction.

HEALTH AND WELFARE

Before 1949 Shandong was particularly hard-pressed by the pressure of population on the land; by the common occurrence—especially since the latter half of the 19th century—of floods, droughts, dust storms, excessive soil salinization and alkalinization, and insect infestations; and by frequent military and civil disturbances. Few serious attempts were made by officials of either the Qing (Manchu) dynasty (1644–1911/12) or, later, by the Republic of China to ameliorate the difficult social conditions of the peasant population. With the exception of missionary-financed and missionary-controlled undertakings in areas under foreign influence or administration, such as Qingdao, Yantai, and Jinan, modern intensive health care facilities were virtually nonexistent, and there was only token support for public higher education. Water supplies, sanitation facilities, and public housing were similarly inadequate to the needs of the populace, and public health services were neglected and understaffed.

Since 1949 the public health services in both rural and urban areas have been improved, and formerly common ailments such as kala-azar (a severe infectious disease transmitted by the sand fly), leprosy, and a variety of nutritional-deficiency diseases have been eliminated. All large and medium-size cities now have adequate water-supply systems, often built in conjunction with multipurpose water-conservancy schemes to improve and stabilize the watersheds of nearby rivers. Along with water supply, the construction of sewage-treatment facilities in many cities has helped raise public health standards. The commercialization of health care systems in the 1990s caused difficulties for many rural people who could not afford the services. More recently, efforts have been made to reestablish public health care and social security systems.

Not only has extensive tree planting enhanced the beauty of most Shandong cities, but "greening" has been officially designated a primary task of urban reconstruction in order to ameliorate the effects of the harsh climate and to improve health conditions. Afforestation efforts in Qingdao have been especially extensive; tree coverage in and around the city now exceeds one-third of the municipality's total land area. In Jinan a greenbelt has been built on the site of some dilapidated sections of the ancient city wall. Along with urban reforestation, recreational facilities have been expanded, improved, and made readily available for public use.

EDUCATION

Most of Shandong's institutions of higher education are located in the provincial capital, Jinan, with smaller or special-purpose schools scattered widely throughout the province. Among those in Jinan are Shandong University (established 1901), Shandong University of Traditional Chinese Medicine (1958), and Shandong Normal University (1950). Qingdao is China's major centre for research training in marine science and technology; institutions include the Institute of Oceanology of the Academia Sinica (Chinese Academy of Sciences) and the Ocean University of China (1924), which is under the jurisdiction of the national-level Ministry of Education. Other major institutions include the China University of Petroleum (1953, East China campus) in Dongying, the Shandong Agricultural University (1906) in Tai'an, and the Shandong University of Technology (1956) in Zibo.

CULTURAL LIFE

Shandong is the ancestral home of both Confucius and Mencius. Its rich cultural and folklore tradition is most clearly evidenced in the temples, shrines, legends, and cults associated with Mount Tai and with the temple, tomb, and ancestral home of Confucius and the Kong family (Confucius's lineal descendants) at Qufu, northeast of Jining. Most of the temples, shrines, and their surrounding areas either have survived or have been restored, renovated, and converted to public parks so as to assure their preservation as important symbols of the national cultural heritage. Both Mount Tai and the Qufu sites were designated

UNESCO World Heritage sites, in 1987 and 1994, respectively.

Mount Tai—known also as Dongyue, or "Eastern Mountain," to distinguish it from the southern Mount Heng (in Hunan), the central Mount Song (Henan), the western Mount Hua (Shaanxi), and the northern Mount Heng (Shanxi)—is the most prominent of these five sacred mountains where the emperors once offered sacrifices to Heaven and Earth. It was also the place where for centuries Buddhists, Daoists, and Confucianists built more than 250 temples and monuments to honour deified historical personages and to immortalize the sacred presence and supernatural powers of the supreme mountain deity of Mount Tai. The mountain was deified at least as early as Han times, and in the Song dynasty (960–1279) it was elevated by the Zhenzong emperor to the position of "Equal with Heaven." Incantations and prayers offered to the deity of Mount Tai by countless emperors are inscribed in stelae along the ascent to the summit, and temples are distributed in Tai'an and on the mountain itself.

The Temple of Confucius, Confucius's tomb, and the residence of the Kong at Qufu are also maintained as national historic monuments. Both the temple and the Kong residence are laid out with elaborate temples, monuments, pavilions, and gates and have collections of stelae dating in some cases from the Han dynasty.

Many famous temples, hot springs, shrines, parks, lakes, and museums are frequented by the populace in other locales. In Jinan—a city famous for its hot springs, where for centuries poets, scholars, and officials enjoyed diverse pleasures—several new parks have been built and old buildings restored. Qingdao, known as the most pleasant beach resort in North China, is also famous for its parks and for Mount Lao, which lies a short distance to the east-northeast along the coast. Coastal resorts also sprang up on the northern shore of the Shandong Peninsula—for example, at Penglai (with its renowned Penglai Pavilion complex) northwest of Yantai, Yantai itself, and Liugongdao Island at Weihai.

Shandong's cuisine constitutes one of the distinctive cooking styles of the country. It is notable for its use of a wide variety of seafood, especially in coastal areas, as well as onions and salt. Inland, in the Jinan area, dishes tend to feature meats and soups. Whereas coastal cooking typically consists of quick stir-frying or deep-frying, Jinan-style dishes commonly are stewed or slow cooked. Another notable feature of Shandong cuisine are its steamed breads, which often are served in lieu of rice.

HISTORY

A Neolithic culture—known as the Longshan because of archaeological remains discovered near the township of that name—existed on the Shandong Peninsula in the 3rd millennium BCE. It played a key role in the establishment of a common rice-based cultural grouping that apparently spread along the Pacific seaboard from the peninsula to Taiwan and to the area that is now eastern Guangdong province.

Western Shandong formed part of the territory of the Shang dynasty (c. 1600–1046 BCE). By the Spring and Autumn (Chunqiu) period (770–476 BCE) it had become the centre of political and military activity that resulted from the eastward expansion of the Zhou dynasty, following their conquest of the Shang. A small state in southwestern Shandong was Lu, the birthplace of Confucius and Mencius. Also in the "Eastern Territory"—an early name for Shandong—was Qi, extending over the major part of the peninsula; it became an important economic centre, exporting hemp clothing, silk, fish, salt, and a unique variety of purple cloth to all parts of China. Beginning in the Six Dynasties period (220–589 CE), Shandong became North China's leading maritime centre, receiving commodities from the South China coastal area (now Fujian and Guangdong provinces) for transshipment to destinations north and south of the Huang He. Thus, Shandong has been an integral part of China from its very beginning as an organized state.

In 1293 the Grand Canal, running generally north to south, was completed, making western Shandong a major inland trading route. Yet even after completion of the canal, maritime trade remained important to Shandong, and the peninsula retained its dominant economic position. In the great agricultural areas of the province, however, early deforestation and the long-established practice of clearing land for cultivation without providing for flood prevention and control measures led to serious and ultimately disastrous erosion and wastage of valuable agricultural land.

In the 19th century, these problems were worsened by shifts in the course of the Huang He. From 1194 until the early 1850s, the Huang He followed the original bed of the Huai River along the Shandong-Jiangsu border before emptying into the Yellow Sea. After 1855, when a series of devastating floods was followed by extensive dike construction, the river changed to its present course some 250 miles (400 km) to the north. Hardships and food shortages from floods and other natural calamities increased in intensity throughout the 19th and 20th centuries. This resulted in a substantial emigration of Shandong peasants to the Northeast (Manchuria) and to Inner Mongolia and Korea, with more than four million people emigrating between 1923 and 1930.

In the closing decade of the 19th century, Shandong came under the influence of German, British, and Japanese interests. It was occupied briefly by Japanese troops after the Sino-Japanese War of 1894–95. In 1897 Germany landed troops, and in 1898 a treaty was signed by which China ceded to Germany, for 99 years, two entries to Jiaozhou Bay and the islands in the bay and granted the right to construct a naval base and port, Qingdao. Germany used Qingdao as a base from which to extend its commercial influence throughout the peninsula; it developed coal mines and constructed a railway (1905) from Qingdao to Jinan. Similarly, in 1898 Great Britain obtained a lease for Weihaiwei (present-day Weihai), another strategic port near the northern tip of the peninsula. This was in response to the Russian occupation of Port Arthur (now the Lüshunkou district of the city of Dalian). With the advent of World War I, Japan took over German interests in the peninsula and in 1915, as one of its infamous Twenty-One Demands, compelled the Chinese to give official recognition to the renewed occupation. Taking up the Shandong question, the imperialist powers decided in 1919 to grant Japanese occupation, which Japan maintained until 1922.

In the Sino-Japanese War of 1937–45, even though the Japanese had gained control of most of Shandong by the end of 1937, they miscalculated Chinese strength and suffered a serious defeat—their first of the war—at Tai'erzhuang, in southern Shandong, in 1938. In the postwar struggle between the Chinese communists and the Nationalists, Shandong came under communist control by the end of 1948.

GUANGDONG

Guangdong (conventional Kwangtung) is the major province of southern China. It is the southernmost of the mainland provinces and constitutes the region through which southern China's trade is primarily channeled. The capital is Guangzhou (Canton), at the head of the Pearl (Zhu) River Delta.

Historically, Guangdong and Guangxi to the west often were jointly governed. Guangdong was first administered as a separate entity in 997 CE; it was from this time that the term Guangdong ("Eastern Expanses") began to be used. Guangdong has its own physical and cultural identity. Its topography separates it somewhat from the rest of China, and this factor—together with its long coastline, its contact with other countries through its overseas emigrants, and its early exposure to Western influence through the port of Guangzhou—resulted in the emergence of a degree of self-sufficiency and separatism. Guangzhou long dominated the province to an unusual extent, though that dominance has lessened somewhat as Hong Kong has been reintegrated back into China and cities around the Pearl River Delta (notably Shenzhen) have risen in prominence. Guangdong's area measures about 76,100 square miles (197,100 square km). Its population numbered 93,570,000 according to a 2007 estimate.

LAND

Guangdong has one of the longest coastlines of any Chinese province, fronting the South China Sea to the southeast and south (including connections to the special administrative regions of Hong Kong and Macau). It is also bounded by the Zhuang Autonomous Region of Guangxi to the west and by the provinces of Hunan and Jiangxi to the north and Fujian to the northeast.

RELIEF

The surface configuration in Guangdong is diverse, being composed primarily of rounded hills, cut by streams and rivers, and scattered and ribbonlike alluvial valleys. Together with the Guangxi region, Guangdong is clearly separated from the Yangtze River basin by the Nan Mountains, the southernmost of the major Chinese mountain ranges running from east to west. The greater part of eastern Guangdong consists of the southerly extension of the Southern Uplands, which stretch down from Fujian and Zhejiang provinces. A series of longitudinal valleys running from northeast to southwest extends as far as the vicinity of Guangzhou (Canton). Smooth, low hills cover about 70 percent of the province. Most peaks range in elevation from 1,500 to 2,500 feet (450 to 750 m), with a few reaching 5,500 feet (1,675 m) or more. Level land is primarily found in the alluvial deltas, formed where rivers empty into the South China Sea.

DRAINAGE

Of great extent and importance in Guangdong is the Pearl River Delta. Measuring about 2,900 square miles (7,500 square km), it is marked by hilly outliers and by a labyrinth of canalized channels and distributaries totaling some

1,500 miles (2,400 km) in length. The delta marks the convergence of the three major rivers of the Xi River system—the Xi (West), Bei (North), and Dong (East) rivers. The Pearl River itself, extending southward from Guangzhou, receives the Dong River and opens into its triangular estuary that has Macau (west) and Hong Kong (east) at its mouth. Entirely rainfed, these rivers are subject to extreme seasonal fluctuations, and they collect so much water that, anomalously, the Xi system discharges six and a half times as much water annually as the Huang He (Yellow River) although its basin area is only about half as large.

Altogether, Guangdong has some 1,300 large and small rivers. The Han is the most important river outside the Pearl system. Other important rivers and lowlands are located in the southwest. The middle and lower courses of many of these rivers have become seriously polluted since the late 1990s, caused by vast quantities of untreated sewage and wastewater pouring into them from the province's rapidly growing urban and industrial areas.

CLIMATE

Since much of Guangdong lies south of the Tropic of Cancer, it is one of the Chinese provinces with tropical and subtropical climates. The average July temperature in the Xi River valley, which is 82 to 86 °F (28 to 30 °C), is little different from temperatures in the lower

The Pearl River flowing past Guangzhou, Shandong province, China, before emptying into the South China Sea. China Tourism Press/Riser/Getty Images

Yangtze and on the Huang He, but the average January temperature is considerably higher, ranging from 55 to 61 °F (13 to 16 °C). Except at higher elevations, frost is rare, so that almost the entire province lies within the area where two crops of rice can be grown. True winter does not occur in the province, but the hot summer varies in length from about 10 months in the south to 6 months in the north.

The rainfall regime shows a pronounced summer maximum, with the rainy season lasting from mid-April, when Guangdong starts to be dominated by moisture-laden tropical air masses from the Equator and the Indian Ocean, until mid-October. More than half of the total precipitation falls between June and August. The months between July and September form the main season for typhoons (tropical cyclones), which ordinarily are accompanied by heavy rains and widespread destruction. The driest period is from December to February. Guangdong's annual rainfall is approximately 60 to 80 inches (150 to 200 cm), decreasing with distance from the coast to the northwest but increasing with altitude and exposure to the prevailing summer monsoon winds.

SOILS

In general, the province's soils are poor, as high temperatures and plentiful rainfall result in podzolization (bleaching) and leaching. Almost all of western Guangdong is covered with mature red soils, whereas the rest of the province is covered with a mixture of old and young red soils that usually have been subjected to a high degree of podzolization. In the wettest and hottest parts of Guangdong, lateritic (heavily leached, iron-bearing) soils are common; like the red soils, they do not resist erosion and require substantial fertilizing for cultivation. Yellow soils are found in the wettest and coolest parts of Guangdong, occurring in small pockets of flatland with imperfect drainage.

Of more limited distribution but of greater economic significance are the alluviums deposited in the river valleys and deltas. As a result of the cultivation of rice, the alluviums have developed special morphological characteristics, the most striking of which is the formation of iron hardpans (hard impervious layers composed chiefly of clay) in the zone of the fluctuating water table.

PLANT AND ANIMAL LIFE

Abundant moisture, moderate to high temperatures, and variegated physiography support Guangdong's luxuriant and highly diversified plant growth. Broad-leaved evergreen forests, intermixed with coniferous and deciduous trees, originally covered much of the land, while a more tropical type of vegetation predominates on the south coast. With the exception of the more remote mountainous areas, much of this natural vegetation cover has been stripped by fire and by the use of trees and shrubs for fuel. This circumstance, together with millennia of uninterrupted cultivation, has resulted in much of the natural vegetation now taking the form of secondary forests of hardwoods and horsetail pine. On the more severely eroded hills, coarse grasses and ferns have taken hold. Bamboo groves, varying greatly in height and extent, are widespread, particularly in humid river valleys. The most productive and least disturbed forests cover the mountainous areas. Certain trees, notably camphor, have been revered and protected for centuries and are found around cultivated fields. Since 1949, massive afforestation programs have been undertaken. In the highlands, where coniferous and deciduous species thrive together, the broad-leaved evergreen forests are characterized by tropical oaks, tan oaks (oaks that yield tannin), and chestnut oaks (or chinquapins). The more significant coniferous species of economic value include horsetail pine, Chinese fir, and Chinese hemlock. Some of the species of cypress and pine are little known outside China. Truly tropical monsoon rainforests are common in the south.

Among the mammals found in Guangdong are many tropical bats, and squirrels, mice, and rats of many species are abundant. Insectivores are generally more diverse than in other regions of China, and carnivores are exemplified by civet cats and small-clawed otters. Types of birds vary according to habitat. In the tropical forest, wildfowl, peacocks, and silver pheasants are common. Reptiles are more restricted in distribution. Guangdong has a number of pit vipers, including the huge and deadly Chinese vipers and bamboo vipers, as well as non-poisonous pythons, which can grow up to 20 feet (6 m) long. Insects of every description—crickets, butterflies, dragon-flies, grasshoppers, cicadas, and beetles—are found in profusion. Amphibians include ground burrowers and many types of frogs and toads. Tigers, rhinoceroses, leopards, wolves, bears, and foxes once roamed the hills of Guangdong, but their numbers have been decimated by forest fires, persistent deforestation, and hunting; they are now considered to be nearly extinct in the area. In the tropical monsoon forest, how-ever, a great number of animals, many of which live in the trees, still remain. In addition, dozens of natural protection zones have been set up in the province to provide refuge for those endangered species.

People

Guangdong is the second most populous political unit in China, behind only Henan province in the north. It also has one of the highest population densities in the country.

Population Composition

Guangdong is populated largely by the Han (Chinese), the other ethnic minori-ties totaling only a tiny portion of its population. The Yao are the largest eth-nic minority in Guangdong and are concentrated principally near its north-western border in autonomous counties. A heavily Sinicized group, the Zhuang, live in northwestern Guangdong in Lianshan. Another group, the She, live in the northeast and in the north around Shaoguan, notably in an autonomous county west of the city. The Jing were transferred to Guangxi in 1965, when the multinational Dongxing (now Fangcheng) autonomous county in extreme south-western Guangdong changed its provincial jurisdiction. The so-called Boat People—the Tan (Dan) or Tanka (Danjia in the Cantonese language)—are not officially designated as a national minority. Whereas some scholars believe they are descendants of aboriginal peo-ple, others regard them simply as a people who live on boats and speak Cantonese. They generally live along the rivers in the Xi-Pearl basin as well as along the coast.

The relative ethnic homogeneity pre-vailing in Guangdong stands in contrast to the great diversity of dialects and lan-guages. By far the most important of these is Cantonese, spoken in central and western Guangdong. Once thought to be a dialect of Chinese, Cantonese is now considered to be a language in its own right. There is considerable variety among the Cantonese speakers, but the form spoken in Guangzhou is generally regarded as the standard. Hakka is another important language, which predominates in the north and northeast areas of the province. Offshoots of Hakka are common in central Guangdong. A third major language, Southern Min (Minnan), is spoken mostly along an eastern coastal area centred on Shantou (Swatow).

In addition to these Sinitic languages, there are the languages and dialects of the ethnic minorities. New scripts have been created for a number of these languages. They not only are taught in minority-area schools but also are used in conjunction with Chinese in official communications in minority communities.

Ancestor worship, folk religions, and the institutional religions of Daoism, Buddhism, Christianity, and Islam coexist in the province, as they do in most places in China. Among these religions, ancestor worship has the most pervasive influence. Although some folk religions are national in outlook, others are of a more regional or local character, such as the worship of Tianhou Shenmu, the goddess of fishing and navigation. With the possible exception of Muslims and Christians, people in Guangdong are polytheistic, visiting temples or priests of different faiths as occasions demand.

SETTLEMENT PATTERNS

About two-fifths of the people of the province live in villages, which remain the basic functional units in the countryside. The greatest numbers of villages are in the fertile river deltas and along the waterways. To an even greater extent, towns and cities are located in the deltas and coastal areas and along major communication lines. The most highly urbanized area within the province is the Pearl River Delta, where the great majority of the population lives in urban areas. Guangdong is a relatively highly urbanized province for China, with its largest urban agglomeration centred on Guangzhou. However, Shenzhen and Shantou are major metropolises as well, and Foshan, Shaoguan, Jiangmen, Zhuhai, and Zhanjiang are important municipalities. Guangzhou and Zhanjiang (on the Leizhou Peninsula in the southwest) were designated "open" coastal cities in the early 1980s and have become central to the planning of the province's economic future. Also at that time, Shantou (on the eastern coast) and Shenzhen and Zhuhai (situated near Hong Kong and Macau, respectively) were designated special economic zones, each becoming a major economic influence in the region.

DEMOGRAPHIC TRENDS

Guangdong's population has grown dramatically since 1980, nearly doubling in size since then. This increase is largely because of the influx of millions of people who work in the factories of the coastal cities. Some two-thirds of the province's residents are now classified as urban. In addition to the growth of Guangdong's permanent population, there also has been a significant rise in the number of people who spend part of the year there in factory jobs before returning to their home provinces.

ECONOMY

For centuries the economic foundation of Guangdong was primarily agriculture, but that sector's proportion of the provincial economy has been declining since the mid-1980s. In part, this is because rapid urbanization from the late 1980s has encroached on the croplands around major municipalities, seriously reducing agricultural production there. In addition the relative value of manufactured goods in the provincial economy has risen dramatically since that time.

AGRICULTURE

Rice is the leading crop. Since less than one-fifth of the land is under cultivation, agriculture is of necessity extremely intensive; but the limited extent of sown land available is partly offset by repeated use of it. Progress in irrigation and flood control has made water control possible for almost all of the cultivated area, producing good rice yields. Farming and irrigation have become increasingly mechanized, with more reliance placed on the use of chemical fertilizers.

Two crops of rice a year can be grown on most cultivated land, and in the Pearl River Delta three crops are not unusual. Thus, although average yields per harvest are below the national average, annual yields exceed the average. Although food-grain crops occupy almost all of the total cultivated area, the industrial and fruit crops grown on the remaining land are of national importance. Guangdong annually produces much of China's total output of sugarcane. In tropical Guangdong a number of industrial crops are successfully raised, including rubber, sisal, palm oil, hemp, coffee, and black pepper. Other traditional agricultural products include sweet potatoes, peanuts (groundnuts), and tea. No less than 300 types of fruits are grown, among the more representative of which are citrus, litchi, pineapples, and bananas.

Guangdong, with its long coastline, produces about one-fifth of China's fish. Fish production accounts for as much as one-third of the income of some localities. More than 400 species of saltwater fish, including yellow croaker, white herring, mackerel, golden thread, and pomfret, are caught from numerous fishing ports. Fish breeding in ponds or along riverbanks and seacoasts has flourished.

RESOURCES AND MANUFACTURING

In the first half of the 20th century, Guangdong experienced modern growth as Guangzhou developed into an industrial, commercial, and transportation centre. But because of the paucity of its iron deposits, Guangdong received only scant attention during the First Five-Year Plan (1953–57). The discovery of other mineral deposits, however, prompted the development of some heavier industries, including metal and petrochemical processing, the manufacturing of machinery, and shipbuilding and ship repairing. A large proportion of these industries is still concentrated in Guangzhou.

Coal reserves and manganese deposits are located mainly in the north and northeast near Shaoguan and Meizhou, although some lower-grade coal is found on the Leizhou Peninsula. Oil shale deposits have been discovered near Maoming, just north of the peninsula. Tungsten, which is associated with bismuth, molybdenum, and tin deposits, is mined near the Jiangxi border, where uranium is also found. The province has reserves of germanium and tellurium and produces some lead and antimony.

Light industry has always been of significance in the province. Apart from handicrafts, light industry—especially food processing and the manufacturing of textiles—accounts for a large section of industrial production. After three of China's first four special economic zones were established in the province in the early 1980s, light industrial production grew dramatically, especially the manufacturing of garments, shoes, and soft drinks. However, since the turn of the 21st century, the proportion of the output value for light industry in the provincial economy has decreased dramatically compared with other quickly developing industrial sectors, notably electronics and information technology. Other major manufactures include automobiles and motorcycles, electric machinery, petrochemicals, building materials, paper, and pharmaceuticals. A large proportion of these industries are export-oriented, notably those factories established in the three special economic zones.

TRANSPORTATION

Economically and culturally, the different regions of Guangdong are linked by the waterways of the Pearl River system. In addition, a number of coastal and international shipping routes are variously linked to more than 100 large and small ports. The leading ports, including Huangpu (Guangzhou's seaport), Zhanjiang, and Shantou, are of national significance. Water transportation accounts for more than two-fifths of Guangdong's total traffic tonnage. The waterways are maintained by continually dredging, widening, and clearing the channels.

Connections with other provinces depend principally on land transportation. Guangdong has developed one of the best highway networks in China, running primarily along river valleys. Interprovincial links, both for highways and railroads, usually run north-south.

The vital Beijing-Guangzhou railroad was double-tracked in the early 1960s. Another major north-south line, from Beijing to Kowloon (Jiulong) in Hong Kong, was opened in the mid-1990s. The low priority placed on east-west transportation is indicated by the absence of a railroad running parallel to the Xi River and by the fact that the Guangzhou-Zhanjiang line was opened only in 1963. However, this line, connected with a line (completed 1956) that runs northwest to Litang in Guangxi, links the province by rail with its western neighbouring province. A new railroad connecting Guangzhou with Shantou via Meizhou (north of Shantou) opened in the mid-1990s and was extended eastward into Fujian province in 2000. In addition, a number of express highways have been built connecting Guangdong's major cities and Hong Kong and Macau with neighbouring provinces, except the island province of Hainan.

Guangdong provides a crucial link in China's domestic and international civil aviation routes. Air services connect the province to numerous international cities. To cope with the increasing traffic, Guangzhou's Baiyun airport has been enlarged and modernized.

GOVERNMENT AND SOCIETY

The administrative system in Guangdong has undergone many changes since the establishment of communist rule in 1949.

CONSTITUTIONAL FRAMEWORK

Autonomous administrative units were created in the early 1950s for areas with large ethnic minority populations. The status of Guangzhou was changed in 1954 from a centrally administered municipality (*tebieshi*) to a prefecture-level municipality (*dijishi*) under the jurisdiction of the provincial government. Guangdong is subdivided into twenty other prefecture-level municipalities in addition to Guangzhou. Guangdong is further divided into districts under the municipalities (*shixiaqu*), counties (*xian*), autonomous counties (*zizhixian*), and county-level municipalities (*xianjishi*). Rural administration was reorganized in 1958 when communization replaced the administrative villages, market towns, and municipal districts. In 1980–81 the government implemented a policy of greater decentralized economic management, and the communes lost their administrative role.

HEALTH AND WELFARE

In general, hospitals, clinics, and many health stations, including maternity centres, are available at the local level. Better-equipped and better-staffed hospitals are maintained at the county and provincial levels. Medical education has been greatly expanded and includes a university devoted to Chinese medicine (acupuncture and herbal medicine). Many short-term medical-training classes are organized for health workers assigned to rural areas. The development of medical services, coupled with the general improvement in sanitation and health education, has succeeded in eliminating many previously common diseases such as malaria, schistosomiasis, and filariasis.

EDUCATION

Education, health, and other social conditions in Guangdong have generally been improved since 1949. There are now many more kindergartens and nurseries for preschool education, secondary schools, and postsecondary schools and universities. Repeated campaigns have succeeded in reducing illiteracy throughout the province. Special attention has been given to the education of the ethnic minorities. New schools, including a national minority college, have been established in minority communities. Dozens of higher learning institutions are located in different cities in the province, notably in Guangzhou, including Sun Yat-sen University (founded 1924), South China University of Technology (1952), Jinan University (1927), and Guangzhou University of Chinese Medicine (1956).

CULTURAL LIFE

Guangdong has long been noted for the distinctive cultural traits of its people, as evidenced by the variety of dialects spoken. Guangdong is famous for its two types of local opera: the Yue Opera and the Chao Opera, which are popular among the Cantonese and Fujianese communities. Guangdong also has some characteristic puppet plays. The hand puppets of Guangzhou are distinguished by their size—they are between 3 to 4 feet (about 1 m) high—and by the beautiful carving of their wooden heads. Many places in Guangdong have distinctive forms of folk art; examples are the woodcuts of Chaozhou and the stone engravings of Shunde.

Cantonese food is widely recognized as among the most distinctive in China and is the best-known Chinese cuisine worldwide. It is characterized by the use of a variety of fresh ingredients, minimal seasoning, and quick cooking (typically, by stir-frying). Living in a coastal province, the people are particularly fond of seafood. Especially in winter, the "big-headed fish" (tench) is often served raw in a fish salad—a departure from habitual Chinese culinary practice. Some other food habits, such as the eating of newborn rats, monkey's brain, and fried snake, are regarded as revolting by most Chinese in other provinces. Chinese who have returned from Southeast Asia have popularized the chewing of betel nut wrapped in cockscomb (Celosia cristata) leaves. Special congees (rice or millet gruels) and soups with different ingredients are also often served in Cantonese cuisine.

Guangdong is a province where lineage—an important social institution in

China—has been emphasized. The importance of ancestry is often reflected in the settlement pattern of lineage groups. The inhabitants of many villages belong exclusively to one or two lineages. In such villages, community and lineage organizations are virtually identical. Conflicts between lineages were once common and often took the form of community strife, with bitter vendettas sometimes lasting for long periods of time.

With the founding of the new regime in 1949, systematic efforts were made to change these cultural patterns in accordance with governmental ideology and policy, although in the early 1980s limited religious practice was again allowed. On the other hand, many aspects of traditional culture, especially the folk arts and the theatre, were revived and extolled.

Guangdong has a wealth of tourist attractions. Major scenic areas include Zhaoxing Lake near Zhaoqing, Mount Danxia at Renhua, and Mount Xiqiao at Nanhai. In addition, Dinghu Mountain at Zhaoqing, Ancestral Temple (Zumiao) at Foshan, and the Sun Yat-sen Memorial Hall and Huanghuagang Park in Guangzhou are all noted tourist destinations.

Many of Guangdong's handicrafts are exquisite specialties. These include red sandalwood furniture, rattan chairs, Guangdong embroidery (characterized by the use of handmade silk), drawnwork (a specialized style of needlework) from Chaozhou and Shantou, ivory carvings from Guangzhou, pottery from Shiwan, fireworks from Dongguan, and ink slabs from Zhaoqing—all of which are known throughout the country.

HISTORY

Physically separated from the early centres of Chinese civilization in North China, Guangdong was originally occupied by non-Han ethnic groups. It was first incorporated into the Chinese empire in 222 BCE, when Shihuangdi, first emperor of the Qin dynasty, conquered the area along the Xi and Bei river valleys down to the Pearl River Delta. In 111 BCE Chinese domination was extended to the whole of what is now Guangdong, including Hainan, during the reign (141–87 BCE) of the Wudi emperor of the Han dynasty (206 BCE–220 CE). The conquest, however, was not followed by successful colonization, and Guangdong remained part of the empire only politically.

The military and agricultural colonization of Guangdong gradually took place during the five centuries of the Sui, Tang, and Bei (Northern) Song dynasties (i.e., from 581 to 1127). This colonization, combined with increasing overseas trade channeled through Guangzhou (Canton), led to an increase of migration into Guangdong and to the emergence of Guangzhou as a metropolis with a population of hundreds of thousands. At the end of the period, however, Guangdong was still occupied predominantly by its original ethnic population. The region was viewed as a semicivilized frontier, and disgraced officials often were exiled there.

The southward thrust of the Han was greatly intensified from 1126, when the Juchen of the Jin dynasty captured the Bei Song capital at what is now Kaifeng, forcing the Song to migrate south. Another major population movement followed a century and a half later as China fell to the Mongols. These migrations marked the beginning of effective Han occupation and the rapid cultural development of Guangdong. Especially after the 16th century, the growth of population was so fast that by the late 17th century the Guangdong region had become a source of emigration. Migrants from Guangdong moved first to Guangxi, Sichuan, and Taiwan and then in the mid-19th century began to pour into Southeast Asia and North America. Some were also taken as indentured labourers to British, French, and Dutch colonies.

Since the mid-19th century, Guangdong has produced a number of prominent political and military, as well as intellectual, leaders. Many of the leaders of political movements during this period—such as Hong Xiuquan, leader of the Taiping Rebellion (1850–64); Kang Youwei and Liang Qichao of the Reform Movement (1898); and Sun Yat-sen (Sun Zhongshan), who led the republican Chinese Revolution of 1911–12—had associations with Guangdong.

In the 1920s Chiang Kai-shek (Jiang Jieshi) made Guangzhou the base from which his program to reunify China under Nationalist rule was launched. Foreign privileges in the city were reduced, and modernization of the economy was undertaken. The almost simultaneous rise of the communist movement and the advent of Japanese aggression in the 1930s, however, thwarted the plans of Chiang and the Nationalists. From 1939 to 1945, the Japanese occupied southern Guangdong province. After World War II the conflict between the communists and the Nationalists erupted into full-scale civil war and continued until the communist victory in late 1949.

SICHUAN

Sichuan (conventional Szechwan) province is located in the upper Yangtze River (Chang Jiang) valley in the southwestern part of the country. Sichuan is the second largest of the Chinese provinces. The capital, Chengdu, is located near the centre of the province.

From economic, political, geographical, and historical points of view, the heart and nerve centre of Sichuan is in the eastern Sichuan Basin area, also called the Red Basin (Hongpen). Its mild and humid climate, fertile soil, and abundant mineral and forestry resources make it one of the most prosperous and economically self-sufficient regions of China. The area has been seen by some as China in a microcosm and is often viewed as a country within a country. The Chinese call the basin Tianfu Zhi Guo, meaning "Heaven on Earth."

Sichuan's area measures approximately 188,000 square miles (487,000 square km). Its population as estimated in 2007 numbered 81,690,000.

Land

Sichuan is bordered by the provinces of Gansu and Shaanxi to the north, the territory of Chongqing municipality to the east, the provinces of Guizhou and Yunnan to the south, the Tibet Autonomous Region to the west, and the province of Qinghai to the northwest.

Relief

The Sichuan Basin is bounded on all sides by lofty highlands. To the north the Qin (Tsinling) Mountains extend from east to west and attain an elevation between 11,000 and 13,000 feet (3,400 and 4,000 m) above sea level. The limestone Daba Mountains rise to approximately 9,000 feet (2,700 m) on the northeast, while the Dalou Mountains, a lower and less continuous range with an average elevation of 5,000 to 7,000 feet (1,500 to 2,100 m), border the south. To the west the Daxue Mountains of the Tibetan borderland rise to an average elevation of 14,500 feet (4,400 m). To the east the rugged Wu Mountains, rising to about 6,500 feet (2,000 m), contain the spectacular Yangtze Gorges.

In general, the relief of the eastern region of Sichuan province is in sharp contrast to that of the west. The extensive Sichuan Basin and its peripheral highlands predominate in the east; the land slopes toward the centre of the basin from all directions. This basin was a gulf of the China Sea in the later Paleozoic Era (which ended about 250 million years ago); most of it is underlain by soft sandstones and shales that range in colour from red to purple.

Within the basin the surface is extremely uneven and gives a general appearance of badland topography. Numerous low, rolling hills are interspersed with well-defined high ridges, floodplains, valley flats, and small local basins. The most impressive portion of the basin's surface is the Chengdu Plain—the only large continuous tract of relatively flat land in the province.

The landforms of western Sichuan include a plateau in the north and mountains in the south. The northern area is part of the edge of the Plateau of Tibet, which consists of highlands above 12,000 feet (3,700 m) and higher mountain ranges. There is also an extensive plateau and some swampland. To the south the transverse mountain belt of eastern Tibet and western Yunnan province rises to an average of 9,000 to 10,000 feet (2,700 to 3,000 m). Trending from north to south is a series of parallel lofty ranges with narrow divides and canyons more than a mile deep. Mount Gongga (Minya Konka), in the Daxue range, is the highest peak in the province, rising to a height of 24,790 feet (7,556 m).

Sichuan lies in a highly active seismic zone. The eastern portion of the province is part of a relatively small crustal block that is being compressed by the mountainous western portion of Sichuan as it is displaced eastward by the constant northward movement of India against southern Asia. Over the centuries

Chinese soldiers search through rubble in Beichuan, Sichuan province, China, after a massive earthquake ravaged much of the province in 2008. Paula Bronstein/Getty Images

this activity has produced numerous strong earthquakes, including one in 1933 that killed nearly 10,000 people and a much more severe quake in 2008 that caused tens of thousands of deaths, hundreds of thousands of injuries, and widespread damage in the affected area (including Chengdu).

DRAINAGE

Seen from the air, the principal drainage pattern of the eastern section of Sichuan has the appearance of a leaf with a network of veins. The Yangtze—flowing from west to east—is conspicuous as its midrib, and the main north and south tributaries appear as its branch veins. Especially important are the Jialing and Min river systems in the north. The distribution of these veins is primarily concentrated in the upper, or northern, half of the leaf.

The four main tributaries of the Yangtze are the Min, Tuo, Jialing, and Fu rivers, which flow from north to south. Most of the major streams flow to the south, cutting steep gorges in the west or widening their valley floors in the soft sediments of the Sichuan Basin; they then empty into the Yangtze before it slices its precipitous gorge through the Wu River below Wanxian (now in Chongqing municipality). Within the basin most of the rivers are navigable and are a common means of transportation.

SOILS

Sichuan has six major soil regions—three in the east and three in the west. In the east they include the highly fertile purple-brown forest soils for which the Red Basin is named. This group of soils rapidly absorbs and loses water, and it erodes easily. The other eastern soils consist of the noncalcareous alluvium and rice paddy soils of the Chengdu Plain and other river valleys and the yellow earths of the highlands and ridges. The alluvial soils are the most important group agriculturally, as they are highly fertile and are formed mainly from the rich black soils washed down from the Tibetan borderlands. The yellow earths are usually gray-brown in colour, are generally less fertile, and are agriculturally unimportant. The three major groups of soils in the west are the degenerated chernozem (dark-coloured soils containing deep, rich humus) soils of the Zoigê Marsh (Songpan Grasslands), the alluvial soils of the numerous valleys, and the podzolized (leached) gray-brown soils of the mountain slopes.

In Sichuan a form of soil erosion known as soil creep has developed. On hillsides where the surface slopes are composed of smooth sandstones, the covering soil gradually slides downward under the influence of gravity. In many places the thin surface soils have been completely removed, leaving only bare rocks. When the surface rock is composed of comparatively rougher shales, the soil is less easily moved.

CLIMATE

The eastern basin area and the lower western valleys are sheltered from cold polar air masses by the surrounding mountains. The climate is therefore milder than would be expected and is similar to that of the Yangtze delta region. The eastern basin has more than 300 frost-free days annually, and the growing season is nearly year-round. In the west the sheltering effect of the mountains is evident from the contrast between the perennially snowcapped peaks and the mild weather prevailing in the valleys beneath them. During the summer, in the month of July, the mean temperature is about 84 °F (29 °C) in the south and lower than 68 °F (20 °C) in most parts of the west. During the winter the mean temperature in the west decreases northward from 54 °F (12 °C) in Xichang to 18 °F (-8 °C) in Qianning.

The eastern rainy season begins in April and reaches its peak during July and August. Annual precipitation (generally as rain) measures about 40 inches (101 cm) annually. The east is noted for its frequent fogs, its many cloudy days, the relative absence of wind, and the high relative humidity. The extent to which the region is overcast is reflected in the saying, "Sichuan dogs bark when they see the Sun." Precipitation is lower in the west than in the east. The average total of about 20 inches (50 cm) falls mainly during the summer and early autumn, and there is heavy snowfall in the mountains during the winter.

PLANT AND ANIMAL LIFE

There are four major vegetation regions in Sichuan: the pine-cypress-banyan-bamboo association of the basin area, the dense mixed association of coniferous and deciduous trees in the eastern highlands, the grasslands of the northwest, and the dense coniferous forests of the western highlands. Sichuan's great differences in elevation, its low latitudinal position, its diversified topography, and its high rainfall make the area what has

Giant panda cubs play at the China Giant Panda Protection and Research Center in Sichuan province, China. Scientists estimate there are about 1,600 giant pandas living in reserves in the mountains of the province. China Photos/Getty Images

been called a paradise for botanists. Extensive forests grow on the upper slopes, and lush growths of rhododendrons are found below those forests, though still at high elevations; arid vegetation prevails on many canyon floors.

One of the outstanding features of vegetation of Sichuan province is its division into vertically differentiated zones. Cypress, palm, pine, bamboo, tung, and citrus fruit trees grow below 2,000 feet (600 m), while between 2,000 and 5,000 feet (600 and 1,500 m) there are evergreen forests and oaks. From 5,000 to 8,000 feet (1,500 and 2,400 m) the vegetation is characterized by dense groves of mixed coniferous trees. Between 8,500 and 11,500 feet (2,600 and 3,500 m) there is a subalpine zone of coniferous forest, while above 11,500 feet there are alpine zones of scrub and meadow up to the snow line, which occurs at 16,000 feet (4,900 m). One of the unique vegetational features is the presence of the dawn redwood (*Metasequoia glyptostroboides*)—a tree previously believed to be extinct—in the zone of mixed conifers.

Two of the most interesting indigenous animal species are the panda, or bear cat, and the *lingyang* (a special species of antelope). Both inhabit the highlands of western Sichuan, and both have become endangered because of overcutting of the vegetation that is the mainstay of their diet. However, the province is best known as the principal home of the world-famous and highly endangered giant panda, whose habitat is now largely confined to a series of protected areas in the mountains of central Sichuan; these reserves collectively were designated a UNESCO World Heritage site in 2006.

PEOPLE

Sichuan was the most populous province in China until Chongqing and adjacent areas were separated from it in order to create the independent province-level municipality in 1997. It still has the fourth largest population of all the provinces.

POPULATION COMPOSITION

Sichuan also has one of the most diversified ranges of ethnic groups in all of China, including Han (Chinese), Yi (Lolo), Tibetans, Miao (Hmong), Tujia, Hui (Chinese Muslims), and Qiang peoples. Most of the Han—who constitute the major part of the population—live in the basin region of the east. The Yi reside in the Liangshan Yi Autonomous Prefecture in the southwest, while the Tibetans are distributed in the plateau region of the west. The Miao live in the southern mountains, near Guizhou and Yunnan provinces. The Hui are concentrated in the Zoigê Marsh grasslands of the northwest and are also scattered in a number of districts in the east. The Qiang are concentrated in the Maoxian-Wenchuan area on both banks of the Min River.

The majority of the non-Han ethnic groups are fiercely independent and have maintained their traditional way of life. In most cases, they practice a mixture of agriculture, animal husbandry, and hunting. Among the Han there has been an influx of people from various neighbouring provinces, particularly from Hubei and Shaanxi. This immigration was especially intensified in the early part of the 18th century, as a result of the massacre of the people of Sichuan by a local warlord. The immigrants brought with them agricultural techniques that are reflected in the heterogeneity of present cultivation patterns.

There are three major linguistic groups: the Han, who speak Southern Mandarin; the Tibeto-Burman group, including the Tibetans and the Yi; and the Hui, who also speak Southern Mandarin but use Turkish or Arabic in their religious services. The Han practice a mixture of Confucianism, Buddhism, and Daoism. They do not maintain rigid boundaries in religious belief. The Tibetans follow their own form of Buddhism. Many people in the northwest profess Islam, while some hill peoples of the southwest practice traditional beliefs.

SETTLEMENT PATTERNS

As one of the most densely populated provinces of China, Sichuan may be compared to the Yangtze River delta and the North China Plain. Its population is unevenly distributed, however, with most people concentrated in the eastern part of the province. The majority of the population is rural. There are comparatively few large villages and nucleated hamlets, except for the provincial and prefectural capitals. In the hilly regions, farmsteads are scattered through generally small and irregular terraced fields. In the Chengdu Plain, the larger field units are commonly square or oblong in shape, and the farmsteads are surrounded by groves of banyan, cypress, mimosa, palm, or bamboo.

Most urban settlements give the appearance of being compactly built. Generally, the houses have only one story. There are no yards or sidewalks in front of the houses, which abut streets that are narrow and often are paved with limestone slabs. One of the outstanding features of urban settlement is the concentration of cities on river terraces, notably along the Yangtze River. Because water transportation is vital, large cities are always found wherever two major streams converge. Examples of such cities are Luzhou, at the juncture of the Yangtze and Tuo rivers, and Leshan, at the confluence of the Dadu and the Min. The principal characteristic of these urban sites is that their areas are limited by their locations, so that urban expansion is hindered; in addition, the hazards of flooding are always a problem. Chengdu, the provincial capital and Sichuan's largest city, is located in the centre of the Chengdu Plain.

ECONOMY

Sichuan, occupying an important position in the upper reaches of the Yangtze River, is the strongest province in western China in terms of overall economic strength. The Sichuan Basin has a good natural environment, abounds in specialty products, and commands an ample labour force. Despite having been reduced in size and population when its eastern part was made into Chongqing municipality in 1997, Sichuan is still one of the country's major provinces in terms of population, resources, economic development, and technological advancement. Its outputs of grain, meat, rapeseed, and silkworm cocoons are ranked among the highest in China. Completely integrated industrial sectors produce high-quality machinery, electronics, metallurgical products, chemicals, building materials, foodstuffs, and silk. Economic growth has been especially pronounced in Chengdu, Deyang, Leshan, Mianyang, Neijiang, Panzhihua, and Xichang.

AGRICULTURE AND FORESTRY

Most of the population of Sichuan earn their livelihood from agriculture, and a large portion of the provincial exports are agricultural products. Cultivation is characterized by the diversity of crops, intensive land use, extensive terracing, irrigation, the cultivation of *zaisheng dao* ("rebirth" rice), and the special methods of soil culture, fertilization, composting, and crop rotation.

The basin area of eastern Sichuan is extensively terraced and is often called a "land of one million steps." The terraces are of varying dimensions but are commonly long narrow strips of land that

frequently have rather steep slopes. They are easy to construct because the bedrock is soft and weathers easily. Even 45-degree slopes have tiny steps of terraced land.

Irrigation is widely practiced in the terraced fields, and numerous methods and devices are employed. Among the most spectacular is the ancient Dujiangyan irrigation system of the Chengdu Plain, which dates to the Qin dynasty (221–207 BCE); it captures the torrential flow of the Min River and guides it through an artificial multiplication of channels into numerous distributaries along the gently graded plain. Annual dredging keeps the river level constant. The system—part of a regional World Heritage site designated in 2000—is not only the oldest but also the most successful and easily maintained irrigation system in China. It has freed the plain from the hazard of floods and droughts and ensured the agricultural prosperity of the basin. A special landscape feature of the eastern basin is the *dongshuitian* (literally, "winter water-storage field") system, in which large tracts of terraced fields are left fallow during the winter season and are used for the storage of water that is needed in the paddy fields in the spring; from the air they resemble a mosaic of broken mirrors.

Crops range from those of subtropical climates to those of the cool temperate zone. Although Sichuan is generally classified as a rice region, it is also a leading producer of such crops as corn (maize), sweet potatoes, wheat, rapeseed, *gao-liang* (a variety of grain sorghum), barley, soybeans, millet, and hemp and other fibre crops. Tropical fruits—such as litchi and citrus—grow together with the apples and pears of cool temperate climates. Other principal cash crops include sugarcane, peanuts (groundnuts), cotton, tobacco, silkworm cocoons, and tea.

Sichuan is a national leader in the total number of its cattle and pigs. It is the only region in China in which both water buffalo of South China and oxen of North China are found together. Pig bristles from Sichuan have been an important item of foreign trade for years. About half the inhabitants of the west are pastoral. Their animals include cattle, sheep, horses, donkeys, and yaks.

Sichuan is second only to China's Northeast as a lumber region. Valuable forests are located on the peripheral highlands that surround the basin area and on the numerous hills within the basin. Western Sichuan still has much of its original forest cover. The most important products from the forests are tung oil, white wax, and various kinds of herbs.

RESOURCES AND POWER

Mineral deposits are abundant and varied. They include both metallic and nonmetallic deposits, such as iron, copper, aluminum, platinum, nickel, cobalt, lead and zinc, salt, coal, petroleum, antimony, phosphorus, asbestos, and marble. The production of brine salt is the most extensive mining activity. Petroleum and

natural gas are often located together and are widely spread throughout the province, especially in the Zigong area. Natural gas has been used for centuries in the production of brine salt. Most coalfields are located in the eastern and southern mountain areas. The most important iron deposits are along the southern and western plateau areas; those of the western sector are of high-quality titaniferous magnetite associated with vanadium. Some placer gold is panned along the Jinsha ("Gold Sand") River. Other valuable minerals include tin and sulfur.

Power is generated from a variety of small- and medium-sized thermal and (in the mountains) hydroelectric plants scattered throughout the province. Power supplies are sufficient for local needs, and the excess is added to the national grid for consumption farther east.

MANUFACTURING

There has been considerable industrial development since the 1950s, and Sichuan has become the most industrialized province of southwestern China. The most important industries include iron and copper smelting, the production of machinery and electric power, coal mining, petroleum refining, and the manufacturing and processing of chemicals. Other important products are aircraft, electronic equipment, textiles, and food. Sichuan is also known for its cottage industries. It has a long history of silk production. Also produced are handwoven cloth, embroidery, porcelain, carved stone, bamboo mats and carved bamboo, and silver and copper items. In addition, such local products as distilled liquors, Sichuan peanuts, and cured meats (notably ham) are known nationwide.

TRANSPORTATION

Of the problems facing Sichuan, none is more important and more acute than that of transportation. For centuries, travel into or out of the province has been extremely difficult; the main entrances were the dangerous Yangtze Gorges in the east through Chongqing, a treacherous plank road across the mountains in the north, and the deep canyons and swift currents of the Dadu and Jinsha rivers in the west. Since the 1950s great efforts have been made to improve transportation. Railways have been built across the mountains, and steel bridges have been constructed over rivers in the west.

Water routes are the most important means of transportation. Of the approximately 300 streams in the province, the Yangtze River is the most significant, traversing the entire width of the basin from the southwest to the northeast. It is the spinal cord of the river transportation system. In the west, water transportation is difficult and limited except in the lower reaches of the Anning and Dadu rivers.

Railways are important for the transportation of bulky products. Since the 1950s, railway construction has included the Chengdu-Baoji route—the first to cross the Qin range—which connects with the principal east-west Longhai rail line and thus links Sichuan to both northwestern and coastal China; and the Chengdu-Chongqing line, which links the Chengdu Plain with the Yangtze River. To the south there are railways to connect Sichuan with Yunnan (Chengdu-Kunming line) and Guizhou and, farther southeast, to Guangxi and Guangdong provinces.

The thoroughly dissected terrain and easily weathered rock structures of the province have made the construction and maintenance of highways costly and hazardous, entailing the constant threat of landslides, the presence of numerous steep slopes and hairpin turns, and the necessity of constructing many solid embankments. Chengdu is the principal highway centre. Major highway routes connect with bordering provinces in the north, Hubei in the east, Guizhou and Yunnan in the south, and Tibet in the west. Express highways linking Chengdu, Chongqing, and other major cities constitute important components of the province's transportation infrastructure.

Sichuan's first commercial air service began in 1937. Since then, commercial flying has grown steadily. Chengdu is the principal air transportation centre.

GOVERNMENT AND SOCIETY

In 1955 former Xikang province, at the edge of the Plateau of Tibet, was incorporated into Sichuan province, and in 1997 the eastern part of Sichuan, centred on Chongqing, was upgraded to China's fourth province-level municipality.

CONSTITUTIONAL FRAMEWORK

Sichuan is now divided into eighteen prefecture-level municipalities (*dijishi*) and three autonomous prefectures (*zizhizhou*). The province is further divided into counties (*xian*), autonomous counties (*zizhixian*), and county-level municipalities (*xianjishi*). These are the most important administrative units because it is through them that the government exercises control.

The autonomous prefectures are the Aba Tibetan Autonomous Prefecture, with its headquarters at Ma'erkang (Barkam); the Ganzi Tibetan Autonomous Prefecture, with its capital at Kangding; and the Liangshan Yi Autonomous Prefecture, with its capital at Xichang. As a rule, the autonomous prefectures represent little more than a symbolic cultural indulgence of local minorities. The actual control of the units is exercised by the central government at Chengdu. The ethnic groups, however, enjoy their own mode of life and preserve their language and cultural traditions with a minimum of interference by the Han-controlled provincial government.

Sichuan province was a leader in the economic reform movement that began in the late 1970s, introducing innovative policies such as the one that linked farmers' incomes to actual output. Three counties in the province became the first areas to dissolve communes, a practice that soon spread nationwide.

HEALTH AND WELFARE

The warm and wet climate of most of the province makes respiratory ailments a major health problem. Because of the severe pressure of the people on the land, the farmers of Sichuan must work extremely hard to eke out a living. The farmers of the Chengdu Plain are the most prosperous and have the highest standard of living. Rural life is harder in the hills surrounding the basin, and the standard of living is considerably lower in the west, where pastoral activities predominate. In the western mountains, many of the people migrate seasonally from the lowlands to the highlands in search of pasturage.

EDUCATION

Sichuan has many institutions of higher education, some of which are important for training China's most talented students. Notable among these is Sichuan University, in Chengdu, which traces its roots to 1902 and acquired its present configuration in 1994 by incorporating Chengdu University of Science and Technology and West China University of Medical Science. The University of Electronic Science and Technology of China and Southwest China Jiaotong University are also important. In addition, there are hundreds of research institutions in the province, and much attention is given to developing science and technology there.

Cultural Life

Chengdu has always played a vital role in the cultural and intellectual life of Sichuan. The city is a haven for intellectuals and scholars, and—with its heavy traffic, rich nightlife, and luxurious surroundings—is sometimes called the "Little Paris" of China. Notable cultural sights in Chengdu include a memorial hall dedicated to the 3rd-century-CE adviser Zhuge Liang and the cottage of the 8th-century poet Du Fu.

The unique form of architecture of the eastern basin is characterized by projecting eaves, gracefully curved roofs, and rich, elaborate roof ornaments. Because there is little wind and practically no snow in the basin, these fragile and extraordinarily beautiful structures and decorations can safely be constructed. The frequent misty rains make it necessary to project the roof eaves over the walls to protect them from the rain.

Tourism is fairly well developed in Sichuan and is of growing importance there. UNESCO World Heritage sites include not only the giant panda reserves and the Dujiangyan irrigation system but also the Mount Emei area and the Jiuzhai River valley. Mount Emei, in the south-central Daxiang Mountains, is one of the

four sacred mountains of Chinese Buddhism; it reaches an elevation of 10,167 feet (3,099 m) at Wanfo Summit. The mountain and the Leshan Giant Buddha (carved into a hillside in the region) were collectively designated a World Heritage site in 2007. The Jiuzhai River (Jiuzhaigou) valley is a beautiful landscape in the Min Mountains of northern Sichuan; it received its World Heritage designation in 1992. All these are popular tourist destinations.

Sichuan is renowned for its hot, spicy cuisine, which features liberal use of hot chili peppers. Garlic and ginger are also common in both vegetable and meat dishes. Peanuts are another common ingredient, as in kung pao (*gongbao*) chicken, a highly popular dish throughout the world.

History

Apart from the provinces of the upper Huang He (Yellow River) valley, Sichuan was the first area of China to be settled by the Han. The first organized Han migration took place in the 5th century BCE. Sichuan was known as the Ba and Shu territory during the Zhou dynasty (1046–256 BCE). During the succeeding Qin dynasty (221–207 BCE) the territory was incorporated within the Qin empire and began to assume considerable importance in China's national life. It was at that time that the Dujiangyan irrigation system was built. In the Three Kingdoms (Sanguo) period (220–280 CE), the

Sichuan region constituted the Shu-Han kingdom (221–263/264), which had its capital at Chengdu. From the end of this period until the 10th century, Sichuan was known by various names and was administered through various political subdivisions. During the Song dynasty (960–1279), four prefectures were established in what is now the eastern part of the province under the name Chuan-Shaan-Si-Lu, which later was shortened to Sichuan. Sichuan was established as a province during the Qing, or Manchu, dynasty (1644–1911/12).

During the early years (1911–30) of the Chinese republic, Sichuan suffered seriously from the feudal warlord system; at one time it was divided into as many as seventeen independent military units, and not until 1935 was it unified under the Nationalist government. During the Sino-Japanese War of 1937–45, there was a great influx of people and new ideas from coastal China, which resulted in extensive economic development. Many factories and trading posts were moved from the coastal area into Sichuan, and a number of industrial centres were established, especially in Chongqing and Chengdu.

Because of its geographic isolation, inaccessibility, extensive area, large population, and virtual economic self-sufficiency, Sichuan has served periodically as a bastion in its own right. The area is easily defensible, and geography has encouraged political separatism. During the war with Japan, Chongqing (then in the province) was the seat of the Nationalist government from 1938 to 1945; the Japanese were never able to penetrate the area.

Economic and population growth were rapid following the establishment of the People's Republic of China in 1949, especially after transportation routes were extended into the province in the 1950s. Chengdu became a leading industrial city. Some military-related projects and institutions were relocated to Sichuan beginning in the mid-1960s, and these also were a great boon to other cities in the province, notably Mianyang. The separation of a large portion of eastern Sichuan to form Chongqing municipality was a significant loss, but the province remained one of the largest and most populous in the country. The 2008 earthquake in central Sichuan not only killed tens of thousands of people but also caused widespread damage in some of the province's most economically active areas, especially Mianyang.

CONCLUSION

China is perhaps the quintessential place on Earth where (at least in large areas of the country) the land shapes the people and the people shape the land. The Chinese people have a deep, ancient, and very particular relationship to this vast and varied land of spectacular mountains and plateaus, great and nearly empty desert areas, and intensely lush landscapes in which they live. On the one hand, they are its victims: Over the centuries many have suffered from the unreliability of the Huang He—aptly nicknamed China's Sorrow—and its great floods or from violent earthquakes, such as those that struck the city of Tangshan in 1976 or Sichuan province in 2008. In this highly agricultural nation, a remarkable amount of land is nonarable (or barely so), and a great many of China's hundreds of millions of farmers depend on unreliable rainfall or must try to till hard, difficult, or even desert soils to make a livelihood.

Yet, in some parts of China, the landscape is so rich and fertile—and where for millennia the land has been so carefully managed—that two and even three crops of rice can be grown each year without exhausting the soil. In many areas the landscape is highly celebrated, and its mountains held sacred; tender appreciation for this beauty is memorialized in the verses of poets such as Du Fu. This beauty is carried over to Chinese cuisine, one of the richest and most varied in the world, which surely reflects the richness of China's natural resources as well.

One cannot think about China without noting the extraordinarily long history of ambitious public-works projects undertaken by the Chinese to master, control, and reshape their land. From the elaborate rice terraces of the south to the Great Wall, the Grand Canal, and, most recently, the Three Gorges Dam on the Yangtze, China's people have not been afraid to assert themselves on the landscapes in which they live. That aggressive drive can also be found in the country's dozens of large and rapidly growing cities, full of energy and economic power but also producing dangerous levels of environmental pollution.

Finally, China's geography has itself played an important role in helping the country's people develop a sense of national identity. China, largely surrounded by mountains, deserts, and sea, was able to isolate itself to a larger degree than many other lands. Even though China faced numerous threats from nomadic invaders in its northern and western regions over the centuries, these incursions generally were short-lived. More times than not, these outsiders eventually succumbed to the assimilating power of the Middle Kingdom and became part of the greater Chinese social fabric.

Official name: Zhonghua Renmin Gongheguo (People's Republic of China).

Form of government: single-party people's republic with one legislative house (National People's Congress [2,980 members[1]]).

Chief of state: President Hu Jintao.

Head of government: Premier Wen Jiabao.

Capital: Beijing (Peking).

Official language: Mandarin Chinese.

Official religion: none.

Monetary unit: renminbi (yuan) (Y).

DEMOGRAPHY AREA AND POPULATION[2]				
PROVINCES[5]	CAPITALS[5]	AREA[3]		POPULATION 2007[4] ESTIMATE
		SQ MI	SQ KM	
Anhui (Anhwei)	Hefei	54,000	139,900	61,100,000
Fujian (Fukien)	Fuzhou	47,500	123,100	35,580,000
Gansu (Kansu)	Lanzhou	141,500	366,500	26,060,000
Guangdong (Kwangtung)	Guangzhou (Canton)	76,100	197,100	93,040,000
Guizhou (Kweichow)	Guiyang	67,200	174,000	37,570,000
Hainan	Haikou	13,200	34,300	8,360,000
Hebei (Hopeh)	Shijiazhuang	78,200	202,700	68,980,000
Heilongjiang (Heilungkiang)	Harbin	179,000	463,600	38,230,000
Henan (Honan)	Zhengzhou	64,500	167,000	93,920,000
Hubei (Hupeh)	Wuhan	72,400	187,500	56,930,000
Hunan	Changsha	81,300	210,500	63,420,000
Jiangsu (Kiangsu)	Nanjing (Nanking)	39,600	102,600	75,500,000
Jiangxi (Kiangsi)	Nanchang	63,600	164,800	43,390,000
Jilin (Kirin)	Changchun	72,200	187,000	27,230,000
Liaoning (Liaoning)	Shenyang	58,300	151,000	42,710,000

PROVINCES[5]	CAPITALS[5]	AREA[3]		POPULATION 2007[4] ESTIMATE
		SQ MI	SQ KM	
Qinghai (Tsinghai)	Xining	278,400	721,000	5,480,000
Shaanxi (Shensi)	Xi'an (Sian)	75,600	195,800	37,350,000
Shandong (Shantung)	Jinan	59,200	153,300	93,090,000
Shanxi (Shansi)	Taiyuan	60,700	157,100	33,750,000
Sichuan (Szechwan)	Chengdu	188,000	487,000	81,690,000
Yunnan	Kunming	168,400	436,200	44,830,000
Zhejiang (Chekiang)	Hangzhou	39,300	101,800	49,800,000
AUTONOMOUS REGIONS[5]				
Guangxi Zhuang (Kwangsi Chuang)	Nanning	85,100	220,400	47,190,000
Inner Mongolia (Nei Mongol)	Hohhot	454,600	1,177,500	23,970,000
Ningxia Hui (Ningsia Hui)	Yinchuan	25,600	66,400	6,040,000
Tibet (Xizang)	Lhasa	471,700	1,221,600	2,810,000
Xinjiang Uygur (Sinkiang Uighur)	Ürümqi (Urumchi)	635,900	1,646,900	20,500,000
MUNICIPALITIES[5]				
Beijing (Peking)	—	6,500	16,800	15,810,000
Chongqing (Chungking)	—	31,700	82,000	28,080,000
Shanghai	—	2,400	6,200	18,150,000
Tianjin (Tientsin)	—	4,400	11,300	10,750,000
TOTAL		3,696,100	9,572,900	1,314,480,000[6]

Population (2008): 1,324,681,000.

Density (2008): persons per sq mi 358.4, persons per sq km 138.4.

Urban-rural (2007[4]): urban 43.9%; rural 56.1%.

Sex distribution (2007[4]): male 51.52%; female 48.48%.

Age breakdown (2004): under 15, 19.3%; 15–29, 22.1%; 30–44, 27.2%; 45–59, 19.0%; 60–74, 9.6%; 75–84, 2.4%; 85 and over, 0.4%.

Population projection: (2010) 1,338,442,000; (2020) 1,407,520,000.

Ethnic composition (2000): Han (Chinese) 91.53%; Chuang 1.30%; Manchu 0.86%; Hui 0.79%; Miao 0.72%; Uighur 0.68%; Tuchia 0.65%; Yi 0.62%; Mongolian 0.47%; Tibetan 0.44%; Puyi 0.24%; Tung 0.24%; Yao 0.21%; Korean 0.15%; Pai 0.15%; Hani 0.12%; Kazakh 0.10%; Li 0.10%; Tai 0.09%; other 0.54%.

Religious affiliation (2005): nonreligious 39.2%; Chinese folk-religionist 28.7%; Christian 10.0%, of which unregistered Protestant 7.7%[7], registered Protestant 1.2%[7], unregistered Roman Catholic 0.5%[7], registered Roman Catholic 0.4%[7]; Buddhist 8.4%; atheist 7.8%; traditional beliefs 4.4%; Muslim 1.5%.

Major urban agglomerations (2005): Shanghai 14,503,000; Beijing 10,717,000; Guangzhou 8,425,000; Shenzhen 7,233,000; Wuhan 7,093,000; Tianjin 7,040,000; Chongqing 6,363,000; Shenyang 4,720,000; Dongguan 4,320,000; Chengdu 4,065,000; Xi'an 3,926,000; Harbin 3,695,000; Nanjing 3,621,000; Guiyang 3,447,000; Dalian 3,073,000; Changchun 3,046,000; Zibo 2,982,000; Kunming 2,837,000; Hangzhou 2,831,000; Qingdao 2,817,000; Taiyuan 2,794,000; Jinan 2,743,000; Zhengzhou 2,590,000; Fuzhou 2,453,000; Changsha 2,451,000; Lanzhou 2,411,000.

Households: Average household size[8] (2004) 3.6, of which urban households 3.0[8], rural households 4.1[8]; 1 person 7.8%, 2 persons 19.6%, 3 persons 31.4%, 4 persons 21.8%, 5 persons 12.4%, 6 or more persons 7.0%; non-family households 0.8%.

Vital Statistics

Birth rate per 1,000 population (2006): 12.1 (world avg. 20.3).

Death rate per 1,000 population (2006): 6.8 (world avg. 8.6).

Natural increase rate per 1,000 population (2006): 5.3 (world avg. 11.7).

Total fertility rate (avg. births per childbearing woman; 2005): 1.72.

Life expectancy at birth (2005): male 70.9 years; female 74.3 years.

National Economy

Gross national product (2006): U.S.$2,641,846,000,000 (U.S.$2,035 per capita).

Budget (2004). Revenue: Y 2,639,647,000,000 (tax revenue 91.5%, of which VAT 34.2%, corporate income taxes 15.0%, business tax 13.6%, consumption tax 5.7%; nontax revenue 8.5%).

Expenditures: Y 2,848,689,000,000 (economic development 27.8%, of which agriculture 8.3%; social, cultural, and educational development 26.3%; administration 19.4%; defense 7.7%; other 18.8%).

Public debt (external, outstanding; 2005): U.S.$82,853,000,000.

ENVIRONMENT

Carbon dioxide (CO_2) emissions from consumption and flaring of fossil fuels (in '000 metric tons of CO_2; 2005): 5,322,690 (of which from: petroleum 16.5%, natural gas 1.9%, coal 81.6%) (% of world total 18.9); *CO_2 emissions per capita* 4.1 metric tons.

FOREIGN TRADE[9]

Imports (2006): U.S.$791,461,000,000 (machinery and apparatus 41.4%, of which electronic integrated circuits and micro-assemblies 13.4%, computers and office machines 5.1%, telecommunications equipment and parts 4.1%; mineral fuels 11.2%, of which crude petroleum 8.4%; chemicals and chemical products 11.0%; metal ore and metal scrap 5.6%; optical devices [particularly lasers] 4.5%).

Major import sources: Japan 14.6%; South Korea 11.3%; Taiwan 11.0%; China free trade zones 9.3%; United States 7.5%; Germany 4.8%; Malaysia 3.0%; Australia 2.4%; Thailand 2.3%; Philippines 2.2%.

Exports (2006): U.S.$968,936,000,000 (machinery and apparatus 43.2%, of which computers and office machines 13.9%, electrical machinery 10.5%, telecommunications equipment and parts 8.8%; apparel and clothing accessories 9.8%; textile yarn, fabrics, made-up articles 5.0%; chemicals and chemical products 4.6%; fabricated metal products 3.7%; iron and steel 3.4%).

Major export destinations: United States 21.0%; Hong Kong 16.0%; Japan 9.5%; South Korea 4.6%; Germany 4.2%; The Netherlands 3.2%; United Kingdom 2.5%; Singapore 2.4%; Taiwan 2.1%; Italy 1.6%.

Food: undernourished population (2002–04) 150,000,000 (12% of total population based on the consumption of a minimum daily requirement of 1,930 calories).

MILITARY

Total active duty personnel (Nov. 2007): 2,105,000 (army 76.0%, navy 12.1%, air force 11.9%).
Military expenditure as percentage of GDP (2005): 2.0%; per capita expenditure U.S.$34.

1 Includes 36 seats allotted to Hong Kong and 12 to Macau.

2 Data for Taiwan, Quemoy, and Matsu (parts of Fujian province occupied by Taiwan), Hong Kong, and Macau are excluded.

3 Estimated figures.

4 January 1.

5 Preferred names in all instances are based on Pinyin transliteration (except for Inner Mongolia and Tibet, which are current English-language conventional names).

6 Total includes military personnel not distributed by province, autonomous region, or municipality.

7 Percentage is rough estimate.

8 Family households only.

9 Imports c.i.f., exports f.o.b.

alluvial Relating to soil or sediments that are deposited by running water.

ameliorate To improve something or make it better.

apex The uppermost point.

arable Fertile land that can be used for growing crops.

cacophonous Harsh and loud sounding.

concave Curved inward.

conceit An organizing theme, concept, or idea.

congeries Collection.

conventional Commonplace.

crenellated Having repeated square indentations like those in a battlement.

disparate Very different in quality, type, or character.

dyestuff Dye; colouring matter.

eddy A current in a body of water such as a river that swirls in a different direction than the main current.

effluent Flowing out.

eluvium Residual deposits of soil, dust, and rock particles produced by wind action.

eradicate To get rid of; to wipe out completely.

fiefdom A feudal state in which peasants can use a lord's land in exchange for service.

hinterland An area far from major cities; a backwater.

homogeneous Of a like nature.

hummock A small, rounded hill.

humus A type of rich, dark earth that comes from the decomposition of plants or animals.

ibex A wild goat with large curved horns that can be found in China.

impervious Impossible to penetrate.

inundate To flood.

jerboa A noctural rodent of the dry sections of northern Africa and Asia. Jerboas, which have long hind legs, are strong jumpers.

lacquerware Items that are made of wood, painted, and then lacquered, or covered with varnish.

levee A high embankment, often made of earth, that is built to prevent flooding.

loess A loose, yellowish brown soil that is found in certain parts of China and that is transmitted by the wind and major rivers.

opium A narcotic substance that comes from the seeds of the opium poppy.

pandit A wise or educated man in India—often given as an honourary title.

placer A deposit that contains small bits of precious minerals, such as gold.

redolent Suggestive.

sorghum A tropical grass that is an important crop in Asia.

stela A carved stone pillar.

steppe A massive flat and treeless area in Asia or southeastern Europe.

stupa A type of Buddhist shrine that is made up of a mound-shaped structure.

sundry Various.

suzerainty A relationship between states in which the international affairs of a subservient state are controlled by the more powerful one.

temporal Concerning earthly, rather than spiritual, matters.

ubiquitous Existing or being everywhere.

urial A reddish brown wild sheep that lives in upland areas of Asia. The males have a beard from neck to chest.

vanguard Soldiers who lead the charge at the head of an army.

FOR FURTHER READING

Barmé, Geremie. *The Forbidden City.* Cambridge, MA: Harvard University Press, 2008.

Belliveau, Denis, and Francis O'Donnell. *In the Footsteps of Marco Polo.* Lanham, MD: Rowman & Littlefield Publishers, 2008.

Berthrong, John H., and E Nagai-Berthrong. *Confucianism: A Short Introduction.* Oxford, England: Oneworld Publications, 2000.

Campanella, Thomas J. *The Concrete Dragon: China's Urban Revolution and What It Means for the World.* New York, NY: Princeton Architectural Press, 2008.

Chang, Leslie T. *Factory Girls: From Village to City in a Changing China.* New York, NY: Spiegel & Grau, 2008.

Chetham, Deirdre. *Before the Deluge: The Vanishing World of the Yangtze's Three Gorges.* New York, NY: Palgrave Macmillan, 2002.

Dillon, Michael. *Contemporary China: An Introduction.* New York, NY: Routledge, 2009.

Dodgen, Randall A. *Controlling the Dragon: Confucian Engineers and the Yellow River in the Late Imperial China.* Honolulu, HI: University of Hawai'i Press, 2001.

Fenby, Jonathan. *Chiang Kai-shek: China's Generalissimo and the Nation He Lost.* New York, NY: Carroll & Graf, 2003.

Gifford, Rob. *China Road: A Journey into the Future of a Rising Power.* New York, NY: Random House, 2007.

Haugen, David M. *China.* Detroit, MI: Greenhaven Press, 2006.

Hay, Jeff. *Buddhism.* Farmington Hills, MI: Greenhaven Press, 2006.

Hessler, Peter. *Oracle Bones: A Journey Through Time in China.* New York, NY: HarperCollins Publishers, 2006.

Hutchings, Graham. *Modern China: A Guide to a Century of Change.* Cambridge, MA: Harvard University Press, 2001.

Lewis, Mark Edward. *The Early Chinese Empires: Qin and Han.* Cambridge, MA: Belknap Press of Harvard University Press, 2007.

Lovell, Julia. *The Great Wall: China Against the World, 1000 BC-AD 2000.* New York, NY: Grove/Atlantic Inc., 2006.

Man, John. *The Terra Cotta Army: China's First Emperor and the Birth of a Nation.* Cambridge, MA: Da Capo Press, 2008.

Meyer, Michael J. *The Last Days of Old Beijing: Life in the Vanishing Backstreets of a City Transformed.* New York, NY: Walker & Company, 2008.

Mohindra, Vandana. *China.* New York, NY: DK Publishing, 2005.

Reader's Digest Association Far East, Ltd. *Treasures of China: An Armchair Journey to Over 340*

Legendary Landmarks. Pleasantville, NY: Reader's Digest, 2004.

Taylor, Jay. *The Generalissimo: Chiang Kai-shek and the Struggle for Modern China.* Cambridge, MA: Belknap Press of Harvard University Press, 2009.

Thubron, Colin. *Shadow of the Silk Road.* New York, NY: HarperCollins Publishers, 2007.

Tsang, Steve Yui-Sang. *A Modern History of Hong Kong.* New York, NY: I.B. Tauris, 2004.

Whitfield, Roderick, Susan Whitfield, and Neville Agnew. *Cave Temples of Mogao: Art and History on the Silk Road.* Los Angeles, CA: Getty Conservation Institute and the J. Getty Museum, 2000.